D1202018

ON THE WAY TO GOD

An Exploration into the
Theology of Wolfhart Pannenberg

David P. Polk

UNIVERSITY
PRESS OF
AMERICA

Copyright © 1989 by

University Press of America,® Inc.

4720 Boston Way
Lanham, MD 20706

Library of Congress Cataloging-in-Publication Data

Polk, David Patrick.
On the way to God : an exploration into the theology of Wolfhart
Pannenberg / David P. Polk.
p. cm.
Reprint. Originally published: Ann Arbor, Mich. : University of
Microfilm Intl., 1983
Bibliography: p.
Includes index.
1. Pannenberg, Wolfhart, 1928–   . 2. God—History of
doctrines—20th century. I. Title.
BX4827.P3P65   1988
230'.044'0924—dc 19   88–27871 CIP
ISBN 0–8191–7229–4 (alk. paper)

All University Press of America books are produced on acid-free paper.
The paper used in this publication meets the minimum requirements of
American National Standard for Information Sciences—Permanence of Paper
for Printed Library Materials, ANSI Z39.48–1984.

To Kitty

confirmation of

the power of love

ACKNOWLEDGEMENTS

Acknowledgment is made to the following publishers for permission to use copyrighted material:

Portions of Chapter 8 reprinted by permission from THE THEOLOGY OF WOLFHART PANNENBERG, copyright © 1988 Augsburg Fortress.

Excerpts from WHAT IS MAN? by Wolfhart Pannenberg, tr. by Duane A. Priebe, reprinted by permission of Fortress Press.

Excerpts passim from THEOLOGY AS HISTORY (New Frontiers in Theology, Vol. III) by James M. Robinson and John B. Cobb, Jr. Copyright © 1967 by James M. Robinson and John B. Cobb, Jr. Reprinted by permission of Harper & Row, Publishers, Inc.

Reprinted with permission of Macmillan Publishing Company from REVELATION AS HISTORY by Wolfhart Pannenberg, tr. by David Granskou. Copyright © 1968 by Macmillan Publishing Company.

Excerpts from GRUNDFRAGEN SYSTEMATISCHER THEOLOGIE I and II by Wolfhart Pannenberg, and OFFENBARUNG ALS GESCHICHTE, 3rd ed., ed. by Wolfhart Pannenberg, reprinted by permission of Vandenhoeck & Ruprecht in Göttingen.

From BASIC QUESTIONS IN THEOLOGY (collected Essays Vol I), by Wolfhart Pannenberg; translated by George H. Kehm. Copyright © 1970 by Fortress Press; reprinted 1983 by arrangement with Fortress Press, Philadelphia. Used by permission of The Westminster Press, Philadelphia, PA.

From BASIC QUESTIONS IN THEOLOGY (Vol. II), by Wolfhart Pannenberg; translated by George H. Kehm. Copyright © 1971 by Fortress Press. Reprinted in 1983 by The Westminster Press by arrangement with Fortress Press. Used by permission.

From THE IDEA OF GOD AND HUMAN FREEDOM, by Wolfhart Pannenberg; translated from German by R. A. Wilson. © SCM Press Ltd. 1973, and published in Great Britain under the title BASIC QUESTIONS IN THEOLOGY, Volume Three. Published in the U. S. A. in 1973 by The Westminster Press. Reprinted and used by permission.

From JESUS - GOD AND MAN by Wolfhart Pannenberg, translated by Lewis L. Wilkins and Duane A. Priebe. Copyright © 1968, 1977 The Westminster Press. Used by permission.

From THEOLOGY AND THE KINGDOM OF GOD, by Wolfhart Pannenberg. Copyright © MCMLXIX, The Westminster Press. Used by permission.

Excerpts from "The Nature of a Theological Statement" by Wolfhart Pannenberg, ZYGON 7, 1972, reprinted by permission of Joint Publication Board of ZYGON.

TABLE OF CONTENTS

FOREWORD

In the nineteenth century Germany became the undisputed center of Protestant theology. This was partly because of the general excellence of its universities, through which Germany led the world in many fields. But it was also partly because theology as a discipline did not lose status as it did elsewhere in the world. Many of the most profound of German thinkers from Hegel to Nietzsche studied theology. Theology was recognized as the field in which questions of ultimate concern were systematically considered in all their breadth and depth.

To be a theologian in that context required both breadth and depth. The range of scholarship to be considered was vast and the analytical and speculative gifts required to bring this vast knowledge into fresh focus were extraordinary. Without the support of the humanistic gymnasia, which offered a background particularly helpful for entry into theological studies, few indeed could have attained these heights.

The continuation of this tradition into the twentieth century has been difficult indeed. The academic disciplines become ever more specialized and separated. Theology is more and more understood as one discipline among others rather than as the place where questions of ultimate importance to all are considered. The greatest theologians of the twentieth century, Karl Barth being the most impressive example, have retained the depth of their predecessors, but have systematically abandoned the effort to relate theology to the whole of human knowledge.

Nevertheless, the Hegelian vision has not died out. Hegel's influence waxes and wanes, but again and again it calls German theology back to the more comprehensive task. Yet on the whole even those who hear its siren call remain quite abstract in their efforts to deal with universal questions. The task of concretely relating theology to the best thinking of the other disciplines seems too formidable, and the theological arguments against the effort remain attractive.

The one twentieth-century theologian to have successfully renewed the nineteenth-century project is Wolfhart Pannenberg. His conversation partners are social scientists and physicists as well as historians and philosophers. His own expertise ranges over the whole of theological scholarship. His analytic and speculative gifts are truly extraordinary.

David Polk has fully recognized the extraordinary, indeed, unique, achievement of Pannenberg. He has approached Pannenberg's work with unusual analytic and speculative gifts of his own, but especially with deep admiration and appreciation. His goal has been, above all, to understand. This book constitutes a lucid and accurate account of Pannenberg's thought based on the most careful study of the texts as well as extensive discussion with the author.

Polk's initial intentions were primarily to expound the coherence of Pannenberg's system and display its adequacy for our time. Much of the book functions primarily in that way. Nevertheless, he came in the end to dissatisfaction with Pannenberg's idea that everything is determined by the power of the future. Whereas Pannenberg finds that compatible with the Biblical understanding of human freedom and responsibility, Polk found it unsatisfactory. Hence, in the end, he parts company and explains the dissatisfaction he feels with this central feature of Pannenberg's system.

Of course, no critique of this sort is in itself decisive. There is always another point of view from which it seems to miss the point or to have assumptions of its own that are not convincing to the advocates of the position criticized. Nevertheless, some critiques are to be taken more seriously than others. Among these are ones that arise from intense and friendly and largely successful efforts to understand. When a student who wishes to agree finds that she or he finally cannot do so, it is worthwhile for others to attend to the difficulty.

Polk's criticism is of this kind. He labored long and hard to find a way of interpreting Pannenberg's vision of the determination of the present by the future that fitted with the concern for human responsibility. That he could not do so is an important fact. His explanation of the problem is worthy of careful attention on the part of all students of Pannenberg.

This book is, therefore, both a fine exposition of Pannenberg's thought and an important systematic critique. The critique does not render the analysis tendentious. Instead the richly nuanced analysis provides the data on the basis of which the critique can itself be evaluated. Enough of comment. The book speaks for itself.

John B. Cobb, Jr.

PREFACE

A work of scholarship may eventually burst forth from its generative cocoon as an expression of individual creativity, but that perception belies the actual dynamics of the productive process. My indebtedness is considerable to those whose varying contributions finally assured that this undertaking would see the light of day.

Foremost among them is John Cobb, who graciously provided the Foreword for this book. His unfailing wisdom and compassion nurtured the work as well as its author through an extended incubation period from its inception as a doctoral dissertation to its present emergence as a published monograph. My sense of gratitude to him rises above mere words.

Wolfhart Pannenberg has been a kind and conceptually rigorous companion in my efforts to systematize his theological program, from those weeks in Claremont over two decades ago when I chauffeured him and his wife around southern California to the semester I spent with him in Munich to the many subsequent hours of probing conversation. He has been generously attentive to my concerns and questions, even when my analyses led to critical judgments with which he did not agree. If I finally stand at a distance from some of his key theses, it is through no absence of effort on his part to persuade me.

Additional expressions of appreciation are in order to more persons than can reasonably be identified here, but they particularly include George Coats, Lewis Ford, James M. Robinson, Jack Verheyden, and Ekkehard Mühlenberg, for their helpful reviews of the work in process; Donald Reisinger, Marjorie Suchocki, and my aunt Mary Burton, for their personal support of inestimable value; and Susan Diamond for her diligent proficiency in preparing this text for publication. I wish also to recognize here the significant support of the members of First Christian Church of Cedar Rapids, Iowa, where I pastored for nearly a decade, and the administration and faculty of Brite Divinity School, Texas Christian University, where I presently teach.

Finally, I cannot begin to verbalize the depth of my affection for the one who patiently and lovingly persevered in support of this long-term endeavor. If, in the end, what we have to fall back on in the weaving of our webs of abstraction is the richness or poverty of our lived experiences, I have been enriched beyond measuring. To one who couldn't care a farthing about the intricacies of theological argumentation, but who lives theology's substance almost instinctively--to my wife Kitty, this now completed project of thought is lovingly dedicated.

1

QUEST

A. Bearings

The contemporary crisis of Christian faith can be identified in a number of ways, but three elements appear to stand out as especially significant. On the one hand, there is a widespread disavowal of the intellectual respectability of that which Christians claim to be truth. If ever there was a time when Christian proclamation was generally received as rationally persuasive, that time is certainly no longer. Of course, there is no denying the fact that Christian theology itself has had a hand in this development. Karl Barth's overturning of the humanity-centered theology of the nineteenth century with his imprisonment of professed truth within a ghetto of revelational positivism has had deleterious repercussions. For if what the Christian proclaims is subject to no external interrogation but is the possession of the faithful alone, then its claim to truth-bearing significance is severely placed in doubt. Whatever additional factors one observes as contributing to the current dilemma of an intellectually suspect faith-stance--the rise of modern scientific method, the concomitant "coming of age" of the Western world and the encroachment of secularism, the collapse of authoritarianism and the shock of relativism--theology cannot forswear its own responsibility in the matter.

Secondly, and hand in hand with the point just made, the reality of God has been radically called into question as a legitimate object of human knowledge or even as an essential facet of Christian understanding. It was not so long ago that the detractors of God bore the brunt of responsibility for establishing the worth of their position. But now the shoe is on the other foot. It is now the theist who is called upon to defend not only the viability of her manner of conceiving of God but even the meaningfulness of speaking about God at all. The dispute is no longer simply over *how* one may conceptualize God but with regard to *whether* one can legitimately do so at all. Again, the Barthian orientation has contributed to this state of affairs, in the emphasis on the exclusivity of Christocentric revelation and the conviction of an otherwise infinite abyss separating God from humankind. It is little wonder that most of the early "death of God" theologians (with the prominent exception of Thomas Altizer) had cut their theological eyeteeth on Barth's dogmatics, and their attempt to lay to rest all references to transcendent deity stemmed not only from their inability to share with Barth the perception of God's revelation in Jesus Christ but equally from their acceptance of the Barthian presupposition that all other avenues to God were closed off as well. Of course, the factors contributing to the current malaise of theism's proponents go far beyond the implications arising within the theological enterprise. But once again, one finds within the theological tradition elements that materially aid and abet the crisis under consideration.

Thirdly, there is the embarrassment to Christianity concerning what to make of the central thrust of Jesus' teaching: the eschatological Reign of God. Indeed the delay of the Parousia, like the poor, we seem always to have had with us. But the eschatological ruminations of Christian thinkers have taken a sharp turn since the recognition by Johannes Weiss and Albert Schweitzer that the imminent inbreaking of the Reign of God stood not on the periphery but at the very center of the message of Jesus, and that the immediate background for that message was the *Weltanschauung* of the Jewish apocalyptic tradition. Schweitzer concluded that the so-called "historical Jesus" after whom so many scholars of the nineteenth century had been searching was in reality a mistaken apocalypticist, and thus of no positive significance for faith in the Christ who is risen in the hearts of women and men.[1] Thus Weiss' and Schweitzer's discovery was filed away under the heading of theological irrelevancy, and eschatology as involving futural expectations concerning the course of human history remained the ill-conceived possession of the literalists and fundamentalists. But the question of the enduring significance of apocalyptic eschatology for Christianity could not be dismissed so abruptly, and it burst forth anew in the debates that were triggered by Ernst Käsemann's call for a new quest for the historical Jesus which he issued to the Old Marburgers in 1953.[2] Therein Käsemann acknowledged the inescapable necessity of confronting the question of the nature of the eschatological vision in Jesus' preaching and activity, precisely as an element of decisive theological importance. The consequence has been a continuing and often fervid reassessment of the place of eschatology, and especially of apocalyptic eschatology, in Christian understanding. If it should seem that this *skandalon* of eschatological thinking is of minor significance in comparison with the previously identified aspects of the current crisis of faith, then one should bear in mind that what is ultimately at issue here involves questions of the very foundation of Christian faith in the historical actuality of Jesus of Nazareth.

The three critical elements noted here are not to be regarded as exhaustive. Neither have they been chosen at random. It is precisely in the work of Wolfhart Pannenberg that these three strands of concern come sharply and provocatively into focus in a theological synthesis of remarkable boldness and penetrating insight.

In the first place, Pannenberg's thought displays a well-honed and thoroughgoing dedication to the canons of rationality with which the broader human community operates. It is his firm conviction that truth must be one,[3] wherefore Christianity cannot make special appeals on behalf of "a" truth that bears no positive relationship to what we otherwise "know." Indeed, Pannenberg embraced Christianity not in a Kierkegaardian leap of faith beyond the bounds of human reason but rather in the emerging recognition that reason reaches its apex just therein. His spiritual pilgrimage was in large part an intellectual one, a quest for a standpoint in which all knowledge hangs together in an all-encompassing unity. To James M. Robinson's observation that "Pannenberg's own road to Christianity had been more one of rational reflection than of Christian nurture or a conversion experience,"[4] Richard Neuhaus adds effusively: "It is in fact hard to imagine a more emphatically intellectual path to Christian affirmation than the one traveled by the young Pannenberg."[5] (Augustine does come to mind.)

One additional facet of Pannenberg's upholding of the intellectual respectability, indeed the rational persuasiveness, of Christian proclamation merits preliminary mention at this point. Pannenberg would maintain that our intellectual pursuit attains completeness only within the framework of a *theology* of reason. This is not to assert, with Aquinas and a host of others, that faith knows some things that reason cannot--such an orientation is indeed a part of the very dilemma diagnosed here. It is rather to affirm that a relationship of *trust* in that to which my reasoning points me is the *sine qua non* of the knowing act. And Pannenberg finds in the content of Christian theology the decisive possibility for identifying in the most adequate way the conditions under which that trust is accurately directed. This is not the *credo ut intelligam* of Anselm. It is not a matter of a faith in search of rational underpinnings but the reverse: rationality in search of the context in which it is truly at home. My reasoning is completed by faith in the certitude of what I presently and provisionally know.[6]

Thus the challenge to the inherent reasonableness of what Christian faith proclaims is straightforwardly engaged by a contemporary theologian who "is a modern man and a rational man before he is a Christian man" and who would maintain "that he is a Christian *because* he is a modern and rational man."[7]   That, by itself, is a promising and provocative development. It calls for careful attention to the specifics of the bold undertaking which is Pannenberg's theology. It also invites careful critical assessment.

In the second place, Pannenberg addresses himself assiduously and fervently to the burning issue of legitimating purportedly meaningful discourse about God. He rejects unreservedly every tendency toward "special pleading" on behalf of God-talk, every well-intentioned endeavor to defend theistic conceptuality by laying claim for it as a realm unto itself. This means especially, for Pannenberg, that theology cannot stand aloof from the atheistic critique of the Christian understanding of God, denying from some transcendent standpoint the validity of atheism's stance. The mistake of dialectical theology, as he perceives it, was to acknowledge the truth of the atheistic argument that all ideas about God are human projections and therefore wrong--and then proceed to overtrump it with a radical *Offenbarungsglaube* in which human "ideas" about God are presumably nowhere present. The only alternative which Pannenberg sees to the resultant dilemma, that talk about God has therein lost its claim to intellectual respectability, is to enter into dialogue with atheism on its own ground, namely, with regard to the question of the adequacy of its anthropological underpinnings. This entails the acceptance of the atheistic view that the conception of God is a product of the human spirit--but not that it is therefore necessarily untrue. The issue for Pannenberg is whether atheism is warranted in maintaining that the idea of God "is an unessential product of the human mind, that is, an idea which is not part of man's understanding of himself which belongs to his essential being."[8] And in the exploration into this crucial question, Pannenberg readily acknowledges that the answer can never be put forth as a bare assertion but must be open to substantive verification.[9]

But the direction in which the answer to the contemporary question of God is to be sought is not along the route of traditional theism. That, Pannenberg maintains, came to a dead end almost two centuries ago in the criticisms of J. G. Fichte (though they were already prefigured in Spinoza), whose insights anticipate the full-blown theory of projection of Ludwig Feuerbach several decades later.[10] Pannenberg's contention is that Fichte's discernment of the impossibility of conceiving God as both infinite on the one hand and highest being and personal consciousness on the other has never since been satisfactorily refuted.[11] The thrust of the matter is that God's infinity precludes the existence of any other whatsoever, for any such existence would be an encroachment upon and denial of that infinity. But to speak of God as highest being entails that God is one being among others, ergo God cannot be an infinite highest being. Furthermore, the notion of consciousness includes the necessary factor of an other, over against which one has

4

consciousness and in relation to which one distinguishes self-consciousness. Personhood is characterized by consciousness. Therefore, likewise, God cannot be infinite person. But Pannenberg insists that a God who is deficient in either infinity or personhood would not be God, wherefore the very concept of God appears to be unthinkable.[12]

The inescapable consequence which Pannenberg draws from this reasoning is that God is not conceivable as a presently extant transcendent being.[13] How, then, is God's reality to be understood at all? It is in regard to this apparent impasse that the third strand of the theological concerns identified here comes into the picture.

For Pannenberg maintains that a viable Christian doctrine of God can only be developed out of a mode of thinking that is fully and firmly rooted in a thoroughgoing eschatological perspective. It is his contention that Christianity's eschatological thrust cannot be casually dismissed, or absorbed into the present as something already realized in authentic existence a la Dodd and Bultmann,[14] nor can it be relegated to the tag end of theological systematization. Pannenberg raises the question, "Can Christianity do without an Eschatology?," and answers it with a ringing "By no means!" Not only is eschatology an indispensable component of the Christian message but it is understood to be "no longer a marginal problem of theology, which one could leave to the last chapter of dogmatics, but the basis upon which everything in Christian tradition is built."[15] And one of the questions of doctrine for which eschatology gains "constitutive significance" is that of God--not only with regard to our knowledge of God but even concerning God's very being.[16] The answer to the question of the reality of God is to be sought within the purview afforded by the cornerstone of Christian eschatology, *viz.*, in Jesus' proclamation of the Reign of God.

The shock of Pannenberg's bold theologizing is encountered precisely in the remarkable integration of intellectual rigor and eschatological earnestness which characterizes his whole output. He contends that, contrary to more commonly held attitudes, commitment to the former requires open and honest consideration of the latter. And eschatology is held to be "intrinsically rational" in its own right, though its content transcends the limits of what reason can straightforwardly articulate.[17]

The doctrine of God which emerges in Pannenberg's conceptual schema as one of the chief fruits of an "eschatologically oriented theology"[18] has not received extended systematic treatment by him but is nevertheless at the very center of his entire work, interpenetrating every other doctrinal exploration. Indeed, Pannenberg himself conveys the impression in the foreword to the first collected

5

volume of his programmatic essays that, although his concept of God came to expression only subsequent to earlier discussions of history, revelation, and Christology, his theology all along has had as its theme the central and foundational issue of the understanding of God.[19] One can interpret the earlier polemical brushfires that were ignited by Pannenberg's theses on God's revelation as but prolegomena to the really crucial issue of his understanding of the reality of God so revealed.

In this regard, I propose to embark upon an extended voyage through the hitherto insufficiently charted seas of Pannenberg's eschatological theology, with his doctrine of God as compass point and ultimate destination. For adequately to comprehend his conceptualization of God and what underlies it entails an exploration through the whole of his theological enterprise, and all of his theological activity points ultimately to this pivotal concept. My aim, in this undertaking, is to lay bare the factors contributing to Pannenberg's exceptional concept of a God whose being is essentially futural, as a basis for analyzing the justifiability of the concept, and to delineate the details of the concept itself in order then to subject it to careful critical scrutiny.

Toward this end, after a brief introduction to Pannenberg's academic pilgrimage,[20] the exploration moves in the second chapter to a consideration of his understanding of the relationship between theology and philosophy, as a substantive background for the subsequent explorations into the details of his theological programme. This encompasses in particular his assessment of the nature of truth and the relationship between faith and reason. Chapter three presents a critical overview of Pannenberg's idea of universal history as necessitated by the quest for meaning in history, including as it does the horizon of the future and the eschatological premise of history's end. Pannenberg's discussions on essential human nature as contributory to the formation of a God-concept, involving such aspects of his theological anthropology as our "world-openness," the nature of personhood, the futurity of freedom, and the enduring human tendency to hope beyond death toward a fulfilling destiny, comprise the scope of chapter four.

There follows in chapter five an analysis of Pannenberg's understanding of history as God's revelation, including especially a consideration of the Old Testament roots of his revelational theses. Chapter six travels into that shadowy region of apocalyptic literature to which Pannenberg ascribes such considerable importance for an adequate understanding of history as universal and, even more crucially, for a proper understanding of the religio-historical background of the life and message of Jesus of Nazareth. The critical assessment of the nature of the apocalyptic world view that emerges here forms a necessary bridge to the discussion in chapter seven concerning the implications of a historically rooted Christology for understanding God, with particular emphasis on Jesus' teaching on the Reign of God and also upon the historically problematic event of Jesus' resurrection from the dead. It is in chapter eight, then, that the precise outlines of Pannenberg's doctrine of God are finally articulated out of this manifold network of interlocking premises and the adequacy and consistency of this theological perspective on God is critically evaluated.

The flow of this essay is intended to facilitate an accurate perception of just what Pannenberg is affirming of God, and why he considers such affirmations to be warranted. The overall structure of this approach can be summarized by pointing up the duality of directions in which Pannenberg moves simultaneously. In the one direction, he seeks to establish what *must* be the case if an intellectually acceptable notion of God is to be put forth at all. That is to ask, what are the issues raised by the quest for genuine knowledge, the concern for meaning in history, the openness of human questioning, for which God's self-disclosure would serve as a sufficient resolution? These conceptual "prolegomena" are explored in chapters two through four. But at the very same time, Pannenberg is exploring the evidences of an actual process of divine revelation in history whose content is seen by him to be strikingly in accord with what this quest for truth, meaning, and ultimate human destiny requires. Pannenberg's understanding of the revelatory process, centering finally in the person and fate of Jesus of Nazareth, is set forth in chapters five through seven. The final chapter explicates the resulting notion of God so revealed, and brings into sharp focus the panorama of critical assessments which challenge the viability of his conceptual vision.

My intent, throughout, is to judge the sufficiency of Pannenberg's insights into the reality of God directly on their own merit. Implied by this statement is the conviction that criticisms which fault Pannenberg's conclusions because ultimately they derive from a point of departure at variance with the critic's will not take us very far. My concern is primarily with the question whether Pannenberg is fully consistent with his own intentionality--whether his conclusions concerning God as the all-determining power of the future, and his specific understanding of the meaning of that notion, genuinely derive from the subject matter with which he is at work. This is especially important inasmuch as Pannenberg would contend strongly that our knowledge of God is to be read off from history as revelatory, and specifically from the person and destiny of Jesus as they definitively disclose the core content of such knowledge. The central issue which focuses the critical argumentation of this study is the degree to which Pannenberg's interpretation of God does justice to the revelatory history he so brilliantly illuminates. Specifically, I am persuaded that Pannenberg brings with him a particular understanding of the nature of divine power which is neither derived from revelation history as that centers in Jesus nor allowed to be sufficiently challenged and reformed by contact with that history, and that, consequently, Pannenberg's related perceptions concerning God, temporality, and change run into conceptual blind alleys. The heart of this challenge to the tenability of Pannenberg's doctrine of God lies in the argument, presented at the end of chapter seven, that Jesus' resurrection, rather than embodying a confirmation of the world view of apocalyptic eschatology, shatters it with the disclosure of God as One whose power is constitutively defined by love rather than in terms of an all-determining control of a yet-undecided future of all that is.

B. Vita

Wolfhart Pannenberg was a remarkably young man when first he attained a considerable degree of theological prominence among his contemporaries in the mid-1960's. Part of this may be attributed to the "missing generation" in German scholarship deriving from the disaster that was National Socialism, but it was also due to the amazingly rapid pace with which Pannenberg developed first as a student and then as a full contributing partner in the ongoing theological dialogue.[21]

He was born in 1928 in the village of Stettin, the son of a German civil servant, and showed early promise of intellectual ability. His adolescent indoctrination in the glories of German nationalism was shattered in the eye-opening demise of the Third Reich and he immediately turned toward the furtherance of his academic studies, sobered and enlightened by what lay behind.[22] After a year at the University of Göttingen, where he studied philosophy under Nicolai Hartmann, and a year at the University of Berlin, he arrived at Basel in 1950.[23] There he came particularly under the influence of Karl Barth's theology,[24] and also Karl Jaspers' philosophy.[25] But he left Basel after one year to take up residence in Heidelberg, where his intellectual pilgrimage received fresh stimuli which were of considerable significance for the direction he was to travel.

At the University of Heidelberg at this time were a number of important scholars in different fields who contributed variously to the progress of the young Pannenberg: the orthodox Lutheran theologians, Edmund Schlink and Peter Brunner; Gerhard von Rad, the Bultmann of Old Testament theology; a rising young Bultmannian New Testament scholar, Günther Bornkamm; his older brother in church history and Luther scholarship, Heinrich Bornkamm; the church historian, Hans von Campenhausen; and the philosopher, Karl Löwith.

An overarching theme which united several among this group in a composite influence upon the course of Pannenberg's studies was that of history. Von Campenhausen several years earlier had lauded Augustine as "the first universal historian and theologian of history of the west" and urged upon the Christian theologian the task of a unified and comprehensive theology of history in the Augustinian spirit, seeing and treating world history as a unity.[26] Shortly afterward, Löwith traced the interpretation of history back to its biblical roots and concluded that meaning in history is indiscernible apart from a context of eschatological expectation--which has no legitimate place in modern historical methodology.[27] Thus he threw down the gauntlet before anyone courageous or foolish enough to attempt to comprehend the whole of history in an interrelated schema from a perspective necessarily within the flow of history itself. Meanwhile, von Rad was well along in his seminal reworking of Old Testament theology which took as its subject matter neither an ahistorical, systematically ordered "world of faith" nor critically derived history of Israel lying behind the kerygmatic texts, but precisely the interpenetration of history and faith which comes to expression in the texts themselves.[28] Any adequate understanding of the message of the Hebrew scriptures, therefore, would henceforth have to come to grips with Israel's own theology of history as an essential ingredient of that community's confessed faith. Not history per se but a "picture" of history was taken to be the proper subject matter of theological investigation. However, even as von Rad was eloquently championing the decisive importance of the Old Testament kerygma for the theological enterprise, his New Testament colleague Günther Bornkamm was earnestly pursuing the historical figure of Jesus that stood elusively behind the kerygmatic portrayals of him in the Gospels.[29] There is no single thread that intrinsically unites these four disparate treatments of the subject of history. Their interconnection is in the fact that they all were heard and absorbed by one who became increasingly convinced that history is a theme with which theology must unavoidably and fundamentally wrestle--and whose resolution of the problem can be seen to involve indebtedness to all four.

Meanwhile, in 1953, Pannenberg completed his doctorate under Schlink, with indebtedness expressed also to von Campenhausen, Heinrich Bornkamm, and Heinrich Vogel as visiting professor. The dissertation was published the following year, as *Die Prädestinationslehre des Duns Skotus*.[30] It is particularly instructive that Pannenberg had turned his attention in the history of tradition to the doctrine of predestination,[31] and that shortly afterward he expanded his concern with this topic beyond late medieval scholasticism to include Luther as well.[32] The implication is rather suggestive that in Pannenberg's intellectual and spiritual pilgrimage the overcoming of the problem of determinism was as decisive for him as the resolution of the question of the nature of evil had been for Augustine, and that only when

9

he had solved this problem to his satisfaction could Christianity be a vital perspective for him. It was crucial for Pannenberg that divine predestination be affirmable without the accompanying concept of determinism.[33] The underlying issue of God's mode of responsibility for order in history has continued to be a concern for Pannenberg throughout his academic career, and remains an element of fundamental importance in his working out the nature of God and God's power.

In 1955, Pannenberg passed his *Habilitation* and was inaugurated into the post of *dozent*, which extended his stay in Heidelberg to a total of seven years. The *Habilitationsschrift*, still unpublished, traced the concept of an analogy between God and the world from early Greek thought through Thomas Aquinas.[34]

During much of this period of study and instruction, Pannenberg came to be involved in a small but vital discussion group that met weekly to explore a range of questions encompassing the whole theological enterprise.[35] Apparently the group had already been formed when Pannenberg was invited to join, and it consisted initially of students majoring in biblical studies. Only subsequently, with the publication of the major fruits of their joint labors in which Pannenberg contributed the introduction and focal essay,[36] did it come to be known against his own wishes as the "Pannenberg Circle." The original participants were Klaus Koch and Rolf Rendtorff in Old Testament, and Ulrich Wilckens and Dietrich Rössler in New Testament. To their number were also added, somewhat later, Martin Elze in church history and the younger Rendtorff brother, Trutz, in theology.[37] All of them went on to receive professorships in the Protestant faculties of various German universities, and have tended to go their separate ways programmatically as well as geographically.[38] But the fact that there no longer exists a conscious identity of purpose among an ongoing circle of discussants should not be allowed to obscure the realization that this enterprise in collective reflection was no incidental venture now abandoned. The dialogical circle reflects rather the essentially social nature of the thinking process and the interdependence of the human quest for truth, which have continued to be constitutive for Pannenberg's work.[39]

Pannenberg accepted a call in 1958 to the *Kirchliche Hochschule* at Wuppertal as professor of systematic theology. Jürgen Moltmann arrived there the same year.[40] Both men were in formative periods of their work at the time, and each undoubtedly drew on the insights of the other in the three years they were colleagues.[41] It was through Moltmann's influence that Pannenberg became exposed to the future-oriented philosophy of Ernst Bloch, to whom he has paid tribute as the one in our time who "recovered the biblical tradition's eschatological mode of thought as a theme for philosophical reflection and also for Christian theology."[42] Pannenberg had already developed a considerable appreciation for the great intellectual synthesis of Hegel during his Heidelberg lecture courses on the history of nineteenth-century theology. Now he investigated the work of a maverick Marxian inheritor of the Hegelian dialectic, one who uniquely integrated Marxism, atheism, humanism, and Jewish messianism in an overarching principle of hope.[43] Though Pannenberg expresses fundamental criticism of Bloch's immanentist vision of the ontological primacy of the future, the thrust of his philosophical explorations did leave a mark on the eventual shape of Pannenberg's conceptualization of God and the future.[44]

Pannenberg left Wuppertal to become professor of systematic theology at the University of Mainz in 1961 and remained there until he accepted a similar post in the newly formed Protestant faculty at the University of Munich in the spring of 1968.[45] At Mainz, the work he had been doing in revelation, Christology, and anthropology began to appear in print in a steady succession of publications that quickly established his reputation as a young theologian of major importance, and as one who could not be pigeonholed into an existing school of thought.[46] It was also while Pannenberg was at Mainz that he entered into dialogue with American currents of thought, lecturing widely in the United States during a semester as visiting professor at the University of Chicago in the spring of 1963, and returning again for part of a year at Harvard and Claremont in 1966-67.[47] And in the academic year preceding this second sojourn abroad, he was joined at Mainz by the American process theologian John Cobb, during which time the two men shared in conducting a seminar on the philosophy of Alfred North Whitehead. Pannenberg's acquaintance with Whitehead's thought is atypical of German theology, which seems so often uninformed about traditions other than its own, but it is typical of Pannenberg's encompassing pursuit of knowledge. The disagreements Pannenberg expresses with Whiteheadian philosophy are certainly greater than the agreements,[48] but an essential point of contact has significantly been made, bringing into potential relationship the disparate philosophical traditions of process thinking represented by Whitehead and Hegel.

During his tenure at Munich, Pannenberg has continued to range far and wide in his intellectual pursuits in a manner that could be expected of one who shares the Hegelian vision of an all-encompassing grasp of unitary truth, but to a degree that is sometimes astonishing. For Pannenberg is a theologian who can feel equally at home discussing with physicists the concept of indeterminacy in natural law and with astronomers their theories concerning the origination of the universe,[49] as well as entering into dialogue with specialists in poetry and hermeneutic on the subject of the function of myth.[50] There is apparently no ceasing in his thirst for interconnections in the appropriation of knowledge.[51]

11

It is this spirit of all-inclusiveness that makes it awkward to single out and treat separately the primary influences on the shape of Pannenberg's theology. Unquestionably he is indebted a great deal to Hegel, but not in such a way that he would represent a complete theological appropriation of Hegel's philosophy.[52] It is rather the case that Pannenberg sees in Hegel a bold attempt at a synthesis of history which is to be emulated but whose shortcomings are to be overcome. It is what Hegel endeavored to accomplish, not the end result, that is of enduring value for him. Beyond Hegel, there are others of influential importance for Pannenberg's understanding of reality who have not been previously mentioned, particularly Wilhelm Dilthey and Ernst Troeltsch. But beyond that, one must be cognizant of the fact that for Pannenberg the whole of the Christian tradition is significant for his work, in light of his conviction that history is *Überlieferungsgeschichte*--the history of the transmission of traditions. Therefore this treatise foregoes any preliminary discussion of the positions of those major predecessors who stand in Pannenberg's intellectual ancestry, for the sake of identifying and assessing the impact of their work on Pannenberg within whatever thematic context that impact is seen to be felt. This procedure facilitates moving immediately into an exploration of the various facets of Pannenberg's theology which contribute in one way or another to his concept of the reality of God.

NOTES

[1]Albert Schweitzer, *The Quest of the Historical Jesus* , trans. W. Montgomery (New York: The Macmillan Company, 1961), pp. 350ff. and ch. 20.

[2]Ernst Käsemann, "The Problem of the Historical Jesus," in his *Essays on New Testament Themes*, trans. W. J. Montague (London: SCM Press, 1964), pp. 15-47. Käsemann's own view that *apocalyptic* eschatology characterized not Jesus but the earliest interpretations of his life and message was subsequently articulated in "The Beginnings of Christian Theology," in *Journal for Theology and the Church 6:*

Apocalypticism, ed. Robert W. Funk (New York: Herder and Herder, 1969), pp. 17-46. (Originally published in 1960.) This is discussed *infra*, ch. 7.

[3]See, e.g., Wolfhart Pannenberg, "What is Truth?," *Basic Questions in Theology*, trans. George H. Kehm (Philadelphia: Fortress Press, 1970, 1971) (hereafter: *BQT*), vol. II, p. 1; "Faith and Reason," *ibid.*, p. 47; and "Christian Theology and Philosophical Criticism," *The Idea of God and Human Freedom*, trans. R. A. Wilson (Philadelphia: The Westminster Press, 1973) (hereafter: *IGHF*), pp. 128f.

[4]James M. Robinson, "Revelation as Word and as History," in *Theology as History* (*New Frontiers in Theology*, Vol. 3), eds. Robinson and John B. Cobb, Jr. (New York: Harper and Row, 1967) (hereafter: *TaH*), p. 11, ft. 31. More recently, Pannenberg has called that conclusion somewhat into question with reference to a significant religious experience at the age of 16, when "on a lonely two-hour walk home from my piano lesson, seeing an otherwise ordinary sunset, I was suddenly flooded by light and absorbed in a sea of light which, although it did not extinguish the humble awareness of my finite existence, overflowed the barriers that normally separate us from the surrounding world." ("God's Presence in History," in *Theologians in Transition*, ed. James M. Wall [New York: The Crossroad Publishing Co., 1981], p. 94.) But in oral conversation, Pannenberg later clarified that recollection with the comment that his intellectual quest was motivated by that experience, which only subsequently was characterized as religious. The experience itself meant that "the intellectual character of the development of my thought was never a matter of disinterested curiosity." (October 21, 1982, in personal conversation with the author.)

[5]Richard John Neuhaus, "Wolfhart Pannenberg: Profile of a Theologian," in Pannenberg, *Theology and the Kingdom of God* (Philadelphia: The Westminster Press, 1969), p. 15. (Hereafter: *TKG*).

[6]For a more detailed discussion of the concept of the provisionality of knowledge and related issues, see *infra*, ch. 2. The endeavor to put forth a theological grounding of reason is no mere passing interest on Pannenberg's part. His single lecture series during his foreshortened visiting professorship at Claremont in the spring of 1967 dealt with this theme, and although he has yet to publish in a systematic way the fruits of his labors in this area, the whole of his work to date may be fairly seen as a continuing manifestation of just this concern, as Neuhaus perceptively has observed ("Profile," *TKG*, p. 43).

[7]Neuhaus, "Profile," *TKG*, p. 50. (Italics mine.)

[8]Pannenberg, "Anthropology and the Question of God," *IGHF*, p. 87. (An ongoing dialogue with atheism is implicit in nearly all of Pannenberg's writings dealing with the question of God.)
One further note is appropriate here, in regard to the quoted content above. Both the original German editions and published English translations of Pannenberg's work contain masculine terminology and pronouns in reference both to God and to persons. These are retained in the present text where direct quotations are involved,

for the sake of accuracy. Otherwise, sex-inclusive (or sex-neutral) language is used herein throughout, including instances of my own translating of quoted passages. Pronouns for God are avoided altogether.

[9]See, e.g., Pannenberg, "The Question of God," BQT II, pp. 206f.

[10]Pannenberg refers time and again to the fundamental significance of the Fichtean atheism controversy for every subsequent conceptulization of God. See in particular: "Person," Die Religion in Geschichte und Gegenwart, dritte Auflage, ed. Kurt Galling et al (Tübingen: J. C. B. Mohr [Paul Siebeck], 1957-65) (hereafter: RGG[3]), V, col. 232; "Types of Atheism and Their Theological Significance," BQT II, p. 197; "The Question of God," BQT II, pp. 202 and 227 f. (ft. 97); and "The God of Hope," BQT II, pp. 234f. and 244f.

[11]In his article on "Person" for RGG[3], completed by 1961, Pannenberg acknowledged that Hegel surmounted Fichte's argumentation through his deeper understanding of personhood (RGG[3], V, col. 232). The same point is made in his monograph on The Apostles' Creed: In the Light of Today's Questions, trans. Margaret Kohl (Philadelphia: The Westminster Press, 1972) (hereafter: AC), p. 28. But he has refined that conclusion in later writing, judging Hegel also to have fallen short of answering Fichte's challenge adequately. "Types of Atheism," BQT II, p. 197: "Even though theism was revived within the nineteenth century, its refutation by Fichte was never surmounted." "The Question of God," BQT II, p. 202: "Ever since Fichte's 'atheistic controversy' in 1799 the traditional concepts of God as the highest being and as personal in nature have been regarded as reifications and anthropomorphisms that are incompatible with God's infinity. These concepts have never completely recovered from Fichte's criticism." Later in that same essay (p. 228, ft. 97), Pannenberg specifically maintains that this is so even with regard to "Hegel's related concept of God as absolute subject." Cf. also his "Person and Subjekt," Grundfragen systematischer Theologie, Band II (Göttingen: Vandenhoeck & Ruprecht, 1980) (hereafter: GsT), pp. 86f.

[12]Pannenberg quotes the passage from Fichte's "Über den Grund unseres Glaubens an eine göttliche Weltregierung" of 1798, which originally touched off the atheism controvery, in "The Question of God," BQT II, pp. 227f., ft. 97: "What then do you call personality and consciousness? Is it not something you have found within yourself and have designated by this name? The fact that you do not at all think of this without limitation and finitude, nor could do so, you can learn from the most cursory attention to the way you have constructed this concept. You make this being, accordingly, by attributing this predicate to a finite being, to a being like yourself, and you have not, as you intended, conceived God, but only reduplicated yourself in thought." The foreshadowing of Feuerbach is obvious.

[13]See, e.g., "The God of Hope," BQT II, p. 235. Cf. also "Anthropology and the Question of God," IGHF, p. 93, and "Speaking about God in the Face of Atheist Criticism," IGHF, pp. 109-112.

[14]Pannenberg, "Can Christianity Do Without an Eschatology?," in G. B. Caird et al, *The Christian Hope* (London: Society for Promoting Christian Knowledge, 1970), pp. 30f. (hereafter: "Eschatology?")

[15]*Ibid.,* p. 31.

[16]*BQT* I, p. xv. Cf. also "Eschatology?," *The Christian Hope*, pp. 31f.

[17]"Eschatology?," *The Christian Hope*, pp. 33f.: "Eschatological ideas can be explained as a rationally lucid projection of the conditions for a final realization of human destiny in the unity of individual existence and social interrelatedness. In this sense eschatology is intrinsically rational, although it expresses that destiny in symbolical terms."

[18]*BQT* I, p. xvi.

[19]*Ibid.,* pp. xv-xvi. In a later essay on how his mind has changed, Pannenberg has observed that although a full-blown doctrine of God actually constitutes the *final* task of Christian theology, nevertheless a deep concern for the achievement of that goal permeated every development of his theological insights from the very outset of his work. ("God's Presence in History," in *Theologians in Transition,* ed. James M. Wall [New York: The Crossroad Publishing Co., 1981], pp. 94-96, 98f.)

[20]For an insightful and engaging depiction of Pannenberg the man, see Neuhaus' illuminating "Profile," *TKG,* pp. 12-24.

[21]That Pannenberg's star was somewhat slow in rising on this side of the Atlantic was considerably due to unfortunate delays in getting his works into translation. Particularly he was overshadowed on the popularizing front by his one-time colleague Jürgen Moltmann, who though two years older than Pannenberg was two years slower in finishing his academic studies and in receiving an appointment to a university professorial chair, and whose widely acclaimed *Theology of Hope* was already the inheritor of Pannenbergian insights--previously published, but less quickly translated into English.

[22]And also, eventually, by Hans von Campenhausen's theological interpretation of the calamity, in the guise of an address on "Augustine and the Fall of Rome" delivered as the Rectoral Address when the University of Heidelberg reopened after the war. (Reprinted in his volume of collected writings entitled *Tradition and Life in the Church,* trans. A. V. Littledale [Philadelphia: Fortress Pres, 1968], pp. 201-16.) Von Campenhausen called for the renewal of Augustine's programme of an all-embracing theological interpretation of history as an esential ingredient of any subsequent theology. Concerning the influence of this call upon the direction taken by Pannenberg in his own developing orientation, see Robinson, "Revelation as Word and as History," *TaH,* pp. 7ff.

[23] Such peregrinations are not the mark of an indecisive mind but are rather typical of the diligent German student, who seeks the benefit of exposure to the insights of more than a single faculty.

[24] Although Pannenberg himself maintains that his theology represents a *tertium quid* beyond the dominant poles of Barth and Rudolf Bultmann, Robinson insists that Pannenberg remains essentially Barthian in his stance, the anti-Barthian polemic notwithstanding. See Robinson, *op. cit.,* pp. 15-21, where he concludes that Pannenberg is the heir rather than the opponent of the Barthian movement. Paul Santmire, in a brief review article, perceptively observes that Pannenberg has "out-Barthed Barth" by taking up the fundamental motifs of Barth's thought and pushing them to an extreme, thereby achieving a new theological synthesis. (*Dialog* 9, 1970, pp. 142-45.) Robert Jenson suggests in one of his books on Barth's theology that Pannenberg is "Barth inside out." (*God after God* [Indianapolis: The Bobbs-Merrill Company, 1969], p. 179.) My intention here is to consider Pannenberg's theology initially in its own right and not as a representation of one or another existing systems of thought. Only out of this vantage point can responsible conclusions be drawn, *a posteriori.*

[25] One of Pannenberg's earliest published articles analyzed Jaspers' interpretation of the nature of myth, though the initial influence of Barth is prominent precisely in his treatment of Jaspers. See "Mythus und Wort. Theologische Überlegungen zu Karl Jaspers' Mythusbegriff," *Zeitschrift für Theologie und Kirche* 51, 1954, pp. 167-85. (Coincidentally, the same issue containing Käsemann's formal reopening of the quest for the historical Jesus.) (Hereafter: *ZThK.*)

[26] Von Campenhausen, *op. cit.,* p. 214(f.). The essay was first published in 1947. (See *supra*, n. 22.)

[27] Karl Löwith, *Meaning in History* (Chicago: The University of Chicago Press, 1949), pp. 5f., 18, 191, 197f. Published in German in 1952 as *Weltgeschichte und Heilsgeschehen.* For a further discussion of Löwith's theses on the philosophy of history, see *infra*, ch. 3.

[28] See, *e.g.,* Gerhard von Rad, *Old Testament Theology,* trans. D. M. G. Stalker (New York: Harper & Row, 1962-65), I, pp. 105-15. (German edition: 1957.)

[29] His *Jesus of Nazareth* (New York: Harper & Row, 1960) appeared in German in 1956.

[30] Göttingen: Vandenhoeck & Ruprecht, 1954.

[31] The choice of the topic does not indicate that Pannenberg was initially intending to become a historian of doctrine. Students in theology in the German universities are expected to orient their dissertation studies toward what has gone before, as essential preparation for later participation in the cutting edge of theological dialogue. Pannenberg himself found it quite singular that he should have so quickly

become the subject of dissertations from America, where the living continuity with previous theological traditions is not so strong.

[32]See "Der Einfluss der Anfechtungserfahrung auf den Prädestinationsbegriff Luthers," *Kerygma und Dogma* 3, 1957, pp. 109-39 (hereafter: *KuD*).

[33]See *ibid.*, pp.136f.

[34]Elizabeth A. Johnson has given careful attention to this early work of Pannenberg in "The Right Way to Speak about God? Pannenberg on Analogy," *Theological Studies* 43, 1982, pp. 673-92.

[35]One is tempted here to draw a further parallel with Augustine and his dialogical circle at Cassiciacum.

[36]*Offenbarung als Geschichte,* edited by Wolfhart Pannenberg in association with Rolf Rendtorff, Trutz Rendtorff, and Ulrich Wilckens (Göttingen: Vandenhoeck & Ruprecht, 1961) (hereafter: *OaG*). In English: *Revelation as History,* trans. David Granskou (New York: The Macmillan Company, 1968) (hereafter: *RaH*). The third German edition (1965) also contains an untranslated "Afterword" by Pannenberg.

[37]A major influence upon the direction of the group's deliberations was certainly von Rad's exploration of Israel's understanding of history as grist for theology's mill. Indeed, early estimates of Pannenberg's programme tended to designate it as a systematic theology consciously rooted in (von Radian) Old Testament exegesis, representing a pivotal shift from Bultmannian theologies oriented primarily toward the New Testament. But there is far more to Pannenberg's innovative theologizing than simply or even primarily a systematization of the implications of Old Testament interpretation. And there is justifiable disagreement as to whether Pannenberg truly represents a legitimate inheritance of von Rad's views on history and theology. (See Robert North, "Pannenberg's Historicizing Exegesis," *The Heythrop Journal* 12, 1971, pp. 385f.) Particularly one finds a fundamental discontinuity in their respective evaluations on the attitude toward history in the Jewish apocalyptic tradition, as will be explored in chapter six.

[38]This has involved, in part at least, a matter of moving out from under Pannenberg's shadow. The biblical scholars Rendtorff and Wilckens were particularly incensed at being unfairly maligned as merely exegetical supporters for Pannenberg's already developed system. On the other hand, Trutz Rendtorff later joined Pannenberg at the University of Munich as his colleague in systematic theology. Rössler, incidentally, shifted fields after his doctoral work on apocalyptic tradition and is now in practical theology.

[39]On this point, see, *e.g.,* Neuhaus, "Profile," *TKG,* p. 23.

[40]Another major Old Testament scholar, Hans Walter Wolff, was Rector at Wuppertal when the two young theologians arrived, and he left there at the same time

as Pannenberg to take a professorship at the University of Mainz. He went on to become von Rad's successor at Heidelberg.

[41]In private conversations with me, each man minimized the contribution of the other toward his own work. There is reason to believe that this is somewhat less justified in Moltmann's case and that the borrowing of ideas was greater on his part. Hans Walter Wolff, again in private conversation, has observed that although the two men came together out of differing backgrounds and interests, they shared a common concern which deeply motivated their overlapping efforts: adequately to comprehend Old and New Testament exegesis theologically, and as a unity.

[42]"The God of Hope," *BQT* II, p. 238.

[43]Pannenberg demonstrated his interest in Bloch's thought in his contribution to the *Festschrift* published in honor of Bloch's eightieth birthday, *Ernst Bloch zu ehren,* ed. Siegfried Unseld (Frankfurt: Suhrkamp Verlag, 1965)--which surprised not a few people in that nearly half of those who were thus paying their respects to his work were Christian theologians. Moltmann has actually gone much further into Bloch's messianic utopianism than Pannenberg, having published essays on Bloch from as early as 1960, and having devoted a seminar in the 1962-63 winter semester at Wuppertal to Bloch's magnum opus, *Das Prinzip Hoffnung.* The title of Moltmann's own initial major work, *Theology of Hope,* bears a conscious relation to Bloch's, and the fifth German edition contains an appendix expressing Moltmann's half of an ongoing dialogue with the philosopher of hope. ("Hope and Confidence: a Conversation with Ernst Bloch." This was not included in the translated edition, but it is available in Moltmann's *Religion, Revolution, and the Future* [New York: Charles Scribner's Sons, 1969], pp. 148-76.) The two men later became colleagues at the University of Tübingen.

[44]The actual relation between Bloch's and Pannenberg's thought will be treated in context.

[45]The faculties in religion at the various state-supported universities in Germany are typically either Protestant or Catholic, depending upon the confessional orientation of the area in which that particular one is located. Mainz has, for some time, been the single exception. But one additional university, Munich (München) in heavily Catholic Bavaria, in 1967 added in a spirit of intellectual ecumenicity a second, Protestant, religious faculty. Pannenberg's interest in sharing in the formation of a Protestant faculty in a predominantly Catholic school can be seen as but one further indication of a strong desire to expand the quest for the truth of Christian faith beyond sectarian boundaries that would imperil its essential oneness.

[46]James M. Robinson has observed that the perspective of Pannenberg and his "circle" represents "the first theological school to emerge in Germany within recent years that is not in one form or the other a development of the dialectic theology of the twenties." ("Revelation as Word and as History," *TaH* , p. 13.)

[47] It was also Robinson who was apparently the first one in this country to recognize Pannenberg's emerging significance--as early as 1960. See John Cobb's review of the circumstances of this discovery in "A New Trio Arises in Europe," *New Theology* No. 2, ed. Martin E. Marty and Dean G. Peerman (New York: The Macmillan Company, 1965), pp. 257-63. The Lutheran journal *Dialog* listed Pannenberg on its masthead as a contributing editor with its premiere issue in 1962, and began publishing his essays in translation in the following year.

[48] Pannenberg's most extended discussion of process thought is in "Atom, Duration, and Form: Difficulties with Process Philosophy," *Process Studies* 14, 1984, pp. 21-30, where he objects particularly to A. N. Whitehead's "atomistic ontology" (p. 22) as inappropriately one-sided and unable to "do justice to wholeness as a metaphysical principle on equal dignity with that of individual discreteness" (p. 27).

[49] *E.g.,* his "Kontingenz und Naturgesetz," in Pannenberg and A. M. Klaus Müller, *Erwägungen zu einer Theologie der Natur* (Gütersloh: Gütersloher Verlagshaus Gerd Mohn, 1970), pp. 33-80.

[50] "The Later Dimensions of Myth in Biblical and Christian Tradition," *IGHF*, pp. 1-79. (See Preface, p. vii.)

[51] Cf. Neuhaus' revealing depiction of how Pannenberg and his wife go about visiting an art gallery ("Profile," *TKG*, pp. 17f.): "Preparations constitute a model of thoroughness which should be emulated by only the more hardy of travelers. There is extended research, followed by strategy meetings and the procurement of equipment covering most every conceivable contingency. It is worthy of a quartermaster's preparations for a major assault. The pace of the excursion itself is breathlessly intensive, everything must be seen and seen carefully. The merits of a painting are discussed with reference to its historical context, the phase of the artist's political development, and the history of its ownership."

[52] Pannenberg's understanding of the relation between philosophy and theology precludes that, as will be discussed in the chapter following.

19

2

THEOLOGY AS TRUE PHILOSOPHY

A. Encounter

"What has Athens to do with Jerusalem?" asked Tertullian rhetorically. What indeed!, echoed Barth. Answers Pannenberg: nothing less than everything.

The issue, for Pannenberg, turns around the problem of the presumed universality of the truth with which theology deals. That is to say, theology's truth must be valid universally, all-encompassingly, or it cannot claim validity at all. And this brings theology directly into competition with the activity of philosophy, which has also, until recently, tended to claim comprehensiveness for the scope of its work. Inasmuch as these two closely related but distinct disciplines overlap so extensively in their mutual concern, inasmuch as both intend to speak truthfully about the nature of that which is, their differing perspectives on the truth cannot simply be ignored, or set beside each other with equal validity. To do so would call seriously into question the essential unity of truth.

Pannenberg came only belatedly to give explicit formulation to his understanding of the relationship between theology and philosophy, although this understanding can be seen to have implicitly undergirded his earlier writings to a considerable extent.[1] In an essay first appearing in 1968 entitled "Christian Theology and Philosophical Criticism,"[2] he crystallized his interpretation vis-a-vis a trio of options which he found it necessary to reject. It will prove helpful to examine these three criticized alternatives as prelude to unpacking Pannenberg's own distinctive position.

21

1) Opposition. Theology so emphasized the primacy of pure revelation that it denied the significance of philosophy for theological reflection altogether. As represented particularly in its Barthian form, this stance resisted any opening toward philosophical justification of theological affirmations and denied even a point of contact for theological statements in philosophy.[3] The consequence was a plethora of bald truth claims, based in the authority of revelation alone, which stood in *a priori* judgment upon all non-theological assertions. Theology went its own way, independent of any and all philosophies which could be dismissed as irrelevant to the theological task.

To begin with, Pannenberg ardently repudiates the idea that revelation can be defended on purely authoritarian grounds. The possibility for that was exploded by the Enlightenment emancipation of the human mind from absolute dependence upon sacred tradition, through its disclosure of the essentially irrational character of authoritarian belief.[4] On the contrary, revelation, if it is to be received as such, must be open to the confirmation of the truth of its content. Revelation's authority can only reside in its demonstrable truth and not vice versa.[5] To reject the possible importance of philosophy's investigation into the truth of reality which revelation purports to disclose, on the ground of the overarching authority of that revelation itself, is therefore seen to be fundamentally a mistaken methodology.

In this respect, Pannenberg insists that a purported revelation of God to which the biblical tradition witnesses "cannot be isolated by an act of irrational and arbitrary choice from the sphere of other religions and their claims to be revelations."[6] Rather, the truth status of that Judaic-Christian revelatory claim is to be established only by comparison with those competing assertions, and such a comparative study can be carried out only on the basis of a philosophical theory of religions in which the meaning of "revelation" is empirically ascertained, not postulated *a priori.* "Thus the theology of revelation," says Pannenberg, "always implicitly assumes an understanding of revelation and religion, that is, a philosophy of religion. At this point theological thinking which is self-critical has no alternative but to deal explicitly with philosophical problems."[7]

Pannenberg makes two further observations concerning the inescapable link between theology and philosophy. Inasmuch as theology conveys a word of revelation not only about persons but also about the world and history, it is making assertions that impinge upon the sphere of scientific and philosophical inquiry. And the implicit assumption that the theologian's statements in these areas are reconcilable with the truth of non-theological assertions about the same matters in an assumption which "itself must become the object of theological reflection, for otherwise the truth of all theological statements remains undecided."[8] This means for Pannenberg then that theology must actively participate in the realm of philosophical discussion in order to unpack that premise of unity and defend its own truth claim. Finally, theology is challenged to be articulate about the meaning of the language it uses, and this requires an entering into the philosophical discussion concerning criteria for linguistic signification.[9]

2) Ethical complementarity. An emphasis developed in Protestant theology, present already even in Melanchthon, upon the ethically centered content of theological statements, and this led to a marriage between theology and philosophy in the area of specifically ethical considerations. Nineteenth-century inheritors of the Kantian reduction of theology to ethics did not simply continue that reductionist process but, in dependence upon Kant, did proceed to restrict philosophy's theological relevance to the field of ethical concerns. One important strand which emerged out of that crucible was what Pannenberg calls an "ethically based supernaturalism," traceable through Ritschl and Herrmann and represented presently in the existentialist interpretation of the Bultmannian school. This approach sought in ethics a common ground shared by both disciplines, supplementing the human ethical dichotomy, which philosophical ethics could identify but not resolve, with a solution offered through divine revelation. Heidegger's analysis of the human existential situation was received into the theological task as a decisively significant philosophico-ethical prolegomenon to the theologian's work proper.[10]

Pannenberg criticizes this concentration upon ethics as the exclusive point of interrelationship between philosophy and theology on three counts. In the first place, theological assertions decisively transcend merely ethical considerations, calling for an understanding of all that is, of reality as a whole. The Bultmannian approach illegitimately brackets out the question of world-understanding, within which human existence has its place and ethical concerns have their meaning.[11]

In this regard, then, the division between an understanding of the world and an understanding of one's self becomes utterly untenable. Bultmann's classic separation of kerygmatic world- and self-understanding, in which the former is regarded as time-bound and mythical and the latter as enduringly valid, simply cannot be maintained. That kind of dichotomizing between two dimensions of primitive Christian perspective which Bultmann's demythologizing program undertakes ignores the crucial factor that "self- and world-understanding always belong together."[12]

Finally, Pannenberg points to the tendency within this perspective to lose sight of the social nature of human existence, in

23

concentrating all too characteristically upon the private ethic of one's individual existence. My essential solidarity with the world has as its corollary my solidarity with the social context within which my individual identity is gained, and this in turn requires that the question of selfhood be raised in association with concerns that go beyond the horizon of the ethical into that of the socio-historical and ontological.[13]

3) **Dependence.** Liberal theology in the nineteenth and twentieth centuries responded to the Enlightenment critique of authority by seeking support for its tenets in one or another philosophical system from which it borrowed rationalist concepts that provided the extra-theological (and extra-revelatory) context for its affirmations.[14] Although Pannenberg does not explicitly say so, it would appear that he does not regard this as distinctively different from a much earlier development in which theology carved out an enclave within its own domain for a *theologia naturalis*, a Christian philosophical system which was independent and preparatory to the work of revelatory theology per se.[15] In either respect, there is involved a dependent relationship of theology upon a body of philosophical concepts which pave the way for its articulation of its own higher truth.

Pannenberg is critical of this approach for a variety of reasons, though he reacts to it more by implication than by direct encounter. He suggests, for example, that there is an unavoidable transitoriness about individual philosophical systems which render them inappropriate for undergirding a theological orientation. Every philosophical construction forms only a single rational model, whereas the religious traditions with which theology grapples remain capable of being interpreted by a wide variety of such models.[16]

Furthermore, the idea that the insights of philosophy might simply serve as the handmaiden of theology has become a theologian's pipedream, since philosophers equally lay claim to the universal validity of their own insights into truth, without the need for the capstone of theological disclosure. Both disciplines claim universal scope for the truth they seek to impart, wherefore each one invariably is faced with the necessity of critiquing the other in light of its own alleged comprehensiveness. Complementarity among the two perspectives is ruled out by virtue of the fact that a co-ordination of the two into a single unified field of view that would encompass and supersede both denies the implicit universality of each.[17] And Pannenberg maintains that the unity of God which revelation discloses, along with God's significance as the origin of all that is real, requires that a theology which corresponds to it be equally universal or give up its claim to intellectual integrity.[18]

Coupled with this is the insistence that God's unity can only be thought of as a "unity which unites all that is," which requires theology's own involvement in the philosophical domain of metaphysics and therefore makes competition rather than dependent co-ordination between the two disciplines inescapable: "By considering the being of that which is--the common element in all that is real in all its diverse forms--philosophy is already pursuing the question of the unity which unites all that is, and thereby competes with what theology says about God."[19]

But what of that previously noted acknowledgment that a theology of revelation does indeed always implictly presuppose some philosophy of religion? Does that not suggest a factor of philosophical dependence? Not so, for Pannenberg, for such a concession

> . . . does not mean that theology has to accept any philosophy as an authoritative basis for its own work. Rather, in each particular case it has to test whether or not the categories and judgment of the philosophy of religion which are available to it are appropriate to its own subject matter in any particular case, and *in some circumstances it must develop its own alternatives.*[20]

This latter clause particularly opens up the direction of Pannenberg's own formation of a more viable alternative for understanding theology's relation to philosophy, to which we now turn.

B.   Denouement

The concept of truth's unassailable unity has been recurrently alluded to, and it serves as the point of departure for Pannenberg's unpacking of how theology and philosophy may be seen to stand in relation to truth.

The crux of the matter, as already indicated, is that the truth of reality which human knowledge endeavors to encompass must in some way to realizable as a unified whole. That is not to deny the actuality of diversity and distinctiveness--Pannenberg's position would not appear to be subject to Hegel's indictment of Schelling's Absolute as a night in which all cows are black. It is rather to affirm that of two logically or factually contradictory interpretations of what is real, one or both must be false. The truth of what is embraces all that is, is therefore universal in scope and cannot admit of any "additional" piece of "truth" that is excluded from its entirety. There can be no plurality of particular truths that defy an ultimate unity encompassing them. Thus the claims of the Christian message to embody truth about humanity, the world, and God cannot stand in impervious isolation from all other explorations into truth, as if those claims dealt only with particular truths of a particular people with a particular history and destiny. To the contrary, the impact of the truth claims of Christianity is universal in scope, inasmuch as they deal with God as unitive.[21]

Therefore, Pannenberg contends, theology can neither be nor contain within itself a "Christian philosophy" which exists alongside other forms of philosophy possessing equal right, for such a discipline "must either be classified and categorized by the philosophy which reflects upon the unity of the truth as a subordinate form of the knowledge of truth, or else it must assert its own right to be considered the 'true' philosophy."[22]   Pannenberg is able to find the resolution to that dilemma in only one direction:

> The conflict between theology and the philosophy which distinguishes itself from theology is unavoidable, so long as philosophy does not itself become theological, or theology remains unable to convince us that it is true philosophy. The conflict between them is inevitable from their nature, because both can be taken seriously only in so far as they lay claim to the whole and undivided truth.[23]

Theology as "true philosophy"--that is Pannenberg's counter-proposal.[24]   Theology is to do philosophy's job, only better. The implication here is that philosophy, left to its own resources of rational reflection, cannot complete its own task of comprehending the nature of reality, the being of beings. Pannenberg inisists that the theologian is called to enter into a dialogue with philosophy not only with regard to how the phenomena identified by philosophy are to be interpreted but even concerning what the phenomena are themselves.[25] All the work of the philosopher is to stand under the "meta-criticism" of a theology whose own form becomes that of reflective philosophical thought, surrendering all appeals to authority.[26]

What this entails is that Pannenbeg, as theologian qua philosopher, would seek to carry on a dialogue with philosophy which not only would endeavor to relate philosophical concepts to theological understanding but would also see the concern of philosophy, to know the truth, as addressed and *completed* by the work of theology.[27] It is not that theologians depend upon the work of philosophy as a foundational prolegomenon upon which they build. Rather theologians have before themselves the task of enabling philosophers to be more adequate in their own philosophizing. In that process, substantial use is indeed made of the history of the philosophical tradition, but only insofar as elements within that reflective tradition are persuasive in their own right and not simply pieces of some normatively adhered-to system.[28]

The most important direction in which Pannenberg pursues this understanding would appear to lie in his conviction that what theologians presume to know through their attention to what history discloses is not

26

simply extraneous to truth but fundamentally constitutive of it. This does not consist simply in a priority of revelation over reason in the appropriation of what is true, for whether a particular "revelation" can lay claim to being a disclosure of truth must always be rationally confirmable, as has been previously stated. What is at stake here is something more crucial. It is the insistence that the particularities of history are of primary importance vis-a-vis the conceptual universals with which the philosopher deals, so far as knowledge of the true is concerned. The truth of what is universally knowable purely through the reasoning process demands extension and completion by what is accessible only through a concrete consideration of the historically particular. Inasmuch as theology's true subject matter consists initially of facts of history,[29] its domain embraces that missing piece of the conceptual puzzle without which philosophy by itself remains ever less than "true" philosophy.

Augustine was the first to become fully cognizant of this distinction but he perceived its implications differently. Yes, the truths with which Christianity is especially concerned are truths of history, but they are therefore inaccessible to the reasoning intellect. For reason deals with that which originates in the bodily senses or the intuitions of the mind and is oriented toward the universal. Those truths which are historical are by their nature particular, and therefore beyond the scope of rational apprehension. The only means of grasping them was understood by Augustine to be an act of faith that accepts the authority of the tradition that transmits them.[30] It is precisely the legitimacy of this authority that has been called into question by the Enlightenment, wherefore theology's claim to be dealing with any truth at all would seem to be decisively in jeopardy.

Pannenberg rejects such a conclusion on two counts. In the first place, he is openly supportive of an additional fruit of the Enlightenment reorientation of human knowing: the rise and development of tools of historical-critical research on the basis of which the traditions of history can be rationally explored. Although he has no compunction about critiquing several of the methodological tenets of modern historiography, Pannenberg is nevertheless firmly wedded to the utilization of that approach as the sole access to the history that lies behind us.[31] Of even more basic significance however is his denial of the self-evident adequacy of Augustine's particular (and Platonic) understanding of the nature of reason as incapable of grasping the historically singular. The concept of what constitutes reason has had its own history of change and development, and the limitation of reason to a knowledge of universals has not always been maintained.[32] Especially this understanding of the nature of reason is tied to the Greek idea that truth itself is always universal in character, and it is just such an idea as this that Pannenberg's theology decisively calls into question.

27

In one of his most important earlier programmatic essays, "What is Truth?,"[33] Pannenberg presented the thesis that the Western understanding of the nature of truth has not one but two distinctively different roots out of which it has grown and which have variously and unevenly formed the context for theology's work: on the one hand, the Greek; on the other, the Hebraic. The exploration into their distinctiveness is pivotal for Pannenberg's thought. Following the path laid out by Hans von Soden in his epochal chancellor's address at Marburg in 1927,[34] Pannenberg points out the different underlying meanings of the Hebrew word for truth, *emeth*, and the Greek word used to translate it, *aletheia*.

Emeth conveys a significance of establishing, standing firm, sustaining. "*Emeth* means the reliability, the unshakable dependability, of a thing or word, and thus also the faithfulness of persons."[35] A person's words are *emeth* insofar as they prove trustworthy. Moreover, *emeth* is not there once and for all, as a timelessly valid state of affairs, but must always and again *happen*. Pannenberg repeats von Soden's observation that truth for the Israelites is "reality (which) is regarded as history . . . not something that in some way or another lies under or behind things, and is discovered by penetrating into their interior depths; rather, truth is that which will show itself in the future."[36]

Greek truth, on the other hand, *is* rather than happens.[37] *Aletheia* conveys a sense of that which is timeless, imperishable, *ungeworden* . It is the "unconcealedness" of that which unchangingly stands behind the changing appearance of things, "always identical with itself as that which is hidden behind the flux of sense-appearances."[38]

Pannenberg sees a decisive point of contact between these two concepts in the shared understanding that truth involves a matter of constancy, *Beständigkeit.* Nevertheless, even here a distinction is implicit. For the Israelite, the guarantee of endurance and stability is not a presently accessible facet of experience. The truth of the God of Israel who is understood to grant and establish *Bestand* is yet open to the confirmation of that truth--because, inasmuch as history is still underway, the unquestionableness of God's constancy and reliability is not yet an established fact.[39] Therefore, the truth of God "will first prove itself through the future" wherein God's trustworthiness in granting *Bestand* is definitively disclosed.[40] In the meantime, truth's constancy is accessible "only by trusting anticipation of the still-outstanding proof, and that means precisely, by faith,"[41] in contrast to the Greek understanding that the unchanging character of truth renders its fullness accessible to the logos of human reason. The underlying difference here is that for the Greek mind truth entails enduring constancy by necessity, whereas, for the Hebrew, truth's constancy is contingent, based on the faithfulness of Israel's God. This does not require, however, that Israel had no

28

experience of truth. On the contrary, Israel continually rooted its trust in its God precisely in its history in which "preliminary proofs" of divine constancy were already at hand.[42]

It is the unfortunate case, so Pannenberg maintains, that Greek thought has been the basic point of departure for the development of Western conceptuality, almost to the complete exclusion of the Hebrew contribution, so that even the basic questions arising in rational reflection are formulated according to greek ways of thinking and the biblical witness is then brought into this mold. The fact that there arose in the Old Testament its own distinct understanding of the nature of truth has for the most part been ignored in the history of Western thought. Pannenberg calls for a reversal of this orientation, in order that one may move into Greek conceptuality from out of the horizon of biblical consciousness.[43] Such a move is not proposed gratuitously. It is Pannenberg's contention that there are impasses in Greek thought which arise out of its abridged view of reality, and which do not admit of resolution within its own perspective. But that fact alone does not warrant substituting the Hebraic perspective for the Greek. Rather the Hebrew understanding of truth merits acceptance only insofar as it continuingly proves able to appropriate for itself the Greek view of reality in such a way as not to exclude its valid insights but to receive them into its own purview while dissolving[44] the aporias of the Greek understanding into a more encompassing whole.[45]

Pannenberg emphasizes three areas where this self-substantiation of the Hebraic view of truth particularly breaks out into the open, surpassing the insufficiencies of the Greek. These constitute, at the same time, instances of the sort of theological engagement of philosophy that he is championing, and each one has a decisive bearing on the question of an understanding of God.

1) Experience of truth and the problem of subjectivity. What grounds the truth claims of the knowing subject? What criteria establish the agreement of thought with that which truly is? For the Greek, the question was readily resolved in the recognition that the knower was essentially passive in the experiencing of the true. Truth imparted itself to the observer in a person's passively received sense impressions. But there gradually emerged in Western consciousness the conviction that reason is not an act of pure reception but involves a creative act on our part. This movement raised the issue of the source of truth: Is it to be found within the understanding reason itself? Is truth anything more than an expression of the knower? The problem that comes to the forefront here is that of the wholesale *subjectification* of truth which discloses a yawning gap between human thought and extrahuman reality. How, if at all, is the gap to be bridged?

29

Pannenberg traces out an answer which first takes shape in Nicholas of Cusa and continues down through Descartes and Kant to German Idealism: the presupposition of the reality of God as the objective ground of the idea of truth as conformity. The point here is not the adequacy of such philosophical explorations, though Pannenberg would appear also to want to maintain that. The essential point is that there arises out of Greek conceptuality a movement of the mind which goes beyond the limits of that conceptuality, in the direction of the biblical idea of God.[46]

Pannenberg now proceeds to take the matter one crucial step further: the movement to a subjectification of truth is indeed to be viewed as a proper outgrowth of the biblical understanding of reality. This is discerned in the recognition that "truth, which is originally God's truth, must be preserved in the world through people, in the sense of a responsible shaping of the world by God's measure." This includes not only the truth of verbal expression but especially that of human conduct. "That truth proves itself in conduct and thus has a personal character demonstrates once more that in the subjectification of truth elements of the biblical, historically determined concept of truth have come through." But human conduct is "true" only insofar as it is "in harmony with God's truth, to which the world as a whole is indebted for its origin."[47] This leads Pannenberg finally to the position that

> . . . human conduct is true only when it occurs in view of the unity of the world, for only thus does it occur in view of the Creator who grounds, in the Creator's fidelity, the unity of the world. And only in the one who grounds the unity of the world can we find the God in whom the truth of our own conduct and thinking has its criterion.[48]

Thus, for Pannenberg, the issue of the experience of truth flows eventually into the closely related question of the nature of truth's unity.

2) Unity of truth and the problem of historical change. How does the overarching oneness of truth encompass the contingencies of historical change? To the Greek mind, change was excluded from truth's unity; permanent unchanging truth was set over against historical flux, which was extraneous to it. But there is in this perspective, Pannenberg suggests, a hidden impasse: the occurrence of unconcealment implies a historical aspect to truth. The Greeks disregarded this "event character of truth" as a tendency contrary to the intent of their conceptuality.[49]

The Hebrew mind, on the other hand, emphasized the historicness of truth as the keystone of its understanding. "Here, true being is thought of not as timeless but instead as historical, and it proves its stability through a history whose future is always open."[50] With the subjectification of truth in the West came a concomitant recognition of the essential historicness of human thought, in the realization that all human affirmations of the true are inescapably timebound, historically conditioned. And with this development, the ultimate unity of truth is once again thrown into question. The Greek solution that the genuinely true transcends temporal considerations is seen to be untenable, whereas the orientation of the Hebraic consciousness that unity is to be sought in the totality of historical process addresses the question in a promising way:

> In this situation, unity of truth can now only be thought of as the history of truth, meaning in effect that truth itself has a history and that its essence is the process of this history. Historical change itself must be thought of as the essence of truth . . .[51]

So also a viable concept of God that is continuous with the Hebraic perspective must be one that does justice to the understanding of an essential "historicness"[52] [*Geschichtlichkeit*] of the very truth of God.

The crucial point that Pannenberg is insisting upon here is that truth must be intrinsically inclusive of change, of the process of history. Indeed, to repeat, with emphasis, truth's essence *is* historical change! Truth is history, history is truth. The one is not extraneous to the other. The Hebrew view of reality denied the Greek supposition that truth is to be sought as something lying behind, or underlying, the process, insisting instead that truth is to be found in and as the process itself. So would Pannenberg endeavor to be loyal to this insight. His success in doing so is not simply to be assumed.

3) Essence of truth and the problem of appearance. There is a third area of conflict which has been spelled out by Pannenberg which perhaps ought to be understood as merely another way of expressing the issue just explored, but to which he has devoted separate and extensive attention. I also shall treat it separately here. It is the problem of the (unchanging) essence of what is real and its (changing) appearances, and the "Hebraic" perspective Pannenberg offers toward its resolution is slightly in tension with the preceding paragraphs.

In his essay on "Appearance as the Arrival of the Future," Pannenberg traces back to Greek thought a troubling dichotomy between that which enduringly is and that which varyingly appears, in which the former is self-sufficiently indifferent toward the latter and the latter contributes nothing to the truth of the former.[53] The issue, as Pannenberg pursues it here, does not turn simply on the matter of the truth of change; it concerns the question of the nature of the relationship between a universal and its individual embodiments. The history of

Western thought brought about a repudiation of the dichotomizing tendency in Greek conceptuality, but the underlying problem remained unsolved even in those interpretations which sought to express a fundamental identity between the *eidos* and the individual instances in which it is concretely encountered. That, also, is one-sided, Pannenberg maintains, for the interpretation does not do justice to the sense that the *eidos* is not exhausted in any particular appearance; the difference thus breaks out anew.[54] "The question is raised as to whether the unity of the identity and nonidentity of appearance and being is accessible to a more penetrating description."[55]

Pannenberg finds a possible solution for that not by building directly upon the Hebraic perspective of reality but rather by drawing out a particular, crucial aspect of the ministry of Jesus, which can be seen to stand in direct continuity with Jesus' own Hebraic context. The argument turns on the "well-known and controversial problem of the relation of the futurity and presence of the Reign of God" in Jesus' ministry.[56] Pannenberg rejects as unconvincing the reductionist interpretations that eliminate one or the other of these two foci from Jesus' message, countering with the following explication:

> . . . in the ministry of Jesus the futurity of the Reign of God became a power determining the present. For Jesus, the traditional Jewish expectation of the coming Reign of God on earth became the decisive and all-encompassing content of one's relation to God, since the coming Reign of God had to do with the coming of God himself. Thus, obedience to God . . . became turning to the future of the Reign of God. But wherever that occurs, there God already reigns unconditionally in the present, and such presence of the Reign of God does not conflict with its futurity but is derived from it and is itself only the anticipatory glimmer of its coming. Accordingly, in Jesus' ministry, in his call to seek the Kingdom of God, the coming Reign of God has already appeared, without ceasing to be differentiated from the presentness of such an appearance. . . . The difference between Jesus' present and the Father's future was ever and again actualized in the surrender of the man Jesus to the coming Reign of God that he proclaimed, insofar as it was the future of another. Jesus pointed away from himself; therefore, the interpretation of that which appeared in him must go beyond the appearance of Jesus, to God, whom his message concerned. . . . And yet, precisely in Jesus' *pointing* away from himself to God's future did this future as such become present in and through him. The appearance of God in this man, which transcends his finite existence, means, just because of this, an existence of God in him, a oneness of God with him. This coming-to-appearance of God in Jesus has thereby a different meaning from the epiphanies of gods in human or animal form, of which we hear, e.g., in the history of Greek religion. There, any particular form of the appearance, being replaceable, remains external to the essence of the deity, just as in Plato or Parmenides, its appearance remains nonessential to true being. In the ministry of Jesus, on the contrary, the God of Israel, the future of his Reign, comes definitively to appearance once. He manifested himself in this single event conclusively and for all time, and just for this reason only

once. . . . The finality of Jesus' ministry is based on its eschatological character, on the fact that through it the ultimate future of God's Reign becomes determinative of the present and therefore becomes present. Appearance and essential presence are here one. Is not this character of the appearance of God in Jesus--as opposed to the different religio-historical background of the Platonic-Parmenidean relation between appearance and true being--also relevant for considering the problem of appearance in general?[57]

It is a remarkable tour de force, modestly presented a la Kierkegaard as a sort of "project of thought." The specifics of the proposal will occupy our attention at greater length in the chapter on Pannenberg's Christology. For the present, the emphasis must be placed on the manner in which Pannenberg endeavors to work through an interpretation of the history of Jesus that, rather than depending on borrowed philosophical categories of understanding, facilitates the philosophical enterprise itself--in suggesting that here "two elements are united which have again and again broken apart in philosophical reflection," namely, "the effective presence of what appears in the appearance, and its transcendence of the individual appearance."[58] The thrust of these reflections is that, derived from the model of Jesus' ministry, one may designate appearance as the present occurrence of a futural essence.[59]

But is this proposal really thoroughgoing enough? In the two previous instances, we have found Pannenberg countering and surpassing Greek conceptuality with insights brought forth out of the Hebrew tradition. In this instance, the solution to a particular impasse in the Greek philosophical tradition is found not in a characteristically Hebrew mode of conceptuality but rather in a bold interpretation of a sequence of historical events arising out of a Hebrew matrix. The root question to be raised is whether the interpretation itself derives also from the conceptuality of that matrix. There is some reason for doubting that it does. Particularly the very conceptual terminology that Pannenberg retains, appearance and that which appears, is basically Greek in derivation. Does the thrust of the solution proposed here stand in contrast to the previously observed tenet that truth (essence?) is to be found in the historical process (appearance?) itself? The cruciality of the question seems to turn on the precise nature of the example that Pannenberg has put forward: it is *God*, in the mode of God's Reign, who is said to come to appearance in the history of Jesus. What, then, is the relationship between the affirmation that truth is historical and the corollary consideration that truth is ultimately the unitary truth of God? Is God historical? Or is God the non- or trans-historical who appears within history? In what way is the truth "which will show itself in the future,"[60] and which is affirmed here already to have penetrated fully into the present, a truth above and beyond the reality which is history itself? The question, with its various ramifications, will be explored herein in due course. It is raised here simply to indicate the insufficiently resolved tension that surfaces in Pannenberg's delineations of a presumably Hebraic context of philosophical reflection.

To return now to the initial considerations which prompted these explorations: it would appear in the light of Pannenberg's emphasis on the truth-bearing particularities of history and his attendant championing of Hebraic over Greek categories of conceptuality that what is basically being expressed in his denial of any possible dependence of theology on philosophy is a repudiation of philosophy as intrinsically *Greek* in derivation. To say "no" to any theological reliance upon philosophy essentially amounts to a rejection of the conceptual primacy of Greek modes of thinking. To say "yes" to theology's interpenetration of philosophical issues is to affirm theology's own Judaic heritage as a bearer of fundamental insight into the very structure of reality. The theologian is called upon to "out-philosophize" the philosopher in getting back to a more embracing and incisive context for articulating and probing the philosopher's root concerns. Pannenberg is deeply appreciative of, though by no means completely wedded to, the philosophy of Hegel precisely because he has seen in Hegel a breaking of the bonds of Greek conceptuality in favor of greater openness to the Old Testament tradition. But criticisms arise even here, as I shall continue to point out, inasmuch as not even Hegel is credited with any sort of philosophically authoritative interpretation of the Hebraic strand of his conceptual tradition. Of course the question must also be raised as to whether some other philosophical orientation than Hegel's may have penetrated more consistently into the Hebraic tradition of thought--as well as whether Pannenberg himself carries off that penetration adequately and consistently.

C. Truth Entire

The premise of the essential unity of truth necessarily encompasses truth in its entirety. I have identified one crucial implication of that for Pannenberg, insofar as competing claims to embrace the whole of truth are concerned. With regard to Pannenberg's championing of the Hebraic view of truth over that of the Greeks, another aspect of this issue rises to the surface--an aspect which becomes problematic precisely because of the perspective on truth reflected in Hebraic thought.

For, with respect to the Greek understanding of the true, the whole of what is genuinely true is unchangingly at hand. The vagaries of historical process in no way alter or contribute to the essentially true; they only variously disclose it. And what is thus disclosed cannot, strictly speaking, be said to have a history. It is characterized as transhistorical.

But with regard to the approach to truth rooted in the Hebrew tradition and foundational for an adequately grounded Christian theology, the history of truth is essential to truth itself. And inasmuch as history is unfinished, the whole of truth is not yet at hand. It is not presently at my disposal, not a proper object of human thought. Precisely because this whole of truth as historical is still outstanding, the unity of truth as a unity of all that is is not an extant reality.[61]

Pannenberg credits Hegel with having decisively taken up this insight into his system. Hegel's philosophy

> . . . is distinguished from other philosophies of history by the fact that truth is not to be found already existing somewhere as a finished product, but is instead thought of as history, as process. "The truth is the whole."[62]

And only in light of the end of the historical process does this wholeness of truth become discernible.

Pannenberg finds significant concurrence here with the biblical understanding of truth.[63] On the one hand, there is the common recognition that truth is not timelessly unchangeable but rather a process which runs its couse. This leads, on the other hand, to the insight into the essential futurity of ultimate truth. Hegel's thesis approximates the biblical perspective in the implication that

> . . . the unity of the process, which is full of contradictions while it is under way, will become visible along with the true meaning of every individual moment in it, only from the standpoint of its end. What a thing is, is first decided by its future, by what becomes of it.[64]

Inasmuch as the whole is incomplete, the true meaning of any of its parts is yet to be definitively disclosed. As Hegel maintained, the truth arrives conjointly with the end.[65]

But Hegel was unable to carry through this insight with sufficient consistency, insists Pannenberg. For he had at hand no other option than to regard his own philosophical standpoint as the terminus of the process in order to conceive the unity and truth of the process, thus surrendering the horizon of the future from his purview. This radical contemporizing of eschatology brought Hegel into contradiction with his own intention, inasmuch as future truth is necessarily excluded from his system.[66]

With what, then, is Pannenberg himself left? Inasmuch as the history of what is true is yet under way toward its own embracing and illuminating unity, all human "knowledge" of the true has the present character of provisionality. Knowledge is necessarily anticipatory of the outcome in the light of which all preliminary affirmations of the truth of what is will find their proper place in the whole.[67] Therefore any absolutizing of a presently held declaration of truth would constitute a misrepresentation of the inescapably provisional character of all present claims of knowledge.[68]

Nevertheless, the limitations on human access to truth imposed by the anticipatory and thus provisional character of knowledge do not necessarily have the last word, even for the present moment. For Pannenberg considers the implication inherent in the understanding of thinking as a process of striving beyond itself toward its goal: the presence of truth is presupposed precisely by the consciousness of its lack.

> The insight about the thorough-going anticipatory structure of all thought can be maintained only on the condition that consciousness can nevertheless be certain of the presence of the truth. If it is correct, however, that we have access to the truth only in anticipation, then the truth's presence can be conceived, from its side, only as an anticipation in the sense of a pre-appearance [*Vorschein*] of that which has ultimate validity and of the whole constituted by the end of all history. Nevertheless, it would not necessarily call into question the presence of the truth if there should be given an experience of a pre-appearance of the ultimate which so far has not been superseded and which is at least not involved in any inherent necessity of being superseded. There would prove to be a pre-appearance of this sort if there were one which would not be superseded, but would rather, as the entrance of the ultimate into history, constitute its wholeness from that point. But this statement is again an anticipation whose validity can only be proved in the future.[69]

The idea introduced here is one dealt with elsewhere by Pannenberg under the designation of "prolepsis." This involves the understanding of a pre-actualization, within the course of history, of the final truth which characterizes the whole of history from the standpoint of its end. What is significant at this juncture is that Pannenberg brings up the idea here not as an answer to the problem of the provisionality of knowledge but as an indication of a possible direction in which an answer may be sought--and the concluding sentence in the quotation above is meant to be taken quite seriously. I will examine in detail, in chapter seven, Pannenberg's defense of the resurrection of Jesus as the event within history which ostensibly provides a prolepsis of ultimate truth. What initially is of concern here is the manner in which he proposes the formal idea of prolepsis: he is laying out the theoretical conditions according to which a resolution, in principle, to the problem deriving from the provisionality of

36

knowledge might be forthcoming. Whether or not it is substantively forthcoming is another matter.

Likewise, it is crucial in this context to point out the relevance of these considerations for an understanding of the reality of God. In Hebrew tradition, God, according to Pannenberg, is only understandable as that one in whom the unity of truth is established. This point of view appears to function axiomatically for him: "God is not thought of as God at all if he is not thought of as the unity which unites all that is."[70] Inasmuch as the unity of truth is attained only through the process of history and with the end of that process, and inasmuch as the future of that process is yet open,[71] the truth of God's unifying actuality is decisvely at stake. Only a God who embraces everything can be the truth itself, and therefore "every representation of God is to be tested as to whether it permits understanding reality as a whole, and thereby satisfies the unity of truth."[72] But initially we are not confronted here with an actual doctrine of the reality of God. We are confronted rather with a positing of conditions for the possibility of having knowledge of the truth of God, and of truth at all. *I.e.,* God is properly to be conceived as that one who, in bringing truth into a unified whole, functions as the guarantor of truth--but only, thus far, as the appropriate direction in which an answer to the question of the possibility of knowledge is to be sought, not yet as definitively given in and for knowledge. That is to say, God as the ground of truth and thus of knowledge is posited as a conceivable reality whose own veracity is yet to be sought out and authenticated--by attention to the particularities of history in which the truth of God's unifying activity is or is not preliminarily disclosed. For the moment, the act of adopting the premise of God as the one unifying source of the whole of what is real "can only mean having an open question, not an actual knowledge of God."[73]

D. Knowledge, Faith, and a Theology of Reason

The insistence that the true must encompass the whole of history, coupled with the resulting emphasis on the present incompleteness and provisionality of all acts of knowing, leads Pannenberg to a provocative synthesis of the categories of faith and reason. It takes the shape of an asseveration that the movement of faith forms the essential criterion for the rationality of reason itself. We can best get to the heart of this pivotal insight by considering first Pannenberg's understanding of the nature of faith and its relationship to knowledge, moving thence into his proposal for an eschatological theology of reason.

Faith can be understood either in the narrower, Reformers' sense as *fiducia*, trust, or it can be understood in a broader sense as *fides,* including within itself the motifs of trust, knowledge (*notitia*), and assent (*assensus*).[74] Pannenberg tends most often to follow the former line of thought, regarding faith as an attitude of trust in the reliability of what history ostensibly discloses. But the act of trust is not to be isolated from the ground of trustworthiness in the object of one's trust. The question is that of the nature of the access to that basis for faith.

Pannenberg adamantly repudiates the view that faith can legitimately function to ground that knowledge which constitutes the content of faith, in the sense that the believer comes to know the truth of the object of one's trust in the very act of trusting.[75] Such fideistic circularity tends to make the decision of faith the very ground of faith, and this understanding fails to do adequate justice to the sense that faith is directed toward a truth "outside myself" (*extra me*).[76] It is that objective truth, which is presupposed both for knowledge and for faith as trust, that holds the place of priority with regard to either. Theology cannot limit itself to an explication of the faith one proclaims, but must also address itself to the question of what legitimately sustains one's faith. Therefore, writes Pannenberg elsewhere,

> . . . theology has to deal with the presupposition of faith, with the truth and reliability (already presupposed in the act of faith) of the "object" on which faith depends. Of course it can do this only in a provisional way. The truth or untruth of faith is not decided primarily in the act of faith; rather this decision depends on faith's object, which contains the promise in which faith trusts, and which is also the object of theological knowledge. Only in this way does faith depend on a truth *extra se.* . . . Therefore it is the business of theological knowledge to confirm the truth which is presupposed for faith and on which it trusts.[77]

The position which Pannenberg takes is that faith thus rests upon the logical, though not necessarily the psychological, primacy of knowledge--predominantly "historical knowledge."[78] For faith "has its basis in an event which is a matter for knowing," not merely for believing; faith cannot take the place of knowledge on that score.[79] Faith does not become superfluous because of this, inasmuch as the decision as to whether I will commit myself trustingly to what confronts me in the act of knowing must still be made. The issue, for Pannenberg, is that the decision be made as intelligently as possible, and he understands the task of theology to be the providing of that rational groundwork whereby the appropriate reasons are forthcoming for the decision of faith.[80] "Knowledge," therefore, "is not a stage beyond faith, but leads into faith-- and the more exact it is, the more certainly it does so."[81]

There is, however, a crucial distinction which must be maintained. Historical knowledge "assures faith about its basis"[82] but is not itself that basis. This means, on the one hand, that faith is hardly invulnerable to the shifting sands of critical historical inquiry. Trust is directed toward historical data with regard to which we never have more than greater or less probability of knowledge.[83] But on the other hand, Pannenberg insists, faith is never tied completely to any particular, momentary state of knowledge, inasmuch as its roots are in the history which knowledge mediates and not in the knowledge which is doing the mediating. The "certainty of faith" does not become a "historical certainty,"[84] given the mutability of all results of historical research. Nevertheless, Pannenberg suggests, in the act of trusting, "faith goes beyond its own criteria, abandoning not only self but even the particular form of knowledge of its object from which it started, and laying itself open to a new and better knowledge of the truth on which it relies.[85] The reason for this is that faith is understood to be able to transcend its own picture of a historical event, mediated through a particular form of historical knowledge out of which it has arisen, because its true foundation is the event itself and the God who is revealed therein.[86]

Is Pannenberg taking away with the left hand what he is giving with the right? *Does* rational historical inquiry really have the capacity to make a substantive difference in the shape of faith--to the extent, for example, that it might *deny* rather than assure faith its basis? Pannenberg openly concedes that possibility.[87] The conflict between the act of trust and what knowledge communicates about the event(s) on which trust is founded could conceivably be so unequivocal and complete that the possibility for holding one's faith with intellectual integrity would be nil. But even beyond the lack of anticipation of the emergence of such a prospect in the future, there remains the recognition that even *that* state of knowledge would be equally circumscribed by its provisionality and open to further correction in its own future. Thus, once again, though historical knowledge serves as the essential avenue of access to that which grounds faith, and is therein indispensible for faith, no one particular form of historical knowledge is in itself the immutable basis which would sustain or utterly suspend that faith.

But the relationship between faith and knowledge has still another important dimension for Pannenberg, insofar as the logical primacy of knowledge over faith is understood to be encompassed in turn by an act of trust in the future on which both ultimately depend. The need for the development of that additional dimension was recognized as early as 1963, when Pannenberg observed in the untranslated Postscript to the second edition of *Offenbarung als Geschichte* that his understanding of the nature of human knowledge called for a full-blown "theology of reason."[88] The project is still under way, though the outlines of such a venture appeared in a 1965 essay on "Faith and Reason"[89] and formed the basis for a lecture series at Claremont in the spring of 1967. From these two sources, the fundamental shape of the proposal is readily identifiable.

The decisive breakthrough with regard to an understanding of faith was made in the Enlightenment repudiation of authority as a basis for assent to truth claims. The consequence of this development is that there can no longer be a legitimate conflict between reason and faith in terms of faith as authority. But an understanding of the nature of faith is not the only term in the dialogue which has shifted. Reason too has a history, and inasmuch as theology alone sees its task as directed toward a resolution of the tension between reason and faith, the process of sifting through the disparate meanings attached to "reason" is a valid one for theology to pursue. And given the lack of a monolithic constancy and absoluteness about any single understanding of reason, the theologian has every responsibility to view and judge distinctive concepts of reason and affirm that one which can be seen to be the most legitimate.[90]

Toward that aim, Pannenberg isolated three typical forms of reason in his essay on "Faith and Reason," but he expanded and slightly altered the typology in his more extended treatment of the subject in his lecture series two years later. It is the latter which the following summary primarily reflects.[91]

1) Receptive reason. For Plato, knowledge was understood to be the consequence of *anamnesis*, recollection. The mind is illumined by the self-revelation of being (Ideas), an illumination already operative in a human being in the pre-existence of one's soul. All "learning" is understood as the recalling in memory of an idea of truth eternally present within us. Aristotle retained the emphasis on the receptivity of the intellect in somewhat altered fashion. Persons possess a passive intellect which receives knowledge through being illumined by the active intellect which is divine and immortal. The fundamental premise basic to both, and to Greek philosophy in general, according to Pannenberg, is once again that truth is eternal, unchanging, in abstraction from the ongoingness of the temporal processes of change. A further problem arises with regard to the lack of noetic significance of any autonomous reflection by the human subject on sense data: the transition from sense perception to conceptual cognition happens rather automatically.

This emphasis on the mind's receptivity to given truth continues down through Augustine, Thomas Aquinas, and Nicholas of Cusa, with the major shift being the introduction of the direct role of God as the illuminating source of truth. The perspective reaches its apex in modern thought with British empiricism, with the source of the mind's receptive activity now understood as sense experience. Knowledge is dependent upon a conformity of ideas with the object of sense perception.

2) Creative *(a priori)* **reason.** Kant made unavoidably clear the necessity of facing the contribution of the perceiving subject, which did not involve a negation of receptive reason so much as a surpassing of it which incorporated it. The fundamental Kantian critique of receptive reason's basic inadequacy was that everything we point to as given is already perceived in a creative way; all our knowledge begins with experience but does not necessarily arise therefrom. The contribution of the human subject to knowledge is that we provide the synthetic *a priori* structures of the mind in its operations which are presupposed in every act of experiencing. The new discovery here is that imagination is already constitutive for sense perception, providing the synthesis whereby the multiplicity of perceptions achieves unity.[92]

But problems arise even here. The *a priori* were regarded by Kant as complete once and for all, failing to allow for the dynamic of historical process and ignoring the fact of the creative multiplicity in the productivity of imagination (*i.e.,* the possibility of the actuality of a variety of *a priori* structures in different persons of different cultural epochs). There is the failure to perceive that imagination is an ongoing process.

3) Reflective reason. Hegel moved beyond Kant in elevating the role of the creative imagination and recognizing more fully the continuing dynamic at work within it. For Hegel, reflection must be an ongoing activity, a dialectic in which the continual encounter of reflection with its limitations, its momentary inadequacy, urges the reflection forward into a new reflective operation which utilizes the immediately foregoing accomplishment as the departure point for the next stage of the dialectic movement. Reflection continually reveals the limitation of each stage of understanding, the inadequacy of the moment's knowledge for its object, and thus drives beyond each moment's contradiction between thought and thought's intention.

The fundamental movement of the dialectic is that sense impressions, at the outset, are themselves empty and abstract. Sense perception introduces identifiable content, but at the expense of an accompanying contradiction between the thing-in-itself and thing-for-myself as perceiving subject. The understanding attempts to explain the divergence, and does so by employing subjective notions (laws, etc.). Thus there occurs a turning inward; unity is to be sought within. So now the development must take place in terms of self-consciousness as the key to its unity with objective consciousness.

Reason arises beyond mere understanding as the achievement of knowledge through the surrendering of the particularity of an individual's self-consciousness in order to overcome the contradiction between the in-itself and for-others. The result is reason's fulfillment in *Geist,* the in-and-for-itself, which reason apprehends as the truth, and which entails the reunification of objective consciousness and self-consciousness. But the fundamental problematic in this schema is that the whole process of attainment of truth depends upon the possibility of the surrendering of particularity--which is precisely what seems to fail to take place. Universal truth, as common Spirit, is apprehended only from individual perspectives. *Individual* reason is never really superseded. Human reason is related to, and tries to get at, this universal final truth which underlies everything, but its grasp is always particular, partial, and anticipatory. Individual reason remains historically conditioned, and therefore cannot get hold of absolute truth absolutely and unconditionally.

4) Historical reason. The insight developed by Wilhelm Dilthey regarding the historicity of reason forms a basic component in Pannenberg's understanding and will be examined more fully in the chapter following, in respect to the concept of the futural dimension of the category of "meaning." But the outlines of the position must be introduced here, for the turn taken by Dilthey is basic to the understanding of reason which Pannenberg is most concerned to uphold.

Dilthey recognized that reason itself is historical in that it develops within the course of human history and has as its proper object the understanding of the meaning of that history. For truth has to do essentially with historical events and the question of an event's truth is at root the question of what it ultimately signifies. But the meaning of an event is not something intrinsic to the event itself. It has to do rather with how that event is understood to be related to other events. Every individual experience has its meaning only in connection with the totality of other experiences to which it stands in relationship--and thus, ultimately, for Dilthey, with life as a whole. Within any present moment of experience, the reasoning process is unavoidably incomplete and provisional, for it is directed toward a yet outstanding future which moves it beyond where it presently is. Reason points ahead in anticipation of its own eventual fulfillment.

It is this understanding of reason as historical, presently provisional, and futurally oriented, which Pannenberg sees as leading into the horizon of eschatology already present in faith.

> Faith is not the only thing that has a relationship to the future in that as trust it anticipates something future and unseen. Rather, a fore-conception of the future is constitutive for reason, too, conceived in its historic openness, because it is only an eschatologically (because temporally) constituted whole

that yields the definitive meaning of everything individual . . . . The creative character of the productive imagination seems to draw its vitality from this fore-conception. Conversely, the eschatological structure of reason opens up room for faith's talk about an eschatological future of the individual, the human race, and the world as a whole. Such talk cannot any longer be cast aside as contrary to reason.[93]

Faith and reason are brought together, therefore, by their mutual directedness toward an eschatological unity of reality as a whole which is both the object of the act of trust and the presupposition for the ongoing process of reasoning. A theology of reason properly recognizes that reason is eschatologically grounded and qualified, inasmuch as the whole of history is the premise of the reasoning activity which always implicitly anticipates it. But faith remains distinct from reason, all the same. "Faith is explicitly directed toward that eschatological future and consummation which reason anticipates" and from which reason derives, whereas reason carries its "anticipation of a final future constituting the wholeness of reality" only as an implicit presupposition.[94]

The truth of this interpretation of the nature of reason is understood by Pannenberg to lie in the recognition that the structure of human thought as proceeding by imaginative anticipation toward encompassing truth corresponds to the structure of reality itself as momentarily incomplete and anticipating its final consummation. Therefore, "because this future is not alien to reason, but is rather its origin from which it implictly always derives, faith cannot stand in opposition to reason."[95] Quite to the contrary, one significant function of faith would be to liberate reason to its full dimensionality of future relatedness, so that reason can go beyond its attention solely to past and present realities and recognize its proleptic character in regard to its imaginative anticipations of meaning. Insofar as faith as trust takes the promise of a futural unity of reality and relies thereon, it undergirds the reasoning process in the hope for its success. It is in this way that "faith can confirm itself as the criterion for the rationality of reason, just by its orientation toward a final, eschatological future."[96]

E. Truth and Verification

There remains yet to be considered under the rubric of theology as true philosophy Pannenberg's thoroughgoing willingness to endeavor to defend the cognitive significance of theological statements against the demands of language philosophy, explicitly in contradistinction to the irrational "retreat to commitment" championed by the theology of the Word of God. The crucial outlines of that defense were developed in a paper presented in the fall of 1971 on "The Nature of a Theological Statement."[97]

Pannenberg notes there that scientific inquiry proceeds by positing hypotheses--and generally speaking all statements are hypotheses, even theological ones. They are open to the determination of their truth or falsity. Any statement must in principle be open to the possibility of checking its claim to truth. Belief statements are not to be regarded as merely performative, expressing the intention of the believer to commit himself or herself in a certain direction, because they contain a cognitive element with their complex intention, and to dismiss that would render the commitment element meaningless. This cognitive element of a belief statement can become the object of theological reflection, which will include the question of whether the cognitive claim is true or false. Theology has to admit as pertinent, criticisms of faith's truth claims, and attempt to answer them.[98]

Pannenberg accepts three basic postulates that relate to the "scientific" character of the theological discipline: the non-contradictory character of theological statements (God is not beyond logic); the "unity of the subject matter distinguishable from the statements about it" (God is other than affirmations about God); and finally, the point at which these two issues decisively merge, the necessity of "control," of ascertaining appropriate means of "checking" the truthfulness of faith statements.[99] Specifically the avoidance of the problem of rational confirmation of the legitimacy of God-talk is no longer possible, because "statements which in principle do not allow for a critical inquiry are no statements at all and can no longer be taken seriously as claiming anything with regard to truth."[100]

But how does this apply to talk about God? Pannenberg acknowledges that statements referring to God cannot be tested directly because, on the one hand, "the reality of God is still debated," and, more significantly I think, "it would go against his divinity as being the all-determining reality if he were at man's disposal like a finite reality which is available at man's pleasure."[101] But that is not yet the whole of the matter. There is a second alternative: statements which cannot be tested by direct inspection of their truth may be investigated indirectly, "by an examination of the consequences that can be derived from them"--and, with regard to God-talk, "statements about divine reality and actions are testable by reference to their implications for the understanding of finite reality insofar as God is maintained to be the all-determining reality."[102] To the degree, then, that one can indicate that the content of God-statements "is really of determinative significance for all finite reality as it is available to our experience," such that "nothing real can be fully understood in its particular reality without reference to the presumed God" whose presumed reality "opens up a deeper understanding of reality"--to that degree, "one can speak of a corroboration or confirmation of theological assertions."[103]

The problem of course, once again, is that the totality of reality is not yet accessible for investigation of the traces of God's all-determining power, because it is presently incomplete. "The totality of everything real is given only in the form of an anticipation of the universe of meaning as implied in present experience."[104] It is only in religious experience that this anticipatory thrust becomes thematic,[105] producing its enduring forms in the historical religions and their philosophical ideological offshoots.

> Thus, the totality of all finite reality that should provide the criterion for statements about divine reality is accessible only by subjective anticipations of the universe of meaning that tacitly and by implication determines all experience but becomes explicit as subject matter in religious experience. Hence, the religions constitute the immediate object of theological investigation . . . Theology, then, deals with hypotheses on the adequcy or inadequacy of religious traditions with relation to the implications of meaning in all other experience, first at the time of the historical origin of a particular religion and continuing until the present day.[106]

The latter sentence is crucial. The point is that the truth claim of a particular religious perspective is understood to be supported to the extent that it proves able "to investigate the continously changing experience of reality."[107]

Finally, then, Pannenberg turns to the question of verification per se, rejecting the arbitrary restriction of verification to empirical observations and holding out instead for a broader use of the term along the lines of "provisional corroboration" that he has been setting forth. In this respect, even John Hick's "eschatological verification,"[108] seemingly so close to his own perspective, is accorded only guarded approval, inasmuch as it does not serve anyone any present purpose. The conclusion with which he ends is a moderate one, fully in accordance with his perspective on the provisional and anticipatory character of all present expressions of truth.

> Certainly, a final verfication of theological statements by whatever means will remain unattainable before the final advent of the kingdom of God. But a provisional corroboration of theological hypotheses seems to be within reach and will be possible to the same degree that they illuminate the problems of the religious traditions and the implications of meaning in present experience.[109]

F. Summary and Critique

The basic movement of Pannenberg's conceptualization of the appropriate relationship between theology and philosophy in their joint pursuit of truth, and the implications arising therein with respect to his understanding of the truth of God, can now be summarized.

The premise of truth's ultimate unity entails that theology cannot simply be dependent upon the tenets of a philosophical system but must itself become philosophical and embrace philosophical pursuits into the nature of truth. The implied primacy of theology over philosophy consists essentially in an affirmation of the supremacy of the Hebraic understanding of truth over that of the Greeks, and the impetus to that judgment is derived from the recognition of the capacity of Hebraic understanding to resolve impasses which have come to light in the tradition of Western conceptuality that has been predominantly rooted in Greek modes of thinking. For the attention of the Hebrews to the historicity of truth and the conviction that constancy and stability are contingent upon a futural confirmation penetrate the dilemmas arising in Greek thought with regard to the increasing recognition of the role of subjective human thinking and acting as contributing to the becoming of truth and with regard to the necessity to take historical change seriously as somehow intrinsic to truth.

But this realization that truth embraces the historically particular and not simply the cosmicly universal gives rise to the consequence that the whole of truth which is theology's as well as philosophy's goal is not presently accessible, inasmuch as the whole truth of what is included within the historically particular must embrace the yet outstanding future of history. Thus an end of the historical process is a premise of the possibility of truth's being one and whole. For the present, one can have only anticipatory cognition of what is ultimately and embracingly true, wherefore all knowledge of the true is presently provisional and open to futural correction. The only possible resolution to this provisionality of knowledge would be if there were discernible within history a proleptic occurrence of that truth which will emerge in unified fullness when history arrives at its final destiny.

The implications of this understanding are that faith as trust is directed toward the assurance that truth as the unity of all that historically becomes will ultimately prevail, but such trust legitimately can be held on to only if the course of history itself can be understood to impart and sustain that trust, wherefore the faith of the believing theologian relies upon the work of critical historical inquiry into the events of the past as the only avenue of access to faith's proleptic ground. But respectively, a theology of reason is called for wherein reason is properly understood to be grounded in the future of truth toward which the trust of the theologian is directed, wherefore faith critiques and sustains the rationality of reason itself. Furthermore, theological statements are not strictly verifiable in the present, for their ultimate object, the futural unity of truth, is not presently at hand. But they are provisionally corroborated indirectly through

46

attention to the observable consequences derived from them and through consideration of their capacity to open us up to a deeper understanding of reality.

God is properly to be understood as the source and guarantor of truth as unified and entire. According to Hebraic understanding, God is conceivable only as that one who provides truth its basis by granting constancy and stability to the direction of the historical process, and by leading history to its "true" destiny. Inasmuch as truth and history are not extraneous to one another, there is a certain "historicness" attaching to the truth of God, which always must prove itself anew in the future of unfolding history. Therefore the truth of God as the "uniting unity of all that is"[110] is that which can show itself only in the future. It is presently inaccessible in any absolute way inasmuch as the truth of the unity God is understood to provide is not presently actual. Therefore God's ultimate truthfulness is apprehensible only anticipatorily, through attention to what history preliminarily discloses concerning its ultimate destiny, and possibly by means of a "prolepsis"--a "happening in advance" of a truth yet outstanding. In the meantime, talk about God is cognitively valid to the extent that such affirmations prove instrumental in disclosing the meaning of history more encompassingly than is possible without them.

The program thus advanced is a bold and far-reaching one. Pannenberg is to be generously commended for the depth of philosophical understanding and the breadth of awareness of the philosophical tradition which he brings to the difficult task of elevating the activity of the theologian to philosophical respectability. He has staked out a large and perilous territory for himself in striving for a sense of conceptual unity among conflicting strands of tradition, and he moves about within it with great intellectual dexterity. Nevertheless, awe must be tempered with critical reflection, and there are important questions to be raised and criticisms to be advanced with regard to the procedures of thought which have been set out in this chapter.

1) Concerning Pannenberg's rejection of theology's dependence upon or complementarity with philosophy, two criticisms arise. First, his emphasis upon the transitoriness of philosophical systems, in contrast to the enduring capacity of a religious tradition to be interpreted by a variety of such models, tends to overlook the fact that the *theologies* which interpret their religious tradition are transitory as well. It is the *basis* of a specific theological orientation, in the tradition it seeks to articulate, which can lay claim to a certain ongoing constancy, not the theological orientation itself--as Pannenberg fully acknowledges in his extensive and informed criticism of the continuing history of theological reflection. For this reason, it seems inappropriate to contrast theology and philosophy on this score. Both theology and philosophy stand provisionally and insufficiently before the truth they seek to encompass,

and neither is ultimately able to transcend completely its transitoriness. Even so, of course, a theological system will find itself all too readily surpassed by subsequent developments in the process of philosophy. But theology's goal is only to latch on conceptually to eternal truth, not to become that truth. Its ultimate surpassability does not negate its present, provisional relevance and partially truth-bearing character.

2) Secondly, there is a bothersome circularity about denying theology's complementarity with philosophy on the basis of the understanding that God is the unifying unity of all reality and therefore the single goal of two essentially competitive quests. The (presumably revelatory) content of theology as it develops its reflective work becomes in retrospect the basis for marking out the boundaries for that work. But does one really grasp that pivotal truth already independent of influence from philosophy, or is it mediated precisely by a particular understanding which one has previously inherited from a philosophical source? That is to say, does Pannenberg not deny the legitimacy of his objection to complementarity by virtue of the very fact that the concept which he calls on to substantiate the impossibility of complementarity is itself derivative from a particular philosophy--*i.e.,* that of Hegel?

3) Given Pannenberg's insistence upon developing theology itself as "true philosophy," the question must continuingly be raised as to the innate philosophical soundness of the specifics of his theological program. This can only be done contextually, of course, so that an answer to the question cannot be offered and defended until the direction of Pannenberg's interpretation of reality, divine and otherwise, has been set forth.

4) A second question must be kept carefully in mind as well, with regard to the consistency with which Pannenberg faithfully adheres to the presuppositional grounds of theological understanding which he has laid out: I will be concerned particularly to identify, in due course, the extent to which Pannenberg incorporates concretely the insight into historical process and change as *constitutive* for ultimate truth.

5) Additionally, the question of whether Pannenberg is actually successful in developing a theology with no borrowed philosophical presuppositions must be continuingly confronted. I have already had one occasion to voice this concern above. The issue is not immediately whether theology *can* make do on its own, independent of philosophy except in those instances when it consciously tests particular philosophical categories and judgments and appropriates them as its own. The issue advanced here is whether Pannenberg succeeds in carrying off this proposal. As the specifics of Pannenberg's theology emerge, the question of whether his perspective is captured by unobserved philosophical presuppositions--which he brings with him in

his investigation of history rather than reads off from that investigation--must ever be at hand.

6) Substantively, there is a quite problematic condition imposed on the very *possibility* of the truth which theology and philosophy endeavor to grasp: that history *must* come to a consummating, unifying end. Pannenberg unblushingly has "cosmic" history in mind here, the wrapping up of all finite reality into an ultimate whole. In this perspective, one conceivable possibility is eliminated as an absolutely necessary non-truth, namely, that the process itself is endless. But must the end of history function necessarily as a condition for the possibility of truth at all? Is an eschatological point of view to be rationally defended on the diametrically reversed grounds of "either eschatology or nonsense"? We will need to be on the lookout for internal substantiation of the legitimacy of that premise. For the moment, I will simply ask whether this understanding is unequivocally essential to the Hebraic understanding of truth's historicity and the openness of the historical moment to futural confirmation. Once again, *must* the truth that bestows *Bestand* be one in which the historical process is brought into a unified whole, or is this a looking at the Old Testament too thoroughly through Hegelian spectacles? *I.e.,* Pannenberg has already observed one fatal flaw in Hegel in his lack of openness to a yet outstanding future beyond his own philosophy, but does he fail to observe another equally fatal one in regard to that absolute insistence on terminal unity?

7) Finally, a question must be posed which Pannenberg does not directly consider, namely, whether a self-consciously *philosophical* system of thought may have emerged in the West's conceptual history which can be seen to have greater continuity with Hebraic modes of thought than with Greek. If so, would this not overcome the remaining barrier to consideration of a legitimate complementarity between theology of philosophy, and provide the possibility of a utilization of philosophical categories concerning the way in which all events occur as instrumental for unpacking the meaning to be discovered in the paticular events of history with which the theologian is concerned?

NOTES

[1]See, *e.g.,* "The Crisis of the Scripture Principle," *BQT* I, pp. 1f. (Originally a lecture delivered in 1962.)

[2]*IGHF*, pp. 116-43. First published in *Revue de Theologie et de Philosophie* 18, 1968, pp. 249-71.

[3]"Christian Theology and Philosophical Criticism," *IGHF*, p. 119.

[4]See "Faith and Reason," *BQT* II, pp. 50-52. The insistence that the Christian shares necessarily in the implications deriving from the Enlightenment heritage is a theme to which Pannenberg returns again and again. Cf., *e.g.,* his "Response to the Discussion," *TaH*, pp. 226f., where he identifies Barth's resistance to this changed intellectual climate as the fundamental reason for his turning away from the "theology of the Word of God" of his one-time theological mentor. It is also salient to note that he does not exempt the Bultmannian stream of "Word of God" theology from that indictment.

[5]Pannenberg's explication of this understanding is explored in chapter five. The emphasis on theology's responsibility for engaging in this truth-confirming task consitutes the thrust of Pannenberg's analysis of "The Nature of a Theological Statement" in *Zygon* 7, 1972, pp. 6-19. That argument is examined within the present chapter.

[6]"Christian Theology and Philosophical Criticism," *IGHF*, p. 120.

[7]*Ibid.,* p. 121.

[8]*Ibid.*

[9]Ibid., pp. 121f.

[10]*Ibid.,* pp. 118f. There would seem to be a possible continuity here with Tillich's method of correlation in which the theologian endeavors to give answers to questions which it is the philosopher's task to identify. (See Paul Tillich, *Systematic Theology* [Chicago: The University of Chicago Press, 1951-63], I, pp. 59ff., especially p. 63.) But Tillich does not limit this correlation to ethical matters, and Pannenberg does not directly give consideration to Tillich's methodological proposal. The reason for this may lie in the fact that Pannenberg's own resolution of the issue is actually very similar to Tillich's--especially in Tillich's insistence that the theologian may properly be engaged in the philosopher's own analytical task.

[11]*Ibid.,* p. 122.

[12]Pannenberg, *Gottesgedanke und menschliche Freiheit* (Göttingen: Vandenhoeck & Ruprecht, 1972) (hereafter: *GmF*), p. 55, my translation. (Cf. *IGHF*, p. 123.) Pannenberg goes on to explain that "it is unhistorical to state that one is obsolete, while the other can be adopted as it stands. Man's struggle for an appropriate understanding of himself comes about largely when he comes to terms with his

relationship to the world, and when he achieves this his relationship to himself also changes. Man's changing of the world brings about a change in man himself." (*IGHF*, p. 123.)

[13] *IGHF*, pp. 123f.

[14] *Ibid.,* pp. 117f.

[15] *Ibid.,* pp. 127f.

[16] *Ibid.,* pp. 134f.

[17] "The conflict between theology and philosophy cannot be resolved by according to each their own particular and separate field of operations. The traditional division between natural and supernatural knowledge and themes breaks down against the fact that an inquiry concerning the nature of things must by its very origins regard itself as definitive and exclusive, and incapable of being complemented or superseded by anything different. But neither are philosophy and theology able to treat each other as different perspectives of a single truth, because the question of the way these two distinct perspectives are to be co-ordinated into the one truth is an inevitable one." (*Ibid.,* pp. 128f).

[18] *Ibid.,* p. 128. See also "The Crisis of the Scripture Principle," *BQT* I, p. 1, where Pannenberg already maintains that theology "includes all truth whatever" inasmuch as theology speaks of God as the "power that determines everything that exists." Pannenberg's justification for such an assertion is explored in chapter eight.

[19] *Ibid.,* p. 130. Again, the justification given for that theistic definition will be subsequently dealt with herein.

[20] *Ibid.,* pp. 120f., italics mine.

[21] Pannenberg's summary judgment on the matter: "The question regarding the truth of the Christian faith is not concerned with a particular truth of one kind or another but with truth itself, which in essence can only be one." ("What is Truth?," *BQT* II, p. 1.) It is important to point out at this juncture that truth's necessary unity stands basically as a premise for Pannenberg which does not receive undergirding elaboration. Truth *must* be one--that appears to stand as self-evident for him. The truth of truth's unity, of course, is not something that currently exists as an attainable object of human knowledge; it remains a yet unattained goal of the ongoing historical process. (See, *e.g.,* "Christian Theology," *IGHF*, pp. 129-32, and the summary statements in "What is Truth?," *BQT* II, pp. 26f.) Thus the unity of truth is theology's goal while at the same time the *premise* of truth's (ultimate) unity is the basis for theology's understanding of its relation with philosophy. A presumed unity is the criterion for theology's repudiation of all merely external relations with philosophy but that unity is not a *given* for theology and philosophy; it is rather a datum arising within the theological enterprise. Thus Pannenberg's demarcation of theology's boundaries

51

arises *a posteriori*, and an inescapable circularity of method is evident. Of course, it can readily be proposed to the contrary that the only alternative to Pannenberg's premise of truth's unity is a condition of intellectual chaos, a conceptual nihilism, inasmuch as truth's *dis*unity would render everything--and therefore nothing--possible. That accords with the essential point that Pannenberg intends to make: the premised (and promised) unity of truth is what alone makes a coherence of meaning possible. The alternatives are therefore clearly drawn: either theology and philosophy deal with an all-encompassing truth, wherefore their claims equally to speak the truth must be adjudicated, or else neither one really has anything significant to say at all.

22*IGHF*, p. 129. The earliest, though undeveloped, reference to the notion of theology as endeavoring to do the work of the "true philosopher" is in "On the Theology of Law," from 1963. (Pannenberg, *Ethics*, trans. Keith Crim [Philadelphia: The Westminster Press, 1981], pp. 34f.)

23*IGHF*, p. 129.

24It is interesting that Pannenberg nowhere seriously considers the first alternative proposed--that philosophy itself might become theological.

25*Ibid.*, pp. 136f. Cf. also "Anthropology and the Question of God," *IGHF*, pp. 91f., and *AC*, p. 34.

26". . . the integration into itself of philosophical criticism by theology can take place only as a 'meta-criticism' of philosophy. But this 'meta-criticism' can do justice to the arguments of philosophy only if its own form is that of reflective philosophical thought. It is possible to rebut the philosophical criticism of religious traditions only if the thinking which sets out to vindicate the religious tradition becomes philosophical in its turn, and above all renounces any appeal to authoritative data and sources of any kind." (*IGHF*, p. 137.)

27Pannenberg pursued just this enterprise when he appeared before a meeting of philosophers in Basel in 1965 and presented them with a paper on the philosophical problem of the relation of appearance to reality, "Appearance as the Arrival of the Future [*Zukünftig*]," included as chapter four of *TKG*.

28*IGHF*, pp. 120f.

29See, *e.g.*, "Redemptive Event and History," *BQT* I, p. 15; "Hermeneutic and Universal History," *ibid.*, p. 131; "The Revelation of God in Jesus of Nazareth," *TaH*, pp. 128f.; *Jesus--God and Man*, trans. Lewis L. Wilkins and Duane A. Priebe (Philadelphia: The Westminster Press, 1968) (hereafter: *JGM*), pp. 28-30; *AC*, pp. 10-12.

30See Augustine, *Enchiridion*, iv, and *Of True Religion*, xxiv, 45, and xxv, 46. See also Robert E. Cushman, "Faith and Reason," in *A Companion to the Study of St. Augustine,* ed. Roy W. Battenhouse (New York: Oxford University Press, 1955), p.

298. For Pannenberg's brief discussion of Augustine on this matter, see his "Faith and Reason," *BQT* II, pp. 48f.

31"... we do not have to reckon with a second way to reliable knowledge of the past alongside that of historical-critical research . . ." ("Redemptive Event and History," *BQT* I, p. 53.)

32"Faith and Reason," *BQT* II, pp. 54ff.

33"Was ist Wahrheit?," first appearing in *Vom Herrengeheimnis der Wahrheit: Festschrift für Heinrich Vogel*, ed. Kurt Scharf (Berlin: 1962), and originally delivered as an address in November, 1961. *BQT* II, pp. 1-27.

34Hans von Soden, *Was ist Wahrheit? Vom geschichtlichen Begriff der Wahrheit*, Marburger akademische Reden 46 (Marburg: 1927).

35"What is Truth?," *BQT* II, p. 3.

36Von Soden, *op. cit.*, p. 15, as quoted in *BQT* II, p. 3.

37The English translation (*BQT* II, p. 4) misses this distinction. See "Was ist Wahrheit?," *Grundfragen systematischer Theologie* I (Göttingen: Vandenhoeck & Ruprecht, 1967), p. 204: "Von der *aletheia* kann man nicht im Sinne des israelitischen Wahrheitsgedankens sagen, dass sie *geschieht*.. Sie *ist* vielmehr." (Emphases are mine.)

38*BQT* II, p. 4 (and f.).

39"That is true which confers stability and thus proves itself as stable. Accordingly, the truth of God proves itself by the fact that ultimately he alone is able to guarantee stability." (*Ibid.*, p. 6.)

40*GsT* I, p. 206, my translation.

41*BQT* II, p. 7.

42*Ibid.*, pp. 6-8. Concerning the latter point: "Previous experience of the constancy of a man or even of God is always, for the Israelite, a presupposition, the ground of faith. Israel always lived from the experienced faithfulness of its God, and precisely through this, its history, is it called to entrust itself to its God for the future, too." (*Ibid.* p. 7.)

43*Ibid.*, pp. 10f. In observing that "the history of the Western consciousness of truth" traverses a path "from the Greek to the Old Testament idea of truth" (p. 10), Pannenberg would appear to have the philosophical contribution of Hegel in mind. He credits Hegel with having raised the question of truth's unity along lines that are continuous with Hebraic conceptuality, with a depth that has not been comparably attained since. See *ibid.,* pp. 21-24. The criticisms raised there concerning the inadequacy of Hegel's endeavor to encompass the entirety of truth are explored in the section following.

[44]The German word *aufheben* is what is intended by this word. The term, as Pannenberg uses it here (*GsT* I, pp. 208, 209), has strong Hegelian overtones. It conveys the sense of the abolition or nullification of some concept not by its exclusion from the system but through its being transformingly elevated into a more embracing synthesis of understanding--fulfilling its intent in a higher concept while denying its own conceptual sufficiency.

[45]*BQT* II, pp. 9, 11.

[46]*Ibid.,* pp. 11-18.

[47]*GsT* I, pp. 215f., my translation.

[48]*Ibid.,* p. 216, my translation. See also theses 1-3, *BQT* II, pp. 26f.

[49]*BQT* II, p. 19.

[50]*Ibid.,* p. 9.

[51]*Ibid.,* pp. 20f. See also theses 4-5, p. 27.

[52]*Ibid.,* p. 10.

[53]*TKG,* pp. 128f.

[54]*Ibid.,* pp. 129-32.

[55]*Ibid.,* p. 132.

[56]*Ibid.,* p. 133.

[57]*Ibid.,* pp. 133-35.

[58]*Ibid.,* p. 135.

[59]*Ibid.,* pp. 140f.

[60]Pannenberg quoting von Soden, *BQT* II, p. 3.

[61]See "What is Truth," *BQT* II, pp. 20-22; "Christian Theology," *IGHF*, pp. 130-32 and 142f.

[62]"What is Truth?," *BQT* II, p. 21. The quotation is from G. W. F. Hegel, *The Phenomenology of Mind*, trans. J. B. Baillie (New York: Harper and Row, 1967), p. 81.

[63]Gerhard Sauter has criticized Pannenberg on the grounds that his dependence on Hegel has clouded his vision of the perspective of the Old Testament. Truth as the disclosure of the whole from its result forth is understood by Sauter to be purely Hegelian, in distinction from the Old Testament in which truth is viewed rather as constancy and durability (*Dauer, Bestand*), as "that which has a future." (Sauter, "Fragestellungen der Christologie," *Verkundigung und Forschung* 11:2, 1966, p. 60.) But Sauter has failed to perceive that for Pannenberg there is indeed a crucial inner connection between these two: it is only in light of the end that the constancy of God's truth can be definitively maintained. Sauter's question does remain, however, as to the extent to which the inner connection is already present in the Old Testament.

[64]"What is Truth?," *BQT* II, p. 22.

[65]See Hegel, *The Phenomenology of Mind*, pp. 81f., and *Science of Logic*, trans. W. H. Johnston and L. G. Struthers (New York: The Macmillan Company, 1929), vol. II, p. 484.

[66]*BQT* II, p. 22. Pannenberg does acknowledge, in another context, that the implicit thrust of Hegel's system is such as to call into question Hegel's own conclusions in this regard. Inasmuch as every concept (*Begriff*) remains for the present merely an anticipatory "forecept" (*Vorgriff*), there is an openness to the essential futurity of truth with which Hegel himself did not follow through. ("The Significance of Christianity in the Philosophy of Hegel," *IGHF*, pp. 175f., ft. 96.)

[67]See "What is a Dogmatic Statement?," *BQT* I, pp. 204f.; "Nachwort," *OaG*, pp. 146f.; *AC*, p. 8.

[68]See *BQT* II, p. 20.

[69]"On Historical and Theological Hermeneutic," *BQT* I, p. 173.

[70]"Christian Theology," *IGHF*, p. 130.

[71]Summary theses four and five, *BQT* II, p. 27.

[72]Summary thesis three, *ibid.*

[73]Summary thesis two, *ibid.*, p. 26.

[74]"Insight and Faith," *BQT* II, pp. 30f.

[75]This is the position taken, *e.g.,* by Paul Althaus in his response to *Offenbarung als Geschichte* ("Offenbarung als Geschichte und Glaube. Bemerkungen zu W. Pannenbergs Begriff der Offenbarung," *Theologische Literaturzeitung* 87, 1962, pp. 321-30) (hereafter: *ThLZ*), and to which Pannenberg replies in "Insight and Faith."

[76]"Insight and Faith," *BQT* II, pp. 31, 34.

[77]"Response to the Discussion," *TaH*, p. 271.

[78]"Insight and Faith," *BQT* II, pp. 32f., 35; "The Revelation of God in Jesus of Nazareth," *TaH,* p. 129.

[79]"Revelation," *TaH*, p. 128.

[80]"Response," *TaH*, pp. 270f.

[81]"Revelation," *TaH*, p. 129.

[82]"Response," *TaH*, p. 269.

[83]*Ibid.,* p. 273.

[84]*Ibid.*

[85]*AC*, p. 12.

[86]See *OaG*, pp. 101f. (The translation of the key sentence in *RaH*, p. 139, has garbled the meaning.) See also the extended footnote on this proposal, *RaH*, p. 157, n. 15, and more recently, the discussion in "Wahrheit, Gewissheit und Glaube," *GsT* II, pp. 233f.

[87]"Response," *TaH*, p. 274.

[88]*OaG,* pp. 146f.

[89]*BQT* II, pp. 46-64.

[90]*Ibid.,* p. 54.

[91]The paragraphs which follow have been read by Professor Pannenberg and acknowledged as responsibly reflecting the content of his lectures. The summary has been derived from my own lecture notes.

[92]The possibility of this transcendental unity of apperception is dependent upon the transcendental unity of the consciousness which underlies the whole process of thinking. The apperception of ourselves as unities is implicit in all thinking activity.

[93]"Faith and Reason," *BQT* II, pp. 62f.

[94]*Ibid.*, p. 63.

[95]*Ibid.*, p. 64.

[96]*Ibid.*

[97]*Zygon* 7, 1972, pp. 6-19.

[98]*Ibid.*, pp. 8f.

[99]*Ibid.*, pp. 10f.

[100]*Ibid.*, p. 11.

[101]*Ibid.*, p. 12.

[102]*Ibid.* Concerning this designation of the essential characteristic of God, Pannenberg continues: "At least within the scope of these [biblical and most philosophical] traditions and of the process of their transmission, all other statements about God tacitly presuppose that this name refers to the reality that determines and rules everything."

[103]*Ibid.*, p. 12.

[104]*Ibid.*, p. 16.

[105]Cf. "Christian Theology and Philosophical Criticism," *IGHF*, pp. 142f.

[106]"The Nature of a Theological Statement," *Zygon* 7, 1972, pp. 16f.

[107]*Ibid.*, p. 15.

[108]Only when God's Reign comes, and the content and truth of God's promises are thereby definitively disclosed, will the truth of God's reality be verifiably certain.

[109]*Ibid.*, p. 19.

[110]See "Christian Theology and Philosophical Criticism," *IGHF*, pp. 130 and 131.

3

MEANING, HISTORY AND THE FUTURE

A. Reality as History

"History is the most comprehensive horizon of Christian theology."[1] So begins Pannenberg's sweeping reassessment of the role and responsibility of the theologian in his venturous programmatic essay of 1959 on "Redemptive Event and History."[2] "All theological questions and answers," he continues, "are meaningful only within the framework of the history which God has with humanity and through humanity with his whole creation--the history moving toward a future still hidden from the world but already revealed in Jesus Christ."[3]

This clarion call to take history seriously as the focus of the theological investigation was issued over against what Pannenberg regarded as dehistoricizing tendencies in the dominant strands of recent theological understanding: on the one hand, Bultmann's and Gogarten's existential dissolving of history into the historicity of existence,[4] and on the other, the *heilsgeschichtlich* tradition rooting in Martin Kähler which considers the actual kernel of Christian faith to be suprahistorical. This latter is understood to find its present expression in Barth's interpretation of the incarnation as *Urgeschichte*, "pre-history." The motive common to both orientations is the endeavor to overcome the apparent loss of the category of redemptive event in the context of historical-critical research into the specifics of history.[5] Pannenberg proposes instead that the possibility of preeminent meaning attaching to individual events of history need not be sacrificed before the bar of critical historical inquiry--that, to the contrary, only through encountering the heritage of the past with such means may proclamations of Christian faith become transmittable as truly meaningful.

59

Pannenberg embarks upon this full-scale reversal of recent theological trends with the insistence that the historicity of truth identified previously has as its corollary the essentially historical character of reality itself. History is understood to be "reality in its totality";[6] it "characterizes reality as a whole."[7] As in the case of truth's inescapably historical nature, so here also Pannenberg finds the primary rootage for that pivotal assertion in the historical consciousness of ancient Israel. Israel is distinguished from its neighbors in the ancient Near East "by the fact that it experienced the reality of its God not in the shadows of a mythical primitive history, but more and more decisively in historical change itself."[8] Nor does this begin merely with the prophets: contra Eliade, Pannenberg discerns a consciousness of the centrality of history for Israel that reaches all the way back to the beginnings of historical writing dating from the time of David and Solomon. The basis for Israel's understanding of meaning as historical is not to be sought initially in the futural fulfillment of prophetic proclamations, but in something yet more primal.

> The presuppositions of the historical consciousness in Israel lie in its concept of God. The reality of God for Israel is not exhausted by his being the origin of the world, that is, of normal, ever self-repeating processes and events. Therefore this God can break into the course of his creation and initiate new events in it in an unpredictable way. The certainty that God again and again performs new acts, that he is a "living God," forms the basis for Israel's understanding of reality as a linear history moving toward a goal.[9]

There is a very interesting logical progression implicit here. An understanding of the truth of God is not initially read off from the presupposition that reality is historical in nature, but rather the reverse is the case. Reality is seen as historical in light of the conviction that God is ever the source of contingent novelty, wherefore the truth of what is cannot already reside fully in some eternal cosmic order.[10] An *idea* of God, therefore, grounds the historicity of being. Conversely, however, it is only through attention to what history itself discloses that the idea moves from premise to rationally sustainable affirmation. It will be necessary to pay very close attention, in the chapters that follow, to the manner in which Pannenberg carries out that crucial move.

But what now is the structure which that divinely directed history is understood to have? The position which Pannenberg initially adopted centered upon the relationship between promise and fulfillment.

> Within the reality characterized by the constantly creative work of God, history arises because God makes promises and fulfills these promises. History is event so suspended in tension between promise and fulfillment that through the promise it is irreversibly pointed toward the goal of future fulfillment. . . . The tension between promise and fulfillment makes history.[11]

Pannenberg went on then to maintain that the issue of the relationship between the two Testaments is resolvable only in the context of "the consciousness of the one history which binds together the eschatological community of Jesus Christ and ancient Israel by means of the bracket of promise and fulfillment."[12] The relationship of New to Old is found in the recognition that God who is understood to be at work in history remains true to God's promises, thus grounding the unity of history itself.[13]

James Robinson raised a telling objection to this approach, calling attention to the fact that Pannenberg's principle of promise-fulfillment was yet another instance of an unhistorical structure being imposed upon the data of history, "a timeless principle being used to replace the actual history."[14] But Pannenberg had already moved independently to perceive that crucial error.[15] In conjunction with the investigations of fellow Heidelberg Circle member Rolf Rendtorff, he set aside the promise-fulfillment schema in favor of a recognition that history is essentially constituted by a process of *Überlieferungsgeschichte*, a "history of the transmission of traditions."[16] A historical occurrence is understood to bear its significance not *purely* in itself but only in positive or negative relation to the traditions and expectations in which its people live. "The events of history speak their own language, the language of facts; however, this language is understandable only in the context of the traditions and the expectations in which the given events occur."[17] The twin motifs of promise and fulfillment are now recognized as merely one possible rubric under which this transmission of tradition may be carried on, one possible form which the tradition may take and has taken.

We need to perceive more fully yet what this concept of history as *Überleiferungsgeschichte* really entails.[18] First of all, Pannenberg is at pains to distinguish what he regards as his broader use of the term from a narrower usage contained in the approach of exegetical and form-critical research. The "systematic" concept employed here is seen as an extension and transformation of the more restricted methdological concept. Whereas *überlieferungsgeschichtlich* research begins with the final stage of a literary unit and works backwards to earlier written stages and eventually to oral ones, the systematic utilization of the concept works conversely, beginning at the points of origin reached through such a procedure and inquiring about "an *open future* of transformations, mixtures, or ramifications of traditions" that subsequently develop therefrom.[19] Historical-exegetical research employing this concept is understood to be working therefore with only a partial aspect of the more encompassing process.

Secondly, Pannenberg carefully guards against an interpretation of history as a transmission of traditions that would tend to eliminate any emergence of contingent novelty into the historical process. Quite to the contrary, the sense of the ancient Israelites was that history is ever being broken open by new and unpredictable occurrences derivative from God, the repudiation of which would constitute no less than a repudiation of the historical character of reality itself. Thus the sense of the contingency of events remains tied to the very idea of history, so that no new event is ever *fully* interpretable or anticipatable in terms of prior tradition even though initially it is understandable only in the *context* of its transmitted tradition.[20] The concept of contingency expresses therefore the idea of "a future which is not the prisoner of past and present."[21]

Finally, in this perspective event and tradition are not to be understood as separate from one another. The cleavage especially in biblical exegetical studies between the kerygma and a historical-critical conception of the history underlying it is overcome through a recognition that the history of the transmission of traditions includes the eventful origins of those traditions as well as the concrete occasions of their transmitted changes. Pannenberg attributes to von Rad the primary breakthrough in this understanding,[22] but he carries his reflections on the implications of that insight much further than von Rad had been inclined to do--specifically in regard to the question of how a particular event bears an essential relationship with the interpretations arising in the tradition concerning that event. It is the question of how meaning is to be understood in relation to events in history and ultimately to history itself, and it is one that requires a considerable amount of unpacking. To that task I now turn.

B. Meaning in History

Pannenberg has observed that he takes off from a concern for wholeness of meaning in history, not from a concern for *future* per se--as he would characterize other forms of eschatological theology such as Moltmann's.[23] In pursuit of this comprehension of historical meaning, it is remarkable the extent to which he adopts presuppositions from the work of Löwith and Bultmann--moving however to the articulation of quite different conclusions. The third major source of this movement is located in the philosophy of history of Dilthey, which already underlies Bultmann's perspective if not explicitly Löwith's also.

Karl Löwith raised the question of the possibility of finding meaning in history by tracing backwards the theories of history in the West from the nineteenth century to their original roots in the scheme of historical purposiveness found in Judaeo-Christian eschatology. A "philosophy of history," by which he meant "a systematic interpretation of universal history in accordance with a principle by which historical events and successions are unified and directed toward an ultimate meaning,"[24] was understood to derive from and remain fundamentally dependent upon a *theology* of history which interpreted history as a history of fulfillment and salvation. But why "universal" history, why the direction toward "ultimate" meaning? Löwith maintained that the question for a meaning *of* history is motivated by an absence of a sense of meaning directly manifest in historical events themselves.[25] And the search for meaning appeared to him to be indistinguishable from a search for "purpose," wherefore it seemed to be the case that history could be deemed meaningful only insofar as it is directed toward a purpose, a goal--a *telos*.[26] The ultimate meaning of history comes therefore to be focused on a final end arriving at some point in the future, leading to the twin recognition that an interpretation of the meaning of history is necessarily eschatological[27] and that the *future* is the "true" focus of history.[28] It is only within an eschatological scheme of the historical process, anticipating in faith the *telos* or eschaton, that history becomes universal and thereby a bearer of meaning.

But the conclusion which Löwith drew from this understanding was basically negative. Tracing the outlines of past philosophies of history, he perceived on the one hand their failure at providing any *immanent* solution to the meaning of history through any internal scheme of comprehensive order:

> The problem of history as a whole is unanswerable within its own perspective. Historical processes as such do not bear the least evidence of a comprehensive and ultimate meaning. History as such has no outcome. There never has been and never will be an immanent solution to the problem of history.[29]

But he acknowledged on the other hand that for the modern mind, faith in an order of history rooted transcendentally in the promises of God and in the life and death of Christ as "beginning of an end" and "the final answer to an otherwise insoluble question" is no longer a viable prospect.[30] The impossibility of establishing a meaningful plan of history through the use of reason has its counterpart in the impossibility of holding on to an eschatological meaning of history through faith.[31] The consequence of this dilemma was for Löwith, in effect, the recognition that meaning *in* history is not accessible at all. In a brief "Epilogue," he could only call weakly for the possibility of an unconditional, and empirically unjustifiable, hope as a way of anticipating an ultimate fulfillment of history and its meaning.[32]

Pannenberg appears to have accepted the challenge that Löwith threw down, in terms of the insistence on an essential interrelationship binding meaning within history with an overarching meaning of history. The question comes to be raised only at the point of the adequacy ascribable to the modern understanding, and concomitantly concerning the issue of whether an encompassing view of history as universal is not only necessary to meaning but even also possible.

In the Gifford Lectures for 1955,[33] Bultmann tackled the issue of meaning in history with a thesis parallel to Löwith's. The meaning of an event is not to be sought purely in itself, in individual isolation from the larger historical context, but only in relation to the future for which it has importance. Therefore only the future can contribute a horizon of meaning to events within history, which leads to the understanding that an ultimate end of history is presupposed for the possibility of determinations of meaning.[34] But Bultmann carried this concept yet a further step: inasmuch as the future alone will disclose the truth of what already has come into history, therefore one must say that "to each historical phenomenon *belongs* its future."[35] The event itself is incomplete in anticipation of its horizon of meaning. What is made of it is what becomes of it.

It is understandable, viewed from this perspective, why philosophy of history arose for the first time within an intellectual climate informed by Christian thinking, "for Christians believed they knew of the end of the world and of history" as a basis for fathoming historical meaningfulness.[36] But today that claim is untenable, wherefore "the question of meaning in history has become meaningless."[37] For we stand within history itself, and cannot gain a backward perspective upon the whole of history from the standpoint of the end.[38]

Bultmann overcame this impasse by means of his existentialist interpretation of persons and history: I *choose* my future in the present moment of decision, whereby the present becomes eschatologically qualified and in the unity of history is located not in a causal connection of events but in the act of human responsibility.[39]

> . . . the meaning in history lives always in the present, and when the present is conceived as the eschatological present by Christian faith the meaning in history is realised. . . . do not look around yourself into universal history, you must look into your own personal history.[40]

For Löwith, meaning *in* and meaning *of* history are inseparable; for Bultmann, an event and its future are equally inseparable. For Löwith, *meaning* is presently incomplete; for Bultmann, the *event itself* is always yet incomplete, because it *includes* the (ultimate) future of its meaning within itself. This pair of premises also functions, uncritically it would seem, for Pannenberg. The task he set for himself appears to have been only the challenging of Bultmann's, and Löwith's, conclusions, while accepting the authenticity of the way in which the problem had been set forth. *I.e.,* given the inability of Pannenberg to affirm either Löwith's implicit nihilism or Bultmann's existentialist method of exegesis, but given also the legitimacy of the way in which especially Bultmann defined the issue, what alternative resolution could be forthcoming? In pursuit of a solution, Pannenberg turns his attention upon the preceding work of . . . a Hegelian.

Wilhelm Dilthey discerned that, as in the interpretation of a word or a sentence or a text, so in the interpretation of history the hermeneutical principle of a reciprocal illumination between a whole and its parts applied.[41] The experiences of life which collectively constitute history are thus interpretable only within their context as individual life-moments in the larger whole of life. The process is one with a moving edge, inasmuch as later life-experiences are always altering the shape of the momentary whole, casting new light back on earlier experiences and providing them with changed significance. This means on the one hand that an assessment of the meaning of one's life is always retrospective; the new shape of the present is the perspective from which the meaning of the past is determined. It means on the other hand that a momentary sense of integration of meaning is achieved through a combination of memory and anticipation--but this is always only provisional. Later experiences are corrections of false anticipations, shifting the understanding of the nature of the whole. Therefore it became apparent to Dilthey that only from the standpoint of the end of one's sequence of life-experiences, at death, could the true meaning of one's life be legitimately observable. And inasmuch as history is just life in its temporal extension, the writing of history must become essentially biography.[42]

But a problem initially rises here. No one really "has" the whole of one's life at the point of one's death, for the rounding off of one's life in death is precisely beyond one's own experiencing. Heidegger built upon Dilthey's essential insight in his interpretation of the human individual as a "Being-towards death"--that being who alone knows of its coming death and therefore has the possibility of grasping wholeness in advance by anticipating the coming of death in conscious acceptance of it.[43] But Pannenberg cannot remain content with this additional step. On the one hand, anticipatory knowledge remains abstract, and the wholeness which is grasped therein is equally abstract; the real course of our lives in which meaning lies is accessible only in retrospect.[44] Far more important, on the other hand, is the question of whether death really brings a wholeness of meaning. Death is the occasion of the *interruption*, not the fulfillment, of life, shattering into fragments whatever meaning it had. Such a consideration pushes forth the question of whether "the wholeness of human being can find a satisfactory answer only when it is directed beyond death toward the participation of the individual in the destination of mankind as such."[45]

65

This leads to the second problem which Pannenberg sees in Dilthey's understanding of death as the necessary condition for an assessment of meaning. One's life has its own place, in turn, within a larger whole composed of the society of which it has been a part-- ultimately extending even to the totality of humankind and history universally.[46] Death does not close its meaning once and for all; its shifting impact continues to be experienced by others, significantly or negligibly, on into the future. Dilthey recognized, however uncertainly, the truth of this aspect of life's meaning, and at one point dropped a brief hint of the implications of his position: "One would have to wait for the end of history to have all the material necesssary to determine its meaning."[47] But nothing immediately came of it. In Pannenberg, much comes of it indeed.

Pannenberg observes that the background for Dilthey's deliberations was the Enlightenment's displacement of God by humanity as bearer of history, leading to the loss of a sense of historical unity and the onset of historical relativism.[48] It is this movement which he finds characteristic of the endeavor by Christian existentialism to ground the reality of history in the historicity of human existence, but Pannenberg does not take confidence in the prospect that this understanding will be able to sustain itself in emancipation from its original roots in Christian eschatology.[49] If we cannot subjectively provoke the sense of history's unity, what is left? According to the categories with which Pannenberg works, the answer is straightforward: Either the rationally defensible premise of an end of history, or nihilism. Either history is conceivable as proceeding toward a final future of consummation, or it disallows signification in any of its aspects. Either an event faces forward toward an embracing end that ultimately defines it, or it is perpetually incomplete and void of meaning.

C. End of History

The foregoing reflections underlie the tack which Pannenberg takes in his attempt to identify the nature of history's essential significance for theology and the way in which the truth of historical events is properly to be assessed. The direction of that tack can now be sketched in, leading to a careful consideration of what Pannenberg has in mind when he speaks of a consummating end of the historical process.

Pannenberg denies the procedure of positivist historians who accept too uncritically the neo-Kantian distinction between being and value and seek thereby to ascertain bare historical facts independent of an external imposition of meaning.[50] On the contrary, he maintains that there are no such things as *bruta facta* to which significance is then added by the observer.[51] There can be no dichotomy between "inner" and "outer" history in which the one is somehow additional to the other.[52] Rather, every event always already includes its meaning within itself; there is an "original unity of facts and their meaning" with which the historian is called to deal.[53]

> It is simply not the case that one can take uninterpreted [*deutungsfrei*, "meaning-free"], established facts and then subsequently ascribe to them this or that meaning as one wishes, so that one could, for instance, also place a revelatory meaning on the list next to other equally possible meanings. On the contrary, events always bring their original meaning along with them from the context to which they have been assigned by their having happened.[54]

In this process of coming to understanding, word and event are therefore not mutually extraneous. The word of interpretation plays a crucial role in bringing to expression the essence of an event which may lie hidden within it.[55]

Building on the premises from Dilthey and Bultmann which have been identified here, Pannenberg proceeds to make the further move that the meaning inherent to an event, which fully emerges only in the future of its ever expanding context of relationships, is finally discernible only in relation to the whole of reality.

> As long as the future brings something new, reality is not yet complete even in its existence . . . . The anticipation of the whole cannot be evaded, for the reason that the individual entity is not really any more easily available than the whole. Each individual entity has its meaning only in relation to the whole to which it belongs.[56]

The implication of this understanding is twofold. First, an event is open to its own future. If the meaning of an event is internal to that event but that meaning is fully ascertainable only in light of the event's place in the entire historical scheme, then what the event actually *is* is not yet fully decided. The event is yet incomplete, unfinished. The *essence* of an event, in terms of the truth of its meaning, will be determined only by the (final) future in which its destiny is attained. This, Pannenberg contends, is "according to the Biblical understanding, [that] the essence of things will be decided only in the future. What they are is decided by what they will become."[57]

Secondly, it follows therefore that some sort of end of the historical process is presupposed as a necessary condition for the ultimate attainment of the requisite wholeness of history and consequently for meaning. "For the whole of history could only come into view if we knew its end and could understand all that precedes it on the strength of the end [*auf das Ende hin*]."[58] Pannenberg also refers to this end as the "ultimate" or "essential" future,[59] and as "the end of historical time."[60] The point is parallel with what emerged in the previous chapter: just as the eventuality of a final unity embracing the multiplicity of historical truths is a presupposition for the possibility of there being any truth at all, so also is the eventuality of an ultimate end of history a presupposition for the possibility of there being any meaning of experience at all. The logical progression is in principle the same.

But what sort of conceptual sense is to be made of this expectation which is required as a condition for understanding historical reality correctly? Pannenberg has been less than thoroughly clear on this point, and the shape of his ontological interpretation of the meaning of "end" is still in process of developing. He observes at one point that there is no absolute negation of the concept of an end of reality in natural science, that the unending continuation of history is not an established scientific deduction.[61] But he has not consistently maintained that an ultimate end of history has to "require the assumption of an end of the natural universe as well."[62] At one point, Pannenberg singles out for consideration several possible alternatives for understanding:

> In particular, no answer is given to the question of the relationship between the idea of a new creation of the natural world, as the condition of the realization of human nautre, and the physical processes with which we are familiar. Are these processes to come to an end, and are they to be replaced by something quite different? Do these physical processes continue without leading beyond the stage which the realization of human nature has theretofore reached?[63] Must we suppose a "curvature" of time, analogous to the "curvature" of the dimension of space in the theory of relativity? All of these ideas are worth discussion.[64]

Pannenberg has given some degree of attention to the latter proposal. He advanced the idea at the 1971 conference in New York on "Hope and the Future of Man,"[65] suggesting the possibility of "a deformation of the ordinary form of temporal sequence comparable to the contortion of space" in relativity theory.[66] In subsequent discussion there, he spelled this out in terms of the emergence of a different kind of process, not identified by temporal sequence but characterized by a proceeding into the depths of true existence.[67] Telling objections were directed to that thesis, most notably by the theologian-scientist Ian Barbour who rejected as inconceivable the notion of a contortion of time: even in the concept of relativity, scientists do not disavow the fundamental character of the irreversibility of temporality and the inextinguishable distinction between before and after. But Pannenberg continued to defend the possibility in a published conversation conducted several weeks later,[68] though a bit less strongly. In that context, he also gave brief attention to an additional option that he has contemplated: not simply that the process either comes to an end entirely or undergoes some sort of contortion of temporality, but that

> . . . the sequence of events would go on and on as we know it, but without contributing anything further in a decisive way to the meaning of human reality. In my view, this would be difficult to accept because in history as we know it, the on-going forces of time and events change the context of meaning which we experience. If we should imagine that events go on, but no longer change the ultimate meaning, then this would imply a different kind of events going on than the ones we know about.[69]

The struggle with which Pannenberg is wrestling here is to guarantee both the meaningfulness of the "end" as definitive bearer of meaning, beyond which there is no further *essential* development, and yet the legitimacy of a "post-ultimate" reality which is other than static lifelessness: "an eschatological theology that would envision the end just as a stop of the process would have extreme difficulties in understanding that end as eternal life rather than eternal death."[70] His most recent attempt to get around that unpromising prospect came a decade later in his Ingersoll Lecture at Harvard (1983), where he advanced the proposal that the end of time brings a cessation of eventful sequentiality altogether, to be superceded by an eternal simulaneity in which the differences between particular temporal moments are totally dissolved.[71]

In regard to the foregoing, Pannenberg has maintained that the variety of possible conceptions which he has offered concerning the end of history is helpful but not crucial; theology is relieved "of any need to settle for any one particular conception of the end of the world."[72] To the contrary, however, it would appear that the entire thrust of Pannenberg's attempt to go beyond the inadequacies in Hegel, Dilthey, and Bultmann concerning the anticipation of an end as condition for wholeness stands or falls with his success in being able adequately and consistently to conceptualize what that "end" might signify ontologically. If it cannot be rendered cognitively meaningful through at least one viable model, even within the limitations imposed upon reason's provisionality;, one has to wonder how it can function as anything more than a "limiting concept"[73] devoid of genuine content. The implications of this caveat will be addressed more fully in chapter eight.

D. Universal History as Hermenutical Horizon

Theology inquires into history as the avenue of access to the truth of God. In that inquiry it is dealing with transmitted texts which bear this or that tradition of understanding. It is faced with the necessity of interpreting these residues of tradition in the process of a coming to awareness of the truths that it would persuasively articulate. Therefore theology is engaged in hermeneutic, and it must deal with the question of how history and hermeneutic interrelate.

Robinson observes perspicaciously that the dialectical theology of the nineteen-twenties polarized into Bultmannian and Barthian camps, respectively characterized as "kerygmatic theology" and "theology of the word" but equally oriented to the primacy of the concept of God's *word*. Out of that two-pronged heritage a new shape is emerging in German theology, focused on the common theme of the relation between word and *history*. The question, as Robinson depicts it, is not whether one of these will be emphasized to the exclusion of the other, but which category can best provide an overarching point of departure for including and doing justice to the other. One approach, represented by the post-Bultmannians who include Robinson himself among their number, is to understand language itself as fundamentally eventful in character and to accent therefore the linguisticality of all reality. Within that perspective, hermeneutic provides a theological understanding of history by interpreting language as event which recurs in the ongoing translation of meaning. The other approach begins with an understanding of all reality as history, of which a coming to expression in language is but one instance. In this perspective, universal history provides a theological understanding of hermeneutic by interpreting events and the language that transmits them in the context of *Überlieferungsgeschichte*. This latter approach is the one defended by Pannenberg.[74]

By way of penetration into the problem, Pannenberg notes that the contemporary interpreter of past texts--especially where these texts are pieces of the biblical tradition--confronts not one but two gulfs which must be bridged. On the one hand, there is the distance between the present world of understanding of the interpreter and that of the witnesses reflected in the texts, and to overcome that distance is the central concern of hermeneutic. But on the other hand, there is also a gulf which has opened up between the straightforward meaning of biblical writings and the historical events to which they intend to refer. To bridge that gulf is the central problem of historical study.[75] Inasmuch as what is at stake is the bodying forth in contemporary language of the intentionality of the authors of the biblical texts, the two gaps prove to be but different aspects of a single theme.[76]

Pannenberg contends that the perspective of history affords the more embracing approach to the dual problem, because the hermeneutical question concerns only one of the gulfs whereas historical inquiry deals with both. For historians are properly concerned to move beyond the text to the event that lies behind it, and in doing so they are

70

driven toward understanding that event not in its isolatedness but within an expanding context of events and meanings that comes eventually to include the interpreter as well. Ultimately, Pannenberg maintains, historians are led by their concern with continuities of meanings to consider the whole of reality, *i.e.*, they work within the horizon of universal history.[77]

> . . . the hermeneutical outlook apparently moves solely between the past text and the present interpreter, whereas the universal-historical outlook first goes back behind the text, and considers the essential content [*Sache*], i.e., the event being inquired into behind the text, in its universal-historical context of meaning, including also the interpreter's own present era. The universal-historical approach thus makes a detour, the detour of going behind the text to the underlying event which the text attests, in order to build a bridge to the era contemporaneous with the interpreter (or historian).[78]

Precisely as universal history, as reality on its way toward being whole and completed, is history the umbrella for hermeneutic. So long as historians define their responsibilities more narrowly than this, historical science "has no right to view hermeneutic as a mere auxiliary discipline, but will rather itself remain only a branch of hermeneutic."[79]

Pannenberg particularly finds the hermeneutical analysis of H.-G. Gadamer to be of considerable value, especially in Gadamer's description of the interpreter's bringing of past and present into relationship with each other as a "fusion of horizons."[80] In the process of understanding, the interpreter widens her and his own horizon increasingly so as eventually to encompass the initially strange subject matter encountered in the text. Thereby a new horizon is formed, which transcends the particularities of both text and interpreter in an elevation of their respective understandings to a higher universality. Contrary to Gadamer's own conclusions, Pannenberg insists, the very notion of a fusion of horizons thus leads to a consideration of universal history as the most comprehensive horizon of interpretation possible.[81]

> If interpretation has to do with the relationship between the then and the now in such a way that the difference between them is preserved when the hermeneutical bridge is built; and if, further, one must inquire behind the text into its unspoken horizon of meaning, into its historical situation, so that the first task of the interpreter is to project the historical horizon to which the text is native; then the only way that the historical situation of the text can be adequately linked to the interpreter's present is by investigating the historical continuity between the present and the past situation from which the text stems. This means that the text can only be understood in connection with the totality of history which links the past to the present, and indeed not only to what currently exists today, but also to the horizon of the future based on what is presently possible, because the meaning of the present becomes clear only in the light of the future. Only a conception of the actual course of history linking the past with the present situation and its horizon of the future can form the

comprehensive horizon within which the interpreter's limited horizon of the present and the historical horizon of the text fuse together.[82]

Gadamer resisted this thesis as straightforwardly Hegelian, regarding Hegel's approach to be impossible because of the boundary of every encompassing projection by finitude and because of the openness of the future.[83] But Pannenberg considers the dilemmas of Hegel to be surpassable, as we have seen, in the conceptual reserve demanded by the provisionality of an anticipatory "forecept" [*Vorgriff*]. Anticipation of the whole, not a Hegelian closedness of the future, is the mode of access to universal history.[84] The *premise* of an end serves as the basis for imparting meaning to the idea of a universal scope of the historian's responsibility, whereas the actual whole of history must ever remain beyond the direct and definitive grasp of the historian.

Finally, it must be briefly noted that Pannenberg rejects the notion of a peculiarly theological hermeneutic as something distinct from the work of historical hermeneutic generally. The theologian is not allowed to regard biblical texts as special sources to be treated differently from other objects of critical inquiry. There can be, for example, no specially theological hermeneutic of the New Testament texts as witnesses to Jesus.

On the contrary, as explication of the meaning warranted by the history of Jesus itself, these texts allow themselves to be questioned and, if occasion arises, judged critically insofar as the interpretation they offer falls short of or in some other way deviates from the anticipation of meaning that the history of Jesus allows to be advanced for itself. Viewed in this way, no fundamental difference between historical and theological hermeneutic needs to be assumed. The peculiarity of the interpretation of the New Testament texts as witnesses to Jesus can be traced back to the particularities of the history and person of Jesus himself, so that such interpretation constitutes only a special case of historical hermeneutic, not a completely different type of hermeneutic.[85]

The position that Pannenberg consistently adopts is that, conversely, the premise of a totality of history is a condition of all valid inquiry, theological and otherwise, into the meaningful truth of the past.[86]

E.   Principles of Historical Inquiry

Just as the theologian must become philosopher in order that philosophy may be corrected and completed in its pursuit of truth, so must the theologian become historian in order that secular historiography may do its own job more adequately.[87] The basis for this proviso, centering in the thrust toward universal history and the concern for the whole which occupies the theologian, has been sketched in. The specific challenges which Pannenberg puts forth to the canons of historical methodology must now be added to complete the picture.

Pannenberg finds modern historical study to have arisen concomitantly with the human self-insertion into the center of history as the focus and bearer of history's meaning. This led to an identification of anthropocentricity with the very essence of historical method. But Pannenberg wishes to distinguish between a narrower employment of necessarily anthropocentric elements in the structure of methodological principles of historical inquiry, and the broader ingression of an avoidable anthropocentric world view.[88] The principles of historical research developed by Ernst Troeltsch provide a helpful basis for opening up this important distinction, especially the principles of universal correlation and analogy.

Troeltsch's principle of the universal correspondence of all historical phenomena, that "every historical process is reciprocally connected to events in its environment,"[89] is a crucial insight. The insistence on acknowledging interlocking causal relations between events, however inaccessible to direct observation, denies the possibility of delimiting redemptive history to a realm different from the rest of history, a realm characterized by supranatural influences on the course of events.[90] To the contrary, *Heilsgeschichte* is only understandable, if at all, as *Weltgeschichte*,[91] and the theologian's access to the redemptive dimension of universal history can in no way bypass the historian's investigation into the immanent interconnections of historical phenomena: "we do not have to reckon with a second way to reliable knowledge of the past alongside that of historical-critical research."[92] But this thesis of universal correlation takes on a specifically anthropocentric character when the nature of those interrelationships is interpreted as fundamentally *developmental,* as a sort of entelechy in which history is pushed forward by the unfolding of inherent germinal tendencies. To Pannenberg, this tends to stand in opposition to the contingency of events and the openness of the future beyond the influence of the past. He would prefer to employ the concept of a correlation of events in terms of a thoroughgoing changeableness of reality, in recognition of the unfinished character of historical forms, without embracing the anthropocentric principle of entelechy.[93]

Secondly, Pannenberg also endorses Troeltsch's principle of analogy between past events and present experiences--but only to a point. He agrees that the concept of analogy validly expresses an overarching similarity among events despite apparent dissimilarity,[94] but the principle has come to be employed far more strongly than that. For Troeltsch, it was broadened to the postulate of an encompassing homogeneity of all reality, in which all differences between presumed historical phenomena should be comprehended within a context of uniformity. Pannenberg finds this extremely problematic. For this anthropocentric broadening of the principle of analogy, to the end that the individuality of the dissimilar is subsumed under categories of understanding based on present human experience, precisely loses sight of what is most important in historical study. Historical inquiry is constricted by a biased perspective which is thereby unable to give open, honest attention to what the historian is presumably most interested in: *particular* events, lifted out of the mass of surrounding phenomena just because of their distinctiveness.[95] Pannenberg calls for a reduced utilization of the principle of analogy, which does not allow it to stand in the way of being confronted by the unique and the dissimilar in history. Only thereby can historians allow their own merely *provisional* perspectives on the possibilities of historical occurrence to be broken open by their critical confrontation with what history genuinely discloses. Particularly in this respect, one cannot deny *in principle* the possibility that historical research will disclose that a particular event contains decisive revelatory significance for the meaning of existence, though whether that is true *in fact* is yet another matter.[96]

There is one further dimension of historical study which remains to be clarified. It concerns the issue of *how* a universal-historical approach to the phenomena of history can legitimately function for the historian, and the solution to the problem leads--as similarly in the pursuit of truth by the philosopher--to the premise of God's reality as a condition for successful historiography. I have observed that, for Pannenberg, the anticipation of an end of history is fundamental for discerning meaning within history, and that therefore the responsibility of historians is to concern themselves with the whole of reality, universal history. We have seen that problems arise in endeavoring to conceptualize meaningfully the idea of this "end." But careful notice must also be taken of a further threat to the success of this orientation, which deals not merely with the fore-conceptualizable nature of the end but more basically with the very possibility of envisaging an end at all.

The problem centers upon an apparent conflict between anticipatorily embracing the whole of history as a universal context for discerning the truth of God's involvement with that history, and allowing for the freedom of the God so disclosed. If the future is enclosed in the "darkness of God's freedom," then any universal-historical projection of the future course of history and any anticipation of the end of history would seem to infringe upon that divine freedom and therefore deny the reality of the essential core of the Christian faith.

> Here we have an apparently unsolvable dilemma: Either theology ventures upon a revelational-historical conception of the total course of history, in which case it infringes upon the freedom and pure futurity of God. Or theology renounces history as the horizon of its thinking and speaking, in which case

there disappears along with the revelational-historical conception of world events even the content of Christian faith, this content being bound essentially to the revelational-historical understanding of reality: With the surrender of the revelational-historical horizon would fall, in the first instance, the end-historical eschatology and therewith a Christology oriented to the New Testament witnesses.[97]

The specific content of Pannenberg's resolution of this dilemma will occupy our attention in chapter seven, concerning the manner in which "the anticipated coming of the end of history in the midst of history [in Jesus' resurrection], far from doing away with history, actually forms the basis from which history as a whole becomes understandable."[98] What is important for now is to note the structural provision that Pannenberg proposes as the direction in which a solution is to be sought--still as a condition for thought, not yet as a datum read off from history proper.

The minimal prerequisite that Pannenberg elicits turns on the relationship between the contingency and unity of historical events. The projection of a unity of history seems to run counter to the sense that individual events are contingent, that is, that they do not arise necessarily out of their past. The contingency of events requires an openness of future history and therefore would appear to rule out the possibility of genuinely anticipating a particular outcome of the historical process, namely, a unifying end. The resolution of the dilemma is seen by Pannenberg to be forthcoming only if the unity and contingency of events can be understood to derive from the same source, which would have to be transcendent to the course of history itself. The premise is therefore advanced: "The God who by the transcendence of his freedom is the origin of contingency in the world, is also the ground of the unity which comprises the contingencies as history."[99] In such a perspective, unity as continuity is not something enduring out of the past into the future in the sense of development, but is achieved from the future backwards, out of the ultimate faithfulness of a free God who grants not only contingent novelty but a stability of connectedness and order in history.

> By means of such backward linking the continuity of history is constantly reestablished. This is the way in which the faithfulness of God expresses itself. Only in this way, as a backward-reaching incorporation of the contingently new into what has been, but not the reverse, as a predetermining mastery and its effect, can the primary connection of history be conceived without losing its contingency.[100]

The consequence of this reflection is immediately apparent: just as universal history is a necessary focus for the historian, so is the reality of God a necessary presupposition for grasping history in its movement toward universality, and therefore, "since only the concept of God makes it possible to conceive the unity of history in a way that maintains the peculiar characteristics of the historical, it should really be indispensable for the historian."[101]   So is the study of history completed by the historian's adoption of theologically derived presuppositions:

> . . . the theme of the totality of history is a strictly common frame of reference for both historical and theological work. The historian as such may not usually speak explicitly of God, but his work nevertheless remains oriented toward that theme which on its part, justifies speaking about God, viz., the problem of universal history.[102]

It is hardly accidental, it would therefore seem, that Pannenberg understands the consciousness of universal history to have originated within the biblical tradition, specifically in the Hebraic conceptualization of God as source of "ever new, once-occurring events directed toward a final goal."[103]   The specific contours of that contention will recurringly occupy our attention in the chapters following.

F. Summary and Critique

What I have undertaken in this chapter has involved a separation of formal from substantive considerations of an understanding of history as end-directed and encompassed by ultimate wholeness. This procedure is not an entirely accurate reflection of Pannenberg's own approach: the formal and substantive elements are consistently interwoven by him, so that the premise of universal history is rarely set forth as naked postulate but is developed precisely in relation to phenomena within history that tend to substantiate that mode of understanding.[104]   Nevertheless, there is value to be derived from initially discerning the *conditions* for understanding that Pannenberg lays down as he comes to grips with what history discloses. There is an identifiable thread of logic that runs through his reflections on what *must* be the case re history's compass in order that *any* historical meaning be determinable at all, and this logic can be seen to have independent significance irrespective of the capacity of historical occurrences to substantiate the proposed thesis. It is this logic that I have attempted to set forth here.

Israel's consciousness of God as initiator of ever new events led to the conviction that reality is essentially historical in character, moving forward toward a goal. Reality is historical in that what *is* real is not yet fully given in its present immediacy but is accessible only through what becomes of it in its future. For events are necessarily understood to be open to their future of meaning, inasmuch as what an event means is not something extraneously added to it but is constitutive of the event itself, and furthermore in that an event has its meaning not in isolation but only in relation to its environing context which extends ultimately to embrace the whole of reality. Thus an event is completed only through the process of history culminating in a yet outstanding unity and determination of meaning.

History therefore is most adequately to be understood as *Überlieferungsgeschichte*, as a history of the transmission of traditions in which event and meaning are encompassed conjointly. An event occurs and initially has its meaning within the context of a transmitted tradition of understanding but is not bound simply to re-present that tradition--the contingent character of event would deny that. Traditions are ever broken open by new occurrences that give rise to new strands of tradition. The origins and the transmissions of traditions thus interrelate within a single compass of historical understanding. The radical disjunction between history and kerygma is hereby disavowed by a perspective that comprehends both in recognition of their mutual interpenetration and interdependence. History stands in judgment upon the adequacy of a kerygmatic formulation to incorporate the truth of the event which gave rise to it, and yet the event is not something simply external to but *includes* the kerygma as a (provisional) transmission of its meaning.

Inasmuch as an anticipated wholeness of history is the condition for an ultimate determination of meaning, history is interpretable only as universal history. The task of the theologian therefore who would be true to reality as history and the meaning of history is to take seriously the demand for conceiving of universal history, which is possible only under the premise that history points ahead toward a consummating end. The precise nature of this "end" is yet open to question, with respect to whether process continues in any way beyond the termination of historical processes, but the crucial point is that there would be no further contribution to be made with regard to a determination of the meaning of the whole of history and its individual components.

Only if a unifying terminus is anticipatable can history as universal history embrace the task of hermeneutics, for the gulf separating present understandings from past texts can be bridged only by means of a detour that confronts the other gulf between the texts and the events they intend to transmit. Only a perspective which embraces the horizons of the original event and *all* its subsequent interpreters, therefore the perspective of universal history, can do justice to the eventful meanings that underlie and come to expression in transmitted texts. The *meaning* of a text for the present interpreter comes to light precisely through an inquiry into the *reliability* of that text in representing the truth it intends to communicate.

The inquiry into the past of history is possible only through utilization of principles of critical historical methodology but these must be stripped of their accompanying anthropocentric world view in order to be fully viable. The principle of universal correlation between events cannot impose a developmental interpretation upon history, in which the future would be purely an effect of the present. And the principle of analogy, in which possibilities for past occurrences are determined by the scope of present experience, must be limited by the acknowledgment of the provisionality of all present modes of understanding and recognition of the inherently *particular* nature of those past events in which the historian has an interest. The possible *uniqueness* of an event is not to be ruled out *a priori.*

Finally, only if a single, transcendent source of the unity *and* the contingency of history is conceivable is the end and therefore the universality of history a possible anticipation. On that account, the reality of God becomes a premise not only for the theologian but for the historian's understanding of history as well.

The boldness of this transformation of commonly held canons of historical inquiry is to be seen in that theology is bidden to become more rational through a process of understanding in which history is made more theological.   But the inherent persuasiveness of this enterprise is qualified by a number of bothersome considerations which must be introduced into the discussion.

1) Does the Hebrew perspective on the presently unfinished character of reality as history demand the expectation of an eventual unifying consummation? That it came to do so in the history of the Hebrew tradition is a development that will be examined in the upcoming chapters. But does that anticipation *essentially* characterize the Hebrew understanding of history or only incidentally and belatedly do so? There is a possibility that Pannenberg reads the Hebraic tradition too strongly through an influence from Hegel that results in too quick an appropriation of Dilthey's and Löwith's thesis that an anticipatable whole and therefore end of history is a necessary condition for meaning in and of history. Is there, then, an unintended interposing of an external philosophical concept present here?[105]

2) There is a lack of sufficient clarity with regard to the "eventful" character of history as *Überlieferungsgeschichte.* Pannenberg maintains that such an understanding of the reality of history encompasses not only the transmission but also the *origins* of traditions. But are these origins ever anything more fundamental than initial moments in the chain of linguistic transmission? If that were so, there would be no essential difference between Pannenberg and those who accent the "linguisticality of reality." If it is not so, what is the meaning of event vis-a-vis *Überlieferung*? It would appear that Pannenberg's understanding here requires a more adequate grounding in an ontology

that does justice to the whole of reality as a process of events interlaced with the transmissions of their meanings. What we have is a theology in search of a metaphysic, of an ontology of events.[106]

The question emerges in this regard as to whether it is really possible to analyze history without bringing to the analysis some prior ontological understanding of general principles according to which all possible experience is interpretable. A. N. Whitehead raised this problem very tellingly.

> It is a curious delusion that the rock upon which our beliefs can be founded is a historical investigation. You can only interpret the past in terms of the present. The present is all that you have; and unless in this present you can find general principles which interpret the present as including a representation of the whole community of existents, you cannot move a step beyond your little patch of immediacy.
>
> Thus history presupposes a metaphysic . . . . you can only deduce metaphysical dogmas from your interpretation of the past on the basis of a prior metaphysical interpretation of the present.[107]

Pannenberg denies this premise, of course. It represents too sweeping an endorsement of the analogy principle, and it overlooks the problem that we do not really "have" the present all that extensively either. But Pannenberg has not countered with a sufficiently explicit indication of how attention to what history discloses offers a firm possibility for developing a metaphysic of historical reality. Much has been left unexplored in that direction.[108]

3) The concept of the knowledge of an event as a basis for critiquing the sufficiency of the tradition arising in relation to it is plagued by a trio of problems. First of all, one is confronted with a practically infinite inexhaustibility of elements comprising any single "event" of history. John Cobb observes:

> The past is inexhaustibly complex. Even if a group of people should limit themselves to a consideration of the events occurring in a fifteen-minute period in a particular room, and everyone should cooperate for the rest of their lives in seeking to report them accurately, they would touch on only a very small portion of these events in highly selective ways. Their sentences would never exhaust their actuality.[109]

Pannenberg takes account of this in his recognition of the provisionality of all interpretations of historical occurrence. Nevertheless, the premise is maintained that we can know some events well enough to stand in judgment of the tradition that communicates their meaning--and, as will be seen, even well enough to anticipate history's eventual end on the basis of a knowledge of a specific event in its tradition-context. Is this not basing too much in an elusive occurrence which always transcends every endeavor to comprehend it?

Secondly, it would seem that one must choose between affirming the capacity of an event, historically appropriated, to stand in judgment upon its subsequent interpretations, and insisting that an event is yet open to its own futural determination of meaning. Pannenberg attempts to have it both ways, and this is awkard. Either an event is closed and thus can disclose its inherent meaning to future observers, or it is open to its ultimate determination in the future and thus is ambivalent in meaning with regard to its subsequent interpreters. Pannenberg's struggle to hold on to both concepts results in a curious circularity: the anticipation of a final future is the basis for assessing meaning provisionally in the present, but the validity of the anticipation is conversely seen to depend upon being able to understand a particular event (*i.e.*, Jesus' resurrection) as already signifying that the final future will eventually arrive.

Thirdly, if a crucial aspect for grasping the truth of an event is to understand it initially in light of its own *überlieferungsgeschichtlich* context, on what basis can one acknowledge that in a particular instance the event has burst through the bonds of its own inherited tradition and set in motion a new sequence? How does one avoid losing sight of the contingent novelty of a particular event by subsuming it too completely within previously existing tradition?[110]

4) The "ontology of history" called for above would have to include a more thoroughgoing justification for the premise that an event includes the future of its determination of meaning. Why must this be so? Why can one not maintain instead that futural developments and alterations in the assessment of the meaning of a past event are not components of that event but rather *new events* in their own right? To insist that fact and value are inseparable does not seem to require that subsequent instances of *valuation* of a previous event are themselves internal to that event. The direction in which Pannenberg's thesis seems inevitably to move is toward a final unity of events indistinguishable from an actual *singularity of event*, in which the ultimate truth of the whole is a single complex datum incorporating within itself all of its precedent diverity as merely internal aspects of that One. The ontological question to be addressed here is how a unity of events can be consistently conceptualized without eliminating their individuality.

5) Finally, the manner in which Pannenberg brings the premised reality of God into the historical picture is very tenuous. God is conceivable as the resolution of the seeming conflict between the unity and the contingency of events--what is at stake there? The problem is that there is an apparent inconsistency between speaking of a future's

openness (contingency) as well as its eventual closure (unity), and Pannenberg gets around this by suggesting that a single power, God, can be thought as responsible for both. But how can that legitimately be? Does an anticipation of already assured ultimate unity not turn the "openness" of the future into a sham? The proffered resolution to that dilemma is to be found in Pannenberg's concept of the nature of divine causality. Thus the question that is initially raised here will come to receive fuller attention in chapter eight.

NOTES

[1]"Redemptive Event and History," *BQT* I, p. 15.

[2]Originally delivered as a lecture at Wuppertal in January of 1959, the essay appeared in *KuD* 5, 1959, pp. 218-37 and 259-88. The first half, in a translation by Shirley Guthrie, Jr., appeared in Claus Westermann, ed., *Essays on Old Testament Hermeneutics* (Richmond: John Knox Press, 1963), pp. 314-35, but an entire four-page section was omitted for some reason in that translation (cf. *GsT* I, pp. 39-42) and the omission was carelessly continued in the otherwise complete translation appearing in *BQT* I, pp. 15-80. The section contains important work concerning the relationship between history as a whole and the reality of God, as is developed within this chapter.

[3]"Redemptive Event and History," *BQT* I, p. 15.

[4]James M. Robinson observes with penetrating insight in "Revelation as Word and as History" (*Theology as History*, pp. 1-100), that Pannenberg does not regard the historicity of human existence as "a universal ontological reality, but rather as an acquired trait of Western man, the effect on him of Biblical history. Hence it cannot function for him as an all-embracing category as it does for Bultmann." (Pp. 26f.) Cf. "Redemptive Event and History," *BQT* I, p. 35.

[5]"Redemptive Event and History," *BQT* I, pp. 15f. Robinson notes that "the concept of *Urgeschichte,* 'pre-history', was limited to the early Barth, so that the quotation is not as direct a criticism of the Barthians of today as it might seem." (*TaH,* p. 15.) It must be acknowledged, however, that the thrust of Pannenberg's remarks is against a tendency, of which Barth is only one representative, to depreciate history at the expense of *Übergeschichte* (suprahistory), and that tendency does not really appear to have been broken through by the later Barth, as Robinson himself admits (*ibid.*). Robinson finds hints of a movement of Barthians away from a complete

repudiation of the historical-critical method as a way of taking history seriously, but only the faintest of hints in the later Barth himself (such as his implicit praise for von Rad)--certainly not enough to render Pannenberg's judgment of Barth's tendency toward dehistoricizing totally invalidated.

[6]Redemptive Event and History," BQT I, p. 21.

[7]"Response to the Discussion," TaH, p. 241.

[8]"Redemptive Event and History," BQT I, p. 17.

[9]Ibid., p. 18. See also AC, pp. 37f., and "The Crisis of the Scripture Principle," BQT I, p. 12.

[10]This understanding is the reverse of Jürgen Moltmann's erroneous critical judgment that the premise of history as reality as a whole constitutes for Pannenberg a kind of cosmological argument for the existence of God. (Theology of Hope, trans. James W. Leitch [London: SCM Press, 1967], p. 77.)

[11]"Redemptive Event and History," BQT I, pp. 18f. See further, p. 23.

[12]Ibid., p. 25.

[13]Ibid., p. 31.

[14]James M. Robinson, "The Historicality of Biblical Language," in Bernhard W. Anderson, ed., The Old Testament and Christian Faith (New York: Herder and Herder, 1969), p. 128. (Originally published as "Heilsgeschichte und Lichtungsgeschichte," Evangelische Theologie 22, 1962, pp. 113-41 [hereafter: EvTh].)

[15]See "Response to the Discussion," TaH, p. 259, ft. 68.

[16]See "Kerygma and History" (originally published in 1961, in a Festschrift for von Rad), BQT I, p. 90: "Historical process . . . is essentially a process of the transmission of tradition." (Cf. ibid., p. 93.) OaG (of the same year), p. 112: "So is history always even a history of the transmission of traditions." See also "Response to the Discussion," TaH, p. 256, and p. 257: ". . . history seen as the transmission of traditions is the deeper meaning of history in general . . ."

[17]"Dogmatic Theses on the Doctrine of Revelation," RaH, pp. 152f. The same point is made in "Kerygma and History," BQT I, p. 90.

[18]On the wide-ranging significance of this understanding for contemporary theology, see Trutz Rendtorff's discussion in "Überlieferungsgeschichte als Problem der systematischen Theologie," ThLZ 90, 1965, columns 81-98, especially cols. 87-

82

90. Rendtorff calls attention particularly to the integration of *Geschichte* and *Historie* under this unified perspective, col. 88.

[19]"Response to the Discussion," *TaH*, pp. 256f., ft. 63.

[20]Gerhard Sauter's objection that Pannenberg's understanding of history under the motif of *Überleiferungsgeschichte* betrays an inescapable grounding of the "coming" (*Kommende*) in the "having-been" (*Gewesene*), thus denying the possibility of genuine *novum*, fails to take this factor into consideration. (Sauter, *Zukunft und Verheissung* [Zürich: Zwingli Verlag, 1965], pp. 210f.)

[21]*TKG*, pp. 56f. See also "Redemptive Event and History," *BQT* I, pp. 74-76. Moltmann develops this point under a distinction between two different senses of "future," as identified in the Latin words *adventus* and *futurum*. *Adventus* signifies arrival, the coming-on of something not already present, and is the basis for the German word for future, *Zukunft*. *Futurum*, on the other hand, "means that which will be, that which follows from the becoming of being." (Moltmann, "Probleme der neueren evangelischen Eschatologie," *Verkündigung und Forschung* 11:2, 1966, p. 115.) In this latter regard, what happens in the future arises out of the present and can bring forth only "mutations," alterations grounded in *Urpotenz*. But the sense of *adventus, Zukunft,* is that "the future does not follow from the present, neither as postulate nor as consequence, but the present springs out of such a future." (*Ibid.,* pp. 114f.) Moltmann finds the concept underlying *Zukunft* to be a more valid way of comprehending the extent of future's freedom from mere repetition or rearrangement of what already is, and therefore contrasts eschatological theology, which anticipates the arrival of the *novum*, with "futurology," which extrapolates a future from factors and tendencies already emergent in history. (See also Moltmann's "Theology as Eschatology" in *The Future of Hope*, ed. Frederick Herzog [New York: Herder and Herder, 1970], pp. 11-14.) Pannenberg makes this latter point in "Future and Unity" in *Hope and the Future of Man* (hereafter: *HFM*), ed. Ewert H. Cousins (Philadelphia: Fortress Press, 1972), p. 62, but generally does not draw on the *Zukunft-futurum* distinction in his theology. The reason for this would appear to be that he does not recognize *futurum* as a valid category for understanding any aspect of the coming of the future at all, a point which will be developed fully in chapter eight. (Thus, the tendency must be resisted to characterize the present shape of German theologizing as turning on two words for "future" in contrast to its recent debates over two words for "history," *Geschichte* and *Historie*.) The rootage of Moltmann's distinction appears to be found in a brief coment by Emil Brunner in *Eternal Hope,* trans. Harold Knight (Philadelphia: The Westminster Press, 1954), p. 25: "Humanity has a future because it awaits the coming of the kingdom of God in the future coming of its Lord. The life of the world to come as distinct from *futurum* is an eschatological concept; it suggests the realization of hope through an event which springs from the beyond, from the transcendent; not like *futurum*, something which grows out of what already exists."

[22]"Kerygma and History," *BQT* I, pp. 90-93.

83

[23]"A Theological Conversation with Wolfhart Pannenberg," *Dialog* 11, 1972, p. 287.

[24]Karl Löwith, *Meaning in History* (Chicago: The University of Chicago Press, 1949), p. 1.

[25]*Ibid.*, p. 4.

[26]History "is meaningful only by indicating some transcendent purpose beyond the actual facts. But, since history is a movement in time, the purpose is a goal. Single events as such are not meaningful, nor is a mere succession of events. To venture a statement about the meaning of historical events is possible only when their *telos* becomes apparent. . . . If we reflect on the whole course of history, imagining its beginning and anticipating its end, we think of its meaning in terms of an ultimate purpose. The claim that history has an ultimate meaning implies a final purpose or goal transcending the actual events." *Ibid.*, pp. 5f.

[27]*Ibid.*, pp. 6, 18.

[28]*Ibid.*, p. 18.

[29]*Ibid.*, p. 191.

[30]*Ibid.*, p. 197.

[31]*Ibid.*, p. 198.

[32]*Ibid.*, p. 206.

[33]Rudolf Bultmann, *History and Eschatology: The Presence of Eternity* (New York: Harper and Row, 1957).

[34]*Ibid.*, p. 120. Cf. his "Is Exegesis without Presuppositions Possible?" in *Existence and Faith: Shorter Writings of Rudolf Bultmann,* trans. Schubert M. Ogden (Cleveland: World Publishing Company, 1960), p. 295: ". . . what a historical event means always first becomes clear in the future. It can definitively disclose itself only when history has come to an end." This essay originally appeared in 1957.

[35]*History and Eschatology*, p. 129 (italics mine). Cf. also *Existence and Faith*, p. 295: ". . . a historical event is always first knowable for what it is--precisely as a historical event--in the future. And therefore one can also say that the future of a historical event belongs to that event." And finally, "Zum Problem der Entmythologisierung" in *Kerygma und Mythos* VI-1: *Entmythologisierung und existentiale Interpretation (Theologische Forschung 30)* (Hamburg-Bergstedt: Herbert Reich Evangelischer Verlag Gmbh, 1963), p. 22: ". . . the historical meaning of

an event always becomes first understandable from its future forth. The future belongs essentially [*wesenhaft*] to the event."

36 *History and Eschatology*, p. 120.

37 *Ibid.*

38 *Ibid.,* p. 138.

39 *Ibid.,* pp. 140-44. Cf. *Kerygma und Mythos* VI-1, p. 22: "One can speak of the meaning of history only as a meaning of the moment, which is meaningful as moment of decision."

40 *History and Eschatology*, p. 155.

41 See Pannenberg's discussion of this point in "On Historical and Theological Hermeneutic," *BQT* I, p. 162, and "Eschatology and the Experience of Meaning," *IGHF*, p. 200.

42 See "On Historical and Theological Hermeneutic," *BQT* I, pp. 162f., and "Eschatology and the Experience of Meaning," *IGHF*, pp. 200f. For a presentation in English of Dilthey's theses, see the rearranged excerpts from *Gesammelte Schriften* VII in Wilhelm Dilthey, *Pattern and Meaning in History: Thoughts on History and Society*, trans. H. P. Rickman (New York: Harper and Row, 1961), pp. 73-75, 105-09, and 127-31. See also the colection of materials in chapter two under the heading of "The Historical Relevance of Autobiography and Biography."

43 See Martin Heidegger, *Being and Time*, trans. John Macquarrie and Edward Robinson (New York: Harper and Row, 1962), pp. 279ff., especially pp. 303 and 306f.

44 "On Historical and Theological Hermeneutic," *BQT* I, pp. 166f.

45 *Ibid.,* p. 167. See also "Eschatology and the Experience of Meaning," *IGHF*, p. 201.

46 See "On Historical and Theological Hermeneutic," *BQT* I, p. 162; "Eschatology and the Experience of Meaning," *IGHF*, p. 202.

47 Dilthey, *Pattern and Meaning in History*, p. 106.

48 "Redemptive Event and History," *BQT* I, p. 32; "On Historical and Theological Hermeneutic," *BQT* I, p. 164.

49 "Redemptive Event and History," *BQT* I, p. 35.

[50]"The Revelation of God in Jesus of Nazareth," *TaH*, p. 127; "Kerygma and History," *BQT* I, p. 86.

[51]*RaH*, p. 152.

[52]"Kerygma and History," *BQT* I, pp. 90f.

[53]*TaH*, p. 127. See also "On Historical and Theological Hermeneutic," *BQT* I, p. 155, ft. 17; *JGM*, p. 13.

[54]"Insight and Faith," *BQT* II, p. 39.

[55]"Response to the Discussion," *TaH*, p. 260. The implications of this understanding are drawn out in the following chapter dealing with Pannenberg's concept of historical revelation.

[56]*Ibid.*, p. 242. See also "Redemptive Event and History," *BQT* I, pp. 68f.; "Kerygma and History," *BQT* I, p. 90; and "Eschatology and the Experience of Meaning," *IGHF*, p. 210.

[57]*JGM*, p. 169. Cf. "Nachwort," *OaG*, p. 142, ft. 25: History's "individual components do not already bear in themselves what they are in truth. Rather it is decided first from the end forth what the meaning of the whole way and its individual events was." "Dogmatische Erwägungen zur Auferstehung Jesu," *GsT* II, p. 173: ". . . the permanent reality which determines the secret of our existence. . . . will first be *decided* in the not yet completed future of our world. Only on the strength of that can it be said that it is already present in a hidden way. The yet open future corresponds to the hiddenness of the true essence of present reality." See also *AC*, p. 38.

[58]"Heilsgeschehen und Geschichte," *GsT* I, p. 42, untranslated in BQT I. (See *supra*, ch. 3, note 2.)

[59]*E.g.*, "Eschatology and the Experience of Meaning," *IGHF*, pp. 206f. Cf. also *TKG*, p. 59: "To speak of the definitive unity of the world means that all events are moving ahead to meet, finally, a common future."

[60]"Can Christianity Do without an Eschatology?," *The Christian Hope*, p. 33.

[61]"Nachwort," in Ignace Berten, *Geschichte, Offenbarung, Glaube*, trans. Sigrid Martin (München: Claudius Verlag, 1970), p. 132. (hereafter: *GOG*.)

[62]"Can Christianity Do without an Eschatology?," *The Christian Hope*, p. 33.

[63]The translation of this sentence in *IGHF* has been corrected here. Cf. the original "Eschatologie und Sinnerfahrung," *KuD* 19, 1973, p. 44.

[64]"Eschatology and the Experience of Meaning," *IGHF,* p. 199.

[65]The presentations and formal responses, but none of the discussion, have been printed up in *Hope and the Future of Man,* ed. Ewert H. Cousins (Philadelphia: Fortress Press, 1972). (*HFM*.)

[66]"Future and Unity," *HFM*, p. 71.

[67]Because the unpublished discussion there contains the most extensive indication of Pannenberg's reflections in this crucial area, I quote at length from a taped recording of his response to criticisms of his position:

"Will there be a final event? . . . In my lecture I did not speak really of *a* final event, but I tried to distinguish very carefully between what I called the essential future--which is the future of ultimate destiny, of ultimate realization of meaning of our present existence--and those future events which will bring about, which will decide about, that ultimate destiny one way or the other. I think, since the question of the essence of our present lives--that is, of the definitive meaning of our present lives--depends on the course of our lives, but on the other hand cannot just be depending indefinitely, because then our presents would have no meaning at all,--so there must be some future which will decide definitively the meaning of the present, which will decide the ultimate meaning and thus the essence of things present and past. But this does not mean that we would know about the question as to whether such events will go on. I entertain different opinions about that. It would be possible to envisage such a future in which events would go on beyond the point when the ultimate destiny of man will be decided in such a way that it will not be questioned any more by further process." Another possibility is "that events of the kind that we experience now will not continue to happen. Such a possibility would mean that events will continue to happen but that the character--I think this is the most viable possibility for myself--that the character of their sequence will be different, so the character of the event itself will be different, so that we have to envisage, with Teilhard de Chardin, the contortion of time for the future in a similar way that the theory of relativity considers contortions of space in speaking of the universe. So in some way it would be true to say that events will not go on beyond the point of the ultimate realization and decision of the meaning of present and past reality. Something will go on, in the sense that the end is not the death of everything--that would not be eternal life, of course. But still we should think of eternal life in a way different from the process of life which is characteristic of our present experience. And in that way, I would like to think of a contortion of time connected with the future of fulfillment spelled out by the Christian hope. This contortion of time would amount to another kind of process, a process which would proceed into the depths and the mystery of our present life, while our present life in some way proceeds on a superficial dimension. We don't live into the depths, into the mystery, of our lives now. We don't live into that depth of our lives which is the presence of God."

[68]"A Theological Conversation with Wolfhart Pannenberg," *Dialog* II, 1972, pp. 287f.

[69]*Ibid.*, p. 287.

[70]*Ibid.*, p. 288.

[71]"Constructive and Critical Functions of Christian Eschatology," *Harvard Theological Review* 77, 1984, pp. 136-38.

[72]"Eschatology and the Experience of Meaning," *IGHF*, p. 199. Pannenberg has defended his conceptual vagueness regarding the ontological character of history's ultimate future by observing that theologians are not alone in the inclusion of a degree of "mystery" in their theorizing: physicists also share this characteristic! Even so, Pannenberg acknowledges, "one needs to know something about it, though one cannot presume to exhaust it." (Conversation with W. Pannenberg, 10-21-82.)

[73]See Robinson, "Revelation as Word and as History," *TaH*, p. 27, ft. 80.

[74]*Ibid.*, pp. 1-3.

[75]"Hermeneutic and Universal History," *BQT* I, p. 96. Cf. "The Crisis of the Scripture Principle," *BQT* I, p. 6. Concerning the relation of text and event, Pannenberg writes: "The essential content stated by a text is not, of course, always a specific event. That is only the case with texts that speak of occurrences and persons, as well as of their significance. The essential content of a text can also be a mathematical truth, a natural entity, a technical construction, or a philosophical idea . . . . With regard to the biblical texts, however, we have to do in every case with testimonies to specific events and their inherent meaning. The inquiry which presses behind them to their essential content will to that extent be a quest for the actual course of events, and will thus be historical." (*BQT* I, p. 96, ft. 1.)

[76]"Hermeneutic and Universal History," *BQT* I, pp. 97f.

[77]*Ibid.*, pp. 98f.

[78]*Ibid.*, p. 99.

[79]*Ibid.*, p. 103.

[80]*Ibid.*, p. 117. See Hans-Georg Gadamer, *Truth and Method*, trans. Garrett Barden and John Cumming (New York: The Seabury Press), pp. 269-73.

[81]"Hermeneutic and Universal History," *BQT* I, p. 120.

[82]*Ibid.*, p. 129. Pannenberg goes on to remark that "only within the context of universal history can the 'then' of the text be bound to the 'today' of the interpreter in such a way that the temporal, historical difference between them is not eliminated but

rather preserved and bridged over in the nexus of events linking them both." (*Ibid.*, pp. 131f.)

[83]See *ibid.*, p. 122.

[84]*Ibid.*, p. 135; "On Historical and Theological Hermeneutic," *BQT* I, pp. 170f. Cf. especially, on p. 171: "Every such anticipation is conditioned by its standpoint, bound to its location in history. To this extent, it is a *mere* anticipation, and not the whole itself. Nevertheless, to the extent that it is an anticipation, it is the presence of the whole constituted by the future."

[85]"On Historical and Theological Hermeneutic," *BQT* I, p. 155.

[86]*Ibid.*, pp. 151f. and 159.

[87]See Robinson, "Revelation as Word and as History," *TaH*, p. 42.

[88]"Redemptive Event and History," *BQT* I, pp. 39f.

[89]*Ibid.*, p. 40. See Ernst Troeltsch, *Gesammelte Schriften* II (Tübingen: J. C. B. Mohr, 1913), pp. 729-53.

[90]"Redemptive Event and History," *BQT* I, p. 41.

[91]"Welgeschichte und Heilsgeschichte," in *Probleme biblischer Theologie* (Gerhard von Rad zum 70. Geburtstag), ed. Hans Walter Wolff (München: Chr. Kaiser Verlag, 1971), pp. 354 and 361-64.

[92]"Redemptive Event and History," *BQT* I, p. 53 (cf. p. 38).

[93]*Ibid.*, p. 42.

[94]*Ibid.*, pp. 46f.

[95]*Ibid.*, pp. 43-47.

[96]*Ibid.*, p. 61. Richard Rhem has identified the relation of Pannenberg to Troeltsch on the one hand and Barth and Bultmann on the other very perceptively in "A Theological Conception of Reality as History--Some Aspects of the Thinking of Wolfhart Pannenberg," *Reformed Review* 26, 1972, pp. 178-82. The dialectical theologians agreed with Troeltsch that history and the methods by which it is investigated rule out the possibility of understanding history as the locus of God's definitive revelatory activity, and therefore turned away from history toward the transhistorical Word or the historicity of human existence. Thus Barth and Bultmann concurred with Troeltsch's conclusions on the results of historical study and found therein the justification for rejecting it as having no bearing on what is ultimately of importance.

But "precisely where Troeltsch, Barth, and Bultmann were one, Pannenberg parts from all three; that is, at the point of the understanding of the nature of history and the principles by which the past is known . . . . By a critique of Troeltsch's understanding of history and the principles of historiography Pannenberg attempts to do justice to Troeltsch's demand to pursue the historical method while leaving room for a definitive revelation of God in history which Barth and Bultmann in their respective manners recognized as essential to the Christian tradition." (*Ibid.*, p. 182.) This is essentially parallel to Pannenberg's unwillingness to continue dialectical theology's endorsement of atheism's critique of human projective concepts of God. (See *supra*, chapter one, pp. 3f.)

97"Heilsgeschehen und Geschichte," *GsT* I, p. 42 (untranslated in *BQT* I--see *supra*, ch. 3, note 2.).

98"Redemptive Event and History," *BQT* I, pp. 36f.

99 *Ibid.*, pp. 74f.

100 *Ibid.*, pp. 75f. Pannenberg maintains in a footnote thereto that this counts not only for understanding continuities in human history but with regard to natural events as well. Natural laws are to be understood accordingly as expressions of the faithfulness of God. In this respect, Pannenberg denies any dichotomy between history and nature: "nature, too, is to be understood as history." (*Ibid.*, p. 76, ft. 145. See also *AC*, pp. 39-43.)

101 *Ibid.*, p. 76.

102"On Historical and Theological Hermeneutic," *BQT* I, p. 159.

103"The Crisis of the Scripture Principle," *BQT* I, p. 12, where Pannenberg observes further: "The difficulty of speaking of a goal of history as a whole makes it questionable whether universal history can be understood as a unity without the biblical ideas of God." See also "Response to the Discussion," *TaH*, pp. 242-44.

104The manner of presentation employed here would seem to confirm Lothar Steiger's criticism that Pannenberg always considers the "that" of universal history before the "how" of our knowing it. (Steiger, "Revelation-History and Theological Reason: A Critique of the Theology of Wolfhart Pannenberg," in *History and Hermeneutic* [*Journal for Theology and the Church*, Vol. 4], ed. Robert W. Funk [New York: Harper and Row, 1967], pp. 86f.) However, the matter is just not that simple. Pannenberg's approach to the raw materials of his theological interpretation is far more organismic than serial, a factor which constantly frustrates the endeavor to distinguish the presuppositionally given from the empirically (historically) deduced.

105Cf. criticism number six in chapter two.

[106]Allan Galloway repeatedly points to the need for the development of a new, Pannenbergian metaphysics to undergird his theological insights, in his book *Wolfhart Pannenberg* (London: George Allen & Unwin Ltd., 1973). See pp. 71, 83f., 97, 131, and 136f. The question of the possibility of such a venture would seem to turn on the issue of whether eschatology and ontology are to be regarded as mutually exclusive concepts.

[107]Alfred North Whitehead, *Religion in the Making* (New York: The Macmillan Company, 1926), p. 84.

[108]By way of example, one can inquire whether history adequately encompasses "nature" when it is understood as a history of transmission of traditions. How is natural history included here? Is Pannenberg successful with his approach in transcending the nature-history dualism as he intends? He addresses himself very cogently to the way in which nature is to be understood to have a history in his extended essay on "Kontingenz und Naturgesetz" (A. M. Klaus Müller and Wolfhart Pannenberg, *Erwâgungen zu einer Theologie der Natur* [Gütersloh: Gütersloher Verlagshaus Gerd Mohn, 1970], pp. 33-80), but nowhere therein does he deal with this history in conjunction with *Überlieferungsgeschichte*. If natural history stands outside of tradition history, how is the latter the most adequate concept for embracing reality as history?

[109]John B. Cobb, Jr., *Liberal Christianity at the Crossroads* (Philadelphia: The Westminster Press, 1973), p. 27.

[110]Gerald O'Collins raises essentially this question in his chapter on Pannenberg in *Foundations of Theology* (Chicago: Loyola University Press, 1971), on pp. 128f.

91

4

HUMAN QUESTIONING TOWARD GOD

In the pursuit of truth, one comes up against the need to presuppose the unifying reality of God as condition of truth's ultimate existence. In the endeavor to understand history, one confronts the necessity of presupposing a transcendent source of contingency and unity as condition of meaning. So also in attempting even to grasp one's own selfhood, Pannenberg insists that we inescapably face toward God as condition of the essence of human reality. But even here, as there, we only have such a God initially in the form of a question--a necessary but ungrounded presupposition. Before going on to explore how the reality of God can come to function as answer, we need to enter into a consideration of Pannenberg's thesis that the human individual[1] exists as a question mark pointing in the direction of God. This amounts to an exploration into theological anthropology as springboard to a concept of deity.

A.   *World-openness*

Continuous with a number of anthropologists whose insights into human nature he appropriates,[2] Pannenberg proceeds to define our human distinctiveness as a matter of "world-openness."   Greek philosophy portrayed the human being as a microcosm of reality, reflecting the structures of being in the individual's own existence, but this concept has become as strange today as the ancient picture of the cosmos itself. For we no longer presume that our picture of a cosmic order is anything more than a model to be projected and then rejected. On the contrary, modern women and men since Pascal have been characterized by a boundless, formative freedom over against the world, which Pannenberg interprets as an indication of our essential *Weltoffenheit* . This places us in distinction from animals, who have only an environment and are limited to their environment. By contrast, we are not bound to what environs us. Our capacity for novel responsiveness and creativity transcends merely environmental limitations. In this regard, we cannot be said to have our world already at hand; rather it becomes at hand (*zuhanden*) only through our active structuring of it, in the building of an artificial, cultural world. Because of this ongoing creative activity, it is impossible to regard the world as the source of our true determination (*Bestimmung*)--for we determine (*bestimmen*) what is to become of our world.[3]

Therefore we are raising continually a question about our own being, which cannot be answered from the world before us because we are always able to inquire beyond every horizon of the world that discloses itself to us. In our open questioning beyond every answer that is forthcoming to us, we come to be experienced in the form of a question ourselves.

> The designation of this basic structure of man's being as a question which drives toward an answer is not a mere metaphor. For the ability to transcend one's own situation, which characterizes man, is realized in the process of an inquiry, which is also something that underlies every human projection. Every projection is an anticipation of an answer to a question that underlies it. The inquiry is directed toward what is not yet known. Through it man proceeds beyond the realm of the known and thus beyond his own situation. His openness to the world is expressed by the very fact that he is able to make an inquiry and that his life is a process of inquiry that continually drives him on into the open. In questioning the reality he encounters and going beyond its currently given aspects to its very essence through this inquiry, thus disclosing *its* questionableness, man is in the last analysis asking about himself, about his own destination [*Bestimmung*]. Thus it makes good sense to describe man as a question that continually pushes him further into the open.[4]

Thus our world-openness is not only an openness to and for the world but also and essentially an openness *beyond* it.[5] Out distinctiveness from the animals is not to be found merely in the recognition that our world is more vast in scope than their milieu. Rather we remain requisitely open beyond every experience, every situation, every achieved picture of the world and every possible one that we might image. We are utterly directed into the open, with a surplus of drives that surpasses every cultural attainment and presses us ever onward toward something that ever remains undefined. We are open beyond our world because our world is never able completely to satisfy our restless seeking and striving and questioning.[6]

But we do share with animals one important factor. It belongs to the nature of drives, whether animal instincts or human impulses, to be dependent upon that which sustains them. In our case, this entails a sort of dependency characterizable as an infinite "directedness" (*Angewiesenheit*)[7] beyond everything finite toward a sustaining ground which supports both oneself and the world and is not identifiable with anything in the world. In our boundless openness, we are directed ultimately toward that which is over against (*ein Gegenüber*) this boundlessness, which is presupposed by our experience of directedness. It is not the case that I create an imaginary object of my longing beyond every possible thing in the world, a la Feuerbach; rather the premise of that which is over against my directedness provides a basis upon which alone my imaginative representations of this Other can be formed.[8] Thus my unlimited questioning ultimately points me in the direction of God:

> For that to which the human individual is directed in one's infinite striving, language has the term "God." The word "God" can only be meaningfully recovered if it refers to that which is over against the boundless directedness of human life. Otherwise it becomes an empty vocable.[9]

My openness to and beyond the world therefore passes over into an openness *for* God as the underlying thrust to that anthropological insight. Pannenberg concludes: "What is for animals the environment, is for us God: the goal in which alone our striving can find rest and where our destiny [*Bestimmung*] would be fulfilled."[10]

Nevertheless, to maintain that God is the answer presupposed by my unlimited world-openness and infinite directedness cannot constitute any theoretical proof for the actuality of God.[11] To say that I am a question aimed at an answer does not at the same time confirm that a conclusive answer beyond all further questioning is ultimately forthcoming.[12] All that is initially concludable from such anthropological considerations is that the questionableness of human beings in our world-openness constitutes a question about God.

Pannenberg goes on to explore the implications inherent in our culture-producing activity as a further expression of our openness for God. In our openness to the world, we strive to attain dominion over the world, and the form which this takes is culture. That which makes culture possible is our capacity for language, whereby we order and interrelate what we find about us. But we do not remain content merely to create an artificial world of symbols, reflecting a sort of conceptual dominance over our world. Through the use of language we are able to construct

95

outwardly an artificial world of culture by the transformation of our world into new shapes and structures, thus embodying a full-blown dominion over extant reality.[13]

But what really makes us capable of such far-reaching creative achievement? Pannenberg finds the answer in the power of imagination, *Phantasie.* [14] Access to reality, even for the scientist, is opened up through imaginative constructs which are subsequently confirmed or discarded. Models projected by the image-making mind are the means of advance in the comprehension and transformation of the given. This represents a continuing openness in us which pries us out of the already and thrusts us toward the creatively new. Imagination enables us to free ourselves from our own situation and discover creatively that which is unprecedented and novel.[15] Thus it is intimately connected with a characteristic human openness for the future. Through imagination, our questioning world-openness is extended into future-openness.

> Only human beings can experience the future as future, as not yet present. This openness for the future results from world-openness, from our far-reaching freedom from immediate pressure of instinct, and therein the capacity of imagination to free oneself from one's own situation and anticipate the new is also grounded.[16]

But imagination is not merely an active human projection. It also has a passive element, because we are incapable of bringing forth pure flashes of insight underived from some source or other. "The imagining individual more receives than brings forth."[17] And inasmuch as imagination has to do in a special way with our inifinite openness, "through imagination we, in our inwardness, receive from God."[18] God is presupposed therefore not only by our world-openness in questioning but also by our future-openness in imagining, so that "God appears not only as the goal of man's striving in his openness to the world, but also as the origin of man's creative mastery of the world."[19]

Finally, we are able to be related to this presupposed reality over against our questioning and imagining openness only through an act of trust. For the truth of that to which we are directed remains impenetrable in every instance. It does not place itself at our disposal. We live rather from trusting in the reliability of that to which we surrender ourselves in putting ourselves at the mercy of the unknown toward which we are directed. One takes a chance, which is precisely a yielding up of oneself to the uncertainty of the future. And yet there is an enduring tension between the inability of trust to assure itself of the certainty of its object and the dependence of trust upon an experiencing, at least partially, of the trustworthiness of its object. *I.e.,* trust requires a point of departure, though it cannot guarantee its ultimate fulfillment. Where it endeavors to gain such a guarantee, the motif of trust is replaced by one of control, a tendency which is all too characteristic of the human experience. God as the ultimate object of my trust is conceivable as God only in that God is infinitely beyond every finite object which is transformable from an object of trust into something at my disposal.[20]

But this trusting relationship contains another element essential to it. Inasmuch as trust is properly directed toward that which possesses a hidden inwardness, incalculable and inaccessible to external observation, it is inescapably tied up with the concept of the personal. "That that to which we are ultimately directed in the openness of our humanity can only be experienced in the act of absolute trust, and that this source is in its essence a person, are very closely connected.[21] The consideration of trust as a fundamental corollary of our world- and future-openness leads therefore to an inquiry into the concept of personhood as it applies to the human experience.

B. Personhood

If I perceive myself directly as personal and then come to project that personalness upon the object of my infinitely directed trust, I am unable to get around the charge of a fundamental anthropomorphism in my concept of deity, as Fichte so convincingly observed.[22] But is it necessarily the case that I am immediately aware of my own personhood? That I discern my individuality is surely the case, but are these two really one and the same? Pannenberg is convinced that they are not.[23] Personhood entails more than just the recognition of one's separate individual existence, for there are individual "things" as well. It is precisely in contrast to the nature of any thing that the character of the distinctly personal stands out.

Pannenberg maintains that the very concept of personhood is rooted in religious experience. I come to understand myself as person only in believing myself to be encountered by a power which is intrinsically impenetrable and beyond my disposal (*unverfügbar*), and which lays a claim on me. Only in response to that experience do I come to recognize my own corresponding hidden innerness and nonmanipulability, in comparison with the intrinsic accessibility and transparency of things. As the reality that confronts me is untransparent, so do I come to perceive in myself an element that is not accessible to other human beings except insofar as I yield it up myself.[24]

It is not therefore the case, initially, that we perceive God as a Thou in correspondence to our own I. Rather I come for the first time to discern my own I-ness when I experience myself as the thou of God.[25] Pannenberg traces the roots of this discovery to the biblical understanding of God and persons. The thou is a person to me only when I recognize that he or she is not under my control.[26] Biblical individuals found themselves in the presence of a power that continually brought forth new and contingent events that were not under human control.[27] Furthermore, it was in response to this powerful presence that they saw their own and their fellow human beings' nonmanipulability in a new light: the ancient commandment against murder in Israel appears in the tradition to have been motivated by a recognition that we are in the image of this personal power (Gen. 9:6).[28] So also, the repudiation of murder in the Decalogue is presented precisely in the context of a covenantal relationship between the Israelites and their God. They came to take each other seriously because God had taken them seriously. Human life is elevated to a new status in the election covenant,[29] sharing derivatively the character of personhood which God is understood to possess originally.

But Pannenberg has not remained fully content with that description of the nature of our derivative personhood, and he has expanded his interpretation of the essential character of the personal in a direction that is continuous with his earlier position but goes significantly beyond it. To begin with, he comes to observe that personalness is inescapably bound up with freedom, inasmuch as personal power is not confined to what is already in existence but is rather the source of the contingently new. This leads then to the realization that the freedom inherent in personhood connotes an openness to the future:

> Man is free only because he has a future, because he can go beyond what is presently extant [*das Vorhandene*]. And so freedom is in general the power that transforms the present. This means, however, that futurity as a condition of freedom constitutes the very core of the personal . . .[30]

Freedom for the future, freedom to go beyond and transform the present, is thus a hallmark of personhood. But Pannenberg does not stop there. Integrating the consideration of a person's inner impenetrability and that person's freedom beyond what is extant, he takes the further step of asserting that personhood itself remains beyond extant reality:

> . . . a person is the opposite of an existent [*vorhandenen*] being. Human beings are persons by the very fact that they are not wholly and completely existent for us in their reality, but are characterized by freedom, and as a result remain concealed and beyond control [*unverfügbar*] in the totality of their existence.[31]

Where we presume to have an individual person wholly before us as already actual, we cease therein to regard that one as personal. A fully available entity is no thou, but an it, not person but thing. It is entirely the case that human beings are also existent: "their being as persons takes shape in their present, bodily reality,"[32] but what constitutes their personhood is that they are yet more than what is visible therein. The obvious implication of this understanding is that we are not yet fully personal but are on our way toward becoming so.[33]

Pannenberg pursues just this point in yet a further area of reflection, on the relation between the personal and the infinite. He aligns himself with Hegel in denying Fichte's insistence that the idea of the personal necessarily entails the notion of the finite. The issue concerns whether the nature of the I to have a counterpart in a Thou flies in the face of the unbounded inclusiveness of the infinite.

> According to Hegel, the person does not in every respect have its counterpart outside itself, as limitation of its own being; it is rather the nature of the person to be related to its counterpart, even to give itself up to that counterpart and thus to find itself in the other--in the cause which the I serves, in the thing it works on and knows, and in the Thou to which the self is bound in friendship or love. Moreover, a person finds himself again in the other in the degree to which he has surrendered and given himself up to that other. Thus in the personal life the contrast to the other, the limitation, is abolished or overcome. This shows that the person as person is, in his nature, *not* limited or finite. This is not contradicted by the fact that there are finite persons, if their finiteness is to be understood as the limitation of their being as persons. For in fact the finiteness of the human being as person is shown by the circumstance that we only partially overcome the contrast to the other--either the "It" or the "Thou"--and can only partially unite with it. To this extent the finite person is not a person in the full sense. The person as person, according to Hegel's ideas, would be infinite.[34]

It is therefore obvious that, from such a perspective, the personal character of God would not stand opposed to God's infinity. But even more importantly, for the present discussion, human finitude would seem to call into question the appropriateness of fully regarding a human being as personal. The issue has been completely stood on its head. The consequence of such a move is that we are now understood not only to have derived our concept of our own personalness from our encounter with a free, impenetrable, nonmanipulable, infinite power, but we also only have that personalness in a limited, anticipatory way. One might contend therefore that Pannenberg recovers the personhood of God only by eliminating the present personhood of humans. But the thrust of his proposal is actually continuous with a crucial point that he has been concerned to make all along: that we are directed toward the future for the becoming of our essential humanity.

C. Freedom and the Futurity of Essence

Freedom, the future, and our essential being are intimately interconnected for Pannenberg. Very early in his development as a theologian, he offered the observation that freedom is really only present "where essence is actualized." Only where I truly come to find the truth about myself (*viz.,* in Jesus Christ) am I "that at which I am aimed from my origin," and therein, where "the essence of human existence is actualized, is one free."[35] He goes on to distinguish this "essential freedom" from a merely illusory "formal" freedom which one presumes to have as a present capacity or possession.[36]

Pannenberg has continued to remain faithful to this germinal notion. Human freedom is understood to be "the harmony of the individual with his destiny [*Bestimmung*]."[37] It is constitutive of true subjectivity[38] and intimately related to personhood.[39] And yet, strictly speaking, this human freedom which is so fundamental for one's genuine personhood is not something that can be said to be presently extant. Freedom, as something that has to do essentially with the future, is itself truly futural: "the reality of the future and that of freedom belong together, by contrast with what exists here and now."[40] This is understood to be the case because freedom involves precisely the capacity to go beyond what is already extant.[41] To be free is precisely to have a future, not to be trapped in an endless repetition of the already or bound to the forces of the past.[42] In my exercise of freedom, I am always beyond what I previously was, I constantly overtake and transcend myself.[43] Therefore it is necessary to affirm that what I will come to be in my freedom is not something already given; I must first seek, in freedom, the true character of my being which is simultaneously my destiny.[44]

The consequence of these reflections is that I am presently open beyond the extant world for the realization of my own true being as something ever futural to me. The future for which I am open and the essential truth of my own reality are one and the same. Only in the fulfillment of one's destiny "is the essence of man realized; for the essence of man is not to be sought in what is already realized in man, but it still comes to him from his future. The essence of man is the destiny that still lies beyond the empirical content of man's present . . ."[45] It is therefore indeed the final destiny of human existence which is truly free, not the present.[46]

Pannenberg moves on to a consideration of the source of freedom, and finds it impossible to regard freedom as rooted in anything already actual. Especially is it the case that human freedom is not explainable in terms of any present human reality. For "if the origin of freedom is sought in man himself, in what man already was before the act of his freedom, then his being as a person--the subject of his freedom--has already been thought of as an existent being, instead of as a subjectivity which is realized only through freedom."[47] It is rather the case that we always transcend what is extant in the act of freedom, wherefore "the origin of freedom lies in someone or something other than

100

the self which already existed. In other words, human freedom is always received as a gift."[48] But from where does the gift derive? Is it received from other individuals, such that the root of freedom lies in co-humanity? But this does not adequately confront the problem that the other individual needs to be set free also:

> For he too does not derive his freedom from what he already is or was. He can impart only the freedom towards which he himself is open, and which is in the balance at any moment, and must be given and received anew. . . . Since in the end my fellow man is ultimately as dependent as I am upon the gift of freedom, the "thou" of my fellow man cannot be the ultimate basis of freedom. Freedom can continue to flourish amongst men only where its origin lies, independently of the arbitrary desires of individuals, in a commonly recognized truth.[49]

But where can that truth reside? Pannenberg has contended that the direction in which we are open in our questioning and striving beyond the extant world is conceivable as God. The obvious implication therefore is that God is likewise thinkable as the destination of human freedom and also its source. But precisely here a major difficulty arises, for one of the most fundamental characteristics of modern atheism is its denial that the reality of God and human freedom are genuinely compatible. The basic question posed by this "atheism of freedom" is just this:

> Does man, in the exercise of his existence, assume a reality beyond himself and everything finite, sustaining him in the very act of his freedom, and alone making him free, a reality to which everything that is said about God refers? Or does the freedom of man exclude the existence of God, so that with Nietzsche, Nicolai Hartmann and Sartre we must postulate the non-existence of God, not his existence, for the sake of human freedom? This must be the central question by which modern atheism stands and falls. And a decision on this question is an indispensable basic condition, though not a completely sufficient condition in itself, for any justification of our speaking about God.[50]

Only if God is conceivable as essential source of human freedom can God therefore be meaningfully thought at all. What is called for is nothing less than a radical and profound revision of the traditional doctrine of God in light of the problem of freedom,[51] an incisively new formulation of the idea of God which would overcome the antinomies arising out of the notions of divine foreknowledge and predestination.[52] Pannenberg proposes the direction in which such a conceptual revision is to be sought:

> Thought of as an existent being on the analogy of tangible things, God, even if such a God existed, could only belong to the totality of everything with which freedom is concerned. But the basis of freedom cannot be a being that already exists, but only a reality which reveals to freedom its future, the coming God.[53]

101

A God of freedom is therefore a viable concept only insofar as God is understood to be beyond what is presently extant, for "if freedom is the ability to go beyond what already exists, to set it aside or change it, then such a freedom means the ability to go beyond a God who in some sense belongs to the totality of what exists."[54]

Nevertheless, it is not possible to conclude the (non-extant) reality of God as necessary condition of freedom on the basis of such considerations. All that is opened up hereby is the conceivability of a divine origin of freedom. Whether or not such a reality is true is another matter.[55] As in the case of our questioning world-openness and the implicitly infinite and derivative character of personhood, so also concerning the issue of a ground of freedom, we have God only in the form of a presupposition of our own eventual essential completedness. It has still only been ascertained that God is the one about whom the human individual as question is asking in the inquiry into the ground of one's presumed freedom. That God is the corresponding answer cannot be postulated on the basis of the formulating of the question. To state it differently: the ultimate attainment of our destiny is presently a *hope* and not a certainty.

D. *Resurrectional Hope*

We face forward toward a future that is beyond our complete control. In our openness beyond what is extant in the world, we are directed toward the distinctively new which the future brings. We are thus futurally disposed beings. Interest is greatly concentrated on the future; we alone have an awareness of the future through our capacity for anticipation of what is not yet. In our futural emphasis, we try to plan for and secure the outcome of our present experiences. Though we have made great strides in that direction, in the building of culture and the advance of science, complete success ever eludes us. "The essential nature of the future lies in the unpredictable new thing that is hidden in the womb of the future."[56] Therefore our endeavors to calculate where the present is tending are repeatedly being thwarted by unexpected turns of events. Precisely where calculation ceases, hope begins.[57]

Specifically we strive forward toward a consummation of human wholeness, an attainment of our essential destiny, but the wholeness toward which our destiny aims is attainable only beyond death.[58] For death forecloses the expectation of further futural accomplishments. If death is the end, hope is foolish. "How stupid it is to long for an uncertain future that even at best will only bring the grave closer."[59] It is therefore the case that anticipation of ultimate self-realization in the attainment of one's destiny and hope that spans the seeming finality of death are inextricably interrelated: "Whether hope is a meaningful attitude toward existence or the most extreme foolishness is ultimately decided in the question about whether there is something to hope for beyond death."[60] This leads Pannenberg to the consideration that just as it is uniquely characteristic for us to be confronted by the knowledge of the coming of our own eventual death, so also is it characteristic for us to hope that our future is not utterly closed off by death.

> If it is taken seriously, does not the knowledge that death is unavoidable render everything that fills our fleeting days stale and empty? . . . Only the person who is certain of his future can calmly turn to the present day. It is inherent to man to hope beyond death, even as it is inherent to man to know about his own death. The openness to [and beyond] the world, which compels man still to seek his destiny while animals live theirs out without question, also compels him to push the question about himself forward beyond death. For men's question about their destiny finds no conclusive answer in this life, but remains an open question in the totality of every pattern of life. Man's destiny, which is open to the world, leads him to think beyond the world to the vis-a-vis, God. So also his destiny compels him to think about a life beyond death. The two are closely connected.[61]

Pannenberg drives home his point elsewhere in no uncertain terms: "The phenomenology of hope indicates that it belongs to the essence of conscious human existence to hope beyond death."[62] In the human drive beyond every present attainment toward a further and more encompassing self-fulfillment, I am necessarily driven to look past death if my coming to my true self is not ultimately to be thwarted. For only if death is not the final end is an appropriate fulfillment of human destiny conceivable.[63]

But what shape can a fulfilling life beyond death be understood to take? Conceptions about life after death are attempts to express what presently remains inconceivable,[64] and yet it is important to ask "whether or not such conceptions adequately express the motive that gave rise to them, that is, whether they appropriately formulate the destiny of human life that reaches out beyond death and that each individual seeks."[65] To that extent, therefore, a testing of various concepts is possible. The two main ideas of the West have been the Greek concept of the immortality of the soul and the biblical understanding of the resurrection of the dead. Can one of these be seen to correspond more adequately than the other to the anthropological considerations that prompt their being entertained?

Pannenberg observes that the former idea involves a sense of the constancy of a present element in human life, rather than a hope in the coming of something genuinely new. There is the preservation of a kernel of essential humanness, not the expectation of the futural attainment of our essence.[66] Therefore the conviction of our present openness beyond everything extant, including the degree of attainment of our own selfhood, is not justly represented. Furthermore, modern anthropology denies the legitimacy of a distinction in us between body and soul as two separate kinds of reality. We are conceivable only as "a unifed corporeal creature like the animals."[67] Life after death could only be thought of in terms of the "*whole* man,"[68] bodily as well as psychical, in which the full reality of the human is somehow preserved or created anew.

But this is precisely the notion characterized by the biblical metaphor of a resurrection of the dead. The Christian expectation of resurrection includes the understanding that death involves the destruction of present bodily reality, such that hope in the new is essentially involved: "no element of our present human existence can outlast death . . . . Resurrection can only be hoped for as a completely new becoming, as a radical transformation, if not as a new creation."[69] On the one hand, the image does justice to the anthropological insight into the human being as a psycho-physical organism: only if our bodiliness is taken account of is resurrection complete. But on the other hand, there is the thrust toward an ultimate future characterized by genuine newness: "we cannot evaluate this future condition in terms of our present condition."[70]

The consequence of this reflection is not to legitimate the biblical idea of a resurrection from death. It is simply to recognize the degree of continuity between the biblical metaphor and modern anthropological understanding. It is simply to maintain that contemporary anthropological science does not rule out the possibility that resurrection is a meaningful idea.[71]

Pannenberg further maintains that the biblical hope in resurrection commends itself to the contemporary concern over human destiny beyond death in that it expresses the understanding that our ultimate future is anticipated in common with all other people. Resurrection is expected to occur to all people collectively, not to individual people in isolation from others. Therefore this metaphor is able to do justice to the longing for an embracing community of co-humanity, to the idea of an essential thrust toward unity as intrinsic to human destiny.[72] To raise this issue leads us beyond the motif of hope to a consideration of the dynamic at work in us that tends to close us off from the attainment of the essential unity for which we are destined. We are faced with the fundamental conflict of an impulse of world-openness at odds with a resistance characterized by self-enclosedness. Pannenberg's proposed resolution of that tension provides yet another facet of the pluriform thesis that only God is conceivable as the answer to the question that we are.

E. Self-centeredness and the Thrust toward Unity

I am aimed not merely at my own exclusive self-fulfillment, my individual destiny, but even more especially at the fullness of community, my social destiny. In my openness toward the personal other and my own full personhood, I am directed toward a coming to myself which transcends mere individuality in a unity of the individual and the social that does justice to both without sacrificing either. In that the social dimension is inherently a part of the thrust toward complete humanness, we are able to envisage our personal fulfillment only in continuity with the totality of humanity.[73] The concept of the attainment of perfect community belongs unavoidably to one's destiny.[74] The necessity of transcending the isolated self in a unity of the whole is a fundamental element of human existence.

But I am at war with myself. My world-openness which drives me unsatisfied beyond everything extant including myself is countered by a deeply rooted impulse of egocentricity. World-openness is in conflict with self-enclosedness. My striving toward self-assertion and self-establishment is the reflection of a self-centeredness in which I become the center of my own world, disharmonious with the thrust toward openness to the world. I am thus a locus of ambiguity, confronted with dual tendencies and existing in tension between two countervailing forces. Open toward my destiny, I am imprisoned by my ego.[75]

How is the dilemma to be resolved? In escape from the self? No, for then the attainment of one's destiny would no longer be an integration of the self with the larger whole.[76] Perhaps, then, the individual may transcend oneself, by incorporating one's self in a larger totality, extending the ego to embrace all else. But this romantic ideal remains unactualizable: "The ego can never take everything into itself . . . . At least what is accidental, unique, and unforeseeable both in nature and in human history remains beyond its grasp and overcomes the ego again and again with surprises."[77]

The essence of the problem is that the tension between world-openness and self-centeredness, between the social and individual poles of one's destiny, cannot be resolved from within the self. For every successful attempt in that direction would be only a new triumph of my self-centeredness, not a surmounting of it. I would actually have to have my center outside myself in order to overcome the conflict.[78] Thus, the

105

conflict between openness and closedness remains something that I myself cannot bridge.[79]

Pannenberg's penetration of the impasse is accomplished by means of the contention that reality itself would have to co-operate with us in the thrust toward unity. Reality must be on its way toward unity as the condition of our transcending our self-centeredness. The unity of all reality is thus a premise of the achievement of human unity.[80] Inasmuch as God alone is that power who can guarantee the attainment of a unity of all that is, God is therefore presupposed as the source of the harmony between the self and the whole world that we require for the realization of our true destiny. "The directedness of human striving toward God is quite essentially the question of that someone who guarantees the sought unity of all reality and therewith even of our own existence."[81]

F. Subjectivity and the Question of God

Concentration on anthropological considerations reflects Pannenberg's understanding that the question of the reality of God is one that arises distinctively in respect to the fundamental questionablenss of human existence.

> The question about the being of God can only be stated in the form of the question about the being that must always be presupposed by man precisely with respect to his subjectivity: the question about the being to which he is referred for the actual ground of the possibility of his freedom in relation to the world.[82]

This anthropological posing of the question of God is continuous with what Pannenberg discerns as a progressive "anthropologizing of the idea of God"[83] in the West. He traces a movement, beginning already in Plato and reaching a particular plateau of importance with Kant, in which access to God through attention to the natural world is increasingly excluded and God becomes a postulate of the human subject. This has been accompanied by an elimination of the appeal to God as necessary First Cause, not only through the repudiation of the argument itself, deriving particularly from Ockham, but also through the elimination of the need for such an explanation with the rise of Newtonian physics and the establishment of the principle of inertia. Kant saw that the cosmological argument had merit precisely as an expression of an ideal of reason but not directly as an expression of the structure of reality itself--even though humankind could not adequately understand itself in its total existence without presupposing this idea. Thus the understanding of God's relationship with the natural world comes to be mediated through an emphasis upon what is required for our full self-understanding.[84]

Hegel concentrated upon the ontological argument for God's existence as the most crucial one, inasmuch as it alone did not posit the infinite as a condition of the finite but rather proceeded from the idea of the infinite as its point of departure. The essential question arising herein is precisely whether we actually possess the concept of a being whose existence is inseparable from the concept--and does so necessarily, not simply as a mere possibility for thought. Therein the question turns back upon us and once again the conceptualizing of God's being is seen to be linked to an adequate understanding of the truth about ourselves.[85]

The upshot of these considerations is to uncover the fact that the crisis in contemporary God-talk is decidedly more anthropological than strictly theological, wherefore the way back to a meaningful recovery of concepts of God is through a more adequate assessment of our true nature. It is in that direction that the arguments examined in this chapter point, expressing the conviction on Pannenberg's part that theological anthropology can no longer be merely a peripheral issue but finds itself in the position of a "fundamental theology."[86] Concerning the religious dimension of anthropological concerns, he writes:

> If it cannot be shown that the issues with which religion is concerned, the elevation of man above the finite content of human experience to the idea of an infinite reality which sustains everything finite, including man himself, are an essential of man's being, so that one is not really considering man if one ignores this dimension--if this cannot be shown with sufficient certainty, then every other viewpoint with which one may concern oneself in this field is an empty intellectual game, and what is said about God loses every claim to intellectual veracity.[87]

But though anthropology is essential as a point of departure for raising the question of God, that does not entail that the question is answerable through attention to the implications of the truth about human existence. Pannenberg adamantly insists that focusing upon human subjectivity is no sufficient condition for speaking of the reality of God: "Man himself exists as *questioning* toward God. But one cannot simply deduce from the openness of the question that God exists."[88] Nevertheless, Pannenberg's analysis of what is included by the fact of our questionableness goes beyond that merely negative conclusion. There is a rather crucial sense in which the very posing of the question carries with it an underlying rootedness in the answer toward which the question is directed.

Pannenberg pursues this thesis through a consideration of what is entailed by an ability to transcend the horizon of every forthcoming answer with a further question. Does this necessitate the conclusion that all such questioning is inherently nihilistic? Pannenberg denies this. He contends that there is a fundamental difference between questioning that takes place in a sheer vacuum of radical inquiry and questioning which seeks its own ground and source and therefore is determinately directional, aimed at an ultimate answer.[89] "Even if the inquiry which aims at an *answer* must once again raise questions beyond every answer it *achieves*, still such a process of questioning does not for this reason eventuate in the nihilistic consciousness of questionableness which is no longer concerned about finding answers."[90] In recognizing that our essential quest does have reference to something, Pannenberg goes on to observe that "in every question there is always an anticipatory projection of a possible answer."[91] But from where are such anticipations and projections derived? From the questioner? Pannenberg cannot accept that, any more than he can allow imagination to be fully derivable from the imaginer. Rather the *ground* toward which we are infinitely directed must in some way be regarded as antecedent to both the posing of the question and the projection of an answer, as the ground of the possibility of either.[92] The question which characterizes our existence arises only in that we come up against a sustaining ground that enables us really for the first time to formulate the question, and our projections of possible answers arise within that context.

> It would be an abstraction to imagine the questioner as still prior to all contact with the reality he is inquiring about. Rather, the question is always framed only in association with the reality in question. This is particularly true of the question which man not only asks but actually is. In that man's existence is animated by the question about his destination and fulfillment, he is already borne by the reality at which such inquiry is directed. He always already stands in the experience of the reality about which he is concerned in his question--the experience of a non-objective depth of reality, which underlies all extant objects and supports his own life.[93]

What not only completes but even underlies our questioning, therefore, is the *experience* of the reality of the answer in concrete encounter. The truth of God as answer "is not to be derived from man's structure as question, but from his *being met* by the reality that is experienced as the answer to the open question of his existence, and thus claims his ultimate confidence as the ground of his existence."[94] Thus the questioning character of human existence not only presupposes God as the condition for coming ultimately to a fulfilling answer but is rooted in the experiencing of God as the basis for even posing the question.[95] And not only the projected answers but even the question is continually corrected by the encounter,[96] so that it is even necessary to maintain with Barth that the human question is first truly disclosed from the side of the answer.[97]

The impression is strong that a sufficiently penetrating analysis of the human situation will ultimately disclose the truth of God on which the very questionableness of human existence depends.[98] Such a turning inward would represent considerable continuity on Pannenberg's part with Kierkegaard, for whom truth *is* subjectivity, as well as with Bultmann, for whom the truth of God is to be found not in God's activity in the world but in God's calling us to perceive the world in a different light. But Pannenberg is unwilling to go that route. Attention to the implications of our subjectivity, though primary, is not exhaustive: God is conceivable as the experienced answer encountering us as question only if God is identifiable as God of all of reality, even though a knowledge of the world no longer leads directly to a knowledge of God.[99] In this regard, Pannenberg draws out more fully the meaning of the experiencing of God as the ground of our questioning: the concern is not simply with the subjectivity of experience but with the extra-subjective reality of what is experienced, and this directs us necessarily toward the world as the locus of that encounter.

> . . . only in so far as man's statements about God have some points of contact with extra-subjective reality as well, can he assume that he is not trapped in an illusion brought about by the structure of his subjectivity, and instead experiences God as a reality. The divine reality, to which a person whose religion is lively and self-conscious finds himself referred in the structure of his subjectivity, is encountered as a reality only in the context of the experience of the world.[100]

Thus the point of departure is not the whole of the matter. *If* our subjectivity is directed toward the being of God as its underlying condition, *if* our questionableness does indeed arise out of an antecedent experiencing of its answer, that is confirmable only through attention to what is disclosed by all of reality and not simply through attention to anthropological reality. Only if there is discernible the evidence of God at work in the world beyond simply God's undergirding of our open quest for our destiny can talk about God as solution to the human predicament be meaningful. Therefore the question of God arises anew as the issue of whether one can fathom in reality as history the sufficient ground for claiming and proclaiming that our presumed experiencing of God is not ultimately a subjective illusion.

G. Summary and Critique

The West has experienced an increasing anthropologization of the idea of God as the reality of God has become less and less of a crucial factor for explaining the world and functions more and more as a postulate of human subjectivity. Thus the atheist attack upon the legitimacy of God talk is to be confronted at least initially in terms of a concentration upon theological anthropology, upon an analysis of what really characterizes the truth about human existence.

In a number of distinct but considerably overlapping ways, Pannenberg maintains, human beings exist as questions which can only be resolved, if at all, in relation to the reality of God. We are uniquely world-open, driven beyond everything extant in the world and beyond every new horizon to inquire ever further into the open. Beyond every achievement, there is more striving. Beyond every answer that is forthcoming to our restless questioning, a new question can be formulated. In this questioning openness toward and beyond our world, we find ourselves directed toward a reality over against us which sustains us in our quest. In our culture-building transformation of the extant world, we find ourselves dependent upon the power of imagination to envisage the creatively new--a power characterized as much by passivity as by activity and which can only derive from beyond us. In both instances, in our questioning and our imagining, we are open toward the future in a way unique among the animal world, and this future-openness calls forth from us an attitude of trust toward that which is beyond our ability to control and which grounds our continual world-transcending.

But trust immediately calls forth the idea of personhood, for the personal characterizes that which is essentially untransparent and not at someone's disposal. Since a person, unlike a thing, is not fully available to an observer until there is disclosed an externally inaccessible innerness, such a one cannot be totally controlled or manipulated nor can what becomes of the person be calculated in advance, wherefore the only possible attitude thereto is one of trust (or distrust). Personhood, however, is not an original component of our self-understanding. We have come to regard ourselves in personal terms only in being confronted with a power over reality that is discerned to be impenetrable, nonmanipulable, and mysterious. In the encounter, we have found ourselves addressed as thou, and therefore have discovered our own personhood derivatively. Furthermore, inasmuch as personhood remains requisitely open for the contingently new, it is characterized by freedom and therefore by futurity as the condition of freedom--for to be free is to have a future. Therefore the personal, as essentially futural in its exercise of freedom, remains beyond what is presently extant. Finally, personhood essentially must include the motif of infinity, as the overcoming of all limitations that restrict the person from finding oneself completely in the other. Therefore personhood is something we have not only derivatively and anticipatorily but also only incompletely.

The essential futurity of our personhood is of a piece with the basic consideration that what we are intrinsically aimed at in our future-openness is our own destiny which is at the same time our true determination. In my freedom, I reach out beyond myself to the becoming of my true selfhood. The freedom which is constitutive of my subjectivity expresses a harmony of my present existence with my yet to be actualized essence. Thus I am directed in my freedom toward an eventual coming to myself. But this freedom is not explicable in terms of my own present existence, or the existence of other human beings. It can only be understood as gift, and therefore as derivative from the ground which sustains me in the seeking of my destiny.

But our directedness toward the ultimate fulfillment of our destiny is thwarted within a finite lifetime, and death closes the books on the continuing quest. Thus it is inherent in our openness beyond every present reality that we experience a hope beyond death, else we remain ever cut off from the essential truth about ourselves. This hope cannot take the shape of an immortality of the soul, for that fails to do justice to the bodiliness of the whole individual and remains closed to the insight of the attainment of one's destiny as something essentially futural. The biblical concept of resurrection, on the other hand, precisely accords with anthropological considerations concerning the nature of our futural hope: the whole person is taken into account, that which emerges in resurrection life is continuous with the old but characterizable as a "new" creation, and one's destiny is realized not in individual isolation but in the context of the totality of humanity.

In this latter regard, we are aimed toward a destiny that fulfills both our own individuality and a thrust toward community with others. Our openness includes a social dimension. But I am torn by an urge toward self-elevation that stands in conflict with my concern for unity. This conflict between self-enclosedness and world-openness is not resolvable from within my own ego but only, once again, as a gift, from without. Only if the power over reality co-operates with us in our openness toward a community of wholeness is the tension to be overcome. Harmony between the self and the whole as an aspect of our destiny is dependent upon a source of unity beyond us.

In all of these various respects, the questionableness of human life in search of one's own true being points toward the reality of God as the condition of a full self-understanding. Theological anthropology discloses the necessary direction in which the truth of God is to be thought if the reality of God is adequately to be conceived at all. Inasmuch as we are able to question beyond everything extant in the world, God is not conceivable as presently extant. Again, God as the source of the imaginative power in us cannot be identified with any aspect of that over which imagination is constantly at work: reality as it has come to be. God as that toward which we are directed as the ground of our questioning is an object of trust--to the extent that God is conceivable as personal, as possessing a hidden innerness and being beyond our disposal. God is conceivable as God only as the source of human freedom and not as the denial of it. God is conceivable as that one whose power over reality encompasses power over death, granting the legitimacy of hope beyond death and enabling us thereby to attain our ultimate destiny. Finally, God brings each of us to our destiny only in continuity with the whole of reality as the context for our coming to wholeness.

Nevertheless, the reality of such a God cannot be read off from the question-character of human existence. If the truth of such a God is forthcoming, it is only through an experiencing of God in the world which not only points in the direction of the answer but establishes us in our questionableness. What is determined by anthropological reflection on the question of God is this: if God is to lay claim to God's divinity, it is in this wise; if the truth of God is to be found, it will be in continuity with these presuppositions. Beyond this, the question that human life raises and embodies cannot go.

In his engagement with the questionableness of an individual's present being, Pannenberg manifests a penetrating awareness of contemporary anthropological discussion. He appropriates the insights of anthropologists only through critical interaction and not by an appeal to the authoritative weightiness of one school of thought or another. In this process, Pannenberg demonstrates his own rather impressive credentials for encountering a specialist on that scholar's own turf. The theologian must become not only more philosophical and more historical but more anthropological as well. Pannenberg does just that. If it seems remarkable that the conclusions at which he arrives are amazingly continuous with certain elements of the Christian tradition which he is concerned to vindicate rationally, one must recall Pannenberg's insistence that the truth about human existence even as an open question is only fully to be grasped from contact with the answer. Given that proviso, it would appear that the discussion put forward here is out of place--that an unpacking of the nature of God revealed in history should precede a presentation of human life as a question pointing toward God. But that would not be altogether fitting either. For it remains the case that Pannenberg's own involvement in theological anthropology preceded the development of much that is distinctive in his understanding of the truth about God.[101] We must therefore walk a tightrope between reading off of human nature (as from history) a set of conditions which God must exemplify, and seeing anthropological considerations *only* in the light of an understanding of God. The interpenetration of concepts of human beings and God should not be allowed to cloud the realization that, to a large extent, Pannenberg finds in a sort of "pre-theological" reflection on the nature of humanness a sizeable number of pointers that set the compass on the track of God. It is these "psychologically" prior pointers which call forth the following critical reaction.

1) Pannenberg resists the Bultmannian idea of a primacy of the historicity of existence over history itself as the interjection of a historically conditioned understanding of human beings in the place of what actually circumscribes us. It may be that Pannenberg is unconsciously guilty of the same error. John Cobb calls attention to the fact that Pannenberg's understanding of human existence as inescapably directed toward one's future for the locus of one's essential truth and destiny is predicated on the assumption of a "common and universal nature" that may be only the consequence of a particular strand of historical understanding.[102] The thesis which Pannenberg will be found to defend is that precisely this historical tradition opens up access to the truth of the whole, whereby the particular becomes universalized. But a considerable circularity of argument is at work here, in that the universal significance of what comes to expression in the tradition of Christianity is largely grounded in its capacity for providing the ultimate answer to our common human dilemma which has actually been defined within the context of that tradition. Conversely the motif of, say, the Hindu and Buddhist traditions emphasizing a goal of futurelessness is dismissed as erroneous *from the perspective of a definition of human existence informed by Christian thinking.* It remains decidedly questionable whether our futurally open questionableness is as broad a basis for raising the question of God as Pannenberg maintains.

2) Pannenberg's initial distinction between persons and things in terms of the presence or lack of an inaccessible interiority suggests an ontological dualism between subject and object that he may not intend. The reason for raising this matter is that Pannenberg's approach implies a present inexhaustibility and hence futurity of the personal which enables him to postulate the need for a final human destiny in which the goal of our personhood is fully realized, in which the not yet character of the personal is overcome. But what if the unavailability to the external observer of what is real, *in the moment of its becoming,* characterizes *all* that is real, so that objectivity is a *consequence* of subjective being, not a contrast? If that were so, the distinction between personal and non-personal would need to be sought on other grounds, and the momentary unavailability of the subjectively real would not necessarily point to a final *telos* as the condition for recognizing the fullness of personhood.[103]

3) It is not immediately self-evident why the power of imagination, as well as our projections of possible answers to our questionableness, cannot be self-derived. Pannenberg's position here is continuous with his insistence that the contingently new in history cannot be explained as arising out of what already is, but must break in upon it. So also, the contemplatively new is conceivable only as a production of the same source of the novel in history.[104] The issue can be seen here to turn upon the underlying question of the relationship between potentiality and actuality, and therefore is an ontological one. And that leads to the

pivotal question of whether Pannenberg's philosophical reflections on this matter are indeed derivative from, or at least continuous with, Hebraic conceptuality. Does Hebraic thought yield up the ontological insight that the locus of all potentiality is both divine and beyond everything presently actual? One can find roots for this supposition in the biblical understanding of God as originator of unprecendented novelties, as well as in the concept of prophetic *inspiration*: the prophet proclaims not the prophet's own message but an understanding influenced by being open to God's Spirit, wherefore prophetic address is "in-Spirit-ed." However, to affirm that novel notions derive from God does not require that *all* such notions do so. Israel had a tradition of *false* prophecy, for example, for which the claim of divine inspiration came to be denied by the subsequent course of events. It would seem that Pannenberg's contention that potentiality, in the form of the contingently and imaginatively new, can only be located outside of all determinate, extant actuality, remains a problematic thesis which has not been sufficiently grounded with philosophical precision.

4) There is a subtle shift in Pannenberg's treatment of the relationship between freedom and the future which does not seem warranted. To be free is to have a future, to be able to transcend what is already actual and inaugurate novel alternatives. Freedom and the future are therefore intimately interconnected. But does the conclusion follow that the *locus* of freedom itself is necessarily futural? The question is similar to the preceding one, in that Pannenberg does not allow that freedom *over* the present can in any way be located *in* that present. It must derive from that which is beyond the extant, and thus from the future. Freedom to *have* a future shifts over into an equation between the two: it is the future which *is* pure freedom.[105] The implication therefore is that freedom is not something one really "has" in the present but that for which one is open, and receptive. Specifically, in that regard, one is said to be open to one's destiny, and freedom characterizes a harmony with that destiny. But can one be said to be "free" *not* to meet up with one's intended destiny? Is one free to determine a destiny for oneself? But that would presumably constitute a merely formal, illusory freedom, as distinguished from essential freedom. Pannenberg's identification of freedom with future is of one piece with his resolving of the antinomy of history's inclusion of contingency and directedness toward ultimate unity: God must be conceived as equally the guarantor of our attainment of our destiny and the ground of our experience of freedom. The question is whether or not Pannenberg is really successful in carrying this off. The answer to that is to be sought, as in the last criticism of the preceding chapter, in subsequent attention to Pannenberg's concept of how God is causally efficacious.

5) Human life is requisitely open beyond every present for the future. But what sense does this ultimately make if the future for which

we are open, the eventual realization of our true destiny, closes us off from any further future? The question turns, once again, on the cognitive meaningfulness of an anticipatable *end* of the temporal adventure: must it not be conceptualizable in such a way as to allow for a continuing dynamic beyond the *telos* of human life and history? If the final human destiny is no longer to anticipate novelty inasmuch as all is then actualized, how are we (and God, for that matter) to escape the hell of eternal boredom?

The matter turns on the enduring character of hope. Ernst Bloch observes that whereas hope can be disappointed, by destructive developments in the course of history, ultimately it cannot be *annihilated*. [106] Pannenberg would seem to want to affirm this: the destiny for which we seek is somehow *assured* in the experiencing of the Ground of the destiny-open questioning.[107] But if the ultimate content of hope is such as to eliminate the ongoing motif of hope, in that finally there will be nothing further for which to hope, then does that not constitute precisely hope's annihilation?

6) The final point to be raised is more of an *extension* of Pannenberg's anthropological analyses than a direct criticism. It would appear that there is a crucial aspect of anthropological consideration to which Pannenberg has given rather short shrift, but which is implicitly brought to the fore by the ground which Pannenberg does elect to cover. That is, the interrelationship between an intrinsic openness toward the future and the infinity of personhood as complete openness toward the personally other leads inescapably to a consideration of our openness toward the future *of* the other. It is this mode of openness which characterizes the movement of *love*. Is it possible to extend the definition of human existence, as a question for whom the only adequate answer is God, to a further and very crucial motif: *love* as the ultimate truth about human life, which depends upon the reality of a *power* of love as the basis for our coming fully to our loving destiny?

NOTES

[1]A note concerning terminology is necessary at this point. The term used by Pannenberg throughout his reflection on theological anthropology is *"Mensch,"* usually translated as "man" but also encompassing the more-than-masculine images of "human

being" and "person." The latter would seem to serve well the need for non-sexist language here, were it not for the fact that Pannenberg uses the strictly equivalent German term, *Person*, in a very specific way, as will be seen shortly. Consequently, a number of sex-inclusive terms and phrases are employed in this chapter to convey the broader meaning of *Mensch*, including human beings, human life, the human individual, human existence--but also particularly the personal pronouns "I," "we," and "one." "Person" and "personhood," on the other hand, are used here only in reference to the specific meanings they bear in Pannenberg's anthropology (and further on, in his trinitarianism). As previously indicated (ch. 1, note 8), all direct quotations are cited verbatim, with no attempt made to "clean up" the language except in my own translations from the German.

[2]Most extensively Arnold Gehlen, but also Adolf Portmann, Helmuth Plessner, and Michael Landmann. Pannenberg is in considerable sympathy with Gehlen's *Der Mensch*, published originally in 1940 (6th ed.: Bonn: Athenäum-Verlag, 1958). The original insight into our world-openness is attributed to Max Scheler, developed in his *Man's Place in Nature,* 1928 (trans. Hans Meyerhoff [Boston: Beacon Press, 1961]). See Pannenberg's *What Is Man?* (hereafter: *WIM*), trans. Duane Priebe (Philadelphia: Fortress Press, 1970), p. 3, ft. 1; "The Question of God," *BQT*II, p. 216; and *Anthropology in Theological Perspective* (hereafter: *ATP*), trans. Matthew J. O'Connell (Philadelphia: The Westminster Press, 1985), pp. 35f.

[3]*WIM,* pp. 1-7. The book was published in German in 1962, as *Was ist der Mensch?* (Göttingen: Vandenhoeck & Ruprecht), and consists of a series of radio lectures broadcast in 1961-62. Priebe's translation too often slights accuracy for the sake of readability, and therefore most of the quotations in this chapter have been taken directly from the German edition, except where indicated.

[4]"The Question of God," *BQT* II, p. 217.

[5]I have continued to resist utilizing Priebe's translation of *Weltoffenheit* as "openness to the world" for this basic reason that it does not sufficiently encompass what Pannenberg is intending to convey.

[6]*WIM,* pp. 7-9.

[7]The word is regularly translated as "dependence," and *angewiesen* as "dependent," in *WIM* and elsewhere. But I find this problematic. The word as well as the meaning is distinct from Schleiermacher's emphasizing of a feeling of absolute *Abhängigkeit* as essentially characteristic of human beings, and I believe it is important to preserve the distinction. Schleiermacher was referring to an innate consciousness of ontological dependency on our part, upon a reality absolutely non-dependent upon anything outside of itself. Furthermore, this feeling was itself the basis for positing the sure reality of God as co-determinant of the feeling. (See Friedrich Schleiermacher, *Der christliche Glaube* [7th ed.: Berlin: Walter de Gruyter & Co., 1960], para. 4-6.) But Pannenberg is expressing a quite different understanding of the human experience and of God as corollary of our self-understanding. In the first

instance, Schleiermacher contrasts dependence with freedom, whereas it is precisely our freedom of openness beyond the world that generates our *Angewiesenheit* toward God. We do not so much rest upon God as uncaused cause of our contingent being as we reach ahead toward God as *telos* of our becoming and questioning and striving. "Directedness" seems to convey this sense more helpfully. Secondly, the use of "dependence" tends to load the issue illegitimately in the direction of an absolute certainty of God as the supporting ground of our contingent being. But this would be an example of the cosmological argument for God's actuality which Pannenberg refrains from affirming. The way in which Pannenberg endeavors to balance the necessary implication of a goal of our world-open questioning and directedness with the impossibility of deriving God as answer from the human individual as question is examined below, in section F.

[8] *WIM*, p. 10, and "The Question of God," *BQT* II, pp. 220f.

[9] *Was ist der Mensch?* p. 11. (Cf. *WIM*, p. 10.)

[10] *Ibid.*, p. 13. (Cf. *WIM*, p. 13.) See also *JGM*, p. 193; *ATP*, p. 73.

[11] *WIM*, p. 11.

[12] "The so-called proofs for the existence of God do not so much prove the reality of God as the finitude of man and the world. The so-called proofs for the existence of God show only that man must inquire beyond the world and himself if he is to find a ground capable of supporting the being and meaning of his existence. The proofs of God constitute the theoretical formulation for the sort of rising above everything finite to the idea of an infinite reality that goes on in such inquiry. They retain their significance as elaborations of the questionableness of finite being which drive man beyond the whole compass of finite reality. But they do not provide the answer to this question." ("The Question of God," *BQT* II, pp. 223f.)

[13] *WIM*, pp. 14-22. See also *ATP*, ch. 7, where Pannenberg additionally lifts up the value of play in the generating of human culture, pp. 322-39.

[14] *WIM*, p. 23; *ATP*, pp. 377, 381.

[15] Here, as previously concerning our openness beyond the world and our concomitant call to dominion over the world, Pannenberg traces the roots of this insight into the creative nature of imagination to the biblical view of reality. See *WIM*, pp. 11f. and 26.

[16] *Was ist der Mensch?* , p. 21. (Cf. *WIM*, pp. 25f.)

[17] *Ibid.* (Cf. *WIM*, p. 26.)

18 *Ibid.* In *ATP*, Pannenberg calls imagination "a paradigm of the relation between grace and freedom" (p. 381).

19 *WIM*, p. 27.

20 *Ibid.*, pp. 28, 33-38. See also *AC*, pp. 5f.; *ATP*, pp. 231-34.

21 *Was ist der Mensch?*, p. 26. (Cf. *WIM*, p. 33.)

22 See, *e.g.*, "The Question of God," *BQT* II, pp. 227f., especially ft. 97; and "The God of Hope," *BQT* II, pp. 244f.

23 "Person," *RGG* ³, V, cols. 230-35; "Wirkungen biblischer Gotteserkenntnis auf das abendländische Menschenbild," *Studium Generale* 15, 1962, p. 588.

24 "The Question of God," *BQT* II, pp. 228f.; "Person," *RGG* ³, V, col. 232; *WIM*, p. 32; "The God of Hope," *BQT* II, p. 245; *AC*, p. 29; *ATP*, p. 235.

25 See *WIM*, p. 90; "Person," *RGG* ³, V Col. 232; "The Question of God," *BQT* II, p. 230, ft. 99. The history of this notion is carefully explored in *ATP*, pp. 179-90.

26 *WIM*, p. 85.

27 "Person," *RGG* ³ , V, col. 232.

28 "The Question of God," *BQT* II, p. 229.

29 "Wirkungen," *Studium Generale* 15, 1962, p. 588.

30 "The God of Hope," *BQT* II, pp. 245f. (1965). On the relationship between personhood and freedom, see Pannenberg's further discussion in "Man--the Image of God?," *Faith and Reality*, trans. John Maxwell (Philadelphia: The Westminster Press, 1977), pp. 42-49. (hereafter: *FR*.)

31 "Speaking about God in the Face of Atheist Criticism," *IGHF*, p. 112 (1969).

32 *Ibid.*

33 More recently, Pannenberg has modified this perspective on the essential futurity of our personhood with the introduction of yet another crucial term: the *self*. In his "Person und Subjekt" (*GsT* II, pp. 80-95), completed in 1976 and revised in 1979, he advances the notion that it is our genuine *selfhood* toward which we are underway in the course of our existence, and that we are always in process of becoming a person even though we also already *are* so: "Person is the presence of the self in the moment of the I." (*GsT* II, p. 92; see also *ATP*, pp. 236, 240, 528.) The

notion is elaborated at length in his *Anthropology*, where he identifies "true selfhood" as the "destiny" of human beings (*ATP*, p. 114) and characterizes personhood as "human being in its wholeness" (p. 235): in the anticipatory presence of full personhood in each present moment, the whole "appears" already in what yet remains uncompleted (p. 240) and human beings thereby "presently exist as themselves" (p. 527). Pannenberg's discussion of how human identity in its fullness is understood to be constituted dominates Part Two of *ATP*.

[34]*AC*, p. 28 (1972, but extensively incorporating content from the mid-60's).

[35]"Christlicher Glaube and menschliche Freiheit," *KuD* 4, 1958, p. 251.

[36]*Ibid.*, pp. 260ff.

[37]*WIM*, p. 88. See also his "The Christological Foundation of Christian Anthropology," in Claude Geffre, ed., *Humanism and Christianity* (New York: Herder and Herder, 1973), pp. 94-98.

[38]"Anthropology and the Question of God," *IGHF*, p. 92.

[39]"Speaking about God in the Face of Atheist Criticism," *IGHF*, p. 111; *ATP*, p. 240.

[40]*Ibid.*

[41]*Ibid.*, p. 108.

[42]*TKG*, p. 63: "For what is freedom but to have future in oneself and out of oneself?"

[43]"Speaking about God," *IGHF*, p. 113.

[44]*WIM*, p. 140. Pannenberg repeatedly uses the German word *Bestimmung* to designate this dual emphasis. *Bestimmung* contains within itself two rather distinct meanings, "determination" or "definition" on the one hand and "destiny" on the other. Pannenberg finds the two to coalesce in a single concept and not simply in a single word: Priebe captures the meaning perceptively in his explanation of *Bestimmung* as having the sense of "man's destiny which defines or gives content to what man is as man." ("Translator's Preface," *WIM*, p. vii.) What we are is *bestimmt* (determined) only when we attain our *Bestimmung* (destiny).

[45]*JGM*, pp. 192f. Cf. *Thesen zur Theologie der Kirche* (München: Claudius Verlag, 1970), thesis 54, pp. 26f.

[46]*TKG*, p. 121. The notion of the essential futurity of our true being is a pivotal theme of Ernst Bloch's philosophy of hope. See, *e.g.*, *Das Prinzip Hoffnung*

(Frankfurt am Main: Suhrkamp Verlag, 1959), pp. 129ff., 356-68, 1517f., 1625; *Man on His Own,* trans. E. B. Ashton (New York: Herder and Herder, 1970), pp. 52, 59 (from *Geist der Utopie,* 1918); *Philosophische Grundfragen I: Zur Ontologie des Noch Nicht-Seins* (Frankfurt am Main: Suhrkamp Verlag, 1961), pp. 15f., 34-36. But Pannenberg nowhere refers to Bloch's anthropological understanding in his own writing. Whether Bloch has directly influenced Pannenberg's concept of human life as futurely determined, and to what extent, or whether Pannenberg arrived at conclusions similar to but independently of Bloch, remains difficult to assess. Pannenberg maintains that he developed his theological insights on the essential importance of the future prior to acquaintance with Bloch's work, and this is indeed possible. But the most distinctively futural expressions of human personhood and freedom and essence occur in essays written subsequent to Pannenberg's single published engagement with Bloch's thought, "The God of Hope" (*BQT* II), 1965.

47"Speaking about God," *IGHF*, p. 112.

48*Ibid.,* p. 113.

49*Ibid.,* pp. 113f.

50*Ibid.,* p. 106. See also "Anthropology and the Question of God," *IGHF*, pp. 92f.

51"Anthropology and the Question of God," *IGHF*, p. 92.

52"Speaking about God," *IGHF*, p. 107.

53"Anthropology and the Question of God," *IGHF*, p. 93.

54"Speaking about God," *IGHF*, pp. 108f.

55*Ibid.,* p. 114. Cf. the quotation from *ibid.,* p. 106, given above: ". . . an indispensable basic condition, though not a completely sufficient condition by itself, for any justification of our speaking about God."

56*WIM,* p. 42.

57*Ibid.,* pp. 41f.

58*Ibid.,* p. 79. Cf. *JGM* , p. 83: "One may presumably characterize it as a generally demonstrable anthropological finding that the definition of the essence [*Wesensbestimmung:* essential destiny] of man does not come to ultimate fulfillment in the finitude of his earthly life."

59*WIM,* p. 44.

60Ibid., p. 43. See also *JGM*, p. 84.

61*WIM*, p. 44.

62*JGM*, p. 85.

63Pannenberg's theology is not interpretable as a "theology of hope," *per se*. The motif of hope does not play so major a role in his thought as it does for Moltmann. The human being is not predominantly defined as creature-who-hopes, *homo sperens*, even though it is understood to belong to the nature of humans to hope. For Pannenberg, hope is generally spoken of in relation to the question of our destiny beyond death. It is not the most encompassing term that he uses to express the shape of our optimum relation to the all-important future. *Trust* is seemingly the more basic and overarching motif.

64Pannenberg initially acknowledged that all expressions of an expectation of life beyond death are necessarily metaphorical because of the unrepresentable character of that to which the interpretations intend to refer. He has since qualified that reserve with the endeavor to redefine what it is that essentially constitutes "life," of which our finite, physically circumscribed existence is but one (limited) expression. (See "Dogmatische Erwägungen zur Auferstehung Jesu," *GsT* II, pp. 160-73, and "The Doctrine of the Spirit and the Task of a Theology of Nature," *Theology* 75, 1972, pp. 8-21.) Because the context of that discussion has tended to be the question of the cognitive meaningfulness of *Jesus'* resurrection from the dead, and because the issue becomes significant only if one goes the further step beyond the *idea* of a post-mortal resurrection life to the presumed *confirmation* of the idea in the historical event of Jesus' resurrection, I will focus attention on that further development in chapter seven rather than here.

65*WIM*, p. 45. See also *JGM*, p. 86.

66*WIM*, pp. 45f.

67*Ibid.*, p. 47.

68*JGM*, p. 87.

69*WIM*, p. 50.

70*Ibid.*

71*JGM*, p. 88: Such considerations "say enough to indicate that the expectation of a resurrection from the dead need not appear meaningless from the presuppositions of modern thought, but rather it is to be established as a philosophically appropriate expression for human destiny. Thus, precisely today a continuity of our

121

thought with the apocalyptic hope again has become possible at a decisive point, and with this also a continuity with the primitive Christian perception of the event of Jesus' resurrection." Pannenberg does not argue from the reasonableness of the idea of resurrection to the actual truth of Jesus' resurrection. Nevertheless, the conviction that the notion of resurrection is an intelligible one is crucial for providing a necessary point of contact with the historical event under consideration. The point is explored further in chapter seven. (See Sauter's remarks on this score in "Fragestellungen der Christologie," *Verkündigung und Forschung* 11:2, 1966, pp. 57, 59, 61.)

[72] *WiM*, p. 51. Pannenberg goes on to observe also that the resurrection concept is in continuity with the realization that a sense of unity would need to embrace not only humankind but also the world. Inasmuch as "the transformation of men into the fulfillment of their destiny can only make sense in connection with a new creation of the whole world," the biblical idea of resurrection is all the more significant in tying the expectation of final human destiny to the expectation of the end of the old world and creation of the new world. (*Ibid.*)

[73] "On Historical and Theological Hermeneutic," *BQT* I, pp. 176f.; "Future and Unity," *HFM*, pp. 70f.; "Eschatology and the Experience of Meaning," *IGHF*, p. 198.

[74] *WIM*, p. 107.

[75] *Ibid.*, pp. 55f., 58, 63.

[76] *Ibid.*, p. 56.

[77] *Ibid.*, p. 61.

[78] Pannenberg's adoption of Plessner's characterization of human beings as "exocentric" (*ATP*, pp. 37, 68, 105) is complemented by the thesis that this, in turn, points us in the direction of God as that (ostensible) "center" giving "unity and identity" to human existence (p. 480).

[79] *Ibid.*, pp. 59f., 61, 62. (The citations reflect the fact that Pannenberg's chapter on "Selfhood and Man's Destiny" is actually rather repetitive.)

[80] *Ibid.*, pp. 61f.

[81] *Was ist der Mensch?*, p. 45. (Cf. *WIM*, p. 62.) There remains an unresolved tension in Pannenberg's own thought, in that he finds it necessary to retain the notion of *judgment* as an element of God's action in bringing people and history to their consummating destiny. The difficulty arises with regard to the consideration that the image of judgment suggests a separating out of those who are granted participation in God's ultimate reign from those who are excluded. If *all* do not experience the fulfillment of their destinies in community with others and with God, if some are destined instead for being cut off, then it can make no sense to speak of the attainment

of individual human destiny in the necessary context of the *whole*. When pressed on this issue at the New York conference on "Hope and the Future of Man," Pannenberg acknowledged that judgment would not necessarily entail ultimate separation but might be understandable instead in terms of "fire which burns away our separation from God." (Unpublished respnse to the responses.)

[82]"Types of Atheism and Their Theological Significance," *BQT* II, pp. 195f.

[83]"Anthropology and the Question of God," *IGHF*, p. 82.

[84]*Ibid.*, pp. 82-84.

[85]*Ibid.*, pp. 84-86.

[86]*Ibid.*, p. 90. See also *TPS*, p. 422.

[87]"Anthropology and the Question of God," *IGHF*, pp. 88f. It is precisely this concern which led Pannenberg to sally forth into the arena of the anthropological sciences themselves and produce *Anthropology in Theological Perspective*. The key impetus to that "comprehensive, richly textured, and closely argued study," quoting from the book jacket, was Pannenberg's deeply held conviction that atheism's presumed rootedness in anthropological considerations can only be refuted by effectively challenging the insufficiencies of a too narrow perspective on the truly human (*ATP*, p. 16).

[88]"Response to the Discussion," *TaH*, p. 225. See also "Speaking about God in the Face of Atheist Criticism," *IGHF*, p. 114; "Anthropology and the Question of God," *IGHF*, p. 94; and *ATP*, p. 73.

[89]"The Question of God," *BQT* II, pp. 218-20.

[90]*Ibid.*, p. 219.

[91]*Ibid.*, p. 223. "Insofar as a question is a genuine question and asks about something, it already anticipates a possible answer." (p. 224.)

[92]*Ibid.*, p. 222.

[93]*Ibid.*, p. 225.

[94]"Response to the Discussion," *TaH*, p. 225, ft. 2.

[95]So Pannenberg can observe in "Hermeneutic and Universal History," *BQT* I, p. 110, ft. 25, that an understanding of God logically, though not psychologically, precedes an understanding of the self.

[96]"The Question of God," *BQT* II, p. 225.

[97]*Ibid.*, p. 226. The whole of Pannenberg's essay here is basically concerned with identifying the way in which this correlation of answer and question is to be understood, with particular emphasis upon the concept that the answer is to be characterized as personal.

[98]In a somewhat similar vein, Pannenberg observes elsewhere that "the indefinite and undefined primal trust of man *demands* a counterpart in which he trusts." (*AC*, p. 5, italics mine.)

[99]"Speaking about God in the Face of Atheist Criticism," *IGHF*, pp. 106f. See especially p. 107: "the final tenability of any idea of God which is put foward depends in addition upon the understanding of the world, that is, upon how far the God who is asserted is comprehensible as the reality which determines everything."

[100]"Anthropology and the Question of God," *IGHF*, p. 95, with the translation slightly corrected: *verwiesen auf* as "referred to," not "dependent on." So also in "Hermeneutic and Universal History," *BQT* I, pp. 110f., ft. 25: "The objective priority of the understanding of God over the understanding of the self manifests itself in the fact that God is experienced in the world as the ground of a total view of the world and of man in it, in relation to the whole current experience of reality."

[101]The impressive accomplishments of the recent *Anthropology in Theological Perspective* represent for the most part an elaboration on themes previously identified by Pannenberg, insofar as the focus of this exploration is concerned. The *Anthropology* does not bring to light salient new insights into the correlation of anthropological theses and theological affirmations; rather it reinforces, and works from, positions already arrived at. It is one more instance of the remarkable consistency observable throughout Pannenberg's theological pilgrimage to date.

[102]John Cobb, "Past, Present, and Future," *TaH*, pp. 212f.

[103]The suggestion is made because of Pannenberg's abiding concern with the principle of *unity*. A theology that aims at ultimate unity will be better served by the avoidance of unnecessary dualism. The interpretation of reality of A. N. Whitehead offers just such a conceptuality as is suggested here, and although Pannenberg carries on an occasional dialogue with Whitehead's thought, I am not aware that he has given serious attention to its possible informativeness on this point.

[104]See *WIM*, p. 26.

[105]See *TKG*, p. 63.

[106]Ernst Bloch, "Kann Hoffnung enttäuscht werden?," *Auswahl aus seinen Schriften* (Frankfurt am Main: Fischer Bücherei, 1967), pp. 176-81. This was

Bloch's inaugural lecture when he became professor emeritus of philosophy at the University of Tübingen in 1961, originally published in Bloch, *Verfremdungen* V (Frankfurt am Main, 1962).

107Distinctively, as we will see, in what is proleptically actualized in the resurrection of Jesus.

5

REVELATION AND THE OLD TESTAMENT

Christian theology deals with nothing less than the whole of reality inasmuch as the God who is the focus of Christian faith is understandable as God only to the extent that this deity is the creative Lord of all that is. Thus is theology universal in its scope. And insofar as reality is most adequately to be understood in terms of ongoing historical process, theology is occupied with the theme of universal history. And because the human individual is the predominant figure in that history, continually transcending what is found at hand, in unbounded openness toward an ultimate human destiny, theology inquires about the reality of what is over against us which sustains us in that movement. But how does the premise of the God who encompasses all truth and unifies all historical diversity and grounds our quest for self-fulfillment come to be established as anything more than a mere presupposition for understanding and meaning and openness? The answer to this question is to be found in the reality of a divine action of self-disclosure-- in a word, in *revelation*.

Simply to begin by affirming the reality of a divine revelation is not possible for Pannenberg, because of his rejection of any appeal to a pre-Enlightenment authoritarianism and his recognition of the multiplicity of competing revelatory claims among religious traditions. Thus I have postponed an introduction of the theme of revelation in Pannenberg's theology until an important body of "pre-revelatory" considerations in his thought had been laid on the table. But no further penetration into the idea of God can now proceed without raising this decisive theme.

The issue is joined, for Pannenberg, in recognition of the fact that Christians speak of God as having been revealed in Jesus of

127

Nazareth[1] and yet cannot simply let the matter rest there. *Some* reason must be forthcoming as to why it is *there* and not somewhere else that the "true" revelation of God has occurred. And *some* reason must be equally forthcoming as to why one understands *God* to have been revealed therein. One must therefore not only develop an adequate understanding of revelation, in terms of which *Jesus* is identifiable as the decisive locus of revelation, but one must also be prepared to indicate how previous developments paved the way for recognizing that One whom Jesus revealed. This latter concern points emphatically to the crucible of Israelite tradition out of which Jesus came. Therefore attention to the theme of revelation is directed first of all to the Old Testament.

> One cannot understand Jesus' claim unless one realizes its presuppositions, namely, knowledge of God and the anticipation of the future fulfillment of God's will on earth. Israel's God, it is true, does not reveal himself as he really is until the message of Jesus; nevertheless, a knowledge of him is already presupposed for the understanding of Jesus' message. . . . Only through Jesus does it become clear what the God of Israel really is and means. And yet this final understanding presupposes a knowledge of this God prior to it and also a hope for God's presence.[2]

The concept represented here is deftly summarized in Pannenberg's fifth "dogmatic thesis on the doctrine of revelation": "The Christ event reveals the deity of Israel's God not as an isolated occurrence but only insofar as it is a part of God's history with Israel."[3] This opens up for us the direction in which our attention to Pannenberg's treatment of God's revelation must move. I will develop initially, as the theme of this chapter, the way in which Pannenberg's understanding of the *nature* of revelation is derived from his theological appropriation of the Old Testament. The subject of revelation will subsequently be expanded and concretized in the following chapters dealing with the revelatory significance of the message and fate of Jesus as mediated through the Jewish apocalyptic tradition.

A. The Transmission of Revelatory Tradition

Pannenberg has explicitly emphasized the rootedness of his explorations into the concept of revelation in the exegetical work of one of the Old Testament scholars in the Heidelberg circle, Rolf Rendtorff. Denying that the biblical studies in *Revelation as History* were merely exegetical props for his own systematic understanding of revelation, he has insisted that the reciprocity of systematic and historical influences on the work of the circle genuinely characterizes its internal development and that the original impetus to the program stemmed from Rendtorff's attention to Walther Zimmerli's studies on the "word of demonstration" (*Erweiswort*) in the Old Testament tradition.[4]

Zimmerli had discovered during studies on Ezekiel a recurring formula of self-presentation, "I am Yahweh," found within a larger unit which he labeled a "recognition formula": "know that I am Yahweh." The formulae were encountered for the most part at the end of a prediction concerning God's actions in the future course of history, through which the self-disclosure of God's name would be vindicated. Zimmerli identified the larger whole within which the formulae were contained as an *Erweiswort*, of which I Kings 20:28 would be typical,[5] but insisted on form-critical grounds that the shortest form, the self-presentation formula, originally stood independent of the larger unit within which it came to be embedded. The conclusion drawn by Zimmerli was that the primary locus of divine self-disclosure is to be seen in God's presenting godself in the declaration of the divine name. The history subsequently brought forth by God is simply the carrying out of what is implied in the revealing of God's name.[6]

Rendtorff found in Zimmerli's focusing upon the *Erweiswort* a significant breakthrough in the understanding of revelation in the Old Testament. Recognizing the lack of a consistently structured idea of revelation in the Old Testament, and noting that the Hebrew word translated *apokalyptein* by the Septuagint was not theologically oriented but designated an unveiling in an ordinary sense, Rendtorff went on to explore the *concept* of a divine self-disclosure in biblical tradition.[7] He detected three strands of understanding which all seemed to point in the same direction. In the traditions of Yahweh's direct self-manifestations, originally linked with the etiology of a cultic place, there can be seen a development away from the observable appearance itself, as mere introduction, and an increasing concern with what is communicated in the manifestation: a divine promise, which points ahead toward the coming of Yahweh's activity.[8] But partially in opposition to that original emphasis, the mere appearance of Yahweh come to be set over against his making himself "known." Epiphanies are relegated to a preliminary stage, and Yahweh's real self-disclosure comes to be identified specifically with such powerful acts of salvation as the Exodus. Yahweh is known as he establishes himself as defender and helper of Israel in the face of Israel's enemies. Yahweh is therefore the one who is known through the self-authentication of his own power. In time, this comes to be more and more related to the future: the past acts of Yahweh are not forgotten but they are no longer understood as the sole and ultimate self-revelation of Yahweh. New things are expected. Yahweh's full self-disclosure becomes an eschatological fact.[9]

There is yet a third dimension of the Old Testament idea of God's revelation which reflects the same movement: the concept of the "glory" of Yahweh. Yahweh's glory properly belongs to Heaven, so that the becoming visible on earth of the glory of Yahweh is of revelatory significance. Rendtorff discerned three overlapping conceptions. There is an earlier one in which the glory could be perceived by everyone and in which Yahweh is directly revealed in manifestations of divine power. In the priestly texts, for which the glory is of cultic significance, it is manifested in a spatially limited appearance as an unmediated representation of Yahweh. But even here it functions to announce Yahweh's demonstration of power, though only to Israel. Then also especially from deutero-Isaiah onward, Yahweh's glory as the demonstration of divine power becomes the subject of eschatological hope, in which its final ultimate manifestation is awaited as the most imminent and decisive experience of the end time.[10]

Building on these *traditionsgeschichtlich* investigations, Rendtorff then turned to Zimmerli's work on the disclosure formulae and took it to a conclusion Zimmerli had not intended. Insisting that the shorter formula is a reduction of the original, which explicitly oriented the hearer toward the future in which God's promises would be kept, Rendtorff found confirmation of his thesis that revelation had preeminently to do with events of history. He maintained that the name itself, given in the self-presentation formula, is not the primary object of understanding. That is rather the claim of power supported by it and implied in it. One perceives truly that Yahweh *is* God only when one perceives Yahweh's mighty deeds in history, especially in the Exodus but increasingly in events of *future* history.[11]

Only in passing did Rendtorff raise a direct question as to the relation of *word* to event in the understanding of revelation. Having stood Zimmerli's conclusions on their head, it was a simple matter to observe that the word itself, the prophetic word of Yahweh's self-presentation, is not the central locus of revelation, which is rather the event to which the whole *Erweiswort* pointed. Acknowledgment of Yahweh's deity "is not brought about by the isolated word, but by the activity that the word proclaims and sees in its entire context in the historical tradition."[12] Still, Rendtorff granted, there was "no question" but that the word does have an essential connection with the whole revelatory event.[13] In summation, he observed:

> Throughout it is clear that Jahweh is known in his historical acts to ancient Israel and that in them he manifests himself as he is. In the second part [of the essay], it is especially clear that the Old Testament speeches about the revelation of God are more and more anchored in the future. From the time of the political catastrophe of 587 B.C., the conclusive self-manifestation of Jahweh was looked for as the decisive event of the future. The old *heilsgeschichtliche* traditions did not lose their value or importance. On the contrary, they constituted the unconditional presuppositions for the conclusive

revelation of Jahweh in the future. Thus, the process of revelation had begun in the earlier saving acts of Jahweh. In these, Jahweh had always manifested himself as himself, and Israel had lived on this self-revelation of his for centuries. However, the experiences in its history also led Israel to the understanding that the final revelation of God was yet to be expected.[14]

Though the primary thrust of Rendtorff's essay was to show that Israel increasingly looked to its future, and ultimately to an eschatological future, for the conclusive disclosure of the deity of Yahweh, Zimmerli responded with a critique of Rendtorff's elevation of history over word as the locus of revelation. There was obvious justification for this, since Rendtorff's conclusion of the growing focus on futurity was derived from his conviction that the word by itself could not reveal but only point in the direction of where true and definitive revelation was to be found. Zimmerli defended his own interpretation of his exegetical investigations with the contention that the word cannot be reduced to a merely subordinate role. Rather the word of Yahweh is no empty human word but "already occurrence which moves the world and history." The event to which the word of disclosure is directed is to be understood as "actualized word, the proclamation redeemed."[15]

Rendtorff's subsequent response expressed agreement with Zimmerli that what is decisively at stake is the undeniable interconnectedness of word and history.[16] Rendtorff had already developed the thesis that history as *Überlieferungsgeschichte* denies an absolute antithesis between word and event: the history of the transmission of traditions embraces both the events which generate, or fulfill, a tradition of interpretation, and the linguistic formulations which articulate previous or anticipated events.[17] The question is simply which is to be understood as primary for the self-disclosure of God, and Rendtorff continued to maintain that although an event does not depend upon the intervention of a prophetic word in order to become revelatory (the whole of the lived tradition possibly performing that function), the word alone is incomplete without its consummation in the historical consequence to which it is directed.[18] As Robinson points out, the continuing difference between the two biblical scholars is of a piece with the ongoing debate in German theology over the primacy of word or history as the overarching category for an understanding of reality.[19]

Two issues are actually intertwined within the biblical debate, one primarily form-critical and the other primarily theological. The first is the question of the original derivation of the components of the *Erweiswort* : did the self-presentation formula initially stand alone in the tradition, to which the formula of recognition was later added, or is the shorter form "a reduction of the expression to a formulation of extreme pregnancy"?[20] Pannenberg disputes Zimmerli's interpretation on purely form-critical grounds, pointing out that the texts to which Zimmerli points as verifying the antiquity of the short form

> . . . are without exception examples of the formula of recognition "and they will know that I am Yahweh" (e.g., I Kings 20:13, 28). It is very doubtful whether these texts can prove the age of the short form "without additions" in the sense of the "formula of self-presentation," i.e., whether an *originally independent* formula "I am Yahweh" is already presupposed by them. Is it not more probable that these texts represent concisely formulated references to the longer form of the statement that characterizes the name Yahweh more precisely through the use of additional predications? In any case, only statements of the latter type are to be found in the earlier period as *independent formulas.*[21]

But it would appear that the theological question of the definitive locus of revelation need not be resolved on the basis of which formula is earlier in the tradition. For Pannenberg, as Rendtorff, takes notice of the fact that the tradition is not altogether constant concerning how revelation takes place. The relegating of epiphanies to an inconclusive, preliminary status in later tradition is a prime example of this. The inadequacy of an earlier tradition of God's direct self-manifestation is superseded, through a correction *of* the tradition *by* the tradition. Why, then, could one not allow that the formula of recognition represents a later extension of the briefer self-presenation formula, required precisely by Israel's growing awareness that Yahweh's self-declaration could not stand alone but was completed by the historical confirmation of Yahweh's proclaimed deity?

This is the more decisive direction in which Pannenberg's critique of Zimmerli tends to move. For he takes issue with Zimmerli's contention that the promised occurrence of Yahweh's self-confirmation is only "word made reality." On the one hand,

> . . . those words about the future are finally proven to be Yahweh's words only by their coming to pass (I Kings 22:28; Deut. 18:9-22; Jer. 28:6-9). Furthermore, only very few of them occurred exactly according to the prediction. Time and again the course of events surpassed the words, giving them new meaning and a new reference. Under these circumstances one can hardly conceive the events as mere effects of the prophetic word.[22]

The implication is therefore quite obvious that Pannenberg is primarily concerned to defend his position on the basis of what is crucially required in order that one may speak convincingly of a revelation, not on the basis of form-critical or tradition-historical investigations--however supportive they might be. The question to which his theological appropriation of the Old Testament concept of revelation is addressed is whether an instance of Yahweh's self-presentation in word is sufficiently able to bear the freight of definitive self-disclosure, and whether it is not conversely the case that the very essence of what Yahweh discloses in the prophetic word *requires* its being brought to completion in events which manifest the fulfillment of the divine claim.[23]

B.   History   as   Revelation

Inasmuch as theology asks about the God who is presupposed by the universal pursuit of truth and meaning but whose actualized truth is not derivable from the side of the pursuit itself, it is dependent for its completion upon the definitive self-disclosure of the reality in question. Theology has to do ineluctably with revelation. And "for theology to be concerned with revelation means at the very least that it cannot be reduced to insights which can be obtained without the manifestation of divine reality in a historically concrete form."[24] The Christian theologian is directed toward Judaeo-Christian Scripture as mediator of the revelation which is normative for a world-embracing understanding,[25] though the verity of that revelation must be open to its own confirmation and the concept of revelation entertained must be rationally defensible.[26] The primacy of a receptivity of divine truth entails Pannenberg's implicit acceptance of revelation as norm and criterion of the church's dogma and hence, by extension, of theology. [27]

Building on an emphasis of Barth which he traces back to Hegel, Pannenberg takes over uncritically the idea that revelation is the self-revelation of God: what God discloses is nothing less and nothing other than God's own true essence, not various sorts of information about God or the world.[28] This present "consensus" that revelation is God's self-disclosure arose initially out of response to the rejection by the Enlightenment of a "transmission of supernatural and hidden truths" as merely superstition. Revelation was rescued from obscurantism only by limiting its content to "God's *self* -revelation."[29] Pannenberg adopts as fundamental, therefore, the understanding that revelation must entail a "disclosure of essence"; other scriptural references to "revelations" which do not accomplish this are accordingly to be regarded only as appearances or manifestations, not disclosures of the truth about God in the full sense.[30] This leads Pannenberg to the further preliminary observation that, insofar as God is understandable only as a unity, that which discloses the truth about God must reflect that unity itself. Therefore, one may not think with consistency of a plurality of revelations which, by their very multiplicity, would discredit the singular adequacy of any particular one among them. To the uniqueness of the God revealed must correspond the uniqueness of revelation itself.[31] The full implications of this qualification will gradually become apparent.

Pannenberg observes that Scripture has no specific terminology for the self-revelation of God.[32] References to divine epiphanies are excluded as involving only an "appearance" of God and not the full communication of God's essence. Furthermore, following Rendtorff, Pannenberg takes note of the fact that, already within the biblical tradition itself, the epiphanies of Yahweh come to be regarded merely as provisional and displaceable.[33] "Apart from such appearances, however, the terminological investigation into the equivalent of 'to reveal' does not lead, even in the Old Testament, to a tangible solution to the question of God's self-revelation."[34] Beyond this terminological impasse in the Old Testament, is there some other means whereby one can directly lay hold of the self-disclosure of God? Pannenberg considers three possible alternatives and discards them all as inadequate: the direct self-revelation of God through the announcement of God's name, the expression of God's word, and the proclamation of God's law.[35] Always something other than God is communicated. Particularly in the first instance, Pannenberg contends, "the mere announcement of the name 'Yahweh' does not yet reveal what this name comprises."[36] Overemphasis upon the Word as the direct self-communication of God is precisely a characteristic of gnostic thought.[37] Law is not revelation itself but is content which is grounded in revelation.

Perhaps, then, if one cannot speak of a direct self-revelation of God, one might turn instead to the idea of an "indirect" self-communication, a self-disclosure of God reflected indirectly in God's historical activity. Pannenberg proposes: "The totality of God's speaking and acting, the history wrought by God, shows indirectly who God is."[38] But what, exactly, would this mean? Pannenberg gets at this by analyzing the difference between direct and indirect communication. The former immediately has as its content that which it intends to communicate, whereas the latter is initially directed toward something other. Its true meaning is discernible only through penetration to a new perspective, at a higher level.[39] Thus, regarding God, indirect communication does not have God as its content in any direct way, but rather every action of God can indirectly express something about God. That is to say, an event initially discloses simply itself, directly; its content is perceived for its own value. But further reflection occasions a change of perspective: the event is viewed as originating from God, thus casting light back upon God. However, such a concern with a plethora of individual events as reflections of God provides a distorted view. It breaks up the self-revelation of God into individual pieces, none of which provides a full disclosure of God. One must therefore be concerned with the totality of reality as the locus of God's self-revelation in its unity and fullness--either in the Greek way of an enduring cosmos or in the Hebrew manner of reality as history.[40]

Thus Pannenberg arrives at his initial "dogmatic thesis": "According to the biblical witnesses, God's self-revelation has been effected not directly, as in the mode of a theophany, but indirectly, through God's acts in history."[41] Originally this was understood in Old Testament tradition in the sense of Yahweh's past acts of deliverance, especially in the Exodus liberation and the occupancy of the land, but with the prophets, and increasingly from the time of the exile, these previous events lost their character as conclusive expressions of Yahweh's self-vindication as God over all.[42] Israel came to look to the future in anticipation of new activity of salvation in which God's truth would be confirmed. In dependence upon Rendtorff, Pannenberg elevates the concept of Yahweh's *glory* as intimately linked with the definitive self-unveiling of God. In Ex. 14:18 and 16:6, for example, "the glorification of Yahweh through his acts in history is clearly an expression pointing to the indirect revelation of his deity in those acts."[43] But from the time of the postexilic prophets and continuing on through the eschatology of the apocalyptic tradition, the appearance of Yahweh's glory comes to be anticipated as a futural event, as in Is. 40:5 and 43:1ff.[44] Thus, the concept of an indirect revelation of God through history points forward, toward a unity of history in which the unity of God is definitely known, and toward the eschatological establishment of the glory of God.

Pannenberg defends this proposal of the indirectness of God's self-disclosure with the observation that it is precisely characteristic of that which we identify as personal to reveal oneself indirectly, not by way of the immediacy of one's visible appearance but only insofar as one indirectly discloses the truth of one's inner essence through what one does.[45] Continuous with the hidden *Unverfügbarkeit* of personhood is the understanding that the truth of a person is never directly at hand for the other, never immediately available for the other's appropriation, but always must be delivered up by that individual herself. The nontransparency of personhood requires the movement of self-unveiling, and this can only be fully forthcoming through the indirect communication of the self in my activity, not simply in my putting in an appearance, so to speak. As applied to God, Pannenberg observes:

> Where a theophany or a self-presentation of the deity is represented as its self-revelation, the deity *in its appearance* is not yet understood to be a self that is different from its appearance! Only impersonal things may be directly identical with the sheer obviousness of their appearance--and perhaps not even they, insofar as they have an "essence" that remains distinguishable from their mere presence-at-hand. A person, a self, cannot be directly, but always only indirectly, identical with the physical appearance, the existential milieu, and the modes of behavior, in which he expresses himself.[46]

A person's disclosure of himself through the spoken word is not identifiable as the locus of self-revelation because what remains precisely at stake is the degree of truthfulness of word as embodied in deed. The trustworthiness of a person's word about herself is not resolved immediately in the speaking of the word but only through the confirmation of that word in the behavior of the person. In this respect, Pannenberg does not denigrate the significance of word for the concept of indirect revelation; he simply insists that it must be understood to play a secondary, rather than primary, role. Thus the seventh dogmatic thesis on revelation affirms that "the word is related to revelation as prophecy, as instruction, and as report" or kerygma.[47] The word itself is not directly revelatory but rather relates to the revelatory event that precedes, accompanies, or follows it, in which the turth-bearing character of the word is confirmed and even grounded. One does have to reckon with an "intertwining" of prophetic words and events,[48] but not in the sense that the event is an inessential appendage to the word, nor in the sense that the prophetic or kerygmatic word adds something additional to what is contained within the event itself. The word brings to conscious articulation what the event already contains as its own proper meaning. Thus "the word of the kerygma is not first the proper revelatory event itself but is rather a moment of the revelatory event, in that it reports the eschatological occurrence which in itself is God's sufficient self-confirmation."[49]

In response to the criticisms of Hesse[50] and others, Pannenberg adamantly defends the premise that the revelation of God is utterly inseparable from the confirmation of God's deity. Indeed, he acknowledges that "I limit the concept of *revelation* to the *self-confirmation* of Yahweh through his deeds,"[51] and it is this redefining of revelation which gives rise to the provocative second dogmatic thesis concerning revelation as essentially futural. The stance is not taken arbitrarily. Pannenberg observes:

> For philosophy of religion and systematic theology, the question [of revelation] is that of a self-manifestation of divine reality, one which was not only experienced as such by men of earlier cultures at some time or another, but one which is capable of being convincing for our present-day understanding of existence as the deity's self-confirmation of his reality. Against all the deities *claimed* by the religions, the doubt is directed whether they can also be regarded by us as God, as the power over everything.[52]

In the case of the disclosure of God claimed in the Old Testament tradition, what begins as an affirmation of the deity of Yahweh based on an understanding of specific, single events--such as the miraculous deeds of Moses in J (Ex. 7:17; 8:20-22; 9:14) or victory in a holy war (I Kings 20)--is extended by the Deuteronomist tradition into concentration upon a whole connected history as the locus of Yahweh's self-revealing activity, as in Deut. 4:37-40. But subsequent events explode even this understanding and again call Yahweh's deity into question, specifically with the onset of the exile. In this context, the prophetic word turned the eyes of Israel from the past toward the future, toward the expectation of an eventual and unsurpassable vindication of the truth of Yahweh not only to Israel but before all the nations. What was at stake was nothing less than the exclusivity of Yahweh's godhood, which could only be confirmed through the ultimate demonstration of Yahweh's power vis-a-vis the whole of reality.[53]

Thus Pannenberg arrives at the same conclusion from several different perspectives. Inasmuch as God is thinkable only as the unifying power of reality, only the unity of history can definitively confirm and therefore disclose the truth of God's divinity. Insofar as oneness characterizes the essence of God, not individual events but only the ultimate oneness of reality can reflect the truth of God. And insofar as what is presumed to be revealed about God is a Lordship that encompasses all of reality, the present openness of reality as history can only point ahead to an anticipated consummation of reality which would demonstrably reveal the presently disputable reality of God. Pannenberg observes:

> In the history of religions the divine reality is only debatedly at work, and just so may the history of religion be understood as the way of God to God's revelation. First with the revelation of the true nature of the divine will even the question of the existence [*Dasein*] of God finally be decided . . . .[54]

Pannenberg places a tremendous amount of weight upon the central premise that God is understandable only as the "power over everything,"[55] deriving especially from this proviso the direction in which his interpretation of revelation must move. If "the divinity of God is determined by his power over *all* events,"[56] it becomes quite clear that "a single event cannot by itself reveal [as God] the power over all that is real" but rather it is "only justifiable to speak of a single event as an act of God if the power over everything is already known in another way to be identical with God,"[57] *i.e.,* through a view of the *whole* of reality.[58] The logic is clear-cut for Pannenberg: if "an alleged deity" is presumed to be revealed as "really God, i.e., powerful over all things," then the event in which that revelation is forthcoming can only be one in which that power is unsurpassingly confirmed, and only the totality of all events can ultimately demonstrate the truth of that power.[59] Therefore the event which would reveal the essence of God, God's all-encompassing power, would necessarily be that one in which all history is finally realized as a unified whole.

It was in this direction that Pannenberg finds the Old Testament tradition also to have moved--specifically with the emergence of the apocalyptic tradition. For the eschatological emphasis of Jewish apocalypticism represented a sharp focusing of attention upon the final establishment of God's rule upon the earth as the manifestation of God's deity in relation to the whole unfolding of history.

In those prophetic circles which were the starting point of the apocalyptic movement, the whole history of Israel and of the world into the far future was understood for the first time as a continuing totality of divine activity realizing a plan which had been decided at the beginning of creation. Accordingly, God's final revelation, the revelation of his glory, together with the glorification of the righteous, was now hoped for as the End of all occurrence.[60]

Thus Pannenberg reaches the conclusion, continuous with the thrust of Old Testament understanding and what is required by a sufficient concept of revelation, that one must speak of the *end* of history as the actual locus of God's complete self-disclosure.

Since knowledge of God's divinity was no longer expected from single events but from one final occurrence which would gather together all earlier, single events into one single history, this ultimate knowledge had to be placed at the end of all history. Only when all occurrence is ended can the divinity of God be known on the basis of the connection of history. So one may say that only the last, the eschatological, event which binds history into a whole brings about final knowledge of God.[61]

It is this affirmation which is set forth succinctly in the second dogmatic thesis: "Revelation occurs not at the beginning but at the end of revelatory history."[62] The idea underlying it is one to which Pannenberg gave expression rather early in his theological pilgrimage, insisting already in his maiden publication that Christians do not have in their possession the true form of God's oneness: "Christians *wait* with all persons for the futural revelation of the oneness of God at the end of time," though they do so with the provisional knowledge of the identity of the oneness of God with the God present in the transcending event of Jesus' crucifixion and resurrection.[63] This fundamental conviction has received a consistent championing by Pannenberg as he has deepened his insights into the full panoply of concepts which lead to or spring from such an understanding. The implication of such a view is quite apparently a present inaccessibility of the fullness of revelation, and hence a present uncertainty of the very being of God. The most that individuals would have within the ongoing course of history would be merely provisional and supersedable pointers toward the futural disclosure of God's truth, inasmuch as the end wherein revelation definitively occurs is hardly yet at hand.[64] But that is not the conclusion at which Pannenberg eventually arrives. The event in history which is understood to burst through that aporia is the fate of Jesus of Nazareth, and the avenue which leads to that realization is the tradition of apocalyptic.

The details of the move which Pannenberg makes will be examined in chapter seven, but it is important briefly to sketch in the outlines here as the capstone of his revelatory understanding. According to apocalyptic tradition, the universal resurrection of the dead was expected as an accompaniment of the end of history and establishment of God's sovereign rule. The fate of Jesus differs from all other events within history in that the end of history which had been proclaimed in his message of the inbreaking Reign of God, is not only foreseen but proleptically actualized--in the occurrence of his resurrection. The resurrection of one person in the midst of history, precisely continuous with though by no means identical to his own expectations, is a preactualization of the resurrection of all people at the end of history, and thus the deity of God who promises eschatological salvation is demonstrably revealed.[65] This is the understanding summed up in Pannenberg's crucial fourth thesis on revelation: "The universal revelation of God's deity is not yet actualized in Israel's history but first in the fate of Jesus of Nazareth, insofar as therein the end of all events has occurred in advance."[66] The consequences of this apocalyptically oriented assessment of Jesus' significance are spelled out quite cogently:

> History as a whole becomes visible only when one stands at its end. Until then, the future remains always uncalculable. Therefore, only insofar as the completion of history has already stepped into history in Jesus Christ is God conclusively and completely revealed in Jesus' fate. But with Jesus' resurrection the end of history has already happened to him, though for us it is yet outstanding. Therefore--and only under this presupposition--the God of Israel has conclusively proven God's deity in Jesus' fate and is now revealed even as the one God of all people. Only the eschatological character of the Christ-event grounds the fact that no further self-confirmation of God beyond this event will be given: even the end of the world will simply consummate on a cosmic scale what has already happened to Jesus.[67]

Pannenberg is concerned to distinguish this "final, although still anticipatory, revelation" in the fate of Jesus from the manner in which events within history can generally point ahead to the coming ground of their being. In this latter respect, "anticipatory revelations (or better: anticipations of the one revelation) of the power over everything" are discernible, pointing forward to the wholeness of reality to a greater or lesser degree and forming "elements of the whole of all occurrences in which God will be revealed as the power over everything." These Pannenberg refers to as "provisional" and "partial"; single events are always only "anticipations" of the one definitive self-disclosure of God at the end of history, whereas Jesus' resurrection is distinctively a complete preactualization of that final event.[68]

Finally, it is important to take notice of Pannenberg's perspective on the relationship between revelation and faith which comes to expression in the third thesis[69]: "In distinction to special appearances of the deity, revelation in history is open to anyone who has eyes to see. It has a universal character."[70] The point of the statement is that the perception of the revelatory import of historical events is not dependent upon a special spiritual quickening, without which the true meaning would remain hidden from view. In part, this must be so because an unveiling of God could hardly be at the same time, for others, a veiling.[71] But more basically, the ground for affirming the universal accessibility of an event's revelatory significance is to be recognized in the argument that an event's meaning is not something additional to it but rather is contained within it. Therefore the revelatory character of an event is intrinsic to it and available to anyone, not only to the one moved "by faith" to see it that way. To repeat in this context the emphasis discussed in chapter two: faith *arises out of* the perception of the precisely "revelatory" significance of an event, and is properly directed toward the future as the believing anticipation of that to which the event points in its deeper meaning.[72] On the other hand, Pannenberg observes, a revelation of God not universally accessible would amount to its being put forward as having an authoritarian character, not readily open to critical examination and confirmation. Thus he proposes that the program of "demythologizing" must become not less radical but more so, in the direction of a thoroughgoing "depositivization" of the content of the Christian kerygma that would remove all traces of appeal to an authoritarian grounding of its truth-claims.[73] Pannenberg even goes so far as to insist that upon the historian falls the burden of proof for ascertaining whether God is revealed in an event in history--though of course the historian is able to perform this task adequately only upon recognizing a responsibility for taking into account the whole of history in a universal-historical horizon of understanding.[74]

C. Critique and Transition

Pannenberg's argument moves from the premise of revelation as God's *essential self-* disclosure to the recognition of the illegitimacy of a *direct* manifestation of God's essence to a consideration of a different sort of possibility: God's *indirect* self-disclosure through God's actions. Pannenberg finds legitimation of that possibility both in the implications of events of history as indirect communication of the ground of their becoming, and in the direction of Old Testament tradition as coming to reflect just such a knowledge of Yahweh through his deeds in (initially past, but increasingly futural) history. Inasmuch as the God whose reality and power are promised therein is conceivable as deity only if God is the one who is powerful over everything that is, the full self-disclosure of God's being can come only with the confirmation, the self-demonstration, of God's all-encompassing Lordship. Therefore revelation as confirmation of God's true deity can come only with the *end* of history wherein God's unifying and all-determining power is finally decided and decisively manifested. But this is precisely the direction in which the Old

Testament tradition eventually moved, as represented in the emergence of the apocalyptic emphasis upon the eschatological consummation of universal history and vindication of God's deity with the establishment of God's Reign. And the legitimacy of the apocalyptic tradition is grounded in the fate of Jesus as the prolepsis within history of the apocalyptically proclaimed goal of history, the resurrection from the dead. With Jesus has occurred not simply a partial anticipation of futural revelation but a full "happening in advance" of the essence of the End, wherefore the revelation of God *am Ende* is already at hand in the midst of history to anyone who seeks to know of it.

It becomes rather quickly obvious from this concentrated restatement of Pannenberg's argumentation that the validity of his understanding of revelation hinges particularly on the legitimacy of his interpretation of the fate (and, correlatively, the message) of Jesus within the context of apocalyptic tradition. Therefore the analysis emerging in this chapter points us beyond the initial issue of Pannenberg's theological appropriation of the Old Testament to an extended consideration of the credibility of his appropriation of apocalyptic and its presumed authentication in Jesus of Nazareth. A critical assessment of his revelational resolution of the questionableness of human existence, history, and truth can only emerge fully when that further probing has been accomplished. Nevertheless, two critical issues arise already at this juncture, to which we must give our attention. One deals with the relation of Pannenberg's understanding of revelation to the Old Testament on which he endeavors to build so much of his case, the other with the intrinsic validity of the proposal itself.

1) To what extent is this understanding of divine revelation actually rooted in an open-minded, objectively pursued exegesis of Old Testament texts, vis-a-vis the converse dependence of exegesis upon a systematic-theological understanding of revelation? Knierim points to Pannenberg's expression of concern about what would constitute a *presently convincing* instance of God's self-manifestation as an indication that his interpretation of revelation in the Old Testament is predicated on a determinate pre-understanding in terms of which specific texts are valued up or down.[75] Hesse contends that Pannenberg's Old Testament grounding is minuscule--primarily Deuteronomy, the post-exilic prophets, and the apocalyptic tradition--and then attacks the legitimacy even of that rootedness. With regard to the fifth thesis on revelation, he maintains that what emerges in Pannenberg's view of the ground of Jesus' proclamation in its preceding tradition-history is an appropriation not of God's history with Israel in general but of a very delimited tradition of apocalyptic which stands for the most part outside the Old Testament altogether.[76] Of course, there are intrinsic reasons why Pannenberg comes to place so much importance on apocalyptic tradition, as will shortly be manifest. But the impression which emerges

from such criticism as this is that independent, straightforward exegetical work is hardly the bedrock of understanding that it is made to appear. On the other hand, however, one can point to such work as Hans Walter Wolff's analysis of the prophetic understanding of history[77] as solid exegetical support for the direction of Pannenberg's theological appropriation. But that could be somewhat misleading, since already Wolff's own exegesis there betrays the influence of Pannenberg's essay on "Redemptive Event and History."

The issue which emerges from all of this is the question of the role of presuppositions or "preunderstanding," theological or otherwise, in the exegetical task. Bultmann has insightfully developed the thesis that exegesis without presuppositions is impossible, although it is necessary to keep in mind that the preunderstanding which one brings to the text must not be allowed to function as a definitive, unalterable position.[78] I would extend that principle with the further, positive contention that the preunderstanding with which one inevitably confronts the text at the outset must allow itself to be transformed precisely through contact with what the text discloses to the exegetical inquiry, within its total "con-text." This would mean that Pannenberg is not to be faulted for coming to the exegetical task with prior considerations of the direction in which the answer of revelation is convincingly to be sought. The crucial issue rather is whether he sufficiently allows the exegetical process to call into question the adequacy of what he brings with him to the engagement: *i.e.,* the bringing of a *preunderstanding* cannot be allowed to become the imposing of a *precondition.* Pannenberg has endorsed this concept in principle in his insistence, considered in the preceding chapter, that the question which we *are* is fully understand-able only from the standpoint of the reception of the answer. By extension, the reality of revelation must be allowed to burst through the analysis of what a concept of revelation would have to entail. The problem is in knowing when this has fully been allowed to occur. And the debate ranges in part over the degree to which the Old Testament tradition genuinely discloses the eschatological perspective on revelation which Pannenberg finds there, in addition to the question of whether such a perspective is enduringly valid and convincing. So far, the jury of exegesis is still out on the former score. Concerning the latter, the vindication of eschatological revelation is sought by Pannenberg beyond the scope of the Old Testament in which it originally, presumably, arose. It is toward a consideration of that question that this inquiry now moves.

2) The other critical issue which first must be examined concerns an apparent circularity in Pannenberg's designation of the form and content of divine self-revelation: it is on the basis of an understanding of God as "all-determining power" which arises *within* revelation that Pannenberg comes to identify the necessary *locus* of revelation as the end of history, inasmuch as only there *could* such a

deity be conclusively disclosed. The condition by which Pannenberg establishes the essential *futurity* of revelation is the premise of God's all-determining power which in turn is only given *in* that (futural) revelation. By the same token, the definition of revelation as God's self-*confirmation* is rooted in the prior conviction that the essence of God consists in God's being the power over everything: only the confirmation of God's power, accordingly, could truly be a disclosure of such a deity, wherefore history points ahead to the arrival of the End as the only possible basis for speaking of God. But what if reality as history can be more adequately comprehended as supporting a *different understanding of the very nature of divine power*--for example, one in which the steadfast preeminence of God's power is found in God's capacity always to surmount every obstacle history places in the way of God's Lordship and to provide yet new possibilities for our coming into harmony with God's unifying aim? Then not only the content of revelation would be affected by such an understanding but the form and locus as well, in that a final resolution of historical conflict as a *condition* of the divine self-manifestation would no longer be required.[79] This conception would avoid the difficult hypothesis that God's very being demands history's culmination in order to be fully real and manifest. A twofold question arises in respect to this: whether biblical tradition allows or even calls for such an interpretation, and whether this can be seen to be a more appropriate understanding of reality altogether, including divine reality. Both of these aspects of the question will be explored in what follows.

NOTES

[1] "As Christians we know God only as he has been revealed in and through Jesus. All other talk about God can have, at most, provisional significance." (*JGM*, p. 19.)

[2] "The Revelation of God in Jesus of Nazareth," *TaH*, p. 104.

[3] "Dogmatische Thesen zur Lehre von der Offenbarung," *OaG*, p. 107. (Cf. *RaH*, p. 145.) The English translation of *OaG* is of extremely poor quality, so that quotations here are almost always taken from the original.

[4] "Nachwort, " *OAG*, p. 132, ft. 1.

[5]"And a man of God came near and said to the king of Israel, 'Thus says Yahweh, "Because the Syrians have said, 'Yahweh is a god of the hills but he is not a god of the valleys,' therefore I will give all this great multitude into your hand, and you shall know that I am Yahweh."'"

[6]See Walther Zimmerli, *Gottes Offenbarung: Gesammelte Aufsätze zum Alten Testament* (München: Chr. Kaiser Verlag, 1961), pp. 11-40, 120-32, and 133-47. See also Robinson's summary of Zimmerli's insights, "Revelation as Word and as History," *TaH*, pp. 43-46.

[7]See Rolf Rendtorff, "The Concept of Revelation in Ancient Israel," *RaH*, p. 27.

[8]*Ibid.*, pp. 27-29.

[9]*Ibid.*, pp. 29-33.

[10]*Ibid.*, pp. 33-37.

[11]*Ibid.*, pp. 38-43.

[12]*Ibid.*, p. 46.

[13]*Ibid.*

[14]*Ibid.*, pp. 47f.

[15]Zimmerli, "'Offenbarung' im Alten Testament: Ein Gespräch mit R. Rendtorff," *EvTh* 22, 1962, pp. 15-31, especially p. 25.

[16]R. Rendtorff, "Geschichte und Wort im Alten Testament," *EvTh* 22, 1962, p. 622.

[17]R. Rendtorff, "Geschichte und Überlieferung," in R. Rendtorff and Klaus Koch, eds., *Studien zur Theologie der alttestamentlichen Überlieferungen* (Neukirchen: Verlag der Buchhandlung des Erziehungsvereins, 1961), pp. 81-94, especially pp. 89f., 93.

[18]R. Rendtorff, "Geschichte und Wort im Alten Testament," *EvTh* 22, 1962, pp. 623, 629, 635f.

[19]Robinson, "Revelation as Word and as History," *TaH*, p. 61. See his summary of the positions of the two men, *ibid.*, p. 62. Cf. also the specifying of options by Rolf Knierim in his essay, "Offenbarung im Alten Testament," *Probleme biblischer Theologie*, ed. Hans Walter Wolff (München: Chr. Kaiser Verlag, 1971), p. 218: "The discussion concerns the question of where Yahweh is 'seen' or 'known'. There are four alternatives: in his address which promises acts; in the action which follows from the promise; only in the action; or in the tradition-historical unity of both. Both men agree

that the third possibility is excluded. In determining the relation between promise and act, however, Zimmerli leans toward the first alternative while Rendtorff accents the second and, above all, the fourth alternatives."

[20]R. Rendtorff, "Die Offenbarungvorstellungen im Alten Israel," *OaG*, p. 34. The translation is from Robinson, "Revelation as Word and as History," *TaH*, p. 49. (Cf. *RaH*, p. 40.)

[21]*JGM*, p. 128, ft. 30.

[22]"The Revelation of God in Jesus of Nazareth," *TaH*, p. 120.

[23]The most helpful penetration into the impasses of the Zimmerli-Rendtorff debate is to be found in Rolf Knierim's article on "Offenbarung im Alten Testament," in *Probleme biblischer Theologie*, though there are problems in his implied criticism of the Pannenbergian position on revelation. Knierim faults the tendency to concentrate on the Old Testament idea of revelation without specifically focusing on the very word that means "to reveal," and he does so with apparent justification. He insists that the point of departure for an understanding of revelation is to be found in recognizing the basically secular meaning of the word and implications thereof for speaking of a revealing of God. In its ordinary sense in the Hebraic tradition, revelation is "the occurence of the becoming visible of what has been unseen," whether that is the being of the world, a hidden truth, or God (211f.). The unveiling of Yahweh should be understood not in contrast to the common experience of disclosures in the world but precisely in continuity therewith (210-12). But this is very much in harmony, actually, with the point Pannenberg wishes to make about the indirect discernment of God *in* and *through* the historical reality of the world. Knierim goes on to point up the crucial importance of the word in the divine self-unveiling: God is recognizable as *Yahweh* only by means of the prophetic address, so that one credits God rightly for God's saving actions only where they are discernible as the actions of the God Yahweh (222-24). Pannenberg's point, conversely, is that Yahweh is recognizable as truly *God* only through the confirming event, and the question therefore is which one of these motifs is subordinate to the other. Knierim contends that if the name is known already, then either an occurrence or a word can be revelatory, wherefore the debate between word and history is superfluous (224f.), but that precisely fails to take into account the necessity for confirming the truth-claim put forth in the declaration of the name. Finally, Knierim is negative toward the exclusive emphasis upon the realm of history as atypical of the Old Testament tradition: not only history but also *nature* is interpreted by the Israelites as pointing toward the unveiling of Yahweh (228f.). But Pannenberg is concerned to encompass nature within the overarching rubric of reality as history and sees this as derivative from Hebraic conceptuality that "natural events," so to speak, are a part of the history that God has with God's people.

[24]"Christian Theology and Philosophical Criticism," *IGHF*, p. 120.

[25]"What is a Dogmatic Statement?," *BQT* I, p. 187.

[26]See, *e.g.,* "Christian Theology and Philosophical Criticism," *IGHF,* pp. 120f.

[27]See "What is a Dogmatic Statement?," *BQT* I, p. 183.

[28]"Introduction," *RaH,* pp. 4f.; *JGM,* pp. 127f. As Pannenberg observes with a bit of subtle humor, "to locate a theological thought in German idealism is not automatically to condemn it." (*RaH,* p. 5.)

[29]*RaH,* p. 4.

[30]*Ibid.,* p. 9.

[31]*Ibid.,* p. 6. Cf. also *JGM,* p. 129: "The concept of self-revelation includes the fact that there can be only a single revelation. God cannot disclose himself in two or more different ways as the one who is the same from eternity to eternity. When someone has disclosed himself ultimately in a definite, particular event, he cannot again disclose himself in the same sense in another event different from the first. Otherwise, he has not disclosed himself fully and completely in the first event, but at most partially." (It is not immediately self-evident why this must be the case.)

[32]*RaH,* p. 8.

[33]*Ibid.,* p. 125; "Response to the Discussion," *TaH,* p. 233.

[34]*OaG,* p. 12. (Cf. *RaH,* p. 9.)

[35]*RaH,* pp. 9-13.

[36]"Response to the Discussion," *TaH,* p. 233, ft. 11. See also *RaH,* p. 10.

[37]*RaH,* pp. 11f.

[38]*OaG,* p. 15. (Cf. *RaH,* p. 13.)

[39]*RaH,* p. 14.

[40]*Ibid.,* pp. 15f.

[41]"Dogmatische Thesen zur Lehre von der Offenbarung," *OaG,* p. 91. (Cf. *RaH,* p. 125.)

[42]"Dogmatic Theses on the Doctrine of Revelation," *RaH,* p. 126.

[43]*Ibid.,* p. 128.

[44] *Ibid.*

[45]"Response to the Discussion," *TaH*, pp. 235f.

[46]*Ibid.*, p. 236.

[47]*OaG*, p. 112. (Cf. *RaH*, p. 152.)

[48]"The Revelation of God in Jesus of Nazareth," *TaH*, p. 120.

[49]*OaG*, p. 114. (Cf. *RaH*, p. 155.)

[50]Franz Hesse, "Wolfhart Pannenberg und das Alte Testament," *Neue Zeitschrift für systematische Theologie und Religionsphilosophie 7*, 1965, pp. 174-99, esp. 184f. and 195f. (hereafter: *NZsTR.*)

[51]"Response to the Discussion," *TaH*, p. 234, ft. 12. See also p. 232.

[52]*Ibid.*, pp. 231f.

[53]See esp. "The Revelation of God," *TaH*, pp. 121f.; *RaH*, pp. 125-27, 132.

[54]"Reden von Gott angesichts atheistischer Kritik," *GmF*, pp. 46f., my translation. (Cf. *IGHF*, p. 115.)

[55]See, *e.g.,*"Response to the Discussion," *TaH*, pp. 231f., 237, 239, 241, 253, 255f.

[56]*Ibid.*, p. 239.

[57]*Ibid.*, p. 237.

[58]See also *ibid.*, p. 241. Cf. "Kerygma and History," *BQT* I, p. 94, ft. 20: "God can be spoken of only in relation to the whole of reality because, since the critical question of Greek philosophy about the true form of the divine, only one who was the author of all things and all events could seriously be called God. . . . to speak of a deed of God with regard to an individual event means to judge it in its concrete relation to the occurrences of its nearer and farther connections and to history as a whole."

[59]"Response to the Discussion," *TaH*, p. 232.

[60]"The Revelation of God," *TaH*, p. 122. The theme of apocalyptic has been necessarily introduced here in order to facilitate a sequential presentation of Pannenberg's concept of revelation. Critical discussion of the legitimacy of his

appropriation of apocalyptic categories of understanding, however, is postponed until the chapter following.

[61]"The Revelation of God," *TaH*, pp. 122f. So also *JGM*, p. 128: "The more all happenings were perceived in Israel as a single great historical unity, the more the full knowledge of Yahweh became an event that would be possible only at the end of all happenings. Yahweh would complete the entire course of world events, world history, in order that man might thereby know his divinity. Only at the end of history is he ultimately revealed from his deeds as the one God who accomplishes everything."

[62]"Dogmatische Thesen," *OaG*, p. 95. (Cf. *RaH*, p. 131.)

[63]"Mythus und Wort," *ZThK* 51, 1954, p. 185. Already in the previous year, Emil Brunner had noted in *Eternal Hope* that "revelation in the New Testament sense and revelation of the future is one and the same thing," and referred to the coming again of Christ as "this final revealing advent" (pp. 27, 141). Chapter nine is entitled "The Future Advent of Jesus Christ as the Meaning of History," wherein Brunner noted that world history has its ultimate meaning not in itself but in the futural coming of Jesus, the Bringer of the Kingdom of God (p. 86). But Brunner acknowledged that he could only regard the notion of an end of history as a paradox (pp. 130ff., esp. 134).

[64]"If the God of Israel can be revealed as the power over *everything* and thus revealed in his *divinity* only in the totality of all events, but if on the other hand the course of history is not yet complete and all events are not yet gathered up in their totality, then the divinity of the God of Israel is, strictly speaking, not yet revealed but still hidden . . . ." ("Response to the Discussion," *TaH*, pp. 239f.)

[65]See "Dogmatic Theses," *RaH*, pp. 140f.

[66]*OaG*, p. 103. (Cf. *RaH*, p. 139.)

[67]*OaG*, pp. 104f. (Cf. *RaH*, p. 142.)

[68]"Response to the Discussion," *TaH*, p. 240.

[69]I have not devoted separate attention to the remaining, sixth thesis, which states: "The universality of the eschatological self-demonstration of God in Jesus' fate comes to expression in the development of non-Jewish concepts of revelation in the Gentile Christian churches." (*OaG*, p. 109. Cf. *RaH*, p. 149.) The point made therein is simply that the particularity of revelation within a specific strand of historical tradition is understandable as having universal significance only insofar as it can demonstrate its capacity to be taken up within other traditions and speak relevantly to their self-understanding. This is the direction that Pannenberg moves in emphasizing the fruitfulness of Hebraic categories of thought for penetrating the impasses in Greek philosophy, for example, which has been discussed in chapter two.

[70]*OaG*, p. 98. (Cf. *RaH*, p. 135.)

[71]See *RaH*, pp. 7f.

[72]See "Redemptive Event and History," *BQT* I, p. 66; *RaH*, p. 138.

[73]See "Response to the Discussion," *TaH*, pp. 226-30. Richard Rhem has proposed the intriguing thesis that what is really crucial about Pannenberg's doctrine of revelation is not that it occurs indirectly in events rather than directly in Word, but that it is universally available to human reason. It is precisely this latter which sustains theology's claim to be of universal significance, rejecting therewith any special sphere of theological truth illumined by the Spirit. (R. Rhem, "A Theological Conception of Reality as History--Some Aspects of the Thinking of Wolfhart Pannenberg," *Reformed Review* 26, 1972, pp. 186f.) The point is well taken. Certainly what distinguishes Pannenberg the most from his immediate predecessors in the theological arena is his whole-hearted insistence that theology must rationally defend its claim to be speaking a universally valid truth, and only the inherent openness of God's presumed revelation could sufficiently facilitate this understanding. But the unique character of Pannenberg's program is to be found more extensively in the particular conclusions which he has drawn from the indirectness of revelation in history: the essential futurity of both the revelation and the Revealer.

[74]"Redemptive Event and History," *BQT* I, pp. 66f.

[75]Rolf Knierim, "Offenbarung im Alten Testament," *Probleme biblischer Theologie*, p. 206, ft. 1. Kneirim observes: "It is clear that Pannenberg's point of departure leads from the outset to a critical separation between texts that are suitable and unsuitable for the theme [of revelation]." The reference there is to Pannenberg's "Response to the Discussion," *TaH*, p. 231. (See the quotation, *supra*, p. 136.)

[76]Franz Hesse, "Wolfhart Pannenberg und das Alte Testament," *NZsTR* 7, 1965, pp. 191-95, 182.

[77]Hans Walter Wolff, "The Understanding of History in the Old Testament," *Essays on Old Testament Hermeneutics*, ed. Claus Westermann (Richmond, Va.: John Knox Press, 1963), pp. 336-55. Essay translated by Keith R. Crim. Initially delivered as an address in January, 1960.

[78]Rudolph Bultmann, "Is Exegesis without Presuppositions Possible?" *Existence and Faith*, pp. 290, 294.

[79]Such an understanding of the God revealed by history would still contain a provisional, future-directed thrust: further events could conceivably throw this conviction decidedly into doubt. But a terminus of historical becoming is not hereby required; God's powerful transcending of all obstacles to God's Lordship could well be an open-ended process.

6

THE TRADITION OF APOCALYPTIC

An analysis of Pannenberg's theological appropriation of apocalyptic[1] with respect to his concept of God must proceed in a manner at variance with the pattern repeated in the previous chapters. The reason for that is to be found in the fact that Pannenberg rests his case for the legitimacy of his understanding on an interpretation of apocalyptic which has since been fairly thoroughly discredited--and neither Pannenberg himself nor anyone else has adequately entered the breach to repair the damage. Therefore the approach undertaken here will be (A) to begin with a summarization of those aspects of apocalyptic understanding which Pannenberg emphasizes in his theological programme, and (B) to move thence to a consideration of the relevant features of the work of Dietrich Rössler which have tended to serve as support for the position Pannenberg has taken. Recognizing that the critical broadsides leveled at Rössler's contribution have tended to knock the props out from under Pannenberg's apocalyptic appropriation, and taking into account the considerable division of opinion in contemporary scholarship concerning the crucial question of the role of universal history in apocalyptic, the endeavor will be made (C) to provide a textual overview and (D) provisional assessment of relevant themes in apocalyptic literature as a basis for directly engaging Pannenberg's interpretation of apocalyptic in a critical manner. The significance and even necessity of this undertaking will become clearer as an identifiable relationship between apocalyptic thought and Pannenberg's concept of God emerges more fully in the subsequent chapters.

A.   Theological Appropriation of Apocalyptic

When attention is focused upon the apocalyptic hinge on which so much of Pannenberg's understanding of history and revelation turns, a remarkable realization emerges: rarely has so much theological weight rested on a premise so cryptically presented and so minimally defended. Pannenberg actually has very little to say directly about Jewish apocalyptic tradition, though it functions as a crucial element in the overall structure of his theological understanding. And although he manifests considerable exegetical familiarity with Old and New Testament texts and traditions, his direct contact with especially extra-testamental apocalyptic tradition does not explicitly appear to be very extensive. Furthermore, nowhere does he offer a specific definition of what he understands "apocalyptic" to be, though at one point he mentions in passing the particular elements which he regards as essential in the eschatology of Jewish apocalyptic: the Reign of God, judgment, resurrection of the dead, and the end of the world.[2] No grounding of that interpretation is provided.

Fundamentally there are four areas of emphasis that predominate in Pannenberg's direct references to the tradition of apocalyptic, three of them major and the fourth somewhat less so. In the first place, it is to apocalyptic that the Western mind is indebted for our understanding of the universality of history. Therein, the whole sweep of history from the creation to the anticipated end is encompassed for the first time. Whereas the J document ends with the fulfillment of the promise through Israel's reclaiming of the land, and P brings the story to completion with the establishment of the cult, apocalyptic extends its concern to embrace the ultimate fulfillment of Yahweh's promise which is now expected not within history but as history's end.[3] And whereas the covenantal tradition elevated a strand of *Heilsgeschichte* as the locus of God's activity, apocalyptic first carried through systematically the prophetic broadening of God's history with humankind to encompass all the kingdoms of the world--a geographically as well as temporally universal history.[4] It is Pannenberg's contention that only this insight of reality as *"history hastening toward an End"* could compete on the same level of universality with the Greek concept of the cosmos as ever-stable order, and thus come to embrace the whole of reality in a more sufficient way.[5] Contra Bultmann, Pannenberg maintains that the apocalyptic concept of the two aeons did not displace faith in the creative work of God.[6] To the contrary, "the whole history of Israel and of the world into the far future was understood for the first time as a continuing totality of divine activity realizing a plan which had been decided at the beginning of creation."[7] Finally, eschatology, far from contradicting the Old Testament concept of God,[8] is understood by Pannenberg to be discernible already in an "inner-historical" eschatology of the prophets; what is new with apocalyptic is not eschatology per se but an eschatology of the end of history. But this is no more than an extension of a basic aspect of the historical consciousness of Israel which ever involved the anticipation of futural fulfillment beyond all previously experienced fulfillments of Yahweh's promises.[9]

In the second place, it is the apocalyptic tradition which first fully recognizes the character of divine revelation as occurring only *am Ende*, at the end of all events.[10] With this is linked an essential characteristic that revelation is received by the apocalyptic visionary only "proleptically," in anticipation of the end to come and precisely requiring futural confirmation. What was at stake in the apocalyptic visions were proleptic unveilings of the eschatological event which the writers claimed for themselves, but which only the course of history's future could definitely confirm.[11]

Thirdly, there developed in apocalyptic writings the decisive association of an end of the world with a general resurrection of the dead, together with a final judgment. Though there were many variations on a common theme, concerning such matters as what sort of transformation of bodiliness was to be expected and whether judgment preceded or followed resurrection (and therefore whether resurrection was to be of everyone or only of those already judged righteous), the central thread remained consistent: resurrection was understood to take place as a universal phenomenon accompanying the end of history and inbreaking of God's sovereign rule.[12] It is Pannenberg's thesis both that the very notion of resurrection is incomprehensible without its initial apocalyptic horizon of understanding and that the expectation of a futural, end-historical resurrection of the dead is central to apocalyptic thought.

Finally, Pannenberg is concerned to make the point that in apocalyptic writings the content of that which is to be definitively disclosed and even determined at the time of the end already pre-exists in heaven.[13] In their perspective, "that which is to be revealed *on earth* in the future already stands ready in divine concealment ('in heaven')."[14] It is on this basis that he can identify in the apocalyptic tradition a decisive penetration into the nature of time, involving an "interlacing of historical future and hidden present in the eternity of God."[15] But it is precisely such a perspective which would seem to throw into question the sense of history's essential *contingency* that is so dear to Pannenberg, and in an earlier essay he seemed to be cautioning against this aspect of apocalyptic thought.[16] Nevertheless, the (present) heavenly reality of the end-historical future is distinctively accented as a feature of the apocalyptist's understanding.

The point to be scored with this highlighting of apocalyptic traits is not the intrinsic superiority of such a view of reality. Simply taken on its own merits, apocalyptic has no more claim to legitimacy than other interpretations, and in fact contains within its tradition a number of decisively untenable variables. Pannenberg's fascination with apocalyptic rests on other grounds. It is his thesis that the singular

153

interpenetration of Jesus' message and his fate constitutes a retroactive validation of the essentials of the apocalyptic vision of reality. On the other hand, Jesus himself cannot be adequately understood apart from the apocalyptic horizon of his message, essentially with respect to his proclamation of the inbreaking Reign of God. On the other hand, the confirmation of the truthfulness of Jesus' claim provided by the resurrection underwrites the enduring significance of the apocalyptic conceptual framework without which that event of resurrection is incomprehensible.

> Although the apocalyptic concept of the end of the world may be untenable in many details, its fundamental elements, the expectation of a resurrection of the dead in connection with the end of the world and the Final Judgment, can still remain true even for us. At any rate the primitive Christian motivation for faith in Jesus as the Christ of God, in his exaltation, in his identification with the Son of Man, is essentially bound to the apocalyptic expectation for the end of history to such an extent that one must say that if the apocalyptic expectation should be totally excluded from the realm of possibility for us, then the early Christian faith in Christ is also excluded . . . . One must be clear about the fact that when one discusses the truth of the apocalyptic expectation of a future judgment and a resurrection of the dead, one is dealing directly with the basis of the Christian faith. Why the man Jesus can be the ultimate revelation of God, why in him and only in him God is supposed to have appeared, remains incomprehensible apart from the horizon of the apocalyptic expectation . . . . The basis of the knowledge of Jesus' significance remains bound to the original apocalyptic horizon of Jesus' history, which at the same time has also been modified by this history. If this horizon is eliminated, the basis of faith is lost . . .[17]

This is but a brief hint of the relationship between Jesus and apocalyptic which is to be developed in detail in the following chapter. It is introduced here only to indicate the enormous significance that will be placed on such fragile underpinnings. But before continuing the thread of that discussion, it is crucial that we take a detour into an overview of the analysis of the apocalyptic tradition from which Pannenberg's generalizations appear to be drawn, as well as an examination of the criticisms that have been directed toward that analysis, as impetus for working toward a more precise determination of what essentially constitutes that theologically decisive but historically elusive tradition of thought.

B. Apocalyptic and Universal History

One of the doctoral dissertations to emerge from the original Heidelberg group consisted in a bold endeavor by a young New Testament scholar to identify the Jewish theological context of Jesus and early Christianity. In 1957, Dietrich Rössler penned in sweeping strokes an interpretation of what he discerned to be two distinctive strands of tradition, Jewish apocalyptic and Pharisaic orthodoxy, centering upon the pivotal categories of law and history. The dissertation appeared in print three years later,[18] and it is this treatise to which Pannenberg has continued to refer for support for his own understanding of the theological meaning of the apocalyptic tradition. Pannenberg's appropriation of Rössler's theses relates for the most part to Rössler's treatment of the concept of history in apocalyptic, and the discussion here will primarily focus upon that subject and the questions that impinge upon it.

It must be noted at the outset that Rössler's approach is not directly an exegetical one, in which apocalyptic passages are carefully analyzed for their inherent meaning and then conclusions are drawn by an interrelating of those individual exegeses. Rather, he offers sweeping generalizations of identifiable trends and motifs in the literature at hand, for which a varying number of appropriate references are then cited in the footnotes or occasionally quoted in the body of the text. That procedure becomes particularly critical in regard to the manner of his selection of usable sources. Rössler focuses upon the apocalyptic *Gattung*, which he designates as "essentially characterized by revelatory addresses and visions, among whose content mythological representations of history and the world entire stand in the foreground,"[19] and he proceeds to identify three texts as predominantly representative of that *Gattung*: I Enoch, IV Ezra, and II Baruch. Then he turns back around and identifies apocalyptic concepts as those which come to expression in these texts![20] Other texts can be judged to be more or less apocalyptic in nature in terms of their harmony with the conceptuality of these "three great apocalypses." The rationale for this point of departure is baldly set forth: a grasp of the whole is the condition for understanding any of its parts.[21] "The common tradition must first be known before the particular can directly be comprehended therefrom."[22] The unity of apocalyptic is therefore presupposed at the outset as a condition of the inquiry, rather than established as a result of it.

Rössler affirms that the basic theme of Jewish apocalyptic is "history in its entirety": the seer envisions the course of history as a unity, unfolding according to divine plan, as a determinate history from beginning to end.[23] "That history is essentially a unity stands quite clearly in the foreground" of the apocalyptist's interest.[24] This unified history is perceived not in relation to concrete historical events, however, but through various schemes of periodization. In this respect, meaningful connections of events, the unity of history and its goal, come to light precisely through mythological representation as the only adequate vehicle for such expression.[25]

This understanding of history is seen to depend upon two presuppositions: that history *is* a unity, understandable as a whole and therefore providing the framework for the meaning of individual events, and that it is directed toward a goal according to divine plan.[26] The "essential theme" of the apocalyptic texts is precisely *"that* there is this plan of the divine acts in history and *that* God himself is actualizing it."[27] The goal of this unfolding history is salvation: "The eschatological act is the beginning of the time of salvation, and with it history ends."[28] Salvation is not attainable within history; it remains an inaccessible beyond, "only rarely passed over into in individual instances."[29] For the view from within history, salvation is fully futural, and history's meaning is to be seen as a pathway directed toward salvation.[30]

Furthermore, the divine plan of history is presently recognizable to the seer, "fixed in heaven." It is in no way a consequence of human initiative but of God's own acting, in the face of which we are essentially passive. History is thus "the plan of the divine action."[31] On the one hand, this involves an affirmation of divine predetermination, which Rössler acknowledges.[32] On the other hand, there is a sense in which what is yet to occur in the bringing of history to its final destination is already a present reality in heaven, so that what emerges at the end is simply the unveiling on earth of that which is already presently true but hidden from common sight. The seer catches a glimpse of the heavenly secrets, as an anticipatory discernment of what will come fully into view "in the eschatological revelation" at the end.[33]

In summary, Rössler contends that "the most significant characteristic of the apocalyptic scheme of history . . . is unquestionably the fact that here 'history' as one and as entire comes into view."[34] Apocalyptic achieved this "step to universal world-history" in two respects: as a comprehending of the history of the whole world and of the whole flow of time.[35] The distinctive achievement of apocalyptic thought was in fastening together the beginnings in Israelite prophecy and history-writing into a full-blown "universal theology of history" for the first time.[36]

The critical reactions to Rössler's theses have been anything but sympathetic. Philipp Vielhauer curtly dismissed Rössler's work as unworthy of serious attention and no contribution to the apocalyptic debate,[37] thus knocking out the props from under Pannenberg's theology with a single wave of his scholarly hand. But theological misdirections are hardly ever laid to rest so preemptorily. A decade after the original completion of the dissertation, a trio of critical responses by Messrs. Betz, Murdock, and Nissen appeared in print almost simultaneously, attacking Rössler's interpretation of apocalyptic head-on.[38] I will focus selectively on their analyses by attention to six key criticisms that are directly or indirectly relevant to the theme of this discussion.

1) Both Nissen and Betz attack Rössler's narrowness of scope in his choice of apocalyptic texts to be investigated. Nissen is particularly critical of Rössler's principle of selectivity, in allowing theological considerations to dictate a choice of sources which are then utilized to derive particular theological conclusions, thus, in effect, determining the result in advance. Furthermore, Rössler calls in a number of apocalyptic texts in support of his interpretation of the apocalyptic understanding of history and ignores them in his treatment of the apocalyptic concept of law.[39] Betz accurately faults Rössler for ignoring the literature from Qumran, an inexcusable oversight in light of the already emergent scholarly awareness of eschatological emphases in the Qumran community. He further accuses Rössler of a sort of "biblicism" in failing to examine apocalyptic in the *religions-geschichtlich* context of Hellenistic-oriented syncretism within which it originally developed.[40]

2) Betz and Nissen also call into question Rössler's premise of an identifiable unity in apocalyptic. Betz perceives post-biblical Judaism as a highly complex and differentiated phenomenon, making it difficult to single out one isolatable movement to which precisely defined characteristics are explicitly attributable. Furthermore, commonly accepted apocalyptic passages are anything but fully harmonious with each other, signifying that apocalyptic is hardly the homogenous movement that Rössler makes it out to be.[41] Nissen is especially piqued at Rössler's oft repeated phrase "the common apocalyptic tradition," correctly emphasizing that the differences and even contradictions not only between but even within individual apocalypses make it impossible to speak of "the" apocalyptic eschatology in opposition to "the" rabbinic one.[42]

3) Again, both men are concerned to deny the contention that universal history is a central or even merely observable theme in apocalyptic literature. Betz resists the notion that apocalyptic has any positive use for history at all, and relegates world history to merely one area of the apocalyptist's interest among others. The key issue for Betz is that "world history" in its entirety is identical with the "evil aeon," and thus falls under a totally negative judgment. History is not fulfilled in the eschaton, but rather abolished.[43] Nissen's rejection of this thesis is even more sweeping. He maintains that the mythical periods into which apocalyptic divides time do not encompass the whole of history but only the course of history from the pretended time of the apocalyptist forward.[44] More importantly, those visions concerned with *world* history encompass only the time since the Exile, whereas those comprehending the entire *time* of the world concern themselves only with the history and prehistory of Israel. Nissen's summary judgment: "Either history of election or world history, either the encompassing of all time or of all humanity--but not both together."[45]

157

4) Nissen and Murdock maintain that apocalyptic reflects the understanding that God has nothing to do with the present course of history. To Rössler's contention that in apocalyptic thought God is presently acting in history to bring about Israel's salvation, Nissen observes that God is said to have departed for the time being from the course of history:

> The *present*, on the contrary, is void of God's *historical* acts of salvation. Instead, the world powers rule in the present "according to their pleasure," without God and against God, while God stands outside the striving and serenely looks on. In no single vision is it said or intimated that God works *historically* in the time after the Exile. Any reference to God, God's plan and God's activity, is missing all the more in the *mythic-periodic* visions. And therefore there can be no inference that *in these visions* the periods pressed forward toward a goal indwelling them, possesed a meaning or actualized a plan of salvation. The idea of a plan and its historical actualization is known to Judaism and the Old Testament but it has nothing to do with the transmitted apocalyptic schema. What is actually stated there is rather than the epochs in question will unroll thus and so, and after them--at whose end the apocalyptist lives--will the Reign of God follow. What relationship this event has to God's earlier or futural activity. . . is *here* precisely not said.[46]

This is very much the point that Murdock's critique is most thoroughly concerned to set forth. Even though he acknowledges that the apocalyptic schemata presuppose that history is a whole and is directed toward an end,[47] he insists that this history is viewed as inimical to God.[48] Murdock places much emphasis upon the eschatological dualism of apocalyptic, arguing that history as the present evil aeon is a sphere of conflict that threatens God's sovereignty. Only when this aeon is terminated, rather than consummated, with the arrival of the "eschaton" and the inbreaking of the new aeon is god's sovereignty reasserted.[49] Murdock accuses Rössler of ignoring the dualistic aspect of apocalyptic thought.[50] But his own rather arbitrary definition of "eschaton" as a sort of dividing line between aeons which belongs to the present aeon as its end and not to the future aeon as its salvific beginning, and therefore as the goal of history only as *terminus* and not as *telos*,[51] hardly advances the discussion and certainly has no basis in the apocalyptic literature.

5) Murdock pursues his line of thought further with the denial of any sense of historical revelation in apocalyptic. Because there is no continuity between this present aeon and God, history cannot be revelatory.[52] The eschatological revelation, of which the seer has a visionary preview, has no relationship with what happens in history, and the apocalyptist's disclosure of the truth of God is a merely literary, rather than event-ful, link of the present with God's futural unveiling.[53]

> Just as the eschaton cannot be construed as the last link in the causal nexus of history, so the eschatological revelation cannot be interpreted as the final

brilliant burst of light when the last candle is lit at the end of a history-long candlelighting service. That is to say, the eschaton was understood in apocalypticism not as the goal of history, but as the impingement of eternity that destroys history; and the eschatological revelation was understood, not as the sum of all historical revelations, but as the *doxa* of God bursting in upon this aeon of darkness from the aeon of light.[54]

6) Finally, Betz opposes the thesis that apocalyptic bears direct continuity with the tradition of Old Testament prophecy. Apocalyptic is not to be interpreted essentially as an extension of developments within the prophetic understanding for its roots actually lie elsewhere, in wisdom for example, and its distictiveness is in the novelty with which it appropriates older traditions.[55]

Thus the position set forth by Rössler has come under attack on a number of critical issues, which tears at the very foundations of Pannenberg's theological programme. The problem is compounded by the fact that Rössler has committed the cardinal sin of Germanic scholarship: having subsequently shifted professional gears and abandoned the field of biblical study, he has not responded to his critics with a further defense, clarification, or modification of his published theses. The issues have gone begging, and the observation of Martin Seils is explicitly to the point: "It would probably be helpful if the Pannenberg circle expressly and comprehensively verified Rössler's concepts before drawing further such weighty conclusions from him."[56]

In a somewhat restricted sense, Klaus Koch has picked up the gauntlet which has been tossed before the Pannenbergian perspective on apocalyptic. In his "polemical work on a neglected area of biblical studies and its damaging effects on theology and philosophy,"[57] Koch surveys the approaches to the apocalyptic tradition in the past decades and offers his own "preliminary definition" of the subject. In the latter respect, Koch is highly sensitive to the present lack of an adequate overall grasp of what fully and explicitly constitutes apocalyptic. Following von Rad[58] and O. H. Steck,[59] he recognizes emphatically the provisionality of the present state of the discussion and issues a clarion call for a thoroughgoing application of form-critical and tradition-historical methods of examination of the literature as a necessary prerequisite to evaluating the many competing interpretations of apocalyptic that have arisen on the basis of insufficient critical study.[60] In regard to Rössler's contribution, Koch presents a brief resume inclusive of critical reaction,[61] but his subsequent attempt at rebuttal of the three Rössler critics is extremely brief and highly selective, failing to deal in a helpful way with the critical issues highlighted here.[62]

One instance of Koch's support of Rössler is precisely indicative of the divided mind of contemporary apocalyptic scholarship, and that concerns the question of the relationship of apocalyptic to history as universal. Koch contends that Rössler's discovery "that in the apocalypse history has entered the picture for the first time 'as a unit and as a whole', with its 'basis in a predestined divine plan', through which every event acquires 'its non-interchangeable place in the sequence of time', has often been contested since, but never confuted."[63] It is this issue which is central, especially so far as Pannenberg's appropriation of apocalyptic is concerned, and it is around this question that much of the scholarly debate is most significantly joined. A survey of the more important interpretations of this theme in the recent literature on the subject is very illuminating of the absence of a common understanding.

On the one side of the ledger are those whose understanding is essentially continuous with the view shared by Rössler and Koch. D. S. Russell, in harmony with R. H. Charles,[64] credits the apocalyptists with being the first to grasp the unity of history and maintains that history is affirmed rather than rejected by them in the sense of the overarching purposiveness of God that embraces both the present aeon of history and the future age of God's reign.[65] S. B. Frost initially adopted the position that the apocalyptists were the first to endeavor to present an inclusive philosophy of history.[66] Lars Hartman enlarges upon that view:

> To designate the content of these texts as "apocalyptic and eschatological" is almost the same as saying that they are pervaded by a comprehensive view of history. For what is "revealed" is in most cases large or small portions of past history, current affairs and future events. This revealed history is regarded in these texts in a special perspective, viz., how God guides the course of history in one way or another towards a goal which He has determined upon-- that His kingdom shall be established.[67]

So also, Amos Wilder contends that apocalyptic "pioneered the first universal view of history . . . . It took history with utter seriousness, confronting the seemingly total disaster of the present and assigning meaning and hope to it in terms of the wider cosmic drama."[68] O. H. Steck agrees that apocalyptic embraces an all-encompassing view of history, but insists that this is not unique to it: it is already discernible in the deuteronomic tradition, which plays a determinative role in the conceptual framework of almost all subsequent Jewish apocalyptic.[69] Walter Schmitals distinctively highlights the universalistic character of the apocalyptist's interest in all of history as "a continuity which can be viewed as a whole, is complete, and is moving toward a goal,"[70] and maintains that "the Western philosophical and religious interpretation of history unquestionably grew, directly or indirectly, out of the thinking of apocalyptic."[71] Finally, one can observe that even von Rad acknowledges that the notion of a unity of history arises precisely in apocalyptic's "eschatologization of wisdom" in the introduction of the conception of an anticipated end and goal of history.[72]

160

But on the other side are to be found a sizeable number, including several of the foregoing, who insist that history is really of no positive significance to apocalyptic, that, to the contrary, apocalyptic represents a sort of dehistoricizing of the historical realm. Foremost in this group would be Bultmann, who interprets apocalyptic as projecting not a completion of history but its abrupt breaking-off; history is unified only at the expense of a genuine process of historical development and through a surrendering of any historical meaningfulness.[73] Vielhauer emphasizes the sharp dualism of aeons in apocalyptic, and denies the significance of the present one as not holding any positive interest for the acpoalyptist: all the historical distinctions are leveled, and only the coming of the End holds any meaning. The world is not regenerated but rather re-created.[74] Von Rad observes that the particular way in which apocalyptic achieves a unity of history runs directly counter to the prevailing Old Testament sense of history as the locus of God's saving acts. In contrast to the anchoring of the prophetic message in a *heilsgeschichtlich* tradition of determinate saving events, the apocalyptist knows the ground of salvation only as a futural denouement of history which has been set from the very outset. And von Rad is concerned to question "whether behind this gnosticizing interpretation of the calculable ebb and flow there does not stand a fundamentally historyless thinking, because here the experience of the historically contingent scarcely comes to expression."[75] So also, Frost in a later essay contends that apocalyptic actually represents a rejection rather than an embracing of history. Through a process of mythologization of history, the apocalyptist tried to come to terms with history but wound up failing to take it really seriously.[76] He concludes:

> . . . so far from being the first philosophers of history, the apocalyptists are in fact a school of biblical writers who recognized that the burden which Hebrew religion had laid upon history was greater than it could bear. They therefore returned from history to myth, myth in a new amalgam with history, . . . [thereby abandoning] the teleological view of history and with it the attempt to justify in mundane events the ways of God to man.[77]

We have already seen that Betz denies that universal history is actually a "central theme" in apocalyptic thought. Likewise, as previously highlighted, Murdock insists that history has no positive value for apocalyptic and Nissen goes so far as to insist that history in any really universal sense is nowhere embraced by apocalyptic literature. Finally, Paul Hanson suggests that apocalyptic involves not so much the "collapse of the notion of the historical" per se but even more crucially an "abdication of responsibility to the historical realm,"[78] and Schmitals echoes this conclusion in his admission that apocalyptic's "radical dehistoricizing of the future" by virtue of a divine predecision of history's outcome[79] leads ultimately to a "loss of history" on the part of apocalyptic[80] and "the-renunciation of any responsibility for the fate of this world's course."[81]

What emerges from this rapid overview is a rather strong sense of inconclusiveness arising out of contrary, though not altogether contradictory, estimates of the role of history in apocalyptic thinking. The inconclusiveness seems to turn primarily around the question not of whether apocalyptic embraced history in its universality (Nissen excepted) but of whether, in so doing, the specific character of history was eliminated. That is to say, the issue has to do with the meaning that is to be attached to the apocalyptic broadening of a vision of history that encompassed the beginning and the end. On the one hand, then, Pannenberg's position that apocalyptic accomplished the universalization of historical understanding would appear to be essentially unrefuted. But on the other hand, little is gained thereby if that accomplishment has arisen only at the expense of a fundamental dehistoricizing in apocalyptic's view of the world's course.

Is there a way of penetrating the scholarly fog that envelops this question? With the groundwork of form-critical and tradition-historical exegesis just beginning to be laid,[82] any such endeavor at this juncture becomes a very hazardous enterprise. However, recognizing the essential relativity of all momentary stages of advance in the thrust toward historical knowledge, a preliminary investigation of relevant sources is not altogether avoidable or valueless. It is to that task that I turn, as a springboard to proposing a provisional assessment of the features of apocalyptic understanding relevant to Pannenberg's appropriation.

C. Canvassing the Tradition

Koch and Vielhauer both distinguish between apocalypse as a literary genre and apocalyptic as a body of ideas or historical movement which receives expression in that genre.[83] A problematic circularity is observable in that the precise character of those ideas and that movement is identifiable only by extraction from the genre, whereas the very designation of a piece of literature as apocalyptic is considerably determined by the extent to which it embodies various features of apocalyptic thought. Koch calls attention to the widespread literary diversity present in the tradition itself,[84] and Vielhauer is cognizant of the fact that the genre only belatedly took on a common title, with the "Apocalypse" of John.[85] One confronts therefore a diversified tradition of thought which may have only gradually developed out of something originally lacking in unity, and the impulse must be resisted of imposing a unity on the tradition too prematurely.

162

The most crucial aspect of the genre seems to be reflected in the name itself: the apocalypse as a revealing, a vision,[86] specifically one in which the future destiny of humankind and the world is disclosed.[87] On this basis, the extant literature which becomes the primary focus of investigation (and, in turn, from which such an understanding has been derived) comprises Daniel, I Enoch, the Testaments of the Twelve Patriarchs, II Baruch, IV Ezra, the Apocalypse of Abraham, the Testament of Moses, Revelation, and various texts discovered at Qumran. In addition, passages are discernible in other literature which convey a distinctively apocalyptic flavor.

For the purposes of this canvass, however, the selection of texts must be somewhat smaller. The reason for that limitation is to be found in the manner in which Pannenberg appropriates the apocalyptic tradition as theologically significant: his concern is to identify a continuity of Jesus' teaching and understanding with apocalyptic, a continuity that both underlies and is conversely authenticated in Jesus' message and fate. Since that is the case, it is decisively inappropriate to derive an understanding of the apocalyptic perspective that was ostensibly confirmed through Jesus from sources that post-date him. This means that material such as II Baruch and IV Ezra, which scholars generally assign to the Christian era, cannot validly be utilized in this context--until historical criticism has been able to sort out those pieces of that literature whose written or oral history may fairly be seen to reach back before the time of Jesus. Of course, there is an opposite problem to which one must be sensitive as well: apocalyptic literature was generally preserved not in Jewish but in Christian circles, and pre-Christian sources are considerably shot through with Christian emendations. With sensitivity to that problem in mind, the following texts have been employed in this canvass: Daniel, I Enoch, the Testaments of the Twelve Patriarchs, the Testament of Moses, the third Sibylline Oracles, the Psalms of Solomon, Jubilees, and several Qumran texts (1QS, 1QM, and the Zadokite Fragments).[88]

The themes providing the focus of the canvass are substantially in continuity with those upon which Pannenberg directs his attention, though not altogether with the same weighting of emphasis. My concern is primiarily with the question of the attitude of these texts toward history as a whole, with correlative emphasis upon the understanding of that into which history passes or which takes its place (the new aeon, the Reign of God). Interrelated with this are the further issues of the place occupied by the notion of a resurrection of the dead, the implications of a divine determinism, and the nature of the concept of revelation indicated by these texts. Finally, the previously unmentioned figure of the "Son of Man" will receive attention in reference to the discussion, in the chapter following, of the possible significance of this title in the teachings of Jesus.

Daniel. The visions in Daniel embrace the terminus of history's course but not its beginning. The seventy weeks of years (9:24ff.) are only from the ostensible time of the apocalyptist forward, and do not encompass history entire. There is overt reference, however, to God's saving activity *in* past history, specifically in the Exodus (9:15). What is anticipated by the seer is the futural establishment by God of God's indestructible reign which will bring to an end all earthly kingdoms (2:44). In ch. 7, this regnancy, along with "glory," is "given" by the "Ancient of Days" to "one like a son of man" who comes "with the clouds of heaven" (7:13). In both cases, what is established is a reign on earth, through divine intervention, which occurs "at the time of the end" (11:40; 8:19). Only in the final vision beginning at 11:2 is the expectation of a resurrection included (12:2f.), encompassing "many of those who sleep in the dust of the earth" and followed by judgment. All of this is made known to Daniel as "mysteries" revealed by God (2:28, 30), who grants him "wisdom" and understanding (1:17) to discern already that which will come to be "in the latter days" (2:28, 10:14). The concept of divine determinism is explicit in 8:19, in referring to "the appointed time of the end."

I Enoch 93:1-10, 91:12-17, the "Apocalypse of Weeks."[89] History is encompassed by a schema of ten weeks beginning with Enoch's birth. The great King, in unending "glory," is introduced in the eighth week, followed in the ninth by a universal revelation of "the righteous judgment" and a marking of the world "for destruction" (91:13f.). Thereafter a "new heaven" appears, though not specifically a new earth also, and the weeks continue without end (91:16f.). There is no reference to a resurrection. This future yet to unfold is already written in "the heavenly tablets" from which Enoch is privileged to read (93:2f.). Thus, the course of the future is already determinately set.

I Enoch 6-36. There is a great deal of obscurity in these passages. Spatial imagery, rather than temporal, prevails. There is no overview of history at all. The eventual coming of God's judgment is a significant motif (10:11ff., 16:1, 25:4), without, however, any explicit accompanying motif of resurrection.[90] 10:12-11:2 gives a strong implication of the eventual emergence of a situation of perfect righeousness in an earth-paradise, without any sharp historical disconnectedness. A similar image prevails in 25:3-6, which envisages a coming golden age on earth in which God will visit it with goodness and establish God's throne there. Following a judgment, the righteous will inherit the earth and live long, though not eternal, lives in joy and peace. There is no resurrection, no categorical separation of ages per se; history will seemingly go on, only now under God's rule. There is an emphasis here upon God as "eternal King" and "Lord of glory" (25:3, 7), who has

164

already prepared these eventualities for the righteous "and hath created them and promised to give to them" (25:7).

I **Enoch 83-90**, the "Dream Visions." There are two visions here, the first (chs. 83f.) dealing with the first world-judgment of the Flood, and the second (chs. 85-90) embracing in animal symbolism the whole of history from the creation of Adam to a final judgment. There is symbolic reference to God's past saving activity in history, again particularly with regard to the Exodus (89:16-27). The focus is distinctively upon Israel's history. A final struggle between the "sheep" and their enemies issues in Yahweh's intervention (90:15, 18), and after the climactic warfare God erects God's "throne" in Palestine and executes judgment (90:29-27). There is again no specific reference to a resurrection, though 90:33 is possibly a vague allusion to one.

I **Enoch 91-105** (excepting the Apocalypse of Weeks). The unit is explicitly an admonition to the righteous to persevere against adversity, and the motivation given is that only they shall arise to eternal goodness and grace, whereas the wicked will be judged and will perish in wrath. There is no reference to the whole of history, and no overt indication of a coming Reign of a new aeon. That which will come is a day of judgment (91:7-9, 103:8, 102:5), followed by a resurrection of the righteous (91:10, 92:3, 103:4; 100:5), who will apparently inherit a purified earth. The seer lays claim to knowing "a mystery" because he has "read the heavenly tablets" and "seen the holy books" in which that which is prepared for the righteous is inscribed (103:2). So also, the sense of determinism is recognizable in the observation that "the Holy and Great One has appointed days for all things" (92:2).

I **Enoch 37-71,** the "Similitudes."[91] Again, there is an absence of any overview of history. The parables all point toward a coming time in which the righteous will inherit a transformed earth (45:4-5, ch. 58), with no designation of this as a reign of God. There are references, however, to a coming judgment by the Elect One "on the throne of glory" (45:3, 61:8). Resurrection of all the dead (51:1) or only of the righteous (62:15) is affirmed "in those days." References to the Son of Man abound; his role seems predominantly to be as judge, and the title is used as synonomous with the Elect One.[92] A taste of divine predestination is indicated in 41:8. It is said that all the works and creation of the "Lord of Spirits" have been revealed by Him "to the righteous and elect" (61:13), and the author refers also to the present concealing (62:7) and futural revealing of the Elect One (62:1, 3) or Son of Man (62:7).

The Testaments of the Twelve Patriarchs.[93] Only the Testament of Levi surveys history, from his own time (or that of Moses) to the ultimate establishment of a new priesthood, in the imagery of seventy weeks which are only mentioned and not explicated (chs. 16-18). With the raising up of the new priest comes a righteous judgment (18:2) and a heavenly light that brings knowledge and dispels all darkness (18:3f.), accompanied also by the presence of the "glory" of the Most High (18:5-7). There is no resurrection here. Several of the Testaments look forward to the establishment of a rather nationalistic kingdom, messianic in the Testament of Joseph (19:8-12), subordinate to the Levitical priesthood in the Testament of Judah (21:1-5). The Testament of Dan envisages a final warfare culminating in a messianic victory and the establishment of a New Jerusalem, over which the Holy One of Israel shall reign (5:10-13). There is no word of resurrection, and history seems to continue on its course except in a transformed direction. The resurrection of the righteous is affirmed in the Testament of Judah (25:1-5), and a universal resurrection followed by judgment is asserted in the Testament of Benjamin (10:8f.).

The Testament of Moses 1-5, 8-12.[94] Israel's history is surveyed from the passing of Moses down to the Antiochan persecution, with a later addition (ch. 6) encompassing the period of Herod. Furthermore, history is embraced *in toto* by a dating of Moses' death from the creation of the world (1:2) and, later on, by a designation of the subsequent years that are to unfold (10:12) before the coming of the Lord "in the consummation of the end of the days" (1:18). At that prescribed time, "His kingdom shall appear throughout all His creation" (10:1), accompanied by widespread cosmic cataclysm (10:4-6) and succeeded by God's exalting of Israel to heaven (10:8-9). In the meantime, all that transpires in the course of history is completely foreseen by God, who is understood to have "caused all to come forth" (12:4, 13). There is no reference to resurrection in the Testament, nor any sense of an eschatological revealing of God at the consummation of present history.

The Sibylline Oracles, Book III. The oracle surveys the sweep of history beginning with the Tower of Babel and continuing down to the time when desolation will be visited upon the dynasties of the earth, making a shift from past to future tense along the way (162-67). There are two successive references to the coming of an earth-paradise (657-60, 742-59) preceded by widespread combat (652f., 663-68) and, in the latter instance, by a great cosmic cataclysm (672-92). With God's restoration of Paradise God will also "raise up his kingdom for all ages" (767) but no hint of resurrection is given. The mysteries which the oracle receives are understood by him to be completely certain in advance: "nothing fails of its appointed end when He but conceives the thought" (700).

The Psalms of Solomon. Only Ps. 17 is continuous with the literature so far surveyed, in embodying a vision of a coming reversal of fortunes. But the similarities are rather minimal. The psalmist pleads

166

for God to raise up a son of David as king, who will destroy unrighteous rulers, purge Jerusalem of its foreign oppressors, destroy sinners and godless nations, and gather together a holy people whom he will lead in righteousness and will judge. The Gentiles will do obeisance to him and Jerusalem will be sanctified, to which all nations will come to glorify God. But there is no radical upheaval of the course of history: no cosmic cataclysm, no resurrection, not even a transformed earth. There is reference to God's Reign but it is not something to be established; rather it is "for ever" (17:4). On the other hand, the other psalms abound with references to a futural resurrection of the righteous dead, with no indication of any connection with a futural transformation of the world.[95]

The Book of Jubilees. Jubilees, or the "Apocalypse of Moses," is difficult to categorize and even more difficult to assess. The schematized history of seven weeks of years is said to encompass "from the day of creation until the heavens and the earth shall be renewed" (1:29), but the recounting of history actually extends only down to the Exodus. Ch. 23, on the other hand, is a futural look at the end times. But whereas 4:26 envisions Zion as ordained to be the center of a "new creation," the image in ch. 23 is rather one of a gradual regeneration of the present creation. Whereas a destruction of the earth is referred to in 23:18, subsequent verses (23:26ff.) suggest the gradual dawning of a time of great blessing, with no intervening expression of the earth's re-creation. An indication of an eventual resurrection is given in 23:30, but the following verse conveys the distinct impression that it is only of the spirit, sans body.[96] Finally, a remarkable juxtaposition of freedom and divine determinism emerges in 5:13, in reference to the judgment of those "who depart from the path which is ordained for them to walk in." But Jubilees does contain one very important affirmation of straightforward clarity: only here, among all the literature with which we have dealt, does the revelatory *Erweiswort* appear, as a reference to a futural self-unveiling of Yahweh (1:28). The shorter self-presentation formula is found also (1:18).

Qumran literature. The distinctiveness of this material, with regard to the present context, concerns a decisive emphasis upon God's continuing control over the course of history. No overviews of the historical realm have been discovered here, but there is a strong sense of expectation that history is moving toward a climax directed by God. In 1QS, the "Manual of Discipline," matters are understood to proceed "according to the mysteries of God until the End appointed by Him" (3:23).[97] The raging conflict between the two spirits, of light and darkness, has been ordained by God "until the final End" (4:15-17, 25). The Zadokite Fragments acknowledge God's foreknowledge of all events, which occur by God's hand (2:8-10). 1QM, "The War of the Sons of Light Against the Sons of Darkness," depicts in great detail the coming cosmic conflict with which the present course of history will be terminated, and perceives this as eternally encompassed by God's foreknowledge and intent (13:14). But the Scrolls give little attention to the question of what lies on the other side of the great historical divide. The focus is directed rather to the coming of the "end of days" and the "consummation of time,"[98] coupled with references to the presence or "visitation" of God upon the earth at that time.[99] This will amount to a "time of renewal" (1QS 4:25) in the final End, in which human beings will be purified and embued with the Spirit of Truth, and filled with understanding and heavenly wisdom (1QS 4:18-22), but there is no reference to the coming of a divine reign. Furthermore, there are no clear indications of an anticipation of resurrection to be found, though the Hymn Scroll (1QH 11:11-14) may possibly contain such an allusion.

D. A Provisional Assessment

What conclusions are to be drawn from this brief investigation ' of textual material? Particularly, what light is shed on the question of the validity of Pannenberg's interpretation of apocalyptic? What may initially be said, in the way of an attempt at generalization, is this: *there does exist a group of texts displaying a common understanding that the future will be radically different from the present and past, and that God, who will accomplish this world-encompassing transformation, already assures its coming to pass.* Around this core, variations of specific concepts cluster, such as recitations of the movement of history in symbolic terms, images of a coming cosmic cataclysm or catastrophic warfare, references to a transhuman mediator of the historical reversal, expectations of an ultimate divine judgment, the concept of a universal resurrection at the time of the world's transformation (either of all persons, followed by judgment, or of the righteous only, already judged), and widespread diversity of expectation as to the nature of what will follow this climactic complex of events.

To what extent all this can be identified as representative of a specific tradition called "apocalyptic" still remains difficult to assess. The defining of the tradition will depend to a considerable extent on where one elects to draw boundary lines--for one might just as readily say that there exists a group of texts that share the common understanding of a futural universal resurrection of the dead, through a process of selection that eliminates similar texts which do not contain such references. In addition, what we possess is very likely only the tip of a historically submerged iceberg, the residue of a complex process of conceptual development, fragments of a multi-hued tapestry. All designations become rather tentative in the face of that recognition. The proposal that we utilize the term "apocalyptic" to designate the movement of ideas signified in the generalization stated above is therefore done with a sense of caution and a spirit of provisionality, in full awareness of the intellectual spadework yet to be completed.[100] With these reservations in mind, let us consider what implications derive from the investigation here undertaken, in relation to Pannenberg's understanding of apocalyptic.

1) History as universal. A complete overview of the course of world history is a rarity in pre-Christian apocalyptic but it does appear: in the animal symbolism of I Enoch 85-90, implicitly in the Book of Jubilees and the Testament of Moses. The survey of history in Book III of the Sibylline Oracles begins with the Tower of Babel, but otherwise the apocalyptists takes up the story only from their own ostensible time (Daniel, the Apocalypse of Weeks). What must be recognized, however, is that this motif, even where present, does not convey the impression of being of major importance, and it can readily be dispensed with entirely in other texts equally concerned with proclaiming the coming new day. The conclusion is hardly avoidable that apocalyptic discovered the universality of history rather coincidentally, as a by-product of a primary concern to proclaim the certain arrival of a radically new future ushered in by God. To a certain extent, therefore, Pannenberg's point is granted: history as a whole is embraced for the first time when an envisioning of its anticipated consummation arises. But not all the texts are uniform in foreseeing so radical a futural transformation that history ceases; rather it tends to continue, though in more or less altered fashion. Particularly there is no notion of a cessation of all process altogether. History's actual "end" is a concept that can be derived from some texts only with severe difficulty, though history as we presently know it is decisively transcended.

2) God and present history. That God will do a new thing to transform the present course of events is not a denial of God's continuing sovereignty over history but precisely its ultimate championing. The dualism encountered in apocalyptic literature is not ontological, in the manner of Gnosticism, but temporal. Monotheism is an underlying assumption: God is understood to be the one who has ordained the present historical conflict from the outset. God's final victory is assured precisely because God alone is Lord all along. What awaits is God's definitive manifestation of that fact. The entire thrust of determinism, and of the seer's receiving advance information on what will transpire historically, is grounded in the continuing supremacy of God's power. Furthermore, that God is at work already in past history is a motif which, as we have seen, is *not* altogether unknown to apocalyptic literature.

3) The Reign of God. Pannenberg identifies the concept of a coming Reign of God as an essential of apocalyptic thought.[101] On the other hand, D. S. Russell has observed that the phrase "Kingdom of God" nowhere appears in apocalyptic literature,[102] and Martin Rist insists that

169

the very concept is utterly non-apocalyptic.[103] The evidence on this score seems solidly in Pannenberg's favor. Though the phrase itself does put in an appearance only in the Psalms of Solomon (17:4), where it is not specifically characterized as echatological, the underlying idea is widespread. References to the futural establishment of God's Reign as a distinctive feature of the coming transformation of history are explicitly present in Daniel, the Testament of Moses, the Testament of Joseph, and the Sibylline Oracle III. In addition, the image of the coming of the King in glory and the erection of his throne is prominent in nearly all the sections of I Enoch. Although no single pattern completely encompasses all the expressions in apocalyptic literature of what will characterize the so-called new aeon, the motif of the definitive manifestation of God's sovereign Lordship is a major theme.

4) Resurrection of the dead. The literature very extensively reflects an expectation of reawakening to a transformed life as an accompaniment of the new day of history. Variations have primarily to do with whether this is envisaged as occurring to all the dead, prior to the separating act of divine judgment and subsequent condemnation of the unrighteous, or only to the righteous, judgment having already transpired. In either case, it is crucial to note that resurrection is always anticipated as a universal phenomenon in one or the other of these ways, and *almost* always is precisely associated with the irruption of the end time. Two qualifications must be introduced, however: There are descriptions of a futural eschatological occurrence sans resurrection, the Apocalypse of Weeks, the Testament of Moses, and Sibylline Oracles III being the most prominent cases in point.[104] And secondly, the resurrection passages in the Psalms of Solomon present a difficult exception to the general rule: there is no explicit linking there with any eschatological motif. The anticipations of being raised to a new, unending life are devoid of any reference to an accompanying historical consummation.[105] This would seem to call into question the premise that the very concept of resurrection is exclusively an apocalyptic idea. Though it is certainly a central theme, it seems to be neither an exclusive nor an absolutely indispensible one. The possibility of establishing the essential dependence of the very idea of resurrection on the tradition called apocalyptic would seem to depend upon more thoroughgoing research into the relationship of the Psalms of Solomon to that tradition.

5) Divine determinism. This functions as a recurring motif throughout. The affirmation of God's predestining not only the end but all that comes about within history is occasionally explicit. The understanding that God has ordained specifically the shape and time of the end emerges frequently. The image of the seer reading from the heavenly tablets on which the future course of events is inscribed is conditional upon this. History is therefore grasped as a whole for the first time precisely through a repudiation of its contingent uncertainty.

History's yet incomplete unity and wholeness is anticipatorily seized upon through a denial of any meaningful working-out *within* history of that toward which history is tending. Destiny is imposed transcendentally. Our role is to understand, not to act.[106] And time, as marking the passage from the already to the not yet (or the reverse), is reduced to a dramatic device through which the divinely composed script is played out on the world stage. So the conclusion seems clearly warranted that apocalyptic indeed betrays the truth of history, dehistoricizes it in the elimination of future risk and genuine contingency of events, as the price paid for latching onto its universality.

6) Revelation. Revelation as occurring truly at the end of the whole course of historical events, in the sense of the ultimate confirmation of the truth of God's all-encompassing power, is not explicitly present here. The present assurance of the ultimate truth of God, expressed through the perspective of determinism, seems to eliminate the need: the futural certainty of God is claimed already to be. The objection can be raised that only the coming to pass of the proleptically unveiled eschatological End can truly confirm the truth of the seer's claim, and that point would be well taken. But the crux of the matter is that no such sense of the present insufficiency of the seer's disclosure of the truth of God is manifest in the apocalyptic texts themselves. To the contrary, that which is to be definitively revealed in the eschatological future is not the being of God but other realities, such as the "righteous judgment" (I Enoch 91:14) or the Elect One (I Enoch 62:1, 3). Though frequent reference is made to the eschatological coming of the "glory" of God, nowhere does there appear the phrase so significant in the Old Testament, "and then shall the glory of Yahweh be revealed." And the only place in the apocalyptic literature examined here where the crucial *Erweiswort* appears is in Jubilees 1:28; otherwise, the sense that with the coming of the end time the knowledge of Yahweh will be definitively established is not explicitly maintained. On the other hand, the place where that concept *is* distinctly present is in the earlier "proto-apocalyptic" of the Gog-Magog passage of Ezekiel 38-39 and at the conclusion of the apocalyptic prophecy in Joel 3:17. It is as if this theme puts in an important appearance during the earlier, transitional period of apocalyptic's development and then drops out of the heart of the tradition--perhaps as more and more weight comes to be placed upon the sense of historical determinism and the timelessness of the realm of heaven.

7) The Son of Man. This appears as a very minor motif, present only in Daniel and the Similitudes of I Enoch.[107] In the former case, the figure actually does nothing at all except receive the Kingdom. In the latter case, he functions as eschatological judge. In either instance, the phrase designates not a human individual but some sort of heavenly being.

171

The summary conclusion derived from the foregoing, particularly so far as apocalyptic's interpretation of history in relation to God is concerned, does not share Pannenberg's enthusiastic endorsement of the apocalyptic mode of thought. It seems significantly to be the case that apocalyptic does indeed dehistoricize history, precisely in its universal-historical orientation: it closes history off from its yet-upon future, in viewing the future to be as determinately settled as the past. It amounts to a surrendering of the *risk* inherent in historical processes for the sake of an absolute ground of assurance that "everything will come out all right in the end."

In this regard, then, the tradition of apocalyptic would appear to represent the dead end which eventuates when the concern to delineate God's promised future is subjected to precise definition: apocalyptic becomes idolatry. It represents the problem of woman and man as standing before a God who promises trustworthiness and desiring to penetrate to, and grasp unequivocally, the ground of that promise. It is therefore a failure of nerve, an unwillingness to be content with the provisionality of our finite knowledge and with the true contingency[108] of all historical reality. It is therefore, in the final analysis . . . a cop-out!

NOTES

[1]Although there is now a movement away from letting "apocalyptic" serve as a noun as well as an adjective, and no doubt for valid reasons (see, *e.g.,* Paul Hanson's list of defintions in "Apocalypticism," *The Interpreter's Dictionary of the Bible, Supplementary Volume,* ed. Keith Crim [Nashville: Abingdon Press, 1976], pp. 29-31, where "apocalyptic" is always followed by a thus-qualified noun--"eschatology," "movement," "community," "symbolic universe," etc.), the practice earlier in vogue will be retained here. The primary reason is that "apocalyptic" seems to be the only sufficiently accurate translation for both the German adjective *apokalyptisch* and the German noun *Apokalyptik.* "Apocalypticism," as "the symbolic universe in which an apocalyptic movement codifies its identity and interpretation of reality" in Hanson's defintion (p. 30), may eventually come to serve as a generally unifying term, but the scholarly jury is still out on that.

[2]"Eschatology and the Experience of Meaning," *IGHF,* p. 197.

[3]"Redemptive Event and History," *BQT* I, pp. 19f.

[4]"Dogmatic Theses on the Doctrine of Revelation," *RaH*, pp. 132f.

[5]"The Revelation of God in Jesus of Nazareth," *TaH*, p. 133, italics his.

[6]"Redemptive Event and History," *BQT* I, p. 22.

[7]"The Revelation of God," *TaH*, p. 122.

[8]So Bultmann, *History and Eschatology*, pp. 27f.

[9]"Redemptive Event and Hiistory," *BQT* I, p. 23. It is apparent that Pannenberg defines "eschatology" somewhat independently of its rootedness in the Greek adjective *eschatos,* meaning "last." The term takes on the broader meaning of any futural occurrence of a fulfillment of divine promise, which makes it possible to distinguish between a prophetic inner-historical eschatology and a distinctively apocalyptic "end-historical" eschatology that accents the "last" days of the history of this aeon. So also H. D. Preuss understands eschatology to be a legitimate working out of the essential characteristic of Israel's faith as a faith in Yahweh that includes futural expectation as its decisive factor. See his *Jahwehglaube und Zukunftserwartung* (Stuttgart: W. Kohlhammer Verlag, 1968). Eschatology, for Preuss, does signify the coming of a final, conclusive act of God which fulfills history (206-08), but it is essentially continuous with a thrust in Israel's understanding from the outset, so that Preuss can maintain that "eschatology, for the Old Testament, is theology made explicit" (207) and "explication of theology in application to history" (210). The basis for this understanding is explored in the whole of Preuss's book and summarized in the final chapter: "Israel's peculiarity was and is Israel's relation to God. This also was the determining factor for the development of Old Testament eschatology. Yahweh is the God who reveals godself in history, who possesses power and deploys it, who intersperses godself and God's character in this history as the God who is leading things to the goal of God's way. As this Lord, God is . . . necessarily the coming and futural one. . . . Israel therefore hopes primarily for God, not firstly for a happy future, even if both appear within the Old Testament as inseparable. . . . The 'eschatology' of the Old Testament, in the full sense of the word, is therewith the legitimate expression and meaningful development of the future relatedness of Yahweh faith. . . . it is a question namely of the expectation of the final coming of Yahweh . . . " (206f.)

[10]"Dogmatic Theses," *RaH*, pp. 132f.

[11]*Ibid.,* p. 145; "The Revelation of God," *TaH*, p. 112; *JGM*, pp. 60f. See also Wilckens, "The Understanding of Revelation," *RaH*, p. 70.

173

^{12}JGM, pp. 66f., 74f., 78; "Dogmatic Theses," RaH, pp. 141, 146f. The particular meaning which Pannenberg ascribes to this metaphorical image will be explored in the chapter following.

^{13}"Future and Unity," HFM, p. 71.

^{14}AC, p. 172, italics mine.

^{15}Ibid., p. 173. See also the elaboration upon this notion in "Zeit und Ewigkeit in der religiösen Erfahrung israels und des Christentums," GsT II, pp. 199-202.

^{16}"Heilsgeschehen und Geschichte," GsT I, p. 41 (not translated in BQT): The "overview of history" (futural history?) by apocalyptic tends to appear as a "Vorgriff auf" (encroachment upon?) the freedom of God and a "self-assurance of persons against God." Pannenberg continues there: "In that we take the promise from God's hand, so to speak, prescribe to God how the fulfillment must appear, there is already an anthropocentrism at work. . ." Gerhard Sauter has criticized apocalyptic as an attempt to bind the promise of God into an eschatological system in which what is promised is already a (heavenly) reality and has only to be revealed (Zukunft und Verheissung, p. 248). Pannenberg's later writing would appear to be championing that orientation rather than trascending it.

^{17}JGM, pp. 82f.

^{18}Dietrich Rössler, Gesetz und Geschichte: Untersuchungen zur Theologie der jüdischen Apokalyptik und der pharisäischen Orthodoxie (Neukirchen: Neukirchener Verlag, 1960).

^{19}Ibid., p. 43.

^{20}Ibid., pp. 43f.

^{21}This would seem to represent a rather slipshod misappropriation of Pannenberg's understanding of the importance of the whole for discerning individual meanings: it overlooks the fact that we never stand in the perspective of the whole but always must work out "provisional" understandings of unity precisely through an attention to history's individual components.

^{22}Ibid., p. 44.

^{23}Ibid., pp. 55f. In support of that conclusion, Rössler cites a number of apocalyptic texts: Daniel's visions, I Enoch 85-90 and the Apocalypse of Weeks (93, 91:12-17), the Assumption (Testament) of Moses 2-10, Testament of Levi 16-18, IV Ezra 11f., II Baruch 53-71 and 35-40, and the Apocalypse of Abraham 27ff. The list presents a critical problem: as in the case of the three "great apocalypses," so also here, no distinction is made between those apocalyptic texts which can be understood to

174

pre-date the ministry of Jesus and those which are subsequent to him. The latter derive quite certainly from the Christian era, and although a fragment of the Testament of Levi has been discovered at Qumran, there is no evidence that the apocalyptic segment is of that antiquity. The problem emerging at this point is that Rössler makes no effort to discern the role of historical development in interpreting the tradition of apocalyptic, and thus fails completely to distinguish those aspects of apocalyptic which already constitute the conceptual milieu of Jesus from those aspects which have a later derivation--and perhaps involve a counter-influence from Christian interpretations of Jesus' own ministry. Only I Enoch, among the crucial three, is clearly prior to the time of Jesus, and even there the Similitudes (chs. 37-71) present a problem inasmuch as all the sections of I Enoch except that one are discernible in Qumran scrolls. The point of these observations is that one can hardly consider the question of Jesus' indebtedness to apocalyptic thought on the basis of an understanding of apocalyptic derived from a study that makes no effort to isolate those strands of the tradition that are distinctively prior to him.

[24] *Ibid.*, p. 56.

[25] *Ibid.*, pp. 56-58.

[26] *Ibid.*, p. 58.

[27] *Ibid.*, p. 60.

[28] *Ibid.*

[29] *Ibid.*, p. 61.

[30] *Ibid.*

[31] *Ibid.*, pp. 58f.

[32] *Ibid.*, p. 62.

[33] *Ibid.*, pp. 66f.

[34] *Ibid.*, p. 68.

[35] *Ibid.*, p. 111.

[36] *Ibid.*, p. 112.

[37] Philipp Vielhauer, "Apocalypses and Related Subjects: Introduction," *New Testament Apocrypha*, Vol. II, ed. E. Hennecke and W. Schneemelcher (Philadelphia: The Westminster Press, 1965), p. 593: "The entire presentation is so one-sided as to have no longer any value. Since the essential thing in Apocalyptic has been missed out, the

book is scarecely a lasting contribution to the understanding of this religio-historical phenomenon." Vielhauer is apparently referring to apocalyptic's dualistic perspective as the "essential thing."

[38]Hans Dieter Betz, "The Concept of Apocalyptic in the Theology of the Pannenberg Group," *Journal for Theology and the Church 6: Apocalypticism,* ed. Robert W. Funk (New York: Herder and Herder, 1969), pp. 192-207. (The essay circulated in mimeographed form from 1967.) William R. Murdock, "History and Revelation in Jewish Apocalypticism," *Interpretation* 21, 1967, pp. 167-87. Andreas Nissen, "Tora und Geschichte im Spätjudentum," *Novum Testamentum* 9, 1967, pp. 241-77.

[39]Nissen, *op. cit.,* pp. 246f.

[40]Betz, *op. cit.,* p. 198. It is precisely the latter methodological approach that Betz called for in an earlier article "On the Problem of the Religio-Historical Understanding of Apocalypticism," *Journal for Theology and the Church 6: Apocalypticism,* pp. 134-56.

[41]Betz, *op. cit.,* p. 199.

[42]Nissen, *op. cit.,* pp. 244f., 247.

[43]Betz, *op. cit.,* pp. 201f.

[44]But I Enoch 85-90 would represent a significant exception to this, even though animal symbolism stands in the place of periodization as a historical schema.

[45]Nissen, *op. cit.,* pp. 270f. There is an oversimplification here: the only history that the apocalyptists know of prior to the Exile is their own Israelite history! Their particular perspective in seizing upon a thread of meaning in universal history cannot be the basis for denying their concern for history entire. Furthermore, Nissen would have to exclude the Sibylline Oracles (III:97ff.) from apocalyptic consideration to maintain his point of mutual exclusion.

[46]*Ibid.,* p. 272.

[47]Murdock, *op. cit.,* p. 174.

[48]*Ibid.,* pp. 172, 179.

[49]*Ibid.,* p. 179.

[50]*Ibid.,* p. 171.

[51]*Ibid.,* pp. 175-79.

[52]*Ibid.*, p. 180.

[53]*Ibid.*, p. 186.

[54]*Ibid.*, p. 187.

[55]Betz, *op. cit.*, pp. 200f. The issue is peripheral to the concerns of this study but not altogether unimportant. The impetus to the discussion emerged in Gerhard von Rad's suggestion that the roots of the apocalyptic tradition are to be found not in prophecy but precisely in the Old Testament tradition of wisdom. *(Old Testament Theology*, vol. II, trans. D. M. G. Stalker [New York: Harper & Row, 1965], pp. 301-08.) Von Rad's initial concern was to accent what he regarded as a fundamental incompatibility between the orientations of prophecy and apocalyptic, particularly concerning the historical predeterminism of the latter (303f.), and he seemed simply to posit wisdom as the correct matrix of apocalyptic in order to satisfy the need for an alternative derivation (see 306).   But in the fourth (untranslated) edition of that work, von Rad went into far greater detail on the conceptual relationships between the two traditions, noting parallels in regard to the titles of the apocalyptic figures, the importance of knowledge, enlightenment through divine charisma, and a tendency toward dehistoricizing in the concept of historical determinism. *(Theologie des Alten Testaments*, 4th ed., vol. II [München: Chr. Kaiser Verlag, 1965], pp. 316-21.) The latter point is a particularly crucial one, for von Rad's contention is that the Old Testament tradition can hardly be seen to flower into a championing of the historical if both wisdom and apocalyptic represent a "fundamentally historyless thinking" (321). But Pannenberg has offered his own rejoinder to that interpretation, insisting to the contrary that a pretemporal divine determinism of history was a late-blooming mythical thought-form that does not encompass completely the essential wisdom motif that God binds the times together to effect an overarching meaning of history. ("Glaube und Wirklichkeit im Denken Gerhard von Rads," *Gerhard von Rad: Seine Bedeutung für die Theologie*, ed. Hans Walter Wolff [München: Chr. Kaiser Verlag, 1973], pp. 49-54, especially pp. 52f.)   At any rate, the question of the roots of apocalyptic--whether in prophecy or in wisdom, whether purely or primarily within the indigenous Israelite tradition or through major influence from such other sources as Persia--would seem to be a rather premature one to try to answer conclusively at this stage of critical apocalyptic study, although the work of Paul D. Hanson has begun to shed considerable light on that subject. *(The Dawn of Apocalyptic* [Philadelphia: Fortress Press, 1975].) Von Rad himself acknowledges the complexity of growth of that tradition of which only the surface has begun to be scratched by careful form-critical and traditio-historical investigation. *(Theologie des Alten Testaments*, 4th ed., vol. II, pp. 323, 329.) It seems particularly problematic, in von Rad's case, to reject apocalyptic's possible rootedness in prophecy because of a presumed conceptual incompatibility and maintain at the same time that scholarship is still very much in the process of trying to identify what specifically constitutes apocalyptic conceptuality *(e.g., ibid.,* pp. 315, 327).

[56]Martin Seils, review of *Dogma und Denkstructuren* (ed. W. Joest and W. Pannenberg), *ThLZ* 91, 1966, col. 15.

[57] The subtitle of his *The Rediscovery of Apocalyptic*, trans. Margaret Kohl (London: SCM Press, 1972).

[58] "Whoever employs the concept apocalyptic should remain cognizant of the fact that it has not yet been successful to define it in a satisfactory way." (Von Rad, *Theologie des Alten Testaments*, 4th ed., vol. II, p. 315.)

[59] Odil Hannes Steck, *Israel und das gewaltsame Geschick der Propheten* (Neukirchen: Neukirchener Verlag, 1967). Steck maintains that it is still too early to speak of "apocalyptic" as a precise theological position in light of the insufficiency of knowledge about its relationship to other thought-forms in that period of Judaism's history. It may or may not have been, per se, a "particular thought-world" of its own, Steck suggests (193).

[60] Koch, *op. cit.*, pp. 11f., 15, 123f. This is now beginning to be done. A new generation of scholarship in apocalyptic literature has arisen on this side of the Atlantic in the past decade, led particularly by John J. Collins, Paul D. Hanson, and George W. E. Nickelsberg. All future attempts to evaluate the content and meaning of the apocalyptic message will benefit considerably from their careful explorations into the specific textual components of the tradition.

[61] *Ibid.*, pp. 40f.

[62] *Ibid.*, pp. 86-91.

[63] *Ibid.*, p. 42. The quotations are from Rössler, *op. cit.*, p. 68.

[64] Robert Henry Charles, *A Critical History of the Doctrine of a Future Life in Israel, in Judaism, and in Christianity*, 2nd rev. ed. (London: A. and C. Black, 1913), p. 183; *A Critical and Exegetical Commentary on the Book of Daniel* (Oxford: The Clarendon Press, 1929), pp. xxv, cxiv-cxv.

[65] D. S. Russell, *The Method and Message of Jewish Apocalyptic* (Philadelphia: The Westminster Press, 1964), pp. 218, 224.

[66] Stanley Brice Frost, *Old Testament Apocalyptic* (London: Epworth Press, 1952), p. 8.

[67] Lars Hartman, *Prophecy Interpreted* (Lund: CWK Gleerup, 1966), p. 23.

[68] Amos Wilder, "The Rhetoric of Ancient and Modern Apocalyptic," *Interpretation* 25, 1971, p. 443.

[69] Steck, *op. cit.*, pp. 153ff., 192f. Steck adduces Deut. 4 and 28-30 in support of his view, but that is highly problematic. There is no indication in those passages that the *whole* of history as a unity is encompassed.

[70]Walter Schmitals, *The Apocalyptic Movement: Introduction and Interpretation*, trans. John Steely (Nashville: Abingdon Press, 1975), p. 17. (See also pp. 18-20, 31-35.)

[71]*Ibid.*, p. 33.

[72]Von Rad, *Theologie des Alten Testaments*, 4th ed., vol. II, pp. 328f.

[73]Bultmann, *History and Eschatology*, pp. 30, 59. Murdock essentially follows Bultmann here.

[74]Vielhauer, *op. cit.*, pp. 587-93.

[75]Von Rad, *Theologie des Alten Testaments*, 4th ed., vol. II, pp. 320f.

[76]S. B. Frost, "Apocalyptic and History," *The Bible in Modern Scholarship*, ed. J. Philip Hyatt (New York: Abingdon Press, 1965), pp. 99, 105, 110-12.

[77]*Ibid.*, p. 112.

[78]Paul Hanson, "Old Testament Apocalyptic Reexamined," *Interpretation* 25, 1971, p. 478, ft. 19.

[79]Schmitals, *op. cit.*, p. 39.

[80]*Ibid.*, pp. 40, 42, 45, 46, 49.

[81]*Ibid.*, p. 42.

[82]The work of John J. Collins is particularly relevant in this regard. See his trailblazing introductions to the genre of apocalyptic in his *The Apocalyptic Imagination* (New York: The Crossroad Publishing Co., 1984), pp. 1-32, and *Daniel; with an Introduction to Apocalyptic Literature* (Grand Rapids, Michigan: William B. Eerdmanns Publishing Co., 1984), pp. 1-24. In many respects, Collins is not only recategorizing the answers but calling for significant shifts in what questions are properly to be addressed. He is especially critical of the notion that there is one single "apocalyptic eschatology" to be gleaned from the strikingly varied literature that belongs to the genre (see *The Apocalyptic Imagination*, p. 9), though he acknowledges that all the apocalypses "involve a transcendent eschatology that looks for retribution beyond the bounds of history" (*ibid.*).

[83]Koch, *op. cit.*, ch. 3; Vielhauer, *op. cit.*, pp. 582-94.

[84]Koch, *op. cit.*, p. 28.

179

[85]Vielhauer, *op. cit.*, p. 582.

[86]Koch calls attention to the fact that the "discourse cycles" in which this is contained are sometimes only auditions. (*Op. cit.*, p. 24.)

[87]The working definition recently proposed by John Collins extrapolates from a "common core of constant elements" discerned in Jewish, Christian, Gnostic, and Greco-Roman apocalypses to state: *"'Apocalypse' is a genre of revelatory literature with a narrative framework, in which a revelation is mediated by an otherworldly being to a human recipient, disclosing a transcendent reality which is both temporal, insofar as it envisages eschatological salvation, and spatial, insofar as it involves another, supernatural world."* (Collins, "Introduction: Towards the Morphology of a Genre," *Semeia* 14, 1979, p. 9, italics his.)

[88]Collins, on the basis of his genre definition, concludes that the Testaments of the Twelve Patriarchs, the Sibylline Oracles, and the Testament of Moses, as well as I Enoch 91-104, are not in the literary form of apocalypses but nevertheless are related types, containing important features of apocalyptic eschatology. (*Ibid.,* pp. 44-47.) A similar observation is made concerning Qumran material (48), and would also embrace the Psalms of Solomon. All of these texts figure prominently in this analysis, however, precisely because the primary point of orientation is just that apocalyptic echatology which comes to expression both *in* the genre and elsewhere as well.

[89]Individual units of I Enoch are treated here separately, following the identification of sections by R. H. Charles. See Charles, ed., *The Apocrypha and Pseudepigrapha of the Old Testament* (Oxford: Clarendon Press, 1913), vol. II, pp. 168-70. Translations of non-biblical apocalyptic literature are taken from that work, except for Qumran material.

[90]Admittedly, I Enoch 22:9-13 can possibly be interpreted to imply the resurrection of the righteous, but without absolute certainty. The phrase "those who rise," in 20:8, is also somewhat obscure.

[91]The possibility that this section of I Enoch has its origin in the Christian era is suggested by the fact that fragments of every part of the book except this one have been recognized among the finds at Qumran. David Suter's review of the recent literature on the Similitudes ("Weighed in the Balance: The Similitudes of Enoch in Recent Discussion," *Religious Studies Review* 7, 1981, pp. 217-21) reinforces this conclusion on other grounds as well. Suter's own argument that the writing has Jewish, not Christian, provenance also includes the verdict that its date or origin is "not much before" 70 A. D. (p. 218), with which Collins concurs (*The Apocalyptic Imagination*, p. 143). On the other hand, George Nickelsburg offers strong evidence for an earlier date "around the turn of the [Christian] era" (G. W E. Nickelsburg, *Jewish Literature Between the Bible and the Mishnah* [Philadelphia: Fortress Press, 1981], pp. 221-23), so that the question of the applicability of the Similitudes in this study remains open yet.

[92]See especially ch. 62. Cf. also I Enoch 46:1-6; 48:3-7; 63:11; 69:26-29; 70:1.

[93]There appears to be an overlapping of a broad spectrum of material from second century B. C. E. to second and third centuries C. E., with both Christian and Jewish interpolations on what may have once been a consistent unit. The best evidence for antiquity of *part* is the discovery at Qumran of fragments of the Testament of Levi and Naphtali. It would seem that the Testaments as a whole are relatively unreliable as sources for distinctively pre-Christian apocalyptic tradition, though the jury is still out on where the traces of antiquity are precisely to be found.

[94]This title is now in broader usage than the earlier "Assumption of Moses" (see 1:1). Current scholarship is strongly inclined to date chs. 1-5, 8-12 as Maccabean or even slightly earlier, with ch. 6 (and, with less unanimity, ch. 7) introduced by a post-Herodian redactor. See George W. E. Nickelsburg, *Resurrection, Immorality, and Eternal Life in Intertestamental Judaism* (Cambridge: Harvard University Press, 1972), pp. 43-45, and his "An Antiochan Date for the Testament of Moses," in *idem,* ed., *Studies on the Testament of Moses* (Cambridge: Society of Biblical Literature, 1973), pp. 33-37, along with John Collins' response, "Some Remaining Traditio-Historical Problems in the Testament of Moses," *ibid.,* pp. 38-43.

[95]Pss. of Sol. 3:13, 16; 9:9; 13:9-10; 14:2, 3, 7; 15:13-15. No suggestion of the time of resurrection is made either, except in the latter passage where the resurrection is implicitly coupled with "the day of the Lord's judgment."

[96]"And at that time the Lord will heal His servants, and they shall rise up and see great peace. . . . And their bones shall rest in the earth, and their spirits shall have much joy."

[97]Quotations of Qumran materials are taken from A. Dupont-Sommer, *The Essene Writings from Qumran,* trans. G. Vermes (Oxford: Basil Blackwell, 1961).

[98]See, *e.g.,* Zadokite Fragments 4:8-10; 6:10f.

[99]1QS 3:18, 4:18-22; Zadokite Fragments 7:9.

[100]It is perhaps a result of the confusion of competing interpretations that the term "apocalyptic" has been wrenched from its tradition-historical moorings and utilized extensively in current parlance to characterize any and every sense of a coming catastrophic denouement of the historical process.

[101]See *supra,* p. 152.

[102]Russell, *op. cit.,* p. 285. Russell acknowledges, however, that the underlying concept is nevertheless reflected there.

[103]Martin Rist, "Jesus and Eschatology," *Transitions in Biblical Scholarship*, ed. J. Coert Rylaarsdam (Chicago: The University of Chicago Press, 1968), pp. 208f.

[104]Collins makes this point, that resurrection is not an altogether necessary component in the motif of a transcending of death, in "Apocalyptic Eschatology as the Transcendence of Death," *Catholic Biblical Quarterly* 36, 1974, pp. 34-37.

[105]The manner and context in which resurrection is alluded to in II Maccabees (7:9, 11, 23, 29; 12:44) provides no basis for a judgment on whether and to what extent the resurrection hope there is linked with the anticipation of history's terminus or radical eschatological developments.

[106]Collins puts forth an intriguing proposal that the apocalyptic perspective holds determinism and individual human freedom in tension: "In the apocalyptic view, the course of events is predetermined. This does not mean that there is no room for human freedom. People can determine their own destiny by their reactions, but they cannot change the course of events." (*The Apocalyptic Imagination*, p. 87.) The presumption here is that the whole (of history) is constituted by something altogether different from the sum of its parts (human activity, *inter alia*). More attention needs to be given to this thesis by Collins if it is to be rendered persuasive as an interpretation of apocalyptic.

[107]On the strong possibility that the latter are not pre-Jesus in date of origin, see *supra* , ch. 6, note 91.

[108]To claim, as Pannenberg does, that contingency is retained by ascribing it to history's ground of unity--*i.e.,* to God--will be critically evaluated in the discussion of divine causality in chapter eight.

7

JESUS

A. The Significance of the Historical Jesus

The question of the value of the contribution of Jesus of Nazareth for an understanding of the truth of God is one that immediately calls attention to the problem of identifying the extent to which the kerygmatic portrayal of Jesus faithfully communicates the meaning of the history of Jesus. Pannenberg insists that one cannot simply accept uncritically, as the fundamental datum for a Christian understanding of reality, the "kerygmatic Christ" of the apostolic community of faith. Nor can one make that the legitimate beginning point for the development of a Christology that seeks to make clear the relationship between Jesus and God. Precisely such an orientation, however, has been influential in theological circles ever since the work of Martin Kähler,[1] who correctly perceived that the *effect* of a person--in this case, the kerygmatic faith-- belongs to the historical actuality of that person. But that insight into the internal interrelation of an event and its received significance cannot be allowed to obscure the fact that the effects of Jesus are not to be found simply in the apostolic preaching, nor is that which is "truly historic" about Jesus only his personal effect. Though continuity between the two must be acknowledged, there is also the realization that the kerygmatic accounts reflect their own respective situations and individual perspectives, and it is possible, even necessary, to distinguish the figure of Jesus and the outlines of his message from them.[2] This necessity cannot be evaded by elevating a particular moment in the history of the transmission of the kerygma to a position of inviolable dependability. That is rendered impossible by recognition of the fact that the kerygma cannot justify its own existence, nor can any one stage in the development of the kerygma be used as the basis for deciding upon the conceptual adequacy of any other--neither what is crystallized into the

183

canon of the New Testament, for what is at stake there is the question of an underlying unity amid competing and even contradictory formulations, nor any ascertainable "original kerygma," for one has to reckon with an initial multiplicity of interpretations and not a single unified perspective. An evaluation of the truth-bearing character of the kerygma can only be carried out, therefore, in terms of an exploration into the adequacy with which *any* stage of the transmission of tradition legitimately articulates the meaning of the events upon which it is grounded and to which it testifies.[3]

The impetus in this direction is already contained in the kerygma itself, in that what is proclaimed in Christianity are historical events which are not merely the "external occasion" for its rise but also explicitly its "essential content" to which it continues to be related.[4] The question is therefore precisely whether the kerygma is successful in seizing upon the true meaning of those events. And the principle that the meaning of an event is not something external to it, to be affixed by the believing or non-believing observer, but is rather inherent in it, standing in judgment upon all endeavors to perceive it, decisively calls for a continuing critique of all kerygmatic formulations of the meaning of Jesus of Nazareth for humankind.[5]

> Only if the history of Jesus--understood in its original historical context and not as an isolated event by itself--has its meaning in itself will one be able to show, positively, how and to what extent the inherent meaning of the event itself has been unfolded in the various forms of the kerygma and in the language of each new situation in this history of the transmission of tradition in primitive Christianity or, negatively, to what extent a specific form of witness must be judged to be a diminished statement of the Christ-event in this or that respect.[6]

Insofar as that is so, Pannenberg maintains, the inquiry that moves behind the texts to raise the question of the historical Jesus himself is "theologically unavoidable."[7]

The procedure which Pannenberg proposes to follow is one which he calls "Christology from below," which he distinguishes from an approach that takes as its initial assumption--the incarnation of God in this person Jesus--precisely what is to be determined in the historical inquiry. Pannenberg wants to take "the historical man Jesus in his historical singularity" with utmost seriousness, and this rules out presupposing a unity of Jesus with God as the initial context in which that history is probed. One cannot take as one's point of departure the kerygma in which that unity is already affirmed, but must move to an assessment of the legitimacy of that interpretation out of direct consideration of the history to which the concept of incarnation is kerygmatically applied.[8]

184

Wilhelm Herrmann responded to Kähler's emphasis upon the primary significance of the kerygma with a protest against basing one's faith upon that which is itself a product of faith--*i.e.*, the proclamation alone--and which may not be historical fact at all (*except* as proclamation).[9] But Herrmann resisted the conclusion that faith should otherwise be based on the history of Jesus as accessible to historical inquiry, for he could not endorse the principle that faith could be exposed to the inconstancy of scholarly research. Bultmann has continued this line of reasoning in his approach to Jesus in the New Testament. But Pannenberg is insistent that the only way to establish the true significance of Jesus "from his history" is through the utilization of the tools of critical historical study, and he finds support, at least in principle, in the revival of a quest for the historical Jesus among Bultmann's own disciples.[10]

To a considerable extent, Pannenberg's participation in the endeavor to recover the pre-kerygmatic Jesus is continuous with, and dependent upon, the work of the post-Bultmannians in transcending the pitfalls of the "old" question culminating with Schweitzer.[11] Particularly he shares the disavowal of the possibility of reconstructing anything in the way of a biography of Jesus on the basis of the non-chronological sequences of the Gospels. Focus is placed rather on the shape of the teaching of Jesus as reflective of the crucial truth about him, and upon those actions which also exemplify that teaching.[12] What is sought are those essential characteristics of the person of Jesus whose continuity with the kerygmatic formulations cannot be presupposed but must be critically established, and the primary means for accomplishing that search is by employing the fruits of form-critical exegesis.

But Pannenberg's involvement with the new quest is anything but an unqualified endorsement of the way the post-Bultmannians have gone about it. The differences separating them are perhaps as extensive as the common concerns that have brought them to the same task. There is, for instance, the fact that whereas the latter tend to shy away from the consideration that their enterprise is implicitly directed toward a legitimation of the kerygma through Jesus himself,[13] Pannenberg explicitly affirms that "the question about the history of Jesus is inescapable for the legitimation of the kerygma as a message that is derived from Jesus,"[14] for reasons already indicated. Furthermore, Pannenberg is interested not simply in the "understanding of human existence" that emerges in Jesus' own self-understanding but beyond that with "the total historical phenomenon of the figure of Jesus in all its strangeness,"[15] which necessarily includes the historical context within which that phenomenon possesses its own inherent meaning. Finally, the preunderstanding which he brings with him to the task of comprehending the pre-kerygmatic person of Jesus is at variance with

185

the Heideggerian categories of thought employed by the post-Bultmannians. I have endeavored to identify the features of that pre-understanding in the preceding chapters. The extent to which Pannenberg is more successful in allowing the subject of the inquiry to call into question the sufficiency of the categories employed will be considered herein.

Pannenberg is nowhere explicit about the procedures or criteria to be employed in penetrating to the actual history of Jesus, tending instead to build upon the emerging consensus of New Testament scholarship with his own instances of critical engagement where he finds the consensus unacceptable. But one point, on which he is decisively emphatic, deserves special attention. Norman Perrin proposed a trio of criteria to be utilized in determining the authentic teachings of Jesus within the Gospels, two of which are secondary to the principal one that he called the "criterion of dissimilarity."[16] He formulated it thus:

> . . . the earliest form of a saying we can reach may be regarded as authentic if it can be shown to be dissimilar to characteristic emphases both of ancient Judaism and of the early Church, and this will particularly be the case where Christian tradition oriented towards Judaism can be shown to have modified the saying away from its original emphasis.[17]

Perrin openly acknowledged the rationale operative behind his commitment to that criterion with his subsequent assertion that "if we are to seek that which is most characteristic of Jesus, it will be found not in the things which he shares with his contemporaries, but in the things wherein he differs from them."[18] But to presuppose that at the outset of one's inquiry, rather than demonstrate it as a conclusion thereof, is to foreclose in advance on the very possibility that the actual Jesus *was* very much in continuity with the thought-world of his day--and that what may be of preeminent importance in the message of Jesus is not its unprecedented singularity but the manner in which it blended existing tradition with genuine novelty. Particularly given his emphasis on the character of history as that of a continuing transmission of traditions, Pannenberg is predisposed not to isolate the teaching of Jesus from its conceptual context but to grasp its content precisely within the horizons of understanding in which it was formulated--horizons which Jesus himself cannot simply be *presupposed* not to have shared.[19] The point of this difference of approach is especially detectable in considering the question of the extent to which Jesus' mesage is imbued with features derived from the horizon of Jewish apocalyptic, and it is that issue which leaps into focus as we turn to Pannenberg's interpretation of the significant aspects of Jesus' teaching relevant to the truth of God.

B. Jesus, Apocalyptic, and the Reign of God

> The activity and destiny of Jesus naturally have their significance originally on the horizon of the history of Jewish traditions within whose context Jesus appeared. The original significance of Jesus' activity and destiny must be ascertained from this their nearest horizon. Only to the extent that the situation in the Jewish history of traditions out of which Jesus emerged with his message must be seen as determined by Jewish apocalyptic does it become necessary to describe the significance of the activity and destiny of Jesus in relation to the background of apocalyptic theology. This does not mean that the figure of Jesus melts into this background. Rather, it means primarily that his uniqueness is set off from this background.[20]

The process of discerning precisely the relationship between these two--the apocalyptic background and the particular manner in which Jesus critically appropriated it--is one to which Pannenberg, in company with Ulrich Wilckens, has devoted a fair amount of attention. Given the rather common recognition that Jesus was surrounded by an atmosphere of apocalyptic conceptuality that both preceded and followed him, in the message of John the Baptist and in the interpretations of Jesus in the primitive Christian community,[21] Pannenberg regards as "historically not very probable" the thesis of Käsemann[22] and others[23] that Jesus could have stood high and dry on an island of individuality untouched by the waves of apocalyptic lapping all around him.[24] That amounts to an overemphasis on Jesus' unique particularity at the expense of his continuity with his heritage. The issue is hardly resolvable by such a one-sided perspective. On the other hand, the acknowledgment by Bornkamm that Jesus thought and spoke within the context of apocalyptic expectations[25] does not solve but only expresses the crucial problem--of identifying where apocalyptic leaves off and the particularity of Jesus' message and person begins, and of identifying to what extent that particularity can be seen to represent anything in the way of a transcending of its tradition-historical roots.

Pannenberg suggests that Jesus' message is properly to be seen as a sort of "apocalyptically colored prophecy" which had as its fundamental content the "general eschatological expectation of God's reign."[26] He shared with the apocalyptic tradition the anticipation of a Son of Man who would accompany the definitive inbreaking of the consummating rule of God,[27] and he maintained the "apocalyptic scheme of history" in respect to its universal-historical framework, particularly with regard to the expectation of a unifying end of history that God would bring about.[28]

But the primary thread of continuity upon which Pannenberg focuses the greatest amount of direct attention concerns the apocalyptic horizon of Jesus' remarkable claim of authority. This is observable in two respects. First, Jesus presupposes the apocalyptic understanding of the ultimately surpassable character of the Torah in his claim to possess an authority transcending that of the Torah. His word could be set over against the words of the Law only in a context in which the Law could be understood as something less than the eternal will of God, and such a context is precisely to be found in the apocalyptic expectation of an incomparably new and superior act of God that will go beyond every previous manifestation of God.[29] Second, and far more importantly, the form of Jesus' claim is continuous with apocalyptic tradition by virtue of its proleptic structure that required futural confirmation. It was not valid on its own account, for the content of the claim consisted in the announcement of the coming of God's powerful future and therefore was grounded in a historical eventuality grasped in advance. This accords with what is understood to be characteristic of apocalyptic thought, that the disclosure of God's truth in the present is directed toward the futural complex of events in which it will only then be definitively revealed.[30]

That does not entail, however, that Jesus is simply to be understood as a transmitter of apocalyptic concepts. To maintain that would be to err in the opposite direction, of failing to recognize the distinctiveness of Jesus as set off from his apocalyptic background. Jesus was "not an apocalyptic seer"[31] nor were his claims simply a "radicalization" of the claims of the apocalyptic visionary.[32] There are four areas where Pannenberg discerns a profound difference that sets Jesus and his proclamation apart from his predecessors.[33] (1) Jesus forthrightly exposed his own selfhood instead of following the traditional apocalyptic practice of employing a pseudonym.[34] (2) He so greatly emphasized the imminence of the end that he manifested no interest in portraying the path leading up to it.[35] (3) Jesus not only called persons to repentance in preparation for the coming of God's Reign but he claimed for himself a central role concerning the issue of who would receive the gift of eschatological salvation,[36] such that the coming salvation already made its proleptic appearance in him. (4) Finally, Jesus' ministry constituted not only a pre-cognition but even a pre-actualization of the coming end,[37] to the effect that the sharp distinction between the aeons is made to vanish--"whereby the compass of what is possible in apocalyptic theology is clearly overstepped."[38] Radical imminence is singularly conjoined with proleptic presentness.[39]

The question of how to categorize these (and possibly other) aspects of Jesus' departure from his apocalyptic horizon of understanding, in terms of the degree to which he does or does not "spring" the apocalyptic framework or "shatter"[40] apocalyptic conceptuality, is a difficult one to answer. There is a need to delineate more sharply what is meant by saying that Jesus "thought in apocalyptic categories" without actually being an apocalyptist."[41] There is a need to become clearer about how apocalyptic can remain the "intellectual context"[42] of a message that simultaneously breaks open significant aspects of that tradition. To achieve this will depend, to a large extent, not only upon how one understands Jesus' message but upon what one defines as essentially characteristic of the apocalyptic perspective.[43] Are the points at which Jesus burst the bonds of apocalyptic thinking so crucial as to constitute a transcending of his *überlieferungsgeschichtlich* context? But then, what exactly would that mean? Where does emergent novelty within a transmitted tradition pass over into a replacement of the old with the decisively new?

The questions are not raised gratuitously, for the issue becomes critical at the point of determining where Jesus may or may not be understood to have authenticated, rather than superseded, the decisive apocalyptic concept of history as universal and end-directed. Only if Jesus can be interpreted as having fundamentally endorsed the characteristic outlines of the apocalyptic understanding of history can his proclamation and destiny be received as a confirmation of that way of thinking. The issue is resolvable not through the application of broad generalizations but, if at all, only by careful attention to specific features both of the then-current tradition called apocalyptic and of the teaching of Jesus. I have offered a preliminary canvass of the former, leading to a critical assessment of Pannenberg's interpretation and appropriation thereof. It is essential now to turn our attention to Pannenberg's understanding of the latter.

It has been rather universally recognized, since the work of Weiss and Schweitzer around the turn of the century, that the major thrust of Jesus' message centered upon the Reign of God. It is Pannenberg's recognition of the truth of that thesis which has led him to emphasize the pivotal role which the idea of the Reign must play in the whole of Christian theology.[44] For the relationship of Jesus to the coming Reign is not to be understood as merely one factor among others in his proclamation but constitutive of the very heart of it.

> The teaching of Jesus, including his ethical radicalism, was dependent on his message of the imminent Kingdom of God. He viewed every aspect of his life in the light of the imminent end of the world. Every preoccupation was validated or rejected in terms of its conformity to God's action. The coming Kingdom of God--this was the single, pulsating reality of Jesus' existence. All else could be lost, if only this were to be realized. And in the realization of the Kingdom all else would be saved.[45]

Pannenberg suggests that indeed there is, strictly speaking, hardly any novelty of content in Jesus' proclamation--except for an exclusivity of emphasis that took something previously peripheral and turned it into the dominant theme in the light of which all else was to be regarded.[46]

The crucial problem, as Pannenberg sees it, is to grasp how the full complexity of Jesus' understanding of the Reign of God can be comprehended without sacrificing any aspect of it. The difficulty arises in regard to the realization that sayings attributable to the pre-kerygmatic Jesus appear to embrace not only the futural imminence of the Reign but its present presence as well.[47] As we have seen, Pannenberg insists that one cannot perceive the authentic aspects of Jesus' message by dismissing that which he shared in common with the tradition in which he stood. The issue, therefore, is to discern how *both* aspects, the presence and futurity of the Reign, are interrelated in Jesus' message.[48] And the suggestion that Pannenberg makes is that "because the futurity of the kingdom was the general perspective in Judaism, it seems more natural to start with it and then try to understand the presence of the kingdom as the qualification of the present situation by that future."[49]

On the one hand, therefore, the (apocalyptic) futurity of the Reign is understood to be fundamental to Jesus' message:[50] "the future remains future,"[51] and there persisted in his proclamation an openness toward a temporally concrete future in which God's Reign would fully transform the world.[52] The futurity of God's lordship impinging upon the present in Jesus' ministry retained its distinctiveness precisely as futural.[53] The Reign proclaimed by Jesus, as by John the Baptist, was envisaged by him as "imminent" and not as already fully arrived.[54]

But on the other hand, the Reign of God was not only something yet to be expected in the--albeit imminent--future, but something whose power was already being experienced in the present of Jesus. The power of God's future was already presently active.[55] This is particularly noticeable in the communication of eschatological salvation: Jesus "was certain that in his activity the future salvation of God's Kingdom had broken into the present time,"[56] and he directly granted that salvation as already effective to those who accepted the truth of his message.[57] This leads Pannenberg therefore to talk about Jesus' underscoring of "the *present impact* of the imminent future,"[58] and the future of the Reign as "invading" the present.[59]

The question is precisely one of how these two foci are to be brought together into a single, harmonious understanding. How is the Reign of God both a futural reality and presently at hand? Hans Conzelmann advanced the hypothesis that there is reflected in Jesus' parables no sense of an "interval" between the present moment and the coming of God's Reign, and that therefore what characterizes Jesus' eschatology is not simply a matter of "the highest possible degree of imminence" but rather an obliteration of any quantitative sense of temporality: Jesus did not give a new answer to the question of "when" but transcended the question itself.[60] Ernst Fuchs picked up on on this line of approach with the proposal that Jesus actually brought about a new understanding of time, in which the present is seen not as a transition to the future of God's coming but rather as already filled by that future, and therefore in essential correspondence with it.[61] Robert Funk has endorsd this mode of interpretation with an emphasis on Jesus' "naive" understanding of time,[62] for which the future is seen to impinge upon the present and thereby "determines the future trajectory of the present," bringing about a "coincidence of the horizons of time."[63] God's Reign is so near that it "completely overwhelms and dominates" the present, wherefore it can no longer simply be looked for or awaited.[64] And the futural fulfillment of the Reign "will do nothing other than put a period to the present experience of the inbreaking of the kingdom."[65]

Pannenberg is considerably in continuity with the formal aspect of this proposal, but parts company when the particular material element is introduced. That is to say, it is not simply a question of whether Jesus brought a new understanding of time, but of what that new understanding truly was. The question is not whether, for Jesus, the future was understood somehow to penetrate the present, but precisely how that interpenetration is to be comprehended. And Pannenberg finds in the language of "coincidence" and "correspondence" a tendency to dissolve altogether the yet outstanding character of that inbreaking future, resulting in "a deactivation of the tension between the 'already' and the 'not yet' in Jesus' message."[66]

Is a different option at hand, whereby the uniqueness of Jesus' proclamation of God's Reign can be more effectively grasped without surrendering one or another of its components? If the mistake of the apocalyptic tradition was to conceive of the future Reign of God as totally absent from the present, is there a viable way of avoiding the opposite mistake of interpreting God's Reign as *fully* (and only) a qualification of the present? Can Jesus be understood to have anticipated a futurally imminent coming of the Reign of God and yet have equally proclaimed its inbreaking presentness among the lives of those who responded to his message?

Pannenberg's interpretation of Jesus' message of the Reign of God endeavors to do precisely that. The present and future are regarded as "inextricably interwoven"[67] and "intertwined"[68] in the message and ministry of Jesus, without the one being collapsed into, or exhausted by its activity in, the other. For Jesus had a sense that, with his proclamation of the imminence of the Reign, the end had already begun and the Reign of God was already dawning.[69] Thereby the present is to be seen not as independent of God's future but as decisively effected by it,[70] such that the futurity of God's Reign becomes "the power determining the present."[71] Yet the future, as future, does not fade out. Jesus' proclamation pointed ahead to the future consummation and fulfillment of what was beginning to be a reality in his ministry. Therefore, emphasizing the primacy of the Reign's essential futurity, Pannenberg understands that futural consummation not as simply a "period" completing the inner-historical experiencing of God's Reign but as the essential reality of which the Reign's present activity is to be viewed as a "pre-realization" or "proleptic dawning": the end "has happened in advance."[72] Jesus' understanding of time is accordingly seen as one that is able to say *both* "already" and "not yet" with respect to God's inbreaking rule, as proleptically actual in the present and yet to be fully consummated in what is still futural to that present. The future is now, but precisely not limited to the now. It overflows, and it is that overflowing character of God's oncoming Reign which Pannenberg discerns in Jesus' message in his interpretation of a proleptic presence of the ultimate future. Put differently, the waves of the ultimate future are already breaking upon the present shore, as anticipations of the coming tidal crest. Only therein is preserved the sense of the yet outstanding character of the Reign as the destiny of human history which has "taken place only in the form of an anticipation of a future which in its fullness has not yet materialized."[73] In short, the elimination of the forces of destruction and conflict is hardly an experienced *fait accompli*--as Jesus' fate on the cross so decisively conveys.

Pannenberg takes his interpretation of Jesus' message of the Reign of God one further step, in a direction that is of crucial importance for our consideration here. He repeatedly gives expression to a parallelism in which the coming of God's reign is synonymous with the very coming of God.[74] Pannenberg initially finds a basis for this in recognizing that the familiarity with which Jesus relates to God as "Father" characterizes a sense of immediacy that corresponds with his proclamation of the imminent Reign, to the extent that "the nearness to God that is expressed in the address of God as Father is identical with the eschatological nearness of the Kingdom of God."[75] This is then understood as an "eschatological nearness of God," whose own future is of one piece with the future of God's Reign.[76] Therefore what is at stake in the coming of God's Reign is nothing less than the very reality of God.

The earlier writings of Pannenberg do not reflect a sense of the full identity of the being of God with God's Reign, and nowhere does he explicitly say that Jesus' own understanding was constituted by such an equation.[77] But he has gradually come to insist upon the principle that the reality and the power of God are entirely one and the same, wherefore the very being of God *is* God's lordship.[78] This has led him then to draw the conclusion that correctly to penetrate the underlying implication in Jesus' message is to comprehend that the Reign proclaimed by Jesus is indeed nothing less than "God's own ultimate reality."[79]

Beyond Jesus' specific focusing on the inbreaking of the Reign of God as the essential characteristic of his ministry, there are two further points at which Pannenberg has discerned an explicit continuity with the apocalyptic tradition, which have served to reinforce his argument that the proclamation of Jesus was apocalyptically rooted. These involve those sayings attributed to Jesus in which he seems to refer, in distinction from himself, to a Son of Man who will accompany the coming of the final end of the age and will function as judge; and, as previously observed, the unmistakable presence of a proleptic element in Jesus' claim of authority. The former of these has received diminishing emphasis from Pannenberg in the face of contemporary new Testament debate; the latter, however, expresses a particularly crucial factor in the transition to the discussion on Jesus' resurrection that follows.

Scholars have identified three different types of references to the Son of Man in Jesus' teaching in the Gospels: sayings concerning Jesus' own activity in the present; predictions concerning the suffering that Jesus as Son of Man will undergo in the future; and expressions concerning the anticipated coming of the apocalyptic Son of Man. General consensus regards the second group as *vaticinia ex eventu* compiled by the early church, and little support is found for affirming the pre-Easter authenticity of the first group. It is in respect to the apocalyptic Son of Man sayings that most of the current debate has been so intense. Following Bornkamm[80] and Tödt[81] primarily, Pannenberg considers such passages as Luke 12:8 and the parallel tradition in Mark 8:38 (Luke 9:26) to reflect Jesus' own point of view: Jesus anticipated the coming of a transcendent Son of Man as someone other than himself, who would function as judge at the end of the age and confirm Jesus' own decisive role in regard to the decision of admission into the Reign of God.[82] Support for that interpretation is found in the fact that the Gospel tradition maintains the distinction between the two figures in the words of Jesus: surely, had such passages initially arisen within the post-Easter kerygma, no such distinction would ever have been formulated, inasmuch as the tendency within the early Christian community was precisely to perceive the two as identical.[83] The thrust of this aspect of Jesus' teaching, for Pannenberg, is to reinforce the conviction of the apocalyptic rootedness of his message as well as the nature of the interdynamic between future and present already observed in the proclamation of the Reign of God.

Major objections have been raised against the claim of authenticity for this strand of the Son of Man tradition in the Gospels, centering around the twin issues of connectedness and compatibility. Philipp Veilhauer explored at some length the question of the interrelationship between Reign of God and Son of Man sayings both in the Synoptic tradition and in the eschatological expectations of intertestamental Judaism, and arrived at the conclusion that the two concepts do not really have anything to do with one another in either place; they are present in unintegrated fashion, without either contributing meaningfully to the concept of the other.[84] Vielhauer contended that the "unconnected juxtaposition" arose in the post-Easter community as attention came to be focused on the expected arrival of Jesus as Son of Man accompanying the inbreaking of God's Reign.[85] Pannenberg has followed H. E. Tödt in the converse conviction, however, that there is no convincing evidence ruling out the possibility that the two groups of sayings might have initially been brought together in disconnected co-existence in Jesus' own preaching,[86] so long as one were not to repudiate the possible authenticity of the Son of Man sayings on other grounds.

It is precisely on other grounds that the debate really is waged: Vielhauer and company have come to insist upon an essential incompatibility between Jesus' proclamation of the inbreaking Reign and his purported anticipation of a coming Son of Man. The reason for this has already been indicated in the discussion above concerning Jesus' concept of time: anyone who saw oneself in immediate relationship to the already dawning Reign of God could not possibly have looked forward to the coming of an additional eschatological figure yet to be awaited.[87] But there is a fundamental problem of methodology present here: the authenticity of certain sayings is being ruled out on the basis of a theological judgment about the meaning of another element of Jesus' teaching. Jesus *cannot* have spoken of a coming Son of Man because that anticipation is inconsistent with his existentialist understanding of time as disclosed in his proclamation of God's Reign. But this cuts both ways: if the authenticity of these sayings is feasible on the basis of other considerations, then the whole notion of Jesus' attitude toward the future must be rethought along non-existentialist lines, as Pannenberg endeavors to do.[88] And for Pannenberg, the decisive consideration has remained valid that "the characteristic way of speaking of the Son of Man in the third person and thus in distinction from the first person of Jesus could no longer have arisen after Easter."[89]

However, Pannenberg has not been particularly inclined to place a great deal of emphasis upon this facet of historical inquiry. In response to Perrin's suggestion that the Pannenbergian Christological enterprise is crucially dependent upon the authenticity of Luke 12:8,[90] he subsequently maintained that he understands his account of the character of Jesus' message to be relatively independent of the decision as to whether the apocalyptic Son of Man sayings belong authentically to the pre-Easter tradition.[91] Thus, to a certain extent at least, the significance for Pannenberg's theology of the ongoing exploration into this piece of the Gospel account has been somewhat blunted.[92]

But Pannenberg remains emphatic that a Christological appropriation of the significance of Jesus cannot rest content with the mere *claim* of authoritative truthfulness that was so characteristic of his message. The question that must be raised turns on the issue of where the justification for Jesus' claim to authority actually resides. For Pannenberg, it is impossible for the justification to be found within the context of Jesus' own ministry, because of the very nature of the message he brought: inasmuch as Jesus was pointing ahead to the decisive inbreaking of God's eschatological future, the truthfulness of his teaching remained unverified within his own lifetime. Jesus' claim implicitly involved "an anticipation of a confirmation that is to be expected only from the future."[93] It could be legitimated only by virtue of the subsequent course of events to which his message directed his hearers. Therefore in Jesus' claim is to be discerned a proleptic structure corresponding to that of the prophetic word and the apocalyptic vision.[94]

One might affirm to the contrary that an authentication of Jesus' decisive role in regard to the coming of the Reign of God is to be discerned in the power of his activity: the saving deeds of the end time were already occurring through his ministry. This would seem to be the meaning of such passages as Matthew 11:5f. and Luke 11:20. But Pannenberg, following Wilckens,[95] contends that the deeds of Jesus function only as a partial confirmation of his claim: they point to the powerful inbreaking of God's rule but they do not ground Jesus' contention that a person's relationship to the Reign of God will be determined in accordance with that person's response to Jesus himself. The deeds by themselves do not demonstrate unambiguously that Jesus is the key figure in regard to the decision of salvation or judgment.[96]

> Thus the whole of Jesus' work remained aimed at the future verification of his claim to authority, at a confirmation that Jesus himself was unable to offer precisely because and insofar as it involved the legitimation of his own person, which is bound to the arrival of the announced end event. The question about such a future confirmation of Jesus' claim by God himself is held open by the temporal difference between the beginning of God's rule, which was already present in Jesus' activity, and its future fulfillment with the coming of the Son of Man on the clouds of heaven. Even the disciples of the pre-Easter Jesus could only follow his claim to authority in trust of its future confirmation by God himself, i.e., through the occurrence of the end of history.[97]

Jesus' claim to be speaking the truth with authority, and therewith the universal significance of his message concerning God and God's rule, hangs suspended therefore between the first dim rays of the sun beyond the horizon and the full glow of daylight yet to burst forth. Insofar as the end of history has not come to pass, insofar as the eschatological fullness of the Reign of God remains futural, does the claim continue to be without sufficient confirmation? Or has the claim of Jesus been confirmed by God in some other way, continuous with Jesus' expectations but by no means thoroughly identical to them?

The keystone of Pannenberg's theology is his firm insistence that the answer to that question is already at hand, within history, in the event of Jesus' having been raised by God from death[98]--wherein the universal eschatological future awaited by all of humanity is understood to have happened in advance to this one individual. It is therefore necessary at this critical juncture to devote careful and extended attention to Pannenberg's analysis of the meanings inherent in the tradition of Jesus' resurrection and, as an equally crucial area of concern, to examine his defense of the historical authenticity of the elusive event underlying the tradition.[99]

C. The Meaning of the Resurrection

A quarter of a century ago, Richard R. Niebuhr advanced the provocative notion that, far from being regarded as non- or supra-historical, the event of Jesus' resurrection from the dead should be acknowledged by theological reason as paradigmatic for an understanding of events in history and as the key to an understanding of history itself.[100] In many respects, Pannenberg's own theological programme represents a seizing upon and carrying through with Niebuhr's underdeveloped thesis,[101] in his decisive emphasis upon the far-reaching implications of that pivotal event.

According to Pannenberg, the initial reaction of Jesus' followers to the devastating impact of his crucifixion was one of unmitigated despair. The future of the announced Reign had not broken climactically into the present; rather the proclaimer of God's eschatological rule had suffered death at the hands of the powers of this age. The hopes of eschatological consummation seemed shattered by the interruption of the cross. The immediate consequence of Jesus' death was the realization that the truth of his message about the powerful imminence of God had been seemingly repudiated: "After the crucifixion of Jesus the question of the legitimacy of his mission was no longer open; on the contrary, until something else happened, it was negatively decided."[102]

The apostolic community held fast to the conviction that something else did indeed happen, and that something else they called "resurrection"; Jesus had been "raised from the dead." Something seemingly transpired to a number of Jesus' followers which brought them to the shared conclusion that an unprecedented event had occurred in their midst, for which they could offer no other linguistic expression than that which characterized the eschatological expectation of the apocalyptic tradition.[103]

Pannenberg initially acknowledged quite readily that the term "resurrection" is metaphorical in character. It refers parabolically to an event that eludes ordinary human experience, through suggested comparison with the common experience of being awakened and rising from sleep. The term does not fully capture the hiddenness of that unparalleled occurrence; mystery remains, for "the intended reality and the mode in which it is expressed in language are essentially different. The intended reality is beyond the experience of the man who lives on this side of death. Thus the only possible mode of speaking about it is metaphorical, using images of this-worldly occurrences," expressing indirectly "an event that is still hidden to us in its true essence."[104]

This metaphorical character of resurrection language is rooted, on the one hand, in the realization that the inquirer is confronted with "a transformation into a reality which is entirely unknown to us" and not merely the unmetaphorical revivification of a dead person; pictorial language becomes thereby "unavoidable."[105] But even beyond that, on the other hand, resurrection talk is no more metaphorical than all statements of Christology[106] and equally of God,[107] because of the quality of provisionality[108] adhering to all anticipations of the eschatological future. Therefore Pannenberg can call the resurrection "a light which blinds" our understanding, even as Paul was blinded on the Damascus Road,[109] and acknowledge the proleptic character of resurrection talk which retains necessarily an "openness to the future."[110] Accordingly he closed his treatise on Christology with the observation:

> Only the *eschaton* will ultimately disclose what really happened in Jesus' resurrection from the dead. Until then we must speak favorably in thoroughly legitimate, but still only metaphorical and symbolic, form about Jesus' resurrection and the significance inherent in it.[111]

Nevertheless, Pannenberg has strongly resisted the suggestion[112] that the event in question can be translated into other metaphorical language than the apocalyptic language of "resurrection." It is his contention that the term functions in the way of an "absolute metaphor," by which he means "the sole appropriate expression for a definite subject matter, [which] is neither interchangeable with other images nor reducible to a separate, rational kernel."[113]

In this regard, Pannenberg subsequently went even beyond that position with the admission that he may have been wrong earlier in recognizing that all talk of a resurrection is necessarily metaphorical at all. The direction in which he assays to pursue this possible transcending of a reliance on metaphor is toward an expanding of the notion of life itself, whereby our understanding is led beyond the limited horizons of our particular perspective: "Might it not be possible," he asks, "to form a concept of 'life' within which our organic and, at least in more highly organized forms, mortally deteriorating life represents only a special instance?" Were that so, Pannenberg contends, the resulting concept, in "its objective intention, the sense of its designation, would no longer be metaphorical."[114] In his Harvard Ingersoll Lecture, Pannenberg expanded on that suggestion with the proposal to image resurrection life as transtemporal and as no longer dependent on earthly corporeality: resurrection as "coming alive in the eternal presence of God" would involve a self-awareness "restored to the simultaneous whole of our life as it is present to the eternal God" and accomplished through a creative action of God that regenerates in eternity "the totality of our bodily life, as preserved in the presence of God."[115]

But what, precisely, does the singular fate of Jesus subsequent to his death signify? What new understandings of God and Jesus, of history and humanity, emerge out of the matrix of Easter? Concerning the averred unity comprising an event and the meanings inherent within it, what are the interpretive words which adequately and accurately convey the import of this nonpareil occurrence? Six major theses are derivable from the corpus of Pannenberg's theology, in regard to the enduring significance of the resurrection of Jesus.[116] The ensuing paragraphs present a formulation and elaboration of these theses.

1) *If Jesus has been raised from the dead, then in him the end of history has occurred in advance.*[117]

It is Pannenberg's conviction, as we have seen, that in the apocalyptic tradition out of which Jesus' message was shaped, the arrival of the Reign of God in the fullness of its power would be accompanied by the end of history as we know it and by the universal resurrection of the dead. In all probability, therefore, Jesus did not anticipate as his ultimate fate a unique event occurring only to him, expecting instead an imminent resurrection of all the dead that would include himself should his death precede it. Accordingly, the initial interpretation of the disciples, confronted by the risen Jesus, was surely that what they perceived to have happened in him was not to be taken as an isolated occurrence but rather as the onset of the universal resurrection of the dead, as "the beginning of the events of the end of history."[118] They anticipated an immediately unfolding sequence of eschatological events that would embrace everyone. Only gradually did the realization dawn that the end of the world had not really begun in that way. Only belatedly did the kerygmatic community perceive that the resurrection had been a special event happening to Jesus alone.

What, then, is to be made of the fact that the initial understanding of the apostles proved to be in error? Does not the so-called "delay of the Parousia" invalidate the claims of importance attached to Jesus' resurrection? Does not Jesus' imminent expectation, in the final analysis, remain unfulfilled? Pannenberg finds that conclusion unwarranted. He maintains that Jesus' imminent expectation of the coming of God's Reign *was* fulfilled in his own resurrection, even though not at all in the way that he had anticipated.[119] The end event of history--resurrection from the dead--took place *in him*; what yet remains outstanding is but the "universal consequence" of that singular occurrence.[120] In this regard, Pannenberg insists that the difference between the two is only "quantitative," not "qualitative";[121] a "material correspondence" (*inhaltlich Übereinstimmung*)[122] exists between the individual fulfillment of the expectation in Jesus and the yet awaited fulfillment in the ultimate future for all of humanity. The now lengthy delay, he states, is not a refutation of the proclamation of God's Reign "as long as the *unity* between what happened in Jesus and the eschatological future is maintained."[123] The increasing temporal interval is of no consequence because with the pre-occurrence of the end in Jesus, the final consummation "is now no longer bound to any fixed day of an imminent expectation."[124] Essentially, that point of view is deemed acceptable by virtue of the consideration that the matter of *imminence* ceased to be at issue with the fulfillment of the declaration of God's *nearness* in the resurrection of Jesus; with the guarantee of God's powerful presence offered in Jesus' fate, a chronological form of imminent expectation was henceforth rendered superfluous.[125]

The conceptual principle which makes this set of conclusions possible for Pannenberg is, of course, that of *prolepsis*: what occurred in Jesus is understood to be the proleptic actualization of humanity's final destiny.[126] This particular instance of a prolepsis of the future, however, is categorically distinguishable from all others because precisely here, as previously indicated, there is no substantive difference separating the proleptic anticipation and the promised future. This event stands in definite contrast to what Pannenberg calls "broken" or "partial" participations in the eschatological future discernible in prophetic pronouncements.[127] There, the proclamations are surpassable by their fulfillment, because there is only proximate coincidence between them.[128] Uniquely here, that reservation does not apply: "the final event will not bring anything decisively new that was not already anticipated in the resurrection of Jesus. . . . That which happened in him will not be substantively augmented by any further events."[129] Put differently elsewhere, "through the resurrection, the revealer of God's eschatological will became the incarnation of the eschatological reality itself."[130] Because in his resurrection the eschatological consummation had been pre-actualized, any initial distinction between the earthly Jesus' proclamation and the "eschatological reality" was essentially "superseded," in Jesus' own person.[131]

199

2) *If Jesus has been raised by God from the dead, then the claim to authority present in his earthly ministry has been retroactively confirmed.*[132]

Jesus' ministry turned on the enacted pronouncement that the saving power of God was about to break conclusively into the historical arena. His death on the cross was more than an untimely and brutal end to his earthly life--it was an inescapable denial of the legitimacy of his message, for his suffering at the hands of the powers of this age stood in direct tension with the proclamation of the inbreaking Reign of God. The ambiguity with which the message and ministry of Jesus was burdened was dispelled for the first time by his death, in the one direction, and by his resurrection in the other.[133] "Without the resurrection of Jesus his message would have turned out to be a fanatical audacity,"[134] but *with* it, the truth of his preaching and activity was conclusively authenticated. For the occurrence of the anticipated eschatological consummation, even though only in him, displayed conclusively the truth of Jesus' unwavering affirmation that God's powerful presence was near at hand. The resurrection of Jesus represented, therefore, the divine verification of his pre-Easter claim to authority. It placed God's stamp of approval retroactively upon his life and proclamation.[135]

Likewise the pivotal eschatological role affirmed by Jesus for himself, linking a person's response to him to the judgment to be made by the coming Son of Man, was essentially legitimated by God's act of raising him up, so that the early community ceased to maintain a distinction between the Son of Man and Jesus.[136]

3) *If the end of history has proleptically occurred in Jesus' resurrection from the dead, then God is unsurpassably revealed therein.*[137]

> Only at the end of all events can God be revealed in his divinity, that is, as the one who works all things, who has power over everything. Only because in Jesus' resurrection the end of all things, which for us has not yet happened, has already occurred can it be said of Jesus that the ultimate already is present in him, and so also that God himself, his glory, has made its appearance in Jesus in a way that cannot be surpassed. Only because the end of the world is already present in Jesus' resurrection is God himself revealed in him.[138]

An inconsistency is to a certain degree discernible in Pannenberg's writings, concerning the matter of precisely where he actually locates the event of divine disclosure. He can assert, on the one hand, that Jesus' resurrection, because it prefigures history's culmination, "is the actual event of revelation,"[139] though he will also give revelatory weight to his eschatological message on occasion.[140] But he can also develop the thesis, on the other hand, that, strictly speaking, the

200

"final event" of history will itself be "the actual revelatory event," of which the resurrection is but the proleptic anticipation.[141] Günter Klein criticizes Pannenberg perceptively for trying to have it both ways: the resurrection is proleptic revelation of the end, and yet the end first discloses and determines what this and all other events really were--wherefore, according to Klein, genuine revelation prior to history's end is surrendered.[142] However, for Pannenberg, Jesus is affirmed to be already the revelation of God precisely to the extent that the end of history is expected not to "bring anything decisively new" beyond what Jesus' resurrection proleptically actualizes, but will only offer "ultimate proof" of the truth of what has previously been disclosed.[143] The issue turns, once again, on the centrality of the concept of prolepsis: just as Jesus' resurrection proleptically actualizes the end of history, just so does he proleptically disclose the God whose all-determining power is finally settled by history's consummation. One could readily wish for greater consistency on Pannenberg's part in explicitly maintaining this tension in his terminology.

A further, major consequence is derived by Pannenberg from the decisively revelatory character of the resurrection: Jesus' essential unity with God. This point of understanding is a crucial one in Pannenberg's thinking; denying the a priori conviction of Jesus' oneness with God that is presupposed by a Christology "from above," he seeks to establish the principle a posteriori, by elaboration of what is entailed by the notion of revelation. Three steps are involved in the reasoning process,[144] the first being the interpretation of Jesus' resurrection as prolepsis of the end of all history. Second is the declaration that the idea of self-revelation contains within itself the understanding that there can only be one such definitive disclosure; anything in addition would be either superfluous or a denial of the sufficiency of the ostensible unveiling.[145] Thirdly, and decisively, Pannenberg insists that

> . . . the concept of God's self-revelation contains the idea that the Revealer and what is revealed are identical. God is as much the subject, the author of his self-revelation, as he is its content. Thus to speak of a self-revelation of God in the Christ event means that the Christ event, that Jesus, belongs to the essence of God himself. . . . Self-revelation in the strict sense is only present where the medium through which God makes himself known is not something alien to himself, brings with it no dimming of the divine light, but, on the contrary, results in the knowledge of the divinity of God for the first time.[146]

Historically the interpretation of Jesus as one with God occurred as a translation of eschatology into epiphany, through contact with Hellenistic conceptuality: "in Jesus, God himself has appeared on earth."[147] But that represents for Pannenberg a significant manifestation of the essential importance of Überlieferungsgeschichte, for the affirmation of

Jesus' genuine divinity is understood by Pannenberg to be what Christology is fundamentally all about.[148]

The relevance, for our present purposes, of this conviction of Jesus' revelatory identify with God is to be discerned in the concomitant emphasis that *who* or *what* God is is *defined* precisely by the Christ event itself: the *essence* of God is only accessible through the life, teaching, and fate of the one God raised from the dead.[149]

Does the resurrection then merely serve to open our eyes to a truth that was already present but obscured during Jesus' lifetime, namely, that he was one with God all along? No. According to Pannenberg, the resurrection was not only noetically but "ontologically constitutive" for Jesus' divinity.[150]

> Until his resurrection, Jesus' unity with God was hidden not only to other men but above all, which emerges from a critical examination of the tradition, for Jesus himself also. It was hidden because the ultimate decision about it had not been given.[151]

The ultimate decision about the veracity of Jesus' life is, of course, what the resurrection is understood to provide. Are we therefore faced with a reemergence of adoptionism? Pannenberg ardently resists such a conclusion. On the contrary, though Jesus' unity with God is established by the resurrection, "from the perspective of the resurrection, he is retrospectively one with God is his whole pre-Easter life."[152] But how could that be so? The answer is found in Pannenberg's notion of the "retroactive power" of the resurrection event: inasmuch as only the (ultimate) future can be really determinative for what a historical event *is,* the resurrection has the character of resolving retroactively the truth of the pre-Easter Jesus--including particularly the (anticipatory) legitimacy of his claim to authority.[153]

4) *If the end of history has occurred in advance in the resurrection of Jesus, then history is comprehensible as universal history without sacrficing its ongoing provisionality and the quest for the unity of truth is legitimated.*[154]

I have previously set forth Pannenberg's understanding that the possibility of truth demands the premise of an ultimate terminus to history because truth is historical and the meaning of historical events is only decided by their eventual outcome within a framework of eschatological unity.[155] Hegel pursued this avenue of interpretation but wound up in a blind alley because his philosophy foreclosed the contingency of the yet-outstanding future. Pannenberg contends that the event of Jesus' resurrection is the key to encompassing history as universal and end-directed inasmuch as the unifying *ultimum* of all events has broken into the midst of history in that singular occurrence and thus assures the certainty of the eventual outcome. Truth as one, and, concomitantly, history as a whole, are guaranteed in advance *as promise*--whereby Hegel's dilemma is resolved: the horizon of the open future is preserved, the provisionality of futural events is not compromised, by virture of the *proleptic* character of the decisive event.[156] The resurrection therefore does not provide a linchpin for writing a universal history; it only establishes the legitimacy of the hope that "history as a whole" is a meaningful notion.[157]

Pannenberg also explicitly affirms that not only human history but the entire universe (*"das materielle All"*) is "first brought together into the unity of one world through its relation to Jesus"[158] by virture of the resurrection--for the "history" Pannenberg always has in mind is the history of the entire creation.[159]

5) *If Jesus has been raised from the dead, then hope for the fulfillment of human destiny beyond death is authenticated.* [160]

Pannenberg expends much more effort in defending the contemporary viability of the notion of resurrection in general than in establishing this connection per se, but the connection is implicitly present almost everywhere in his writing. And the thread of the argument runs precisely in this direction, in spite of inferences to the contrary. Pannenberg does not derive the legitimacy of Jesus' resurrection from his (extensive) argumentation concerning the preferability of resurrection hope as an expression of transmortal human fulfillment. Rather the historicity of the event independently establishes for him the propriety of the hope. To put it another way, Pannenberg is not claiming that the resurrection (Jesus' and ours) is true because it meets a profound human need, but that the truth of his resurrection is enduringly *relevant* because it addresses that need.[161]

But for *whom* is the promise inherent in Jesus' ultimate fate valid? For whom is the resurrection of Jesus a saving event? For everyone? Or only for those who have made the decision in favor of him and his message? Aspects of Pannenberg's theological anthropology would seem to require the former, inasmuch as Pannenberg has strongly maintained that only if all individuals participate in the goal of consummation is the *unity* of human destiny fulfilled.[162] However, Pannenberg has been reluctant to endorse the concept of universal salvation straightforwardly. In his Christology, he struggled to defend the ultimate unity of humankind while holding back from the implication that all human beings must experience their destiny in the same way, *i.e.,* as an event of salvation.[163] It is only in more recent writings that occasional references to the "universal scope of salvation"[164] are discernible.[165]

Pannenberg has never been reticent to offer his interpretation of the nature of the resurrection life, even when he was emphasizing the metaphorical character of all talk about it. On the one hand, he could readily acknowledge that "the metaphorical character of our speaking about resurrection means that we do not know what sort of reality corresponds to that word."[166] But on the other hand, he has been determined to identify and defend certain facets which have seemed to him basic to any adequate understanding of life on the other side of death--working particularly from Paul's perspective.[167]

Two seemingly contrary motifs have predominated in most of Pannenberg's writings on this subject: the notion of a "radical transformation"[168] and the insistence on the bodiliness of resurrected life.[169] These appear on the surface to be inconsistent with each other, for the emphasis on a radical change would seem to preclude the possibility of retaining any definitive characteristics of life as we presently experience it: there is expected to occur a "new creation,"[170] "a transformation into an entirely new life,"[171] a transformation "so radical that nothing remains unchanged."[172] But Pannenberg, in agreement with Paul, contends that it is "the present mortal body" *to which* the transformation will occur,[173] and that the principle of historical continuity demands a genuine "connection" between beginning and end, however radical the process of change.[174] Pannenberg's reason for insisting that the character of *bodiliness* must provide that continuity appears to be rooted in his opposition to the Greek notion of the immorality of a disembodied soul,[175] along with a strong propensity for attributing some kind of bodiliness to all that is real.[176]

However, Pannenberg has gone on to move in a possibly more fruitful direction beyond his earlier impasse. This has occurred in two respects. In the first place, he has been focusing increasing attention on *life* itself as the fundamental category of understanding to be propitiously probed. In his 1966 untranslated lecture on Jesus' resurrection, he contented himself with a more reserved interpretation of that event: historically one can say "that Jesus--who was dead--lives, without saying precisely what the word 'life' means here, beyond the statement that Jesus has not remained dead."[177] Pannenberg then went on to speak of the resurrection life as "imperishable" or "immortal (*unvergänglich*) in contrast to our present transitory existence, and, most importantly, as "a life in inseparable unity [*in ungelöster Verbundenheit*] with the divine origin of all life."[178] This same theme recurs in a later discussion on the doctrine of the Holy Spirit, where Pannenberg characterizes the new life of resurrection as "life in the full sense," "a true life that persists in communication with its spiritual source."[179] The key component of understanding that emerges here is the notion of a post-mortal experience of fulfilled human destiny in which we are no longer ontologically alien to and alienated from the ground of our being but rather are enduringly and completely united therewith.[180]

The second fruitful development involves a backing away from his earlier emphasis on the fundamentally bodily character of all that is: finding in Einstein's theory of relativity the "autonomous idea of energy conceived of as a field," Pannenberg is now willing to accent *energy* as "the primary reality that transcends the body through which it may manifest itself--a reality that we no longer need to attribute to a body as its subject."[181]

6) *If the resurrection of the dead has taken place proleptically in Jesus of Nazareth, then the essential truthfulness of the apocalyptic expectation is assured.* [182]

The point is more implied than expressed by Pannenberg in his writings, but it is nevertheless a crucial one for the whole pattern of his theological interpretation. The recognition that what happened to Jesus after his death was a foretaste of the definitive consummation of God's Reign along with the universal resurrection of the dead at the close of history entails an endorsement of the Jewish apocalyptic tradition within which Pannenberg finds these eschatological expectations initially to have come to expression. For the event in question remains essentially bound to the apocalyptic horizon of hope from which its meaning is gained within the *Überlieferungsgeschichte*, and toward which its having happened acts as a retroactive legitimation of the "fundamental structure" of the apocalyptic expectation.[183]

There appears to be something of a circularity operative here: the legitimacy of a tradition (apocalyptic) is established by virtue of an event (resurrection) *only* if it is the case that the event is correctly understood by reference to that tradition, and to that tradition alone. Granted, historically the event was interpreted by means of categories derived from that tradition. But it is also granted that the event contained important elements of novelty (resurrection of *one* person, *within* history), which would represent nothing less than a "transformation of the apocalyptic hope."[184] Alfred Suhl has called attention to the problem of how an event can be *essentially* rooted in an existing tradition as the necessary basis for its disclosed meaning and yet at the same time express something fundamentally new.[185] The issue at stake is whether the novelty and uniqueness of the event are indeed not such as to correct, modify, or supersede--rather than confirm--the basic structure of the apocalyptic expectation, including particularly the vision of reality as history hastening toward its ultimate consummation. Pannenberg resists such a conclusion, clinging tenaciously to the ongoing tenability of the apocalyptic tradition as both *überlieferungsgeschichtlich* background for, and authenticated interpreter of, Jesus' resurrection. A more extensive assessment of the adequacy of this affirmation will be offered below--subsequent to, and in light of, an examination of the historical authenticity of the pivotal event called resurrection.

D. The Historicity of the Resurrection

It is a provocative undertaking to derive paradigmatic significance for the understanding of all history from an occurrence whose own actuality is extensively disputed. The issue of the historicity of the resurrection remains unfocused so long as its potential meaningfulness is unperceived. But once the far-reaching implications of the event have been set forth in the way that Pannenberg has developed them, then the defensibility of the resurrection as a real historical happening becomes a matter of crucial importance. If the resurrection of Jesus is nothing more than a "random miracle," it does not really matter all that much whether one can affirm that it genuinely took place. But it is precisely when one claims for it the decisively revelatory and eschatologically proleptic consequences which Pannenberg has set forth that the "historical problem" of the resurrection emerges with inescapable forcefulness.[186]

Following a consideration of preliminary issues concerning the possibility of affirming the resurrection as a historical event accessible to historical inquiry, this section explicates Pannenberg's critical inquiry into the Easter traditions of primitive Christianity, and then concludes with an examination of his provisional conclusions regarding the historian's judgment about what underlies these traditions.

There are three particular barriers which tend to stand in the way of accepting the resurrection of Jesus as a possible occurrence in the past: Is it rationally conceivable? Is it understandable as a specifically *historical* event? Does it fall within the range of the work of the critical historian? Pannenberg is willing to yield to none of these as insurmountable obstacles.

With regard to the first of the questions, I have already had occasion to consider Pannenberg's denial of the absolute applicability of the principle of historical analogy, whereby the *possibility* of a past occurrence would be decided in advance according to its concurrence with the boundaries of present experience.[187] It is inescapable that historians will bring to their investigations some preunderstanding of what their inquiry might uncover. But it is not requisite that they begin with so narrow a perspective that they disallow every possibility of a dead man's being resurrected: the preunderstanding must be allowed to be "modified and corrected in the process of research on the basis of the phenomena examined."[188]   And, as before, the negative prejudgment deriving from lack of identifiable analogy is repudiated by virtue of the recognition that every historical event is distinctively unique ("*einmalig*").[189] Historians ought to be willing to consider *whatever* explanation turns out best to account for the course of events that their inquiry reconstructs.[190]

But what about the objection that the notion of a dead man's being raised is in violation of the laws of nature? Pannenberg insists that the work of the natural scientists cannot be the final court of appeal, for several overlapping reasons: The scientists endeavor to establish laws on the basis of observed data, but do not decree what may or may not be viewed as a datum with which to reckon. Only a partial understanding of the totality of natural law is ever within the scientists' grasp. All that happens--and the validity of the laws themselves--retains an element of contingency. Events do not conform completely to the abstract formulas of law; they are far more complex than that. Finally, natural law deals only in *probabilities* of occurrence, not in possibility or impossibility. Our suspicions about the credibility of a highly unusual occurrence can only be settled by careful historical investigation.   The greater the improbability, the greater is the scepticism of its having occurred and the more pressing becomes the demand for adequate justification of assertions about it--but the issue cannot be circumscribed by a dogmatic scientific prejudgment.[191]

The second barrier involves the question of whether it makes sense to talk of Jesus' resurrection as an event *in history*. If the resurrection is understood as the proleptic actualization of history's terminus, the transitional occurrence which represents the inbreaking of the new aeon, then how can it be affirmed to be real *qua historical*, and open like other events to the investigation of the historian who makes historical judgments through the eyes of the old aeon? Walter Künneth, for example, takes the tack that the resurrection is not a historical but an "eschatological" event,[192] which "essentially breaks the limits of the merely historical."[193] Similarly, Reginald Fuller has argued that the resurrection, though real, is not historical because it stands "at the boundary between history and meta-history, between this age and the age to come"; the resurrection therefore has a "meta-historical character."[194] Pannenberg remains uncomfortable with these notions, on the ground that the real *is* the historical; there is for his understanding simply no other order of "event" than that which transpires within the realm of the identifiably historical, whatever its possible implications for historical transcendence. An eschatological or meta-historical event is an empty concept, an evasive attempt to preserve the truth of the resurrection in a safe haven beyond the canons of critical historiography. "There is no justification for affirming Jesus' resurrection as an event that really happened, if it is not to be affirmed as a historical event as such."[195]

The preceding paragraph already introduces the subject of the third barrier, and already partially obviate it. The historian *can* be seen to have access to the occurrence with which the new aeon ensues just because that event is understood to have happened *as* historical, the only way it could have happened. Furthermore, Pannenberg maintains that the doctrine of incarnation expresses the conviction "that the life of the new creation has begun in the scope of the old world and is perceived even with the eyes of the old self, which are renewed precisely through this perception."[196]

That perspective is particularly important inasmuch as Pannenberg insists that there is no other avenue of access to events of past history in addition to the process of historical research. The notion that a leap of faith, or an appeal to "intuitive certainty" (Althaus, Künneth),[197] or a claim for the self-authentication of a contemporary encounter with the risen Jesus,[198] can independently establish the facticity of a past occurrence is seen as sheer foolishness. To the contrary, "whether or not a particular event happened two thousand years ago is not made certain by faith but only by historical research, to the extent that certainty can be attained at all about questions of this kind."[199] Not only is the resurrection regarded as accessible to historical inquiry, it is accessible *only* thereto and thereby.

It is not at all the case that historians are somehow *required* to affirm the historicity of the resurrection; the evidence at hand might indeed lead them to a different conclusion. All that Pannenberg is demanding is that the historical inquiry be openly and comprehensively pursued, without restrictive preconditions in either direction. And what would qualify as an appropriate designating of the resurrection of Jesus as a historical event? Pannenberg offers a provisional capsule summary:

> If the emergence of primitive Christianity, which, apart from other traditions, is also traced back by Paul to appearances of the resurrected Jesus, can be understood in spite of all critical examination of the tradition only if one examines it in the light of the eschatological hope for a resurrection from the dead, then that which is so designated is a historical event, even if we do not know anything more particular about it. Then an event that is expressible only in the language of the eschatological expectation is to be asserted as a historical occurrence.[200]

Turning to the sources on which any historical investigation of the resurrection basically depends, Pannenberg identifies two separate strands of tradition incorporated into the New Testament texts, which only gradually came to be drawn together into a single unity: the appearances of the risen Jesus, and the discovery of the empty tomb. Given their initial independence, Pannenberg proceeds to examine them separately, beginning with the more illuminating tradition of the post-resurrection appearances.

The point of departure here is found in the Pauline summary in I Cor. 15:1-11, by virtue of the overwhelmingly legendary character of the appearances related in the Gospels.[201] Pannenberg finds Paul's report extremely instructive inasmuch as it includes the narration of first-hand experience, stands in close temporal proximity to the events related, and utilizes transmitted formulas with a claim to considerable antiquity. Furthermore, there would appear to be present in the summary an overt intention to offer proof for the authenticity of the resurrection, since many of the expressed witnesses were still alive at the time Paul was writing.[202]

But if the appearance claims per se can be seen to stand up in the face of investigation, there yet remains the far more crucial issue of how these appearances are to be understood. Pannenberg dismisses the observable corporeality of the subject of the appearances as rather late tradition, heavily emphasized in the Gospels but absent from Paul. Five basic elements seem to comprise the content of the appearances as indicated by Gal. 1:12, 16f., treating the Acts accounts as only supplementary: 1) recognition--the appearing one as distinctly identified with Jesus; 2) the encounter with a "spiritual" body, in contrast to an earthly one; 3) an appearance "from on high," not "on earth"; 4) the occurrence of a "light phenomenon" (re Acts 9:3f.); and 5) the inclusion of an auditory experience of some sort. Pannenberg presupposes these elements, with the possible exception of the fourth, to be valid for apostolic appearance experiences other than Paul's.[203]

Pannenberg moves from content to a discussion of the "character and mode" of the appearances, and offers the interpretation that they "may have involved an extraordinary vision" not shared by everyone present at the scene of the occurrence.[204] Could they have been hallucinations then, purely "subjective" visions with no objectively corresponding datum? Pannenberg repudiates that contention as being an insufficient explanation for the whole sequence of events. On the one hand, there is the matter of the large number and "temporal distribution" of appearances which weighs against that interpretation.[205] But even more importantly, there is the problem of concluding that the appearances would have to be explained on the basis of the disciples' Easter faith, whereas precisely the contrary is the case.[206]

To be sure, Pannenberg tentatively characterizes the experiencing of the appearances as taking the form of "apocalyptic visions,"[207] and emphasizes further:

> That the completely alien reality experienced in these appearances could be understood as an encounter with one who had been raised from the dead can only be explained from the presupposition of a particular form of the apocalyptic expectation of the resurrection of the dead.[208]

This calls glaring attention to the antecedent apocalyptic tradition as possibly providing a sufficient explanation for the emergence and shape of the post-Easter faith of the disciples. A glance at Paul's argument in I Cor. 15:12ff. would seem to lend credence to this position, in the way that the apocalyptic notion of a resurrection of the dead seems to function as the *presupposition* for affirming the fact of Jesus' resurrection.[209] But on closer examination, this line of reasoning will not stand up, by virtue of two fundamental considerations.

In the first place, the logic of Paul's argument is not such as to deduce Jesus' resurrection from the idea of a resurrection of the dead. The *conclusion* is precisely the conviction that the dead *are* raised. Basically the argument can be expressed in the form of a conditional syllogism:

Major premise: If there is no (universal) resurrection of the dead, then Christ has not been raised. (vss. 13, 15b, 16)

Minor premise: But Christ has been raised. (vs. 20a)

Conclusion: Therefore there is a (universal) resurrection of the dead. (vss. 22f.)

However, there is a subtle shift in Paul's actual deployment of the notion of universal resurrection. In the hypothetical clause of the major premise, it is introduced as an *idea,* as an indispensable context for understanding the very notion of a resurrection of Jesus. In the conclusion, it is stated as *fact,* derived from the datum that Jesus has indeed been raised. Thus, there is simultaneously a two-way movement in Paul's argumentation: the (apocalyptic) concept of a universal resurrection of the dead provides the basis for understanding what took place in Jesus after his death, but that which *did* occur in him after his death now becomes the ground for positing the certain, futural fact that the dead will indeed be raised. The apocalyptic tradition is the background for designating the Easter event as "resurrection from the dead," but it does not provide the basis for Paul's contention that the event "resurrection" has actually taken place. His experiencing of a post-resurrection appearance of the man Jesus remains the basis for that.

Secondly, and most decisively of all, one must be willing to recognize that the particular conclusion which Paul and the others reached concerning Jesus' fate beyond death *was not accountable solely on the basis of an antecendent tradition*. Something in the way of novelty had to intervene as a sufficient basis for that conviction, precisely because there was no previous notion within the apocalyptic horizon of expectation embracing the eventuality of an *individual* resurrection *within* history. Something had to have happened, beyond mere reflection upon the meaning of Jesus' life and death, in order to have triggered that unprecedented and decidedly non-traditional interpretation. Therefore, says Pannenberg, "precisely because the resurrection of a single man was quite unfamiliar to the apocalyptic tradition, we must suppose that a special event underlay the apostolic Easter message, an event that caused so decisive a change in the traditional expectation of the End"[210]--and, one hastens to add, so decisive a change in the attitude and faith of the initially downcast disciples.[211]

In shifting focus to the other major strand of tradition, Pannenberg is concerned to point out at the outset that the preceding arguments bear weight independently of any question about the legitimacy of the story of the empty tomb.[212] But Pannenberg does not proceed as though that were indeed the case. Foregoing a primary exegesis of the textual tradition, he opts instead for a careful conjecture about what *must* have been true about Jesus' place of burial given the viability of the resurrection tradition in the kerygma.[213] And one of these conditions is precisely that the tomb would have to have been known to be empty in order for the apostolic interpretation of the appearances to have been convincing. Put conversely, had the tomb been known to be continuingly occupied by the corpse of Jesus, the testimony about a risen Jesus appearing to his followers could hardly have been persuasive.[214]

Pannenberg augments this reasoning with the observation that there are absolutely no traces of any early Jewish polemic denying the tomb's emptiness--which would not be understandable unless the Jews as well as the Christians acknowledged the tomb to be empty.[215] But how does one account for Paul's seemingly telling silence about the empty tomb tradition? Is he not necessarily unaware of it? Would he not have been certain to have employed such a tradition in his defense of the resurrection proclamation, had he known about it? Pannenberg does not believe so. Two separate observations are offered, which are not especially compatible with each other. On the one hand, Paul simply might not have been particularly interested in the "singularity" of this aspect of Jesus' having risen.[216] On the other hand, however, Paul is understood to have stood firmly within a tradition in which resurrection *always* involved the emptying of tombs, wherefore his very silence *implied* the tomb's emptiness. To say otherwise, in this regard, one would have to demonstrate that, in contemporary Jewish circles, an understanding of resurrection as other than completely bodily existed-- and, that Paul stood in that circle.[217]

Willi Marxsen has dismissed the empty tomb tradition as historically unhelpful so far as the resurrection *event* is concerned: the tomb might well have been empty for a wide variety of reasons. Its-- possible but unlikely--emptiness is no *proof* of a resurrection's having happened.[218] Pannenberg would agree that, by itself, it does not stand as proof. His point is that the tradition of its having been found empty reinforces in a vital way the (independent) tradition of the appearances, whereas precisely the *absence* of any tradition of an empty tomb would distinctively tend to call into question the authenticity of the apostolic interpretation of the meaning of the appearances.

For Pannenberg, furthermore, the initial separateness of the two traditions is one more factor in favor of their mutual authenticity. Given the consideration that the empty tomb tradition is rooted in Jerusalem and the appearances traditions were localized elsewhere,[219] their having come together only secondarily lends credence to the legitimacy of both.[220]

The provisional conclusion at which Pannenberg arrives is that the historian, working with an appropriately open perspective toward the data at hand, can indeed, *qua* historian, affirm that an event has occurred in history for which the name "resurrection" is the most accurate designation.[221] Pressed for a more precise indication of what the affirmation encompasses, Pannenberg is finally able only to identify "an occurrence befalling Jesus--to be sure, the *dead* Jesus--after which Jesus was no longer dead." Beyond that, "history guards the mystery of Jesus' resurrection."[222] Even so, the matter is by no means definitively settled for all futural historical research. Within history, all conclusions about history are subject to possible revision, especially one as fundamental and debatable as this. The historical claim, though affirmed as tenable and warranted, remains *"strittig,"* disputable, controvertible.[223]

A number of possible objections can be directed toward this provisional conclusion, however, which seem particularly to impugn its credibility, and which merit careful consideration. In the first place, one may deny that *this* ostensible event, in contrast to all others, can be understood to have occurred at a specific point in time and space, and thus cannot qualify as historical. Gerald O'Collins, for example, maintains that Christ's new mode of existence is one that transcends time and space, wherefore, even though the resurrection "happened," it is not historical--that is, it is not localizable in our space-time continuum.[224] Pannenberg is sensitive to that problem, and probes it perceptively:

Whatever else may also be the case, a historical event must always occur in time and space, and must be affirmed or denied in relation to a *particular* point in time and to a *particular* place in distinction from all others. What can be said in this respect in regard to the event of Jesus' resurrection? First, that it is an event in time. As such, it is at least approximately dateable, insofar as the death of Jesus on the one side and the first appearances and the discovery of the empty tomb on the other side are dateable. Beyond that, can it be said that the event has taken place in space and is therefore localizable? With this question, difficulties arise: On the one hand, it is a question of an event in space insofar as it must in any case have come to pass in Palestine, surely in Jerusalem, and (presupposing the historicity of the empty tomb) in and with this tomb. But on the other hand, other events which occur in space are accustomed to have a continuation in following events which also occur in space, and, to be sure, in a continuing connection with what has come before. On the contrary, Jesus' resurrection, in relation to Jesus himself, has no sequential events in space and, precisely considered, also no immediately sequential events in time. The appearances are no *immediately* sequential events, and their relation to the specific *reality* of the resurrected one is thoroughly problematic: That the Easter appearances, as experiences, were events in space and time need not include that the appearing *reality*-- presupposing that it was no bare hallucination--was, for its part, in space and time. As an event, therefore, Jesus' resurrection is temporally and spatially fixable--but the continuing sequential connection in which events are otherwise ordered, temporally as spatially, evades our view here. Plainly said: The further continuation of the event, insofar as it concerns Jesus himself, remains unknown. If Jesus has not remained dead but is resurrected to a new "life"-- which remains to be understood more precisely--then we can scarcely avoid the conclusion that he has since *vanished* from our world.[225]

But vanished whereto? John Cobb would like to know precisely what has become of Jesus' resurrected body,[226] and suggests that this emphasis on the bodiliness of the resurrection raises "unnecessary difficulties" for Pannenberg.[227] In point of fact, the question is cogent, regardless of the dispute about bodiliness. Simply put: "Where is Jesus now?" Pannenberg's answer is in continuity with the tradition of early Christianity: he has "ascended into Heaven." But with the collapse of the ancient world view, "Heaven" is no longer conceivable as a place. Pannenberg therefore shifts the focus to that term's initial meaning: "Heaven meant the sphere in which God lives. Ascension into Heaven signifies union with God. . . . The life of the resurrected one in Heaven means therefore nothing else than that he lives with God, shares God's life."[228] And where, precisely, is that? The future! Jesus as resurrected has been "removed into God's future."[229] Cobb, however, still objects to this conclusion, because it seems to require that "the future must be posited as already extant or as an eternity alongside of time or abrogating the reality of time in a way that Pannenberg usually wishes to avoid."[230] That this may precisely be the case will be dealt with in the chapter following.

213

But is an *inference* about a presumed event to which there is no *direct* access historiographically permissible? Marxsen contends that the actual event at issue remains hidden from historical perception inasmuch as there is no immediate testimony to the experiencing of the resurrection itself. Paul did not presume to have experienced the resurrection but only its consequences. Positing a particular bridge event between the crucifixion of Jesus and the appearances, Paul offers us only a second-hand reporting of that event by way of an interpretive statement, generated by a process of deduction. And Marxsen insists that it is improper to turn an interpretation into an objective historical fact by inferring something which "must have" happened.[231] He concludes:

> But today we are *no longer* in a position to speak so directly of the resurrection of Jesus as an *event* ; we *must* simply say: *We are concerned with an interpretative statement* made use of by those who reflected on what had happened to them (at that time!). Hence if today we raise the question in *historical* terms (!): Is Jesus risen?--we can only reply: That cannot be established. *In historical terms it can only be established* (though quite reliably) that witnesses, after the death of Jesus, claimed that something had happened to them which they described as seeing Jesus, and reflection on this experience led them to the *interpretation* that Jesus had been raised from the dead.[232]

Pannenberg insists, however, that the nature of the first-hand experiences of the witnesses demands the deducing of the bridge event hidden from human eyes. For:

> . . . the inference has an inner necessity: If Jesus (after he was dead) now lives,   then--before he was seen for the first time as the living one--either he has been resuscitated or (when the manner of his present life excludes that and his death is doubtlessly certain) he has indeed been transformed into another "life."[233]

The logic is persuasive: *If* the disciples and Paul experienced the presence of a living Jesus after his crucifixion, and *if* there was indeed *objective* content to those experiences, then the inference seems unassailable that a genuine though unobserved occurrence transpired at some point between the death and the appearances--as the only plausible explanation for this historical aftermath. Not to make such an inference would seem to amount to a very narrow and arbitrary reductionism in critical historiography.

But is it legitimate to introduce God as a causal agent in the historical process? Marxsen maintains that the notion that God (by having raised Jesus) was the cause of the appearances is beyond the boundaries of reasonable historical affirmation.[234] Robinson objects that "Pannenberg has not yet made fully clear the step from the historical observation that an event occurred in a context in which people believed in God and his action to the theological knowledge by the historian that their belief is true."[235]   Pannenberg's position is essentially that the historian as historian is not required to go that far.   It is at this point that the work of the theologian ensues, in unpacking the implications of what the historian has uncovered.   Once one attempts to characterize *what* the event of Jesus' resurrection actually was, including the explanation--with reference to God--of how it can be understood to have taken place, there "the historically controllable is overstepped."[236]

But if the resurrection in all its unparalleled singularity is to be adjudged as historically credible and not simply rejected out of hand, should it not have to have more going for it than the controversial and indirect evidence Pannenberg puts forth? Cobb puts the question thus:

> Even if we allow the *possibility* of unique events in the past, quite discontinuous with our ordinary experience, should we not require considerably more evidence for their occurrence than for that of more ordinary events? Would not an explanation of past belief in a unique event in terms of more ordinary occurrences have *some* preferability?[237]

Pannenberg would be willing to acknowledge that--*if* it were the case that some such ordinary explanation is genuinely tenable. His fundamental conviction is that there are no sufficiently persuasive interpretations which do adequate justice to all the facts at hand, other than the one which affirms Jesus to have transcended the finality of death by virtue of an event traditionally and appropriately named "resurrection."

E.   Summary and Critique

Because meaning is inherent in an event and not external to it, theology must be willing to probe behind the kerygmatic interpretations of Jesus' life and ministry to the history of Jesus itself, which stands in judgment upon all attempts to transmit its truthfulness.   Such a "Christology from below" confronts unflinchingly the necessary provisionality of all expressions of Jesus' relevance for faith, which are never altogether free of the uncompleted work of historical scholarship. It also, for Pannenberg, calls for attention both to what is discerned as unique in Jesus of Nazareth and to that which he shared with the traditions in which he stood, to the context in relation to which his historical particularity took shape.   And this latter is perceived to be primarily the horizon of Jewish apocalyptic thought.

In the concentration of his message on the coming Reign of God, in his apparent expectation of an accompanying Son of Man, and in the futural thrust and Torah-transcendence of his remarkable claim of authority, Jesus is understood to have lived out of a framework of apocalyptic images. But at the same time, Jesus surpassed the inherited apocalyptic categories in emphasizing not simply the nearness but even the present impact of the future of the Reign of God, in which Pannenberg sees a new understanding of time--one in which the future of God's reign (and, indeed, of God) interpenetrates the present and is proleptically actual therein without surrendering its yet outstanding character as future. Other distinctions, such as Jesus' focus on his own role in the arrival of eschatological salvation and his overcoming of a sharp distinction between the aeons, lead Pannenberg to the conclusion that Jesus overstepped the compass of what is possible in apocalyptic conceptuality but nonetheless remained firmly joined to the fundamental characteristics of that tradition--in particular, to its championing of a unifying end of history that promises to resolve the ambiguities of human existence.

But the truth claims in Jesus' proclamation and manner of life were critically threatened by his suffering of death on a cross: the eschatological hope seemed thereby illusory, negated by history itself. Only a reversal of the judgment of finality that the cross imposed could justify the conviction that Jesus had not been essentially in error about the promise and proleptic dawning of God's Reign. In the various appearances of a death-transcending Jesus to his followers, and in the discovery of the emptiness of his place of burial, both traditions being argued by Pannenberg as historically credible, the assurance of such a reversal is discerned. The resurrection by God of Jesus of Nazareth from death becomes therein the linchpin that holds together the whole Pannenbergian theological enterprise. For, if it is correct to maintain that Jesus has been raised from the dead, then the anticipated end of history has now transpired proleptically (resolving positively the issue of history's possibility of meaningfulness explored in chapter three); Jesus' futurally oriented claim to authority has been vindicated (fulfilling the crucial elements identified in the present chapter); God can thereby be seen to be revealed in Jesus' ministry and destiny (bringing to completion the dynamic of revelation in history articulated in chapter five); the quest for the ultimate unity of truth is legitimated (promising the resolution of theology's concern to embrace truth, examined in chapter two); hope for human fulfillment beyond death is authenticated (answering the questionableness of human existence disclosed in chapter four); and, finally, the validity of the essential apocalyptic vision is assured (completing the groundwork laid out in the first half of chapter six).[238]

The interconnectedness of these theses of meaning centers on Pannenberg's pivotal conviction that not only was the apocalyptic tradition the horizon of understanding within which the early Church interpreted what happened to Jesus that first Easter but that this was the *only* legitimate horizon of interpretation that could do full justice to the

216

content of the event--*in spite of* the singular novelty involved (*one* man being raised, *within* history). Thus the destiny of Jesus as resurrected, though it strains the limits of apocalyptic conceptuality, nevertheless in the final analysis is seen to confirm its essential truthfulness.

We move, now, from the work of summarizing to the task of critical engagement. My critique of Pannenberg's theological appropriation of the history of Jesus will emerge here as a fairly unified argument instead of as a series of separate points of dispute, focusing on the key question of Jesus' continuity with the apocalyptic tradition as disclosed both in his ministry and in the event designated as "resurrection." The issue at stake is precisely the identifiable degree to which Jesus can be said to have confirmed the essential components of that tradition or, on the other hand, to have transcended its orientation in fundamental ways. In short, we have need to explore whether what we encounter in Jesus' ministry and destiny is indeed a *Vollziehung* of apocalyptic, or its *Aufhebung*. On the resolution of this question hinge far-reaching implications for how the reality and power of God are to be conceived.

The core of Jesus' continuity with apocalyptic is discernible in his concentration on the coming Reign of God. As we have seen, although the specific phrase is found in apocalyptic literature before Jesus' time only in the Psalms of Solomon (17:4), the underlying expectation of the futural establishment of God's Reign is a widespread feature of apocalyptic eschatology.[239] Nevertheless, we cannot evade the realization that what was merely one feature among others in the apocalyptic corpus has been moved to the very center of Jesus' proclamation. Pannenberg, of course, concurs. Similarly, the contested but credible authenticity of the eschatological Son of Man sayings attributed in the kerygma to Jesus manifests a link with this same matrix, even if only peripherally. If, on the other hand, Jesus' preaching disclosed no traceable interest in the totality of history, a theme so vital for Pannenberg's perspective, I will let stand for the moment his observation that Jesus was focused so intensely on the imminence of history's end that he had no interest in portraying the path leading thereto.[240] The universality of history is visible therefore, as also so often for apocalyptic itself, only as an implied concomitant of history's awaited consummation.

Even so, the emphasis directed by Jesus toward the *present* manifestations of God's rule already in his own ministry was, to say the least, certainly a surpassing of apocalyptic's implied acknowledgment of God's continuing sovereignty over history. We have found sufficient cause to reject the suggestion that apocalyptic is ontologically dualistic. Its dualism was purely temporally conceived; one God remains supreme over all. Nevertheless, apocalyptic appears to have relinquished any hope that God would manifest that eternal sovereignty *within* the ongoing course of human history--which is precisely what was understood to be emerging with Jesus' ministry. Pannenberg embraces this development with his interpretation of Jesus' new understanding of time, in which God's ultimate and decisive future is seen to become effective already here and now. But is not something more also reflected herein, something perhaps just as crucially important: namely, that with Jesus God was understood to be initiating the transformation of history not simply by its eventual consummation but *from within*, as an *intra-historical process* proleptically actualizing the post-historical *telos*? The hope of significant intra-historical change characterizes the Old Testament prophetic tradition, of course. But this goes beyond that also. What would appear to be new, here, is the dynamic interweaving not simply of future and present but of the *apocalyptic* expectation of an ultimate world-encompasing transformation with the *prophetic* hope for manifestations of God's righteous sovereignty in the very midst of ongoing life. With Jesus, this was no longer an either/or proposition; it was in light of the former that the latter was experienced as viable.

But how was this proleptic dawning of God's world-transforming rule manifesting itself? In what did the proleptic presence of the Reign of God in Jesus' ministry consist? Once again, a fundamental discontinuity with apocalyptic tradition is discernible. For there, it was those who were judged righteous who would be resurrected to participate in God's eschatological reign. In Jesus' ministry, on the contrary, the message was proclaimed with overwhelming consistency that God's Reign is to be the inheritance of forgiven sinners. The shift is not a subtle but a substantial one: God's *mercy*, not God's justice, has become the basic motif in divine judgment.[241] God's merciful love was already known in the Old Testament tradition, to be sure; chapters 3 and 11 of Hosea are prime evidence of that. But in Jesus' teaching and in his way of relating to others, to the extent that this is derivable from the Gospel kerygma, the theme of divine mercy and love has moved to the very center.

So far, the ground covered here would appear to be undisputed territory, so much so that documentation seems superfluous. The issue, rather, is a matter of determining what all of this means for comprehending the precise extent of Jesus' radically new understanding of God's sovereignty in history. For if it is as "abba," father, that God comes to rule; if this father-God can be depicted in parables as a loving parent who unconditionally embraces his wayward son and as a magnanimous host who invites undeserving riff-raff to his feast; and if Jesus is understood to have been doing the will of this loving deity when he socialized with outcasts and forgave broken lives; does this then not betoken something of fundamental importance for discerning *not only*

Jesus' new understanding of time but his new understanding of the Reign of God itself?

He proclaimed the Reign not of an Oriental potentate but of one like a heavenly father. How should God be considered to "rule," as a divine parent? Does such an image call for a rethinking of our notions of divine sovereignty? We have seen that the apocalyptic tradition is shot through with the conviction that everything God has willed will come to pass; divine determinism is the very basis on which the visions of the future are possible. Is this consistent with the motif of God's rule as characterized essentially by merciful love? "Love," Paul observed, "does not insist on its own way." (I Cor. 13:5) If this insight is valid, does it not also have a bearing on our perception of God as love? The image in Hosea of divine parental sway by means of "cords of compassion" and "bands of love" (11:4) seems particularly apt: the poetic metaphor suggests an invisible bond which does not constrain, tie one's hands, but rather finds its potency precisely in the range of options it lovingly allows --as the "prodigal" son of Jesus' parable later experiences. Such a relationship entails *risk*, and essentially so: the behavior of the son embraced by cords of compassion is not circumscribed in advance; it may well move in unexpected directions. And at the very heart of risk is the denial of any role for determinism.

What I am on the track of here is the possibility that Jesus' radical insight into the interweaving of the essentially futural rule of God with the present moment has both *formal* and *substantive* content, in that the Reign of God understood to be proleptically dawning is now to be perceived as *the reign of divine love* in the midst of history--and that such an emphasis on the *loving* reality of God demands a radical rethinking of the nature of God's sovereignty, God's Reign, *i.e.,* God's *power*. In essence, if it is true that precisely *in Jesus* is the truth of God revealed, and that this Jesus pointed in the direction of a God whose very nature is merciful fatherly love, then this would seem to call for a reshaping of our ideas about divine *power* in the light of that disclosure.

What is of pivotal importance here is that once again there are sharp indications in Jesus' ministry and message that a basic dimension of apocalyptic tradition has been modified in a rather fundamental way, in so characterizing the *identity* of the coming Reign that deterministic notions are completely overstepped.[242] Along this same line, Jesus' call for a human response of self-transcending love of God and other persons, though not specifically directed toward socio-political reform, does not reflect continuity with the apocalyptic disinterest in the (prophetic) call for social transformation, which brings us back yet again to the realization that *both* the apocalyptic and the prophetic traditions are traceable in Jesus' ministry.

Finally, then, within this sequence of considerations, the subject of the importance of futural confirmation of the truth of Jesus' revelatory claims remains to be dealt with. We have seen that this is one of the instances of continuity between Jesus and apocalyptic, according to Pannenberg. But this exploration has also previously arrived at the conclusion that the locus of revelation as essentially *futural* is far more characteristic of the prophetic tradition and of "proto-apocalyptic" embedded in the prophetic literature in Ezekiel 38-39 and Joel 3:17 than of the body of apocalyptic literature extant in Jesus' time.[243] It would appear yet again to be the case that a fundamental component of Jesus' proclamation, as characterized by Pannenberg, demonstrates continuity with a tradition different from Pannenberg's identification.

The critical concluscions provisionally derivable from these reflections are twofold: (1) that the designation of Jesus' earthly ministry as "apocalyptically colored prophecy"[244] is a valid assessment only if the *latter* term is allowed as much weight as the former, a tendency not at all prominent in Pannenberg's christological work; and (2) that there appears to be so extensive a novelty in the creative manner in which Jesus appropriated and interrelated these two traditions that one is led to affirm an *Aufhebung* (an abrogation; a transforming annulment) of *both* traditions to a new level of conceptuality. It would seem necessary, then, to speak of a "bursting" of the bonds and "springing" the framework of *both* apocalyptic and prophecy by Jesus. The problem of doing so, as an effective criticism of Pannenberg's interpretation of Jesus, is rendered difficult by the realization that Pannenberg nowhere acknowledges just how extensively Jesus would need to be seen to supersede or depart from a tradition-horizon before that could be judged as a basic denial of its legitimacy per se. Nevertheless, the fundamental discontinuities and new departures which have been lifted up here would seem to necessitate just such a conclusion. Components of apocalyptic eschatology provide a crucial context out of which Jesus' message emerged--but what came to eventual expression therein was not so much its essential fulfillment but its thoroughgoing transformation.

These qualifying remarks, however, have only provisional significance so long as the focus on Jesus and apocalyptic is limited to his message and ministry. For the decisive event which, for Pannenberg, establishes the authenticating link between the Nazarene and the universal-historical perspective of apocalyptic is ultimately his having been raised by God from the dead. The naming of the Easter event as "resurrection" by Jesus' followers is understood to convey accurately and appropriately the continuity of this event with the fundamental components of his pre-Easter proclamation--even though it was at variance with Jesus' own particular expectation. And if the event is named (interpreted) properly as "resurrection," then the consequences of retroactively confirming the essential components of the apocalyptic horizon of meaning, given resurrection's (ostensible) essential link with that tradition, would seem valid.

But is "resurrection" necessarily the appropriate or most adequate category of interpretation for understanding the nature of the elusive event which happened to Jesus after his death? That this characterized the response of the persons initially confronted with the consequences of the event (appearances, with or without the evidence of the empty tomb) is well attested--and there is every reason to understand why this was so, since the notion of resurrection was in fact readily at hand. Given Pannenberg's emphasis upon the primary role of the transmission of tradition in the unfolding of history, this interpretation then comes to be regarded as inseparable from the event so named. But Marxsen has suggested that precisely the handy availability of the interpretive resources of a particular tradition should make us wary of jumping too quickly to the conclusion that this tradition does in fact *offer* the *right* categories for comprehending what has occurred.[245] What if the novelty of the event utterly transcended the available categories-- transformed them by its very novelty?[246] That there was fundamental novelty in the Easter event is one of the bases for Pannenberg's affirming its historical authenticity: it exceeded what was at hand in the tradition, so that it could not simply have been invented by the disciples. But is it not extremely possible that the novelty of the "resurrection" represented as much a shattering of apocalyptic conceptuality as Jesus' message did?

Pannenberg's unwillingness to entertain this possibility seems to be in part an instance of resisting the implicates of his own perspective. Divine promises, for example, may be profoundly overstepped by their eventual fulfillment. Are events not able, precisely in their fundamental *contingency*, to transcend profoundly the existing categories of understanding in which they are embraced? And of even greater import, the fundamental Pannenbergian affirmation that events *themselves* are open toward their own future because they include the future horizon of their ultimately true meaning seems to require that *this* event be so open. That for Pannenberg it is *not* so open, because it uniquely manifests proleptically the ultimate truth of history itself, is predicated on the very basis of the authenticity of *this* horizon of meaning in which it is initially embedded. There appears to be a circularity of argument here: apocalyptic discloses resurrection as essential End-event, which so understood therefore authenticates the apocalyptic identification of its meaning. (If not circularity, then perhaps "eschatological reciprocity.")

Pannenberg acknowledges that a "translation" of the Easter event from apocalyptic categories of conceptuality into some other is in fact possible, so long as the basic message of human life beyond death is not surrendered.[247] But I am not raising here the question of a translation of meaning. I am inquiring into whether the apocalyptic context of understanding must not itself be open to substantive reformulation, if it is arguable that that category was insufficient from the outset.

The link between these reflections and the foregoing examination of apocalyptic in Jesus' message can now be stated squarely: *If Jesus' followers seized upon familiar apocalyptic categories for designating the unique event which transpired in him after his death, whereas Jesus' message and ministry had been decisively stamped by a surpassing of that tradition in crucial ways, then we have cause to ponder whether the initial naming of the Easter event as "resurrection,"* with all that this conveyed traditio-historically, *may represent a retreat from the very novelty which both Jesus' teaching and his fate manifested.* Viewed in this light, the problem of the "resurrection" is that the disciples, encountering anew the reality of a living Jesus after his death, reacted by putting him back into the very categories he had moved beyond-- wherefore, if Jesus' ministry is best characterized as apocalyptic transformed, then designating the Easter event as resurrection represents the faith community's *reapocalypticizing* of Jesus.

Is an alternative possibility of meaning at hand? Yes--in continuity specifically with the reshaping of the image of God's sovereignty in Jesus' teaching. If it is as *love* that Jesus understood the character of God and God's lordship, then what may be seen to have come about on that first Easter is nothing else than *the confirmation of the promise that love is powerful,* that the love which is God is not rendered impotent in the face of Jesus' suffering and death.

Wilckens, in his treatise on resurrection, has emphasized this point that just as Jesus' preaching had focused on "love as the final, decisive power,"[248] so is Easter to be understood as "divine proof. . . that love is all-powerful":[249]

> Paul understands God's *demonstration of power* is his act of resurrection as a *demonstration of the power of love.* The creative power of God, which was shown in the abolition of death in the case of Christ, is thus no longer simply to be seen on its own as a pure demonstration of power, but must be seen as love with its redeeming intention. God's *omnipotence* is thus defined as the *power of love.*[250]

Wilckens does not spell out any sense of what this way of conceptualizing Easter would mean in regard to rethinking in detail our notion of power, and that task is an important one to pursue. At the moment, what is of particular significance to discern is that such an integration of Jesus' message and Easter destiny points not to an apocalyptically derived prolepsis of history's ultimate consummation but to the confirmation, in history, of the power of God's love to surmount every extremity that would defeat it. So understood, the event of Easter properly finds its horizon of meaning not in the old apocalyptic tradition now superseded but directly in Jesus' own life and ministry.

It is in light of this critical insight that we can consider most cogently the criticism by Moltmann that Pannenberg does not do justice in his theology to the fact that it is the *crucified* Jesus who was raised up by God from death.[251] Pannenberg responds by affirming that certainly it is none other than Jesus the crucified one whom God has so vindicated.[252] That, however, fails to get at the heart of Moltmann's weightiest concern, namely, that one do justice in one's theological interpretation to what the cross of Jesus means with regard even to God. For Moltmann, the issue resolved by the resurrection, vis-a-vis the crucifixion, is the confirmation of God's own righteousness which Jesus' having been allowed to suffer unjustly has called radically into question.[253] But we can frame precisely the same issue in a quite different way: that Jesus' dying on the cross, if that is the final verdict, decides negatively the claim in Jesus' activity that the love which characterizes God will prove ultimately victorious, that is, that the Reign of the loving heavenly Father has indeed drawn near, is on the present moment's immediate horizon. It is not, in other words, only *the righteousness of God's power* but *the power of God's* (righteous, or better: *merciful*) *love* that is at stake and which Easter is perceived to confirm.

The consequences of this critique of Pannenberg's investigations into the meaning of Jesus' resurrection can now be summarized in regard to the six major theses identified earlier in this chapter. The second, third, and fifth theses are supported though in altered ways. The claim of Jesus to authority is confirmed through the Easter event: the message of the present availability of God's empowering love was not mistaken after all. God has indeed been revealed in Jesus, but in *both* his ministry and his victory over death's finality--the one as promise, the other as confirmation of the promise's validity. And hope for the fulfillment of human destiny beyond the destruction occasioned by death is authenticated: love wills, and empowers, life. But the first, fourth, and sixth theses have been called very much into question here. I have not championed the apocalyptic anticipation of history's ultimate and unifying termination, having found occasion to loosen the Easter event from those particular moorings by virtue of Jesus' creative transformation of the apocalyptic Reign of God concept. And therefore it is precisely by no means the case that the essential veridicality of apocalyptic's eschatological orientation is perceived therein to have been retroactively authenticated.

223

I have challenged here the structure of meaning Pannenberg has derived from the resurrection of Jesus. I have not, in that process, questioned at all Pannenberg's investigations into the historicity of the event. Indeed the thrust of this entire discussion implies continuity with that aspect of his scholarship. To a considerable extent, that is true. Pannenberg's insistence that the resurrection cannot be relegated to a safe haven untouched by historical inquiry, along with his argumentation for the historical authenticity of the event, comes across as highly persuasive. This is especially true concerning his identifying of the implications of the post-resurrection appearances tradition. It is somewhat less so, however, in regard to his reasoning on behalf of the equal authenticity of the empty tomb tradition. I have noted the tendency to argue by inference and conjecture concerning this facet of the Easter record, and I have observed that support for the tomb's emptiness is derived in part from the consideration that *in the apocalyptic tradition* resurrection is always understood to be accompanied by the tombs' becoming empty.[254] But just this avenue of approach has been vitiated here. Is it not at least conceivable, therefore, that what we encounter in the Easter event breaks through the existing categories of understanding in involving something other than the disappearance and transformed reappearance of the physical body? Additional arguments might be advanced for the tomb's emptiness--for example, the multiple attestation in the tradition that it was one or more *women* who happened upon the discovery, a development which the tradition goes to great pains to devalue.[255] But the fundamental conclusion, that the power of God's love paramount in Jesus' ministry manifested itself anew in his destiny, does not necessarily hinge on the authenticity of the empty tomb. Unless, as Cobb observes, one has other presuppositional grounds for defending the essential bodiliness of what is real,[256] this dimension of the Easter tradition may be expendable.

Much has been touched on in this concluding section that remains rather preliminary at this point. This is to a considerable extent unavoidable inasmuch as the relevance of these critical reflections vis-a-vis Pannenberg's doctrine of *God*, our primary and organizing focus, cannot properly be elaborated upon until that subject is itself fully in view. To such an undertaking we are now in a position, finally, to turn.

NOTES

[1]Martin Kähler, *The So-called Historical Jesus and the Historic Biblical Christ,* trans. Carl Braaten (Philadelphia: Fortress Press, 1964). The original German edition was published in 1892.

[2]*JGM,* pp. 22f.

[3]"What is a Dogmatic Statement?," *BQT* I, pp. 159f., esp. ft. 41.

[4]*AC,* p. 46.

[5]"What is a Dogmatic Statement?" *BQT* I, pp. 196f., 199; "On Historical and Theological Hermeneutic," *BQT* I, p. 149; *JGM,* pp. 30, 48.

[6]"What is a Dogmatic Statement?," *BQT* I, pp. 196f.

[7]"On Historical and Theological Hermeneutic," *BQT* I, p. 149. See also *JGM,* pp. 23f., 27f., 30; "Response to the Discussion," *TaH,* p. 222; *AC,* p. 48.

[8]*JGM,* pp. 33-36. The question of the proper point of departure is hardly that simple, however. One cannot really *begin* with the "historical Jesus" (see "Response to the Discussion," *TaH,* p. 222) because the only avenue of access to him is *through* the kerygmatic formulations--to which the understanding of Jesus' divinity has already been varyingly applied. Thus one must work "from below" only by penetrating a tradition in which a process of moving toward a perspective "from above" can already be seen at work. Pannenberg would be on firmer ground were he to acknowledge more explicitly the role of the apostolic kerygma as the beginning point for any endeavor at critiquing it in terms of its own ground. The relationship is a very complex one: only *through* the kerygma does one have access to the historical ground that is presumed to be accessible to stand in judgment upon that very kerygma.

[9]Wilhelm Herrmann, "Der geschichtliche Christus: Der Grund unseres Glaubens, *ZThK* 2, 1892, pp. 232-72.

[10]*JGM,* pp. 23f.

[11]For a perceptive interpretation of the reasons for the demise of the old quest and the justification of the rise of the new, see James M. Robinson's *A New Quest of the Historical Jesus* (London: SCM Press, 1959), esp. chs. II and IV. Pannenberg tends to work the most positively with the contribution of Günther Bornkamm, *Jesus of Nazareth,* trans. Irene and Fraser McLuskey with James M. Robinson (New York: Harper & Row, 1960).

[12]In the latter case, Ernst Fuchs, for example, concentrates on the conduct of Jesus, particularly as that comes to expression in his celebration of the eschatological meal. See his "The Question of the Historical Jesus" in *Studies of the Historical Jesus*, trans. Andrew Scobie (London: SCM Press, 1964), esp. pp. 19-26.

[13]See *JGM*, p. 24, ft. 13.

[14]*Ibid.*, p. 27.

[15]"On Historical and Theological Hermeneutic," *BQT* I, pp. 149f.

[16]See Norman Perrin, *Rediscovering the Teaching of Jesus* (New York: Harper & Row, 1967), pp. 38-47. The other two criteria are those of coherence and multiple attestation.

[17]*Ibid.*, p. 39.

[18]*Ibid.*

[19]See "What is a Dogmatic Statement?," *BQT* I, p. 198; *JGM*, p. 32. See also John Cobb's criticism concerning the implications of Perrin's procedure in his review article on "Wolfhart Pannenberg's 'Jesus: God and Man'," *The Journal of Religion* 49, 1969, pp. 194f. (Hereafter: *JR*.)

[20]*JGM*, p. 13.

[21]See particularly Ernst Käsemann's "The Beginnings of Christian Theology" and "On the Topic of Primitive Christian Apocalyptic," *Journal for Theology and the Church 6: Apocalypticism*, pp. 17-46, 99-133.

[22]Käsemann, "The Beginnings of Christian Theology," *op. cit.*, pp. 39f.: "while Jesus did take his start from the apocalyptically determined message of the Baptist, yet his own preaching was not constitutively stamped by apocalyptic but proclaimed the immediate nearness of God."

[23]Cf., *e.g.*, Robert Funk's observation in "Apocalyptic as an Historical and Theological Problem in Current New Testament Scholarship," *Journal for Theology and the Church 6: Apocalypticism*, p. 189, that Jesus "bracketed apocalyptic out."

[24]*JGM*, p. 62. Cf. John Cobb's succinct comment in *JR* 49, 1969, p. 195: "If, as Käsemann says, Jesus started from the apocalyptically determined message of John the Baptist, and if, as Käsemann and Perrin agree, apocalypticism dominated the thought of the early Christian community, Jesus' own freedom from conditioning by this apocalypticism would be little short of miraculous!"

[25]Bornkamm, *Jesus of Nazareth*, pp. 66f., 176f.

[26]"The Revelation of God in Jesus of Nazareth," *TaH*, p. 112. See also Ulrich Wilckens, "The Understanding of Revelation Within the History of Primitive Christianity," *RaH*, p. 72.

[27]*JGM*, p. 63; Wilckens, *RaH*, pp. 73-75. On the extent of the role which this actually plays in Pannenberg's thought, see *infra*, p. 194.

[28]"Redemptive Event and History," *BQT* I, pp. 23f., 36. Norman Perrin discerned in Jesus' rejection of a calculating of the time of the end a repudiation of the apocalyptic understanding of history. See his *The Kingdom of God in the Teaching of Jesus* (Philadelphia: The Westminster Press, 1963), pp. 177f., 185. But for Pannenberg, that disinterest in setting forth signs of the end is due to Jesus' sense of its extreme imminence (*JGM*, p. 61); the apocalyptic view of history continued to function as a presupposition of the expectation.

[29]"The Revelation of God in Jesus of Nazareth," *TaH*, pp. 111f. Cf. also the fuller expression of the idea by Wilckens in *RaH*, p. 70: "it is only through an apocalyptic understanding of the Law that Jesus would be able to set the authority of his own 'I' against the authority of the Torah as it is understood in Rabbinic theology. This means that the authority of the Torah does not appear to consist of a once-and-for-all manifestation of the will of God that can allow for all human contingencies. Rather, its authority is conceived of as an expression of the authority of the God who is active in history, and whose self-revelation in his impending eschatological activity of salvation is the goal toward which the just orient themselves in their efforts to keep the Law. The only background that would allow for the development of a polemic against the Rabbinic understanding of the Law as we find it in Jesus' teaching is a system that would direct the God-oriented gaze not toward the Law, but toward history and its end."

[30]*JGM*, pp. 60f., 63; "The Revelation of God," *TaH*, p. 112. See also Wilckens' discussion of what he calls the apocalyptic concept of "proleptic-eschatological revelation" in Jesus' claim, *RaH*, pp. 66, 69f., 76, 78-80. I have already called into question the extent to which the apocalyptic tradition directly reflects an understanding of God's self-disclosure as distinctively futural, such that the implicitly anticipatory element in Jesus' claim of authority would seem to be more at home with the identifiable Old Testament tradition of the *Erweiswort* than in apocalyptic. It is illuminating to realize that the apocalyptic texts to which Pannenberg points as embodying the explicit understanding of a futurity of revelation, as an ultimate disclosure of the "glory" of God, are from the Christian era: IV Ezra 7:42, 9:5; II Baruch 21:22ff. (See *JGM*, pp. 128f., ft. 31.)

[31]"The Revelation of God," *TaH*, p. 112. See also *JGM*, p. 217.

[32]Wilckens, "The Understanding of Revelation within the History of Primitive Christianity," *RaH*, p. 71.

[33]See *JGM*, p. 61, for what follows.

[34]Wilckens observes, *RaH*, p. 69, that this nakedness of the "I" of Jesus "springs the framework" of apocalyptic.

[35]These two points Jesus has in common with John the Baptist, indicating, once again, the relativity of the question of the extent of radicalization of the apocalyptic tradition.

[36]See also "Redemptive Event and History," *BQT* I, p. 23; and Wilckens, *RaH*, pp. 71, 75.

[37]See also "The Revelation of God," *TaH*, pp. 112f.

[38]*OaG*, p. 92. (The translation in *RaH*, p. 127, is substantively in error.)

[39]The third and fourth points are at the heart of Pannenberg's interpretation of Jesus' relationship to the Reign of God and therefore will be considered more fully in the discussion following.

[40]So Peter C. Hodgson, "Pannenberg on Jesus: A Review Article," *Journal of the American Academy of Religion* 36, 1968, p. 383.

[41]*JGM*, p. 217.

[42]*Ibid.*, p. 61.

[43]*E.g.*, Reginald Fuller, in *The Foundations of New Testament Christology* (New York: Charles Scribner's Sons, 1965), p. 130, suggests that Jesus' message is rooted in "the eschatology of a reduced apocalyptic." But reduced from what? And to what degree?

[44]Consider, *e.g.*, *TKG*, p. 53: "This resounding motif of Jesus' message--the imminent Kingdom of God--must be recovered as a key to the whole of Christian theology."

[45]*Ibid.*, p. 102.

[46]"The Revelation of God," *TaH*, pp. 103f., 107f.; *TKG*, pp. 54, 56.

[47]See, *e.g.*, Perrin's thorough analyses of a major portion of the relevant material in *Rediscovering the Teaching of Jesus*.

[48]"Can Christianity Do without an Eschatology?," *The Christian Hope*, p. 30.

[49] *Ibid.*, pp. 30f.

[50] *TKG*, pp. 54, 56.

[51] "The Revelation of God," *TaH*, p. 113.

[52] *JGM*, p. 242.

[53] *Ibid.*, p. 366.

[54] *Ibid.*, p. 255; "The Revelation of God," *TaH*, p. 113. It is remarkable that Pannenberg even interprets the passage dearest to the hearts of realized eschatologists, Luke 17:20f., as referring actually to "the imminent but not definitely dated future" in whose midst one finds oneself. (*JGM*, pp. 226f.)

[55] *JGM*, p. 366; "The Significance of Eschatology for the Understanding of the Apostolicity and Catholicity of the Church," *One in Christ* 6, 1970, p. 415.

[56] *JGM*, p. 217.

[57] *Ibid.*, pp. 227-29.

[58] *TKG*, p. 53.

[59] "Future and Unity," *HFM*, pp. 62, 65.

[60] Hans Conzelmann, "Present and Future in the Synoptic Tradition," *Journal for Theology and the Church 5: God and Christ: Existence and Province*, ed. Robert Funk (New York: Harper & Row, 1968), p. 36.

[61] Ernst Fuchs, "Jesus' Understanding of Time," *Studies of the Historical Jesus* (London: SCM Press, 1965), pp. 104-66, esp. p. 144.

[62] Robert Funk, "Apocalyptic as an Historical and Theological Problem in Current New Testament Scholarship," *Journal for Theology and the Church 6: Apocalypticism*, p. 185.

[63] *Ibid.*, p. 182.

[64] *Ibid.*, p. 183.

[65] *Ibid.*, p. 179.

[66] *JGM*, p. 58. See also "The God of Hope," *BQT* II, p. 237f.

[67] *TKG*, p. 53.

[68] "The Revelation of God," *TaH* , p. 113.

[69] *JGM*, pp. 64, 216f.; "The Revelation of God," *TaH*, p. 112.

[70] *TKG*, p. 54.

[71] "On Historical and Theological Hermeneutic," *BQT* I, p. 178; "Appearance as the Arrival of the Future," *TKG*, p. 133; "Response to the Discussion," *TaH*, p. 267, ft. 77.

[72] "The Revelation of God," *TaH*, p. 113; *JGM*, p. 61. This way of interpreting the presentness of the imminent Reign through the category of "prolepsis" or "pre-happening" is not original with Pannenberg. Rudolf Otto, in *The Kingdom of God and the Son of Man*, trans. Floyd Filson and Bertram Lee-Woolf (Boston: Starr King Press, 1943), p. 109, spoke of the Reign in Jesus' proclamation in terms of a "preliminary dawning": "It was not yet present itself, but it was present as a power effective in advance." H. V. Martin, in "The Messianic Age," *Expository Times* 52, 1940-41, p. 272, referred to the Reign of God as having come "proleptically" in Jesus' ministry. Reginald Fuller has pursued this line of thought the most thoroughly. In his *The Mission and Achievement of Jesus* (London: SCM Press, 1954), p. 50, he wrote of the power of God's Reign as "proleptically operative" in Jesus, though its coming remained "a decisive act of the future." (Cf. pp. 25, 32, 107.) So also, in his later *The Foundations of New Testament Christology* (New York: Charles Scribner's Sons, 1965), pp. 104f., Fuller repeated the emphasis on a proleptic presence of the future Reign, of which Jesus' deeds were present actualizations.

[73] "Can Christianity Do without an Eschatology?," *The Christian Hope*, p. 30.

[74] *E.g.*, "The Revelation of God," *TaH*, pp. 102f., 110; "Appearance as the Arrival of the Future," *TKG*, p. 133.

[75] *JGM*, p. 229.

[76] "The Revelation of God," *TaH*, p. 113.

[77] The closest that he comes to doing so is in *TKG*, pp. 54-56, where he contends that Jesus himself did not actually spell out the implications of his understanding of God because God's being was not a point of controversy among his listeners. But even here he only makes the statement that Jesus saw "God's claim on the world" as something to be viewed "exclusively in terms of" the coming Reign.

[78] "The God of Hope," *BQT* II, pp. 240, 242; *TKG*, pp. 55f.; "Can Christianity Do without an Eschatology?," *The Christian Hope*, pp. 30f.

79"Future and Unity," *HGM*, p. 65. See also "Zeit und Ewigkeit," *GsT* II, p. 197. The observation by John Cobb, in another context, that "the total identification of God with the Kingdom of God is alien" to the New Testament, is no doubt correct. (Review of Gerhard Sauter's *Zukunft und Verheissung, Erasmus* 18, 1966, col. 207.) The question Pannenberg raises is whether a more adequate understanding of what is contained in Jesus' proclamation legitimately leads to the subsequent conclusion that the two are indeed one and the same--whether or not Jesus or the kerygma directly regarded them to be so.

80Bornkamm, *Jesus of Nazareth*, pp. 176, 228.

81Heinz Eduard Tödt, *The Son of Man in the Synoptic Tradition*, trans. Dorothea M. Barton (Philadelphia: The Westminster Press, 1965), pp. 32ff.

82*JGM*, pp. 59f., 62f. So also Wilckens, *RaH*, pp. 73f. Cf. Ferdinand Hahn, *The Titles of Jesus in Christology*, trans. Harold Knight and George Ogg (New York: World Publishing Co., 1969), pp. 22ff.

83*JGM*, p. 59. See also Tödt, *op. cit.*, pp. 57, 229. The direction in which the community moved in its interpretation is plainly visible in the Matthean version of Luke 12:8, where the distinction is eliminated (Matthew 10:32f.).

84Philipp Vielhauer, "Gottesreich und Menschensohn in der Verkündigung Jesu," *Festschrift für Günther Dehn*, ed. Wilhelm Schneemelcher (Neukirchen Kreis Moers: Verlag der Buchhandlung des Erziehungsvereings, 1957), pp. 51-79; see especially Sections II and IV, and pp. 53, 76. So also Hans Conzelmann, *Jesus*, trans. J. Raymond Lord (Philadelphia: Fortress Press, 1973), p. 45.

85Vielhauer, *op. cit.*, p. 79.

86Tödt, *op. cit.*, pp. 332-34. Pannenberg regards Vielhauer's subsequent response ("Jesus und der Menschensohn: Zur Diskussion mit Heinz Eduard Tödt und Eduard Schweizer," *ZThK* 60, 1963, pp. 133-77) not to have substantively weakened Tödt's arguments: see *JGM*, pp. 59f., ft. 22.

87Vielhauer, "Gottesreich und Menschensohn in der Verkündigung Jesu," *op. cit.*, p. 77. Following him, Conzelmann, "Present and Future in the Synoptic Tradition, *op. cit.*, p. 281, and *Jesus*, p. 46; Käsemann, "The Beginnings of Christian Theology," *op. cit.*, pp. 39f.

88See Cobb's critique of this mixing of methods, *JR* 49, 1969, p. 194.

89*JGM* , p. 60, ft. 22.

[90]Norman Perrin, "Putting Back the Clock," review of *JGM, Christian Century* 85, 1968, pp. 1575-76.

[91]"A Theological Conversation with Wolfhart Pannenberg," *Dialog* 11, 1972, p. 291. He remarks there: "I think there is an additional argument for the authenticity of this particular group of Son of Man sayings in that their structure corresponds very closely to other elements of the Jesus tradition that are usually regarded as authentic. The way in which present and future are related is very similar in this group of Son of Man sayings to other elements of Jesus' proclamation. Precisely for this reason the rejection of the authenticity of the Son of Man sayings in itself would not deprive my christology of its historical basis."

[92]Perrin expended a considerable amount of scholarly energy in pursuit of this issue. Nearly all the essays in his volume of collected writings, *A Modern Pilgrimage in New Testament Christology* (Philadelphia: Fortress Press, 1974), deal extensively with the Son of Man traditions. Perrin interpreted all the apocalyptic Son of Man sayings as Christian midrashes on Daniel 7:13 (see especially pp. 34f.), based on the conviction that no general proclamation of a coming Son of Man existed in Jewish apocalyptic (pp. 24ff., 59f.). I have already acknowledged that the Son of Man represents a rather minor motif in the apocalyptic literature extant in Jesus' day. But Jesus himself could conceivably be just as responsible for creatively appropriating Daniel 7:13 as the early Christian community.

[93]*JGM*, p. 58. See also Wilckens, "The Understanding of Revelation within the History of Primitive Christianity," *RaH*, p. 76. Pannenberg's position is developed in critical awareness of the role that Jesus' pre-Easter claim to authority has come to play within the post-Bultmannian contributions to the new quest for the historical Jesus. See *JGM*, pp. 53-58.

[94]*JGM*, pp. 60f., 63. See also the summary paragraph, *ibid.*, p. 66.

[95]Wilckens, *RaH*, p. 77.

[96]*JGM*, pp. 63-65.

[97]*Ibid.*, p. 65. Wilckens had maintained that the proof for Jesus' claim could be given only in Jesus' *Geschick*. (See *OaG*, pp. 59f., the translation in *RaH*, p. 77, is problematic.) Pannenberg qualifies that with the observation that only in retrospect could one conclude that the particularity of Jesus' own fate, *i.e.*, his resurrection from the dead, was interpretable as "the beginning of the end event in his person" and thereby the requisite confirmation of the truth of his message." (*JGM*, p. 64, ft. 37.)

[98]In the architectonic of Pannenberg's Christology, the entire discussion of Jesus' claim of authority occurs as the initial section of the chapter dealing with Jesus' resurrection (*JGM*, pp. 53ff.)

[99] In presenting Pannenberg's interpretation of the significance of the resurrection before dealing with the question of its historical authenticity, I am repeating his own order of the discussion, in *JGM*, pp. 66-106.

[100] Richard R. Niebuhr, *Resurrection and Historical Reason* (New York: Charles Scribner's Sons, 1957). See esp. pp. 3f., 171, 178.

[101] Pannenberg has noted his continuity with Niebuhr's point of view, though with a reservation about the adequacy of Niebuhr's accent upon the role of memory (vis-a-vis critical inquiry) as avenue to historical events. See "The Revelation of God," *TaH*, p. 114, ft. 8.

[102] Quoted from personal communication with Pannenberg by Frank Tupper in his *The Theology of Wolfhart Pannenberg* (Philadelphia: The Westminster Press, 1973), p. 146. Cf. *JGM*, p. 112.

[103] "The Revelation of God," *TaH*, p. 115.

[104] *JGM*, p. 75. See also "The Revelation of God," *TaH*, p. 115; "On Historical and Theological Hermeneutic," *BQT* I, p. 180; *WIM*, p. 53; "Analogy and Doxology," *BQT* I, p. 236; "What is Truth?," *BQT* II, pp. 24f.

[105] *AC*, p. 98.

[106] *JGM*, p. 397.

[107] *Ibid.*, p. 187; "Analogy and Doxology," *BQT* I, pp. 235f. The metaphorical, or "doxological," character of God talk is a facet of Pannenberg's understanding that is dealt with below, in the following chapter.

[108] See *supra*, Ch. 2, Section C.

[109] "Redemptive Event and History," *BQT* I, p. 37.

[110] *JGM*, p. 108. See also "Analogy and Doxology," *BQT* I, p. 236.

[111] *JGM*, p. 397.

[112] Robinson, "Revelation as Word and as History," *TaH*, pp. 35f.

[113] *JGM*, p. 108. See also *WIM*, p. 52, where he speaks of the metaphor of resurrection as an "appropriate and unavoidable image."

[114] "Dogmatische Erwägungen," *GsT* II, p. 168, ft. 4.

[115]"Constructive and Critical Functions of Christian Eschatology," *Harvard Theological Review* 77, 1984, p. 133.

[116]Pannenberg devotes a specific section in his Christology to the identifying of the various facets comprising the "immediate inherent significance" of Jesus' resurrection. (*JGM*, Ch. 2, Section II; the original title of the section, as taken from the German edition, should properly read: "The Significance of Jesus' Resurrection in the Traditio-Historical Situation of Primitive Christianity.") Of the six points identified there, only the first, second, and fourth ones appear to be of fundamental importance with regard to the *continuing* significance of that event, and are appropriately treated in the course of the discussion that follows. I have seen fit to glean from the whole of Pannenberg's writings a somewhat different set of six aspects of the relevance of Jesus' resurrection for the Christian understanding of reality, and believe that these more genuinely convey the role which the resurrection plays in Pannenberg's theological system. The points which he has identified as basic to the initial impact of Jesus' resurrection upon his Jewish contemporaries, however, are listed here for the sake of clarification:
(a) *If Jesus has been raised, then the end of the world has begun.*
(b) *If Jesus has been raised, this for a Jew can only mean that God himself has confirmed the pre-Easter activity of Jesus.*
(c) *Through his resurrection from the dead, Jesus moved so close to the Son of Man that the insight became obvious: the Son of Man is none other than the man Jesus who will come again.*
(d) *If Jesus, having been raised from the dead, is ascended to God and if thereby the end of the world has begun, then God is ultimately revealed in Jesus.*
(e) *The transition to the Gentile mission is motivated by the eschatological resurrection of Jesus as resurrection of the crucified One.*
(f) *Particularly the last consequence throws light on the relationship between the appearances of the resurrected Jesus and the words spoken by him: what the early Christian tradition transmitted as the words of the risen Jesus is to be understood in terms of its content as the explication of the significance inherent in the resurrection itself.* (*JGM*, pp. 66-73.)

[117]*OaG*, pp. 98, 104f., 107 (*RaH*, pp. 134, 142, 146); "On Historical and Theological Hermeneutic," *BQT* I, pp. 179-81; *JGM*, p. 69; "The Revelation of God," *TaH*, p. 117.

[118]*JGM*, p. 66. See also *Ibid.*, p. 106; "On Historical and Theological Hermeneutic," *BQT* I, p. 181; "The Revelation of God," *TaH*, p. 115; "What is Truth?," *BQT* II, p. 24.

[119]*JGM*, pp. 226, 242; "The Revelation of God," *TaH*, p. 114. "But it is true of every 'fulfillment' that it only rarely corresponds exactly to the announcement prior to it." (*TaH*, p. 116.)

[120]*JGM*, pp. 242, 226.

[121]"On Historical and Theological Hermeneutic," *BQT* I, p. 179.

[122]*JGM*, p. 107 (*Grundzüge der Christologie* [Gütersloh: Gütersloher Verlagshaus Gerd Mohn, 1964], p. 105) (hereafter: *GC*). See also *JGM*, p. 243, where Pannenberg speaks of a "parallelism" between "what has already appeared in Jesus" and that which "still lies ahead for all those bound to him in faith."

[123]*Ibid.*, p. 108, italics added.

[124]"On Historical and Theological Hermeneutic," *BQT* I, p. 179. See also *JGM*, p. 242.

[125]*JGM*, p. 243; "On Historical and Theological Hermeneutic," *BQT* I, p. 179, ft. 44; "The Revelation of God," *TaH*, p. 117.

[126]"What is Truth?," *BQT* II, pp. 24f.; "Insight and Faith," *ibid.*, p. 44.

[127]"Response to the Discussion," *TaH*, pp. 262-64. Cf. "On Historical and Theological Heremeneutic," *BQT* I, pp. 179f.

[128]"On HIstorical and Theological Hermeneutic," *BQT* I, p. 180.

[129]"Insight and Faith," *BQT* II, p. 44. See also "Dogmatic Theses," *RaH*, p. 142.

[130]*JGM*, p. 367.

[131]*Ibid.*

[132]*JGM*, pp. 67f., 106, 112, 135; "The Revelation of God," *TaH*, p. 116; "On Historical and Theological Hermeneutic," *BQT* I, pp. 178f.; "Dogmatische Erwägungen zur Auferstehung Jesu," *GsT* II, p. 163.

[133]"On Historical and Theological Hermeneutic," *BQT* I, pp. 178f.

[134]"The Revelation of God," *TaH*, p. 116.

[135]See also Ulrich Wilckens' parallel treatment of this point, in "The Understanding of Revelation," *RaH*, p. 79; *Resurrection,* trans. A. M. Stewart (Atlanta: John Knox Press, 1978), pp. 124-32; and "The Tradition-history of the Resurrection of Jesus," *The Significance of the Message of the Resurrection for Faith in Jesus Christ,* ed. C. F. D. Moule (Naperville: Alec R. Allenson, Inc., 1968), pp. 66, 70. Gerhard Delling concurs in this interpretation, in "The Significance of the Resurrection of Jesus for Faith in Jesus Christ," *ibid.*, pp. 99f.

[136] *JGM*, pp. 68f., 106.

[137] *Ibid.*, pp. 69, 129; "Dogmatic Theses," *RaH*, pp. 143f.; "On Historical and Theological Hermeneutic," *BQT* I, pp. 178f.; "The Revelation of God," *TaH*, p. 125.

[138] *JGM*, p. 69.

[139] *Ibid.*, p. 129.

[140] "The Revelation of God," *TaH*, p. 125.

[141] "Insight and Faith," *BQT* II, p. 44. See also *JGM*, p. 108; "What is Truth?," *BQT* II, p. 25.

[142] Günter Klein. *Theologie des Wortes Gottes und die Hypothese der Universalgeschichte* (München: Chr. Kaiser Verlag, 1964), pp. 38f. (especially ft. 35), 42, 44f.

[143] "Insight and Faith," *BQT* II, p. 44.

[144] See *JGM*, pp. 129f.

[145] *JGM*, p. 129. For the full quotation of the relevant paragraph, see *supra*, Ch. 5, note 31.

[146] *Ibid.*, pp. 129f. See also pp. 323, 367f.

[147] *Ibid.*, p. 69.

[148] See especially "Christologie und Theologie," *GsT* II, pp. 129-45.

[149] *JGM*, p. 130. See also "Christologie und Theologie," *GsT* II, pp. 139ff. I will have occasion in the next chapter to explore the extent to which Pannenberg allows this principle to operate materially in his specific understanding of the nature of divine reality.

[150] *JGM*, p. 224.

[151] *Ibid.*, p. 321. Cf. p. 137: "He was not only unrecognizable before Easter, but he would not have been who he was without the Easter event."

[152] *Ibid.*, p. 224.

[153] *Ibid.*, pp. 135-37, 321; "Dogmatische Erwägungen," *GsT* II, p. 171. "Had Jesus not been raised from the dead, it would have been decided that he also had not

been one with God previously. But through his resurrection it is decided, not only so far as our knowledge is concerned, but with respect to reality, that Jesus is one with God and retroactively that he was also already one with God previously." (*JGM*, p. 136.) Of course, in Pannenberg's schema, this notion of the retroactive signficance of a futural occurrence holds true not merely in the special case of Jesus but for all events whatsoever.

154*JGM*, pp. 388-91; "Dogmatische Thesen," *OaG*, p. 106 (The relevant phrase is inexplicably omitted in the *RaH* translation!); "Redemptive Event and History," *BQT* I, pp. 36f.; "On Historical and Theological Hermeneutic," *BQT* I, p. 181; "What is Truth?," *BQT* II, pp. 26f.; "Kerygma and History," *BQT* I, pp. 94f., ft. 20.

155See *supra*, Ch. 2, Section C, and Ch. 3, Sections A through D.

156"What is Truth?," *BQT* II, pp. 24f.

157See "Redemptive Event and History," *BQT* I, pp. 36-38.

158*GC*, p. 406 (cf. *JGM*, p. 390). See also "Kerygma and History," *BQT* I, p. 94, ft. 20.

159Cf. also "Response to the Discussion," *TaH*, pp. 240f.: The history of Jesus "is itself the event uniting and reconciling all other events to the whole."

160*JGM*, pp. 78f., 83-88; *WIM*, p. 53; "The Revelation of God," *TaH*, pp. 116f.; *AC*, pp. 103, 170. See also *supra*, Ch. 5, Section D.

161Cf. "Dogmatische Erwägungen," *GsT* II, p. 162.

162See *supra*, Ch. 5, Section E.

163*JGM*, p. 88: "The unity of mankind, however, expresses itself in the concept of the resurrection of the dead in that this event is expected as universal fate that will involve all men. Even if the resurrection as a saving event does not happen to every individual, it is still related to the unity of humanity because it is connected with the idea of a universal judgment coming over all men at the end of history in which every individual will be measured in terms of the destiny of man as such." The intended meaning here is less clear than Pannenberg's rather explicit observation earlier in his anthropology: "Only for the person who is in community with Jesus does the resurrection mean eternal life as well as judgment." (*WIM*, p. 81.)

164*AC*, p. 35. "Salvation is only guaranteed to the man who has definite communion with Jesus--and who has through this communion the hope of overcoming death with Jesus. But all other men, too, even those who died before Jesus' ministry, can achieve the salvation which appeared in him--even if in ways which are beyond our comprehension." (*Ibid.*)

165The most explicit indication is found in his presentation at the 1971 conference on "Hope and the Future of Man," to wit: "It takes a resurrection of the dead to have all human individuals of all times participate in the perfect society of the kingdom of God. Only on this condition the destiny of mankind which comprises the total number of its individuals can be claimed to be accomplished. If the social and individual destinies of man condition each other so that they can be realized only together, then the totality of human individuals is required for the realization of the social destiny of man." ("Future and Unity," *HFM*, pp. 70f.) See also the brief discussion *supra*, Ch. 4, note 81.

166"The Revelation of God," *TaH*, p. 115. See also *WIM*, pp. 50f.

167The basis for this is to be found in the recognition that Paul is the only New Testament writer who conveys first-hand information of a post-resurrection appearance. See *JGM*, pp. 76f.

168*JGM*, pp. 76f.; *WIM*, p. 50; *AC*, p. 99.

169*JGM*, pp. 75, 87; *WIM*, p. 50; *AC*, p. 98.

170*WIM*, p. 50.

171*AC*, p. 97, referring to the resurrection of Jesus--but, by extension, applicable to any and all cases.

172*JGM*, p. 76, and also *AC*, p. 99.

173*Ibid.* (both citations).

174*JGM*, p. 66.

175*Ibid.*, p. 87.

176Cobb has observed that, for Pannenberg, "reality is bodily reality and there can be no other." ("Wolfhart Pannenberg's 'Jesus: God and Man'," *JR* 49, 1969, p. 197.)

177"Dogmatische Erwägungen," *GsT* II, p. 167.

178*Ibid.*, p. 168. The same idea appears in Pannenberg's definition (re Paul) of "spiritual body" as "a living being which, instead of being separated from this origin [God's Spirit]--as we are in our present existence--remains united with it." (*AC*, pp. 98f.)

[179]"The Doctrine of the Spirit and the Task of a Theology of Nature," *Theology* 75, 1972, p. 10 (see also p. 21).

[180]A word is in order about the temporal sequence of the sources on which this and the previous paragraph are based. *AC*, which stands in direct conceptual continuity with *JGM* on this subject, was published in Germany in 1972, whereas the lecture of Jesus' resurrection was delivered six years earlier and published in 1968. That would seem to negate the notion of "earlier" and "later" which I am advancing here. However, the lectures on the Apostles' Creed were first delivered in 1965--and I believe their subsequent publication did not occasion extensive revision. Ideas emerging long before 1972 simply were not incorporated into the published text of *AC*.

[181]"The Doctrine of the Spirit," *Theology* 75, 1972, p. 15. Cobb regards this as a significant step that could transcend the "unnecessary difficulties" that Pannenberg creates for the understanding of resurrection. (Cobb, *Christ in a Pluralistic Age* [Philadelphia: The Westminster Press, 1975], p. 253.) Pannenberg's more recent defense of the bodiliness of the resurrection has shifted to a different focus, emphasizing now the comprehensiveness of the divine memory: "every actual event remains present in *all* its aspects to the eternity of God." ("A Liberal Logos Christology: The Christology of John Cobb," in *John Cobb's Theology in Process*, ed. David R. Griffin and Thomas J. J. Altizer [Philadelphia: The Westminster Press, 1977], p. 149, note 21. See also "Constructive and Critical Functions of Christian Eschatology," *Harvard Theological Review* 77, 1984, p. 133.

[182]"Dogmatic Theses," *RaH*, p. 146; "Nachwort zur zweiten Auflage," *OaG*, pp. 141f.; *JGM*, pp. 81-83, 94, 96 (ft. 96).

[183]See especially *JGM*, pp. 82f. The relevant passage has previously been quoted herein, on p. 154. Let the critical reader not be misled by the immediately subsequent observation: "Of course, such considerations in no way decide the question of the truth of the apocalyptic expectation." (*JGM*, p. 83.) The point being scored by this reminder is simply that Pannenberg's discussion of the *meaning* of Jesus' resurrection must yet be completed by considering the decisive question of its *historical authenticity*, in the section which then follows.

[184]"The Revelation of God," *TaH*, pp. 116f.

[185]Alfred Suhl, "Zur Beurteilung der Überlieferung von der Auferstehung Jesu in Wolfhart Pannenberg's 'Grundzüge der Christologie'," *NZsTR* 12, 1970, p. 305.

[186]The point of this transitional paragraph is that Pannenberg would not be concerned to pursue with equal vigor the question of the historicity of the events behind, say, the traditions of Jesus' virginial conception or of his walking on water because the meaning such reported occurrences bear simply does not lead to any similar sort of momentous consequences that he perceives in the resurrection.

[187]See *supra*, pp. 73f.

[188]*JGM*, p. 109 (see also p. 97).

[189]"Dogmatische Erwägungen," *GsT* II, p. 164.

[190]One might add: especially if that singular explanation can be seen to stand in strong continuity with a tradition anticipating it--for that consideration underlies Pannenberg's argument here. But the antecedent *tradition* cannot *establish* the historicity of the event--a point to which I will have occasion to return yet again.

[191]See *JGM*, p. 98; *AC*, pp. 110f.; and "Dogmatische Erwägungen," *GsT* II, p. 164. See also his discussion of the historical contingency of natural law, in "The Doctrine of Creation and Modern Science," *Zygon* 23, 1988, pp. 10f.

[192]Walter Künneth, *The Theology of the Resurrection* (London: SCM Press, 1965), p. 242.

[193]*Ibid.*, p. 31.

[194]Reginald Fuller, *The Formation of the Resurrection Narratives* (New York: The Macmillan Company, 1971), p. 23.

[195]*JGM*, p. 99.

[196]"Dogmatische Erwägungen," *GsT* II, p. 165.

[197]*JGM*, p. 99.

[198]"Dogmatische Erwägungen," *GsT* II, p. 165.

[199]*JGM*, p. 99. So also, *ibid.*, p. 109: "If, however, historical study declares itself unable to establish what 'really' happened on Easter, then all the more, faith is not able to do so; for faith cannot ascertain anything certain about events of the past that would perhaps be inaccessible to the historian." Cf. "Nachwort," *GOG*, p. 136.

[200]*JGM*, p. 98.

[201]John Alsup has dedicated careful attention to a form-critical analysis of the Gospel appearance stories and concluded that, in their earliest discernible structure, they correspond very closely to anthropomorphic theophany stories of the Old Testament and arose independently of the empty tomb tradition with which they were later coupled redactionally. See his *The Post-Resurrection Appearance Stories of the Gospel-Tradition* (Stuttgart: Calwe Verlag, 1975), pp. 265, 269f., and, concerning the latter point, pp. 58, 85-116. Alsup maintains that, in contrast to the "heavenly radiance" type of appearance, reflected in Acts and Paul's writings, these bear no relation at all to the tradition of apocalyptic (p. 265, especially ft. 734). Although

Alsup expressly insists that his analysis cannot be directed toward establishing or denying the historical authenticity of a presumed Easter event behind the tradition, he does conclude finally (273f.) that such is not pointed to by his analysis; to the contrary, the furthest point to which we can reach is the *Gattung* itself "which declared that the risen Lord encountered and re-established fellowship with his own and sent them out in his service" (274). However, he does not offer any suggestion for what triggered the novelty of perceiving *Jesus* to be the appearing one (vis-a-vis a theophany of God disclosing something *about* Jesus), nor does he account for the antiquity, in the form-tradition, of the initial presence of *female* witnesses--away from which the tradition consistently moves in the direction of male apostolic confirmation of the appearances. In this latter regard, Alsup even concedes, concerning the empty tomb narratives, that "in essence this tradition had to be preserved because it is in its origin historically reliable. In spite of the weak position of the female witness in a Jewish-Christian community it could not be displaced, only modified" (106).

[202]*JGM*, pp. 89-92.

[203]*Ibid.*, pp. 92f.

[204]*Ibid.*, p. 93.

[205]*Ibid.*, pp. 96f.

[206]*Ibid.*, p. 96. It is basically this consideration which distinguishes the historical credibility of these reported experiences from subsequent encounters with the presumably risen Christ--*i.e.*, the latter do not historically authenticate Jesus' resurrection in the way the former are understood to do because, in Pannenberg's view, contemporary encounters already presuppose that Easter faith whereas the initial encounters are considered to have given rise to it.

[207]*Ibid.*, pp. 94f.; "Dogmatische Erwägungen," *GsT* II, p. 170.

[208]*JGM*, p. 93.

[209]See *ibid.*, p. 81.

[210]"The Revelation of God," *TaH*, pp. 114f.

[211]*Ibid.*, p. 96.

[212]*Ibid.*, p. 100.

[213]*Ibid.*, pp. 101f.

[214]*Ibid.*, pp. 100f.

215 *Ibid.*, pp. 101, 103; "Response to Dr. J. N. D. Anderson," *Christianity Today* 12, 1968, pp. 682f.

216 *JGM*, p. 100.

217"Response to the Discussion," *TaH*, p. 265, ft. 76; "Response to Dr. J. N. D. Anderson," *Christianity Today* 12, 1968, pp. 682f.

218Willi Marxsen, "The Resurrection of Jesus as a Historical and Theological Problem," *The Significance of the Message of the Resurrection for Faith in Jesus Christ*, ed. C. F. D. Moule (Naperville, Ill.: Alec R. Allenson, 1968), pp. 24f.

219 *JGM*, pp. 102f.

220 *Ibid.*, pp. 104f.

221 *Ibid.*, p. 109.

222"Dogmatische Erwägungen," *GsT* II, p. 168. Cf. similarly the excerpt from p. 167, quoted *supra* on p. 204: "What can favorably be said historically about the event of Jesus' resurrection is therefore that Jesus--who was dead--lives, without saying precisely what the word 'life' means where, beyond the statement that Jesus has not remained dead."

223"Nachwort," *GOG*, p. 139; *AC*, p. 114.

224Gerald O'Collins, "Is the Resurrection an 'Historical' Event?," *Heythrop Journal* 8, 1967, p. 384.

225"Dogmatische Erwägungen," *GsT* II, pp. 166f. Cf. also "Response to the Discussion," *TaH*, p. 266, ft. 76: "the *event* of the resurrection of Jesus, in contrast to the reality which results from this event, has to do with the transition from our earthly reality to that resurrection-reality which is no longer locatable in space." Thus its "initial point" is located in space, and in time.

226John Cobb, "Wolfhart Pannenberg's 'Jesus: God and Man'," *JR* 49, 1969, pp. 197f.

227Cobb, *Christ in a Pluralistic Age*, p. 253.

228"Dogmatische Erwägungen," *GsT* II, p. 170.

229 *Ibid.* The interpretation serves further to reinforce the notion that Jesus' appearances had the character of apocalyptic visions, breaking in from out of the future.

242

[230]Cobb, "Wolfhart Pannenberg's 'Jesus: God and Man'," *JR* 49, 1969, p. 197.

[231]Marxsen, *op. cit.*, pp. 19-24, 30f.

[232]*Ibid.*, p. 31.

[233]"Dogmatische Erwägungen," *GsT* II, p. 166. See also Pannenberg's reply to Marxsen on resurrection as an "interpretive statement" in "Response to the Discussion," *TaH*, p. 266, ft. 76.

[234]Marxsen, *op. cit.*, p. 28.

[235]Robinson, "Revelation as Word and as History," *TaH*, pp. 41f., ft. 119.

[236]"Dogmatische Erwägungen," *GsT* II, p. 168.

[237]Cobb, "Wolfhart Pannenberg's 'Jesus: God and Man'," *JR* 49, 1969, p. 199.

[238]The structure of this book and the identification of six aspects of the enduring significance of the resurrection of Jesus for Pannenberg's theology were worked out independently of this striking interrelationship, of which I became aware only in retrospect.

[239]See *supra*, pp. 169f. On the discussion that follows here, cf. *supra*, pp. 168-72.

[240]*JGM*, p. 61.

[241]Moltmann makes a somewhat similar point in his *The Crucified God*, trans. R. A. Wilson and John Bowden (New York: Harper & Row, 1974), p. 177, distinguishing between the *justicia distributiva* of "legalistic apocalyptic" and the *justificia justificans* of Jesus' proclamation.

[242]Pannenberg's endeavor to evade the notion of determinism by shifting the locus of divine power from past or present to future will be explicated and evaluted in the following chapter.

[243]See *supra*, p. 171. This is a major instance of where Pannenberg's conclusions about apocalyptic motifs rest on the evidence of literature which actually has its provenance in a later era, such as II Baruch. See also note 30 of the present chapter.

[244]"The Revelation of God," *TaH*, p. 112. See *supra*, p. 187.

[245] Marxsen, *op. cit.,* pp. 31f., 42f.

[246] Several of his critics have raised this question of Pannenberg, though only in a very preliminary and unexplored way. See Klein, *Theologie des Wortes Gottes und die Hypothese der Universal-geschichte,* p. 32, ft. 27; Gerald O'Collins, "Christology from Below," *Interpretation* 23, 1969, p. 247, ft. 46, and "Revelation as History," *Heythrop Journal* 7, 1966, pp. 402f.; and Iain Nicol, "Facts and Meanings: Wolfhart Pannenberg's Theology as History and the Role of the Historical-Critical Method," *Religious Studies* 12, 1976, pp. 137f.

[247] "Dogmatische Erwägungen," *GsT* II, p. 169.

[248] Wilckens, *Auferstehung* (Stuttgart: Kreuz-Verlag, 1970), p. 166 (cf. *Resurrection,* p. 129).

[249] Wilckens, *Resurrection,* p. 27.

[250] *Ibid.,* p. 26. I have restored the italics to their original in the German edition, with which the translator has taken careless liberties. See *Auferstehung,* p. 42. For a further discussion of this concept by Wilckens, see also *Resurrection,* pp. 123-30.

[251] Moltmann, *The Crucified God,* p. 166 (and note 13, p. 197), 176f., 181.

[252] "Afterword to the Fifth German Edition," *JGM,* pp. 403f.; "Christologie und Theologie," *GsT* II, p. 139; "Die Auferstehung Jesu und die Zukunft des Menschen," *GsT* II, pp. 176, 182f.

[253] Moltmann, *op. cit.,* pp. 174-78 and chapter 6. Pannenberg has offered the observation that God's very *divinity* (*Gottheit*) is also established in Jesus' resurrection--or, more precisely, the divinity of the Father proclaimed by Jesus as God: "The crucifixion of Jesus calls into question first of all his claim of divine authority but secondly--judged in the light of the resurrection--even the divinity of the Father himself. The resurrection of Jesus is therefore just as constitutive for the divinity of the Father as for the divine Sonship of Jesus. Without Jesus' resurrection, the Father proclaimed by Jesus would not be God." ("Der Gott der Geschichte," *GsT* II, p. 123.)

[254] See *supra,* pp. 211f., and "Response to the Discussion," *TaH,* p. 265, ft. 76.

[255] Alsup, *op. cit.,* p. 106.

[256] Cobb, "Wolfhart Pannenberg's 'Jesus: God and Man'," *JR* 49, 1969, pp. 199f.

8

GOD THE POWER OF THE FUTURE

Our extended voyage through the fecund seas of
Pannenberg's theological creativity has arrived at its port of destination.
Having charted the ideational seascape by letting his quest for a viable
God-concept serve as polar star and guiding principle, we are at the
point of disembarkment. The compass point has become the journey's
end. There remains now the cardinal task of discerning just where it is
that this venture has brought us. This chapter endeavors to map out in
detail the understanding of God which Pannenberg has been in the
process of developing, and to ascertain just how secure a harbor from
the storms of theistic and atheistic controversy it can be seen to be.

A. The Science of God

An examination of the various forms in which the self-understanding of
theology has been embodied in the course of its history has led us to the
conclusion that theology, as it appears in the history of Christian theology, can
be adequately understood only as a science of God.[1]

God is the subject of the theological enterprise first of all as a problem, a
concern, a "thematic point of reference for all its investigations."[2] The
hypothetical character of the idea of God stands in opposition to a
dogmatic orientation toward theology's essential subject matter which is
never able to escape the two-sided trap of positivism and religious
subjectivism. Rather, Pannenberg contends, if the notion of God is to

transcend its status as a projected hypothesis of the theologian qua scientist, that can occur only by virtue of the discernment of its own implications and by substantiation through the experienced reality of persons and our world with which the ostensible reality of God is "co-given."[3]

What stands strongly at the forefront of Pannenberg's consciousness is the serious possibility that atheism may very well have the last word after all, a possibility that must be engaged head on. To be sure, "atheism" is to be spoken of in the plural: the fundamental reasons for repudiating the notion of God are several in number, and atheism emerges never "in general" but always with a specific shape and character. Three in particular occupy Pannenberg's attention.[4]

J. G. Fichte's "atheism of empty transcendence,"[5] already alluded to herein, is the earliest of these and in many respects the most crucial. The transcendence of God is declared to be an empty notion because of the incompatibility of infinity and personhood.[6] What is required by way of response is not an affirmation of the "non-objectifiability" of God a la Bultmann, which focuses on the human relationship with God but does not legitimate how one can properly continue to use the word "God" at all.[7] Theology's challenge instead is to endeavor to develop a way of understanding God's essential personhood which is consistent with God's infinity of transcendence, a process which for Pannenberg can be achieved only if one surrenders the notion of God as presently extant being, as we have seen.

Secondly, however, Ludwig Feuerbach's "atheism of the science of religion" built beyond Fichte in demonstrating the derivation of divine attributes from human projective self-consciousness. The substance of God is declared to be translatable into the highest ideals of human beings alienated from our own true essence.[8] Again, the response of Barth to retreat into a revelation-ghetto of theology "from above," juxtaposing God's transcendent self-disclosure over against all (projective, hence illegitimate) *human* attempts to embrace the truth of God, is viewed by Pannenberg as inadequate: speech about God can no longer claim to possess genuine cognitive import thereby.[9] What is called for is not the denial that the idea of God is a product of the human mind but a consideration of whether it is in fact an *unessential* product of it--"that is, an idea which is not part of man's understanding of himself which belongs to his essential being."[10] On the contrary, Pannenberg wishes to explore, as we have already observed, the critical correlation between human projections of (or: questioning toward) the divine and the ultimate truth that may be determined to coincide with those projections.

Finally, Friedrich Nietzsche's "atheism of human freedom"[11] took the foregoing developments to the pinnacle of atheistic self-expression, by excluding all notions of divine omnipotence in the name of and on behalf of human self-determination. "Here, atheism has developed from a matter of mere enlightenment--as in Feuerbach--into a matter of the will, of self-affirmation."[12] God must be seen to have died, in order that human beings as free agents of becoming and valuing may get up off our knees and be our true selves. The attempt to reconstitute the act of faith in God in a decision of faith, traced through Kähler to Barth and Bultmann, simply reinforces Nietzsche's own metaphysic of the human will. The only viable alternative is viewed by Pannenberg as the pursuit of "a more radical inquiry into being" which explores whether, in fact, God is not the denial of human freedom but, as I have previously noted,[13] its actual ground.[14]

This very rapid overview of the challenge of modern atheisms, bringing together issues already touched on elsewhere in this study, is intended to bring into focus the fundamental task of theology as the science of God, namely, to develop an understanding of God that effectively overcomes atheistic criticisms. What Pannenberg is convinced of is that atheism's negations "are directed only against the traditional concept of God."[15] The open question of what God might be, beyond that tradition, must be answered in the direction of God's non-extant reality as ground of human freedom and essential vis-a-vis to human self-understanding, in such a way that winds up applauding atheistic criticism for not simply having "shattered the shells of inappropriate concepts of God" but precisely having thereby "freed the kernel which can provide the opportunity for some other kind of talk about God."[16]

A major part of the underlying problem, concerning the God-concept so "husked," is its having become enclosed in the hulls of Greek philosophical conceptuality in the first place. Very early in Pannenberg's theological pilgrimage, he examined the assimilation of philosophical notions about God in early Christian theology.[17] There he observed that the contact of Christian conceptuality with philosophical questions about the true form of the divine may have been occasioned, indeed, "by encounter with the Hellenistic intellectual world, but it is also grounded in the biblical witness to God as the universal God, pertinent not only to Israel but to all peoples."[18] He continued:

> The universal claim of the God of Israel first acquired compelling validity for all men by virtue of the fact that first the Jewish and then the Christian mission presented the God of Israel as the true God sought by philosophy. Thus, the claim of the God of Israel to be alone the God to whom all men belong provides the *theological basis* for the fact that Christian faith has to become

involved in the philosophical question about the true God and has to give an account of its answer right down to the present time.[19]

Nevertheless, it is necessary to realize that the biblical witness to God as radically free originator of the ever new, especially including God's covenanting with a community of the elect within history, was utterly lost in the philosophical understanding, so that Christian theology could "link up with the philosophical idea of God only by breaking through it at the same time."[20] The task is seen not as repudiating the philosophical concepts absolutely but as *transforming* them--and instead of, conversely, allowing the biblical witness to be recast inadequately into alien philosophical terms.[21] The process of reworking the categories of Greek philosophical conceptuality has already been discerned in Pannenberg's elevation of the Hebraic notion of truth as eventful constancy over the Greek understanding of timeless self-identity. It is his intention to extend this orientation in regard to such other crucial issues as the nature of God's transcendent otherness, causal efficacy, eternality, freedom--as this chapter will explicitly disclose.

An additional facet of theology as *Wissenschaft von Gott* merits consideration at this point, and that is the thesis, again emerging relatively early with Pannenberg,[22] that statements about God have the character of "doxological" language. This insight has been borrowed from Pannenberg's teacher Edmund Schlink,[23] who developed the expression in opposition to the doctrine of analogical interpretation in which the reality and character of God are read off by analogy from human conduct and understanding. Recognizing that all biblical speaking of God is rooted in the worship of God, Schlink insisted that worshippers, in the act of adoration, surrender up their "I" and therefore, at the same time, surrender the conceptual univocity of their speaking.[24] Therefore, direct analogicity between our words and the truth of God's essence is transcended. Following his teacher, Pannenberg contends that:

> . . . in doxological statements, the otherwise usual sense of the human word is surrendered in its being used to praise God. To be sure, we speak of God's righteousness. But we thereby release this word from the manipulation of our thought, and must learn ever anew from the reality of God what the word "righteousness" properly means. In the act of adoration, our words are transferred to the sublime infinity of God. They are thereby set in contrast to their ordinary meaning.[25]

There are three interrelated directions in which Pannenberg takes this. Doxological statements are never premises from which conclusions can be deduced, for conclusions follow only from unequivocal concepts.[26] The equivocity of God-langugage is closely tied in with the experiencing of the indirectness of God's own activity in history, in which we perceive individual events as the work of God only when we view them in respect to their interrelatedness as part of an ultimate whole--wherefore religious language is understood to be a special mode of speech conveying the depth dimension of all events.[27] And finally, the *proleptic*, provisional, character of statements about God is of a piece with the doxological:

> Dogmatic statements have a proleptic tendency in that they have all of reality, history as a whole, in view, since in Christ, the consummation of history, the future of us all, has already begun. Only this proleptic conception of the whole of reality, whose wholeness was first constituted by the Christ-event, establishes the possibility of speaking of an act of God in this event (and then, retrospectively, in the history of Israel, too) and, on top of that, of specific properties of God's essence. Thus, the doxological element in the dogmatic statement is founded upon the proleptic, and both are interrelated through the universal meaning that inheres in this particular event.[28]

Therefore the degree of correspondence of our words and concepts to the truth of God is yet open, inasmuch as that to which they point is understood to be still out ahead of us, in the ultimate consummation of history.[29]

One further comment is appropriate here. The development of Pannenberg's understanding of what doxological address most properly should be offered up to God by the science of God has been a remarkably consistent one over a period of some three decades of intense intellectual activity--certainly with no fundamental change;[30] equally certainly with novel insights emerging only gradually; but also, as will occasionally be observed, with conceptual variations that call for a sequential rendering of several of Pannenberg's key ideas in order adequately to integrate them into his overall vision of the nature of God.

B. The Future as God's Mode of Being

"Nothing, nothing had the least importance," pondered the condemned Meursault in Camus' *The Stranger.* "From the dark horizon of my future a sort of slow, persistent breeze had been blowing toward me, all my life long, from the years that were to come. And on its way that breeze had leveled out all the ideas that people tried to foist on me in the equally unreal years I then was living through."[31] This bleak wail encapsulates strikingly the nihilism of the early Camus, highlighting as it does the sense of despair that pervades present existence when nothing is seen to be forthcoming from a person's future but emptiness and death. Translated into Pannenberg's conceptuality, the feeling of Meursault is that if there is no guarantor of ultimate meaning, there is no possibility of meaningfulness from moment to moment. Thus is it of "no consequence" to Meursault whether he dies old or young, whether he is to be guillotined for impetuously killing the Arab on the beach--or because he was seen not to be crying at his mother's funeral.

Pannenberg's most provocative challenge to contemporary theology and atheistic nihilism alike is his conclusion that what is "blowing" upon us from out of the future, what we are ultimately on our way toward, is none other than the true God whose very mode of being (*Seinsbeschaffenheit*) is *the future itself.*[32] This thesis has been expressed in Pannenberg's cryptic observation, widely quoted and almost as widely misunderstood, that God, therefore, "does not yet exist"! In context, Pannenberg stated:

> Jesus proclaimed the rule of God as a reality belonging to the future. This is the coming Kingdom. The idea was not new, being a conventional aspect of Jewish expectation. What was new was Jesus' understanding that God's claim on the world is to be viewed exclusively in terms of his coming rule. Thus it is necessary to say that, *in a restricted but important sense, God does not yet exist.* Since his rule and his being are inseparable, *God's being is still in the process of coming to be.*[33]

Much is contained in this brief passage that requires considerable unpacking--concerning God's reality as futural and therefore presently "in process," concerning the inseparability of God's rule and being, concerning the nature of time itself. But adequately to perceive not only the particularities of Pannenberg's horizontalizing of transcendence but also what lies in back of it calls first of all for a consideration of pre-Pannenbergian theological developments which have influenced his angle of vision in this regard as well as earlier insights in his own work which preceded the emergence of the full-blown notion itself. It is precisely on this facet of Pannenberg's work that the impact of the philosopher of hope Ernst Bloch is to be felt--but not of Bloch alone, and, as it turns out, not to very great an extent.

The earliest significant traces of a notion of God's futurity as that impacts on Pannenberg's understanding are to be found, not surprisingly, in the work of the present century's most encyclopedic theologian, Karl Barth. As far back as *Church Dogmatics* II:1, Barth was referring to God's "post-temporality," though this is but one aspect of God's eternity along with God's pre-temporality and God's supra-temporality.[34] God is said to be "after time": "We move to Him as we come from Him and may accompany Him."[35] Although eternity "has and is simultaneity,"[36] the "perfection" of eternity "is God Himself in His post-temporality."[37] "God is the Last as He was the First. He is, therefore, *the absolute, unsurpassable future* of all time and of all that is in time."[38] Inasmuch as God is the post-temporal eternity toward which we are moving,

He is *the God of all hope*. . . . His *is* the kingdom. He *is* the Last. He *is* the One who is all in all. It is only then, at the goal and end of time, that He will be revealed as this and no longer veiled at all. But He is this already in Himself.[39]

Robert Jenson has noted that, in taking up the theme of the futurity of God, Barth (as well as Bultmann also) de-eschatologized hope into an existential event and God's future into abstract futurity.[40] To a considerable extent this is true. In a lengthy "footnote" section to the discussion of God's post-temporality, Barth did endeavor to correct an earlier one-sidedness that overemphasized eschatology as involving a confronting of all moments of time with their eternal "transcendental meaning," and confessed that he had missed "the distinctive feature of [Romans 13:11f.], the teleology which it ascribes to time as it moves toward a real end."[41] Nevertheless, Barth certainly continued to emphasize God and the Reign of God as, in essence, before time and above time as well as at the end of time.

Friedrich Gogarten undertook an exploration into the "pure futurity" (*reine Zukünftigkeit*) of God in his treatise on "man between God and world" published in 1952.[42] Setting forth already the distinction so important later for Moltmann, between future as that which arises out of what has gone before (*futurum*) and as that which "comes to us" as new (*"das Zu-künftige, das uns Zu-kommende"*),[43] Gogarten understands both the Old Testament and Jesus' proclamation to have been oriented toward the latter. The oncoming future, as reality rooted in God's promises, is *"unverfügbar,"* not at our disposal, not subject to the vagaries of our plans and projections, just as God is *unverfügbar* also.[44] Israel laid itself open unconditionally to the future "which is simply the *Zu-kunft* of Yahweh"; for Israel to have faith in Yahweh's promises was precisely to have faith in Yahweh's *Zukünftigkeit.*[45] Gogarten concludes: God is "the purely futural . . . . not only in the future but no less in the past and present. Never and nowhere and in no way can we encounter God than in God's futurity."[46]

Finally, an acknowledgment of the work of Heinrich Ott on eschatology (1958) is also pertinent here, both in his moving of eschatology from a "temporal end-piece of a line of salvation history" to the center of the theological enterprise,[47] and in his decisive coupling of eschatology and the doctrine of God:

God himself is "eschatological," and God's "eschatological character" is nothing other than God's sovereignty. Eschatology is accordingly a (thinking) unfolding of the divine essence, of "what God actually is." An unfolding, as it would certainly appear to us, in a completely determinate sense, in a completely determinate direction: in the direction of the future . . . . *Just because God is the Lord is God essentially the eschatological-futural.*[48]

251

Pannenberg did not move immediately to pick up these threads and integrate them into his own understanding of the God disclosed by the future-oriented processes of history. In the same 1959 essay in which he referred to Gogarten's notion of God's essential *Zukünftigkeit* as an impracticable "abstraction," he recognized the validity of Gogarten's insight into the futural implications of God's promissory trustworthiness[49] and referred in a later footnote to our standing "before the future, before the coming God, who through his coming simultaneously creates the contingent and relates it to what has been."[50] Pannenberg went on in the following several years to expand upon this hint of God's essentially futural character, observing in his theses on the doctrine of revelation that, "to be sure, it is not so much the whole course of history but first its end, as God's revelation, that is one with God's essence,"[51] and beginning by 1963 to use more and more often the phrase, "the future of God." In an essay on the "theology of law," for example, he referred to "the power of the love that streams out from God's future bring[ing] about the community of mankind."[52] In the creativity of love, "God's future gains power over individuals and enables them to fulfill their destiny in relation to one another."[53] Similarly, Jesus, in his proclamation and proleptic inauguration of God's Reign, pointed exclusively "to the *future* of God."[54] The publication of Pannenberg's Christology in the following year included references to "the future of God's lordship announced by Jesus" that shifted subtly over into the phrase (for the first time), "the power of God's future," *die Macht der Zukunft Gottes.*[55] The notion remains undeveloped there. Finally, in regard to this tracing of the "early" Pannenberg, a lecture from that same year (1964) concludes by taking cryptic note of the biblical God who "in his almighty freedom is not among the beings existing in this world [*kein vorfindliches Seiendes ist*], but is the Lord of the future, toward whose coming the world is moving."[56]

It is not so much the case that distinctive stages of understanding are perceptible here. It appears rather that Pannenberg can be seen to be wrestling with the implications of overlapping concerns, three in particular: (1) If God is indeed the guarantor of the unity of universal history, can one properly speak of the full reality of God *within* the context of ongoing, unfinished, non-unified history? (2) If Jesus' teaching and activity are oriented toward an essentially *futural* Reign of God, in what sense can one refer to God in the present? Would not a God whose power is not yet consummated (*vollendet*) be less than God? (3) Since it is the case that in our human questioning we are open beyond everything extant (*vorfindlich*) in our world, must God not be conceived somehow in a manner that transcends everything presently real?

252

The resolution of these aporias is reached in the following year, in Pannenberg's strong and unqualified affirmation that "the power of the future" of which he has begun to speak is not merely *of* God--but *is* God. And the context within which this significant breakthrough is attained turns out to be Pannenberg's contribution to a collection of essays honoring Ernst Bloch on his eightieth birthday,[57] in which he appeared to be manifesting the onset of a major influence from the neo-Marxian atheist philosopher upon his own conceptualizations.[58]

Bloch had discerned that the roots of Marxian utopianism were embedded deep in the soil of Judaeo-Christian eschatology, and he pursued this connection vigorously in his development of a massive, sometimes brilliant, sometimes utterly bewildering "ontology of the not-yet," of the utopian future of all that is in the process of coming to be.[59] Toward the end of his long intellectual career he summed up his vision with the provocative equation, "'S is not yet P,' subject is not yet predicate' . . . . the predicate of the destined *Dass-Grund* of what is presently existent must still be substantially brought forth."[60] Bloch's eschatology of being is carried out, however, with a simultaneous shifting of the locus of God from a presently hypostasized *ens perfectissimum* to the utopian future of the Kingdom itself,[61] and the elimination of deity as a distinct being alongside "God's" Kingdom. In the true evolution of religion, the hope in the coming of the Wholly Other matures to the recognition that "God becomes the kingdom of God, and the kingdom of God ceases to contain a God."[62] For the vacuum left behind by the demise of the God-hypothesis is no monstrous chimera but the open space which makes the kingdom "intentionable" and whose true content is the utopia of the kingdom.[63]

The ontological primacy of the future is grounded in this goal of history toward which everything in the yet unfinished world is being drawn. Essentially, for Bloch, reality is understood to derive from a deficiency of fullness which is not merely a matter of human need but is cosmic in scope. The world issues forth out of a self-propelling drive of non-being toward a completeness of being. Non-being is not merely nothingness but is not-yet-being, containing as such a tension, a thrust toward the realization of what it is deficient in. Human consciousness as future-oriented, as striving toward satisfaction of momentary desires and wants, is but a reflection of this drive of partially-fulled reality toward totally utopia.[64] Thus can Bloch maintain that, strictly speaking, creation occurs at history's end.[65]

Bloch's eschatological/utopian ontology attempts to hold together the dual claim that the ultimate reality of hope's content is *objective* and indeed the very ground of hoping[66]--given the latency of matter to be transformed in the end into its own "bloom," spirit[67]--and that

253

the attainment of the utopian realm depends upon human achievement: the future is open for heaven or hell--acording to us![68]

> [Hope knows] that also latent in the objectively-real possibility, which carries within itself undecidedly both salvation and its opposite, is a "to no purpose" [*ein Umsonst*]. The world process is nowhere won yet; but even so: it is nowhere thwarted yet, and on earth people can be the switchmen of a route that still remains undecided--for salvation, or for disaster. The world remains in its totality the maximally laboring *Laboratorium possibilis salutis.*[69]

Pannenberg began his assessment of Bloch's contribution to the theological enterprise with words of praise and an expression of strong indebtedness. Recognizing the initial recoil triggered by Weiss' and Schweitzer's earlier discovery of the key eschatological element in Jesus, he remarked:

> Perhaps Christian theology will one day have to thank Ernst Bloch's philosophy of hope for giving it the courage to recover in the full sense its central category of eschatology. A temporally understood future remains decisive for such a concept. Bloch has taught us about the overwhelming power of the still-open future and of the hope that reaches out to it in anticipation for not only the life and thought of man but in addition for the ontological uniqueness of everything in reality. He has recovered the biblical tradition's eschatological mode of thought as a theme for philosophical reflection and also for Christian theology.[70]

Pannenberg went on to applaud Bloch for surpassing Feuerbach's "flat" anthropology by lifting up the horizon of a *humanum*-transforming future,[71] and for discerning an eschatological reversal of the idea of creation.[72] Particularly he championed Bloch's transposing the notion of *ens perfectissimum* into a temporal mode and his perceiving its essential connectedness with the ultimate future (of utopia): to *that* extent, as a denial of a *present* "perfect being," Pannenberg acknowledged the truth of Bloch's atheism.[73]

But the applause finally becomes overwhelmed by the accompanying critique. Pannenberg saw as irreconcilable Bloch's appeal to potencies and latencies inherent in the historical process and his accent on the genuine novelty and ontological primacy of the not-yet-real future. "The primacy of the future and its novelty are guaranteed only when the coming kingdom is ontologically grounded in itself and does not owe its future merely to the present wishes and strivings of men."[74] Furthermore, the attempt to retain a meaningful hope in the coming reign of God stripped of the God of the reign appeared untenable, "insofar as the end must be conceived as being numinous in itself."[75] For both these reasons, therefore, the valiant effort to establish the ontological primacy of the future comes to be viewed as inadequate.

What conclusions can be drawn, concerning the extent to which Bloch has been an influence on Pannenberg's theology? One can quite readily propose: very little. Even in this article, the window through which Pannenberg looks in on Bloch's work is a very narrow one,[76] and, as it turns out, very little dialogue with Bloch's ideas is to be found in Pannenberg's later writings. Three facets of the relationship would seem to sum up the matter conjointly: (1) Pannenberg was already moving in the direction of his ideas of God's futurity on the basis of the implications arising within his own work, independently of any influence from Bloch's eschatological philosophy, so that what emerges is a confluence of similar modes of reflection.[77] (2) No substantial indebtedness on the part of Pannenberg to the basic philosophical structures developed by Bloch is discernible whatsoever. (3) Nevertheless--and this is the most important judgment--reading Bloch appears to have opened Pannenberg up to what he was searching for: a notion of the ontological primacy of the future in terms of which he could bring to verbal expression and provisional completion his insights into the futurity of God. From "The God of Hope" onward, and specifically from then, Pannenberg consistently pursues (although in a direction quite distinct from the ontological vision that finally aroused it) a "thoroughgoing-eschatological" transformation of the doctrine of God.

The heart of Pannenberg's justification for affirming the futural character of God's being can be set forth in a very simple syllogism: *the Reign/power of God is future; the being of God is God's power; therefore the being of God is future.* The basis for the first premise has been established in examining the message and activity of Jesus of Nazareth, who proclaimed and proleptically embodied the Reign of God as irreducibly futural. That argument has already been presented in chapter seven, section B.[78] The key component is the other premise: that, as Pannenberg expresses the matter at one point, "a God without power would be a God without reality."[79]

The extent to which Pannenberg endeavors to defend this understanding is scanty indeed. For the most part, he tends to regard the matter as self-evident--even, perhaps, tautological. The closest thing to argumentation, other than the suggestion that Jesus' concentration on the coming Reign implied a unity of God and God's rule,[80] is an appeal to the study of religious ideas:

> God's being and existence cannot be conceived apart from his rule. Or, to put it in the language of the philosophy of religion, the being of the gods is their power. To believe in one god means to believe that one power dominates all . . . . Only the god who proves himself master over all is true.[81]

Other passages expressing this theme merely repeat it, as a given.[82] The flow of the overall logic is cogently apparent in a summary passage from "The God of Hope":

> When the coming kingdom is designated in biblical terms as the kingdom of God, that is out of concern for the ontological primacy of the future of the kingdom over all present realities, including, above all, psychological states. This means that from the biblical standpoint the being of God and that of the kingdom are identical, since the being of God is his lordship. He is God only in the execution of this lordship, and this accomplishment of his lordship is determined as something future. To this extent, the God to whom the hope of the kingdom refers is characterized in a radical and exclusive sense by "futurity as a quality of being."[83]

There are, nevertheless, two other factors that also undergird the necessity for and legitimacy of understanding God as having to do essentially with future. First, the realization that God wil ultimately be *revealed* as God only in the eschatological arrival of God's universal lordship carries with it the implication that God's own being is inseparable from that futural (confirmational)[84] disclosure:

> Is not God God only in the accomplishment of his lordship over the world? This is why his deity will be revealed only when the kingdom comes, since only then will his lordship be visible. But are God's revelation of his deity and his deity itself separable from each other? The God of the Bible is God only in that he proves himself as God. He would not be the God of the world if he did not prove himself to be its Lord. But just this proof is still a matter of the future, according to the expectations of Israel and the New Testament.[85]

Secondly, power and *unity* go together. Insofar as the unity of all contingent reality remains within history an anticipation, not a present attainment, therefore the *power* that unifies all is equally futural. God is unimaginable as an *extant* "unifying unity of the world," since that unity is nowhere presently forthcoming. Therefore God's being is futural.[86]

But what is this future with which God has, essentially, to do? What exactly, *is* it that we are talking about, pointing toward? We are accustomed to thinking of the future in terms of the not-yet-present, in comparison with the past as the no-longer-present. In relation to the present as the temporal moment in which contingent occurrences are concretely becoming, the past would seem to comprise the totality of events already constituted, already decided, and the future accordingly would be seen as the realm of pure potentiality, having no being of its own. The future, on this understanding, is that which has not been decided yet, has not entered into the concreteness of becoming yet. But this is not Pannenberg's perspective at all. As we have seen, the notion of the past as already decided is alien to his understanding: past events are open to their own futural determination of meaning. *All* of history--past, present, and the contingent future not yet emergent--is perceived as a sort of moving front on its way to its destiny in an *ultimate* future which is God *as* the Reign of God.

Therefore it appears that an important distinction between two different modes of being "future" must be recognized. These are by no means identical with the two linguistic expressions accented by Gogarten and Moltmann, *Zukunft* and *futurum*. Indeed, Pannenberg tends not to utilize the latter term at all. In accenting the emergence into history of the contingently new, Pannenberg consistently rejects the possibility of extrapolating the oncoming future from out of tendencies in the present. Instead, the future that breaks in upon each new present moment is a confrontation and not a prolongation, running counter to the present world and transcending trends of development.[87] Nevertheless, two ways of identifying the future are still very prominent, and in fact it is precisely such a distinction which underlies this moment-by-moment arrival of contingent novelty. For one can speak, on the one hand, of the future of history as that which has not yet transpired but one day will, within the historical process itself. Thus viewed, all that has become within history shares the quality of once having been futural. But on the other hand, one can speak of the future of history as *that which is futural to the whole of history.*[88] It is precisely in this latter sense that Pannenberg wishes to develop the thesis that God is futural: God is named as the *ultimate* future, the future even of all that yet remains *historically* futural to our present perspective.[89] God is understood, therefore (though Pannenberg does not specifically use this terminology), as "post-historical," in comparison with historical, future.[90]

This notion of the ontological primacy of an ultimate, potent future of God already engaging the contingent flux of events is perceived by Pannenberg to be thoroughly consistent with--indeed, precisely discernible in--Jesus' focusing on the nearness of the yet-futural Reign of God. The supposition of a dualistic separation of the future of God as some sort of distant beyond, set over against the present as a contradiction of it,[91] is shattered in the face of Jesus' radicalizing of the traditional apocalyptic hope:

> . . . the starting point for Jesus' message was in the Jewish hope for the future Kingdom of God. Jesus' particular emphasis can be understood as a modification of the Jewish hope: God's Kingdom does not lie in the distant future but is imminent. Thus, the present is not independent from that future. Rather does the future have an imperative claim upon the present, alerting all men to the urgency and exclusiveness of seeking first the Kingdom of God. As this message is proclaimed and accepted, God's rule is present and we can even now glimpse his future glory.[92]

Thereby we are opened up to the realization that, as mediated in Jesus' ministry (and authenticated by his resurrection), the ultimate future which is God is immediately at hand to every becoming moment. It is not to be thought of as separated from the now by the length of time remaining to the end, as apocalyptic had reflected.

But after having cleared away the underbrush of possible misunderstanding concerning *which* future Pannenberg is referring to as the locus of God and how immediate it always is to every present moment, we are still confronted with the need for clarifying what is intended by attributing "ontological priority" and "primacy"[93] to this ultimate future of all that is and has been and will yet become. The sources are very slim for accomplishing this. The most important hint is found in a remark that implies essential parallelism between the German adjectives *wirklich* and *wirksam*. Pannenberg offers the provocative observation that "the future is real [*wirklich*], although it does not yet exist [*noch nicht vorhanden ist*]," and precedes that with the suggestion that what is "real," "*wirklich*," is that which is "effective [*wirksam*] in the present moment."[94] Ergo: genuine reality is to be attributed to whatever manifests causal efficacy. And insofar as God is future power, God's future *is even already now* the locus of true reality.

To that assault on conventional conceptuality is added the observation that God is not to be envisaged as future merely in a relational sense, or futural "for the time being," as it were. God is, *in godself*, ultimate future, essential future. The passage which conveys this perception, unfortunately, leaves unexplored and undeveloped much that cries out for deeper clarification:

> Is God future in himself or does he merely appear to be future in relation to our, and perhaps every other, finite standpoint? Obviously, the very idea of future is relative to present and past. So it might be argued that the power of the future is simply the way in which God relates himself to time-bound man. But this is not adequate. We must go farther and say that God is in himself the power of the future. The reason for this is that the very idea of God demands that there be no future beyond himself. He is the ultimate future. . . . In his freedom, God is present to himself and keeps present to himself everything that is past, of which he has been the future. . . . Because there is no future beyond God, his having been the future of his past creatures has not, for him, passed away. He remains the future of the whole of the past and keeps present to himself his having been the finite future of every finite present which has now become past. Thus he keeps his past creatures in the present of his future.[95]

All of this comes to pregnant expression in Pannenberg's explicit identifying of the revealed God of cosmic and human history as *die Macht der Zukunft* : the power of the future. The primacy of the future of God is explicitly a corollary of the primacy of the *power* of the future, which is none other than God in the manifestation of God's Reign. It is therefore less appropriate to say that "God is not yet, but is yet to be," than to realize that God *is*, God exists, "only in the way in which the future is powerful over the present." Remaining always ahead of all speech about God, and outdistancing every concept of God, God is "no thing, no object presently at hand, which man could detach himself from and pass over," nor does God appear as one being among others or as timeless being underlying all that is real; rather, God has being explicitly as "the power of the future."[96]

Pannenberg has subsequently expanded upon this thesis with the observation that the powerful future of God is presupposed to have "concreteness," being regardable as "neither empty category nor bundle of chances."[97] Indeed, that the present is to be comprehended "as an effect of the future, in contrast to the conventional assumption that past and present are the cause of the future," calls for nothing less than "a reversal in all our ontological conceptions"[98] and "a reversal of the time sequence usually presupposed in notions of causality."[99] Although Pannenberg has yet to tackle a thorough conceptual exploration into this theory of ontological relocation, he has more recently begun to refer to the futural Reign as a "field of force" or energy pervading each present, for which the occurrences themselves are a "function" of the field rather than the opposite.[100]

To summarize and point the way forward:

> We thus understand all being and events as eventuating from the ultimate future. . . . In contrast to formulations about natural order, which describe the impact of past conditions on present and future, we have suggested an idea of creation which understands the present--and each present now past--as resulting from its future. This approach to an eschatological doctrine of creation culminates in the idea of divine love. God in his powerful future separates something new from himself and affirms it as a separate entity, thus, at the same time, relating it forward to himself. The autonomous event does not exist in isolation but is creatively related to the freedom of the future. The past is not the dead past. Because of this activity of divine love, we are justified in calling the God of Jesus the living God. He has no unity or being apart from the activity of his life in which he separates another being from himself while still keeping it alive by maintaining its relation to himself.
> The reality of God, then, is the creative arrival of this powerful future in the event of love. In his creative, redeeming, and sustaining arrival, God's future demonstrates his power.[101]

C. The Correlates of God's Powerful Futurity

We are now in a position to integrate the implications arising from the "projects of thought" explored in the earlier chapters of this study, by first giving consideration to the correlates that spring forth from the notion of God as the power of the future and then specifically demonstrating how this overall perspective serves to "solve" the open-ended explorations concerning truth, history, and human subjectivity.[102] What concerns us at this juncture is our discernment of the specific theses which become linked, in Pannenberg's purview, with the ontological shift of focus I have just identified. Particularly, these have to do with God as the source and ground of the contingency and unity of events; the consequent attribution of personal being to God; and the concomitant understanding of eschatological consummation as true creation.

I have previously had occasion to touch on the theme of the unity and contingency of events, in the context of an examination into the work of the historian.[103] The point made there was that the reality of God is to be understood as a crucial presupposition for grasping history in its ultimate universality, as the One who grounds the unity of the historical process without relinquishing its contingent character. But our focus here is on the connection which eventually is developed by Pannenberg between the validity of that idea and the perception of the essential futurity of that presupposed power of contingency and unity. Once Pannenberg has concluded that "it is no longer justifiable at the present day to think of the unity of that which is as a totality existent here and now. . . and to think of the unity which unites this totality as likewise existent here and now,"[104] the way is open to conclude that it is God as power of the future who both generates contingent novelty and assures ultimate cohesion.

The argument thereto finds most cogent expression in an important sequence in *Theology and the Kingdom of God*. There, Pannenberg begins by observing that it is the notion of the contingent character of what happens in history which guarantees "a future which is not the prisoner of past and present."[105] But contingency alone is problematic. The crucial question is whether one can also identify "a unity behind contingent self-expressions. . . . exhibiting some meaningful connection in the sequence of events."[106] One looks to the future for the answer to that, insofar as events are always only linked together into relationships of coherence retroactively. The notion of God as the power of the future is an understanding that the same power which "lets go of itself to bring into being our [contingent] present" is the unifying unity which brings these disparate occasions into the inter-connectedness of a "common future"--the Reign of God.[107] The source of the many is, qua future, the ground of their ultimate oneness. In summary, Pannenberg observes:

Three ideas are essential here: unity, the future, and sovereignty. Sovereignty establishes unity. The coming of God to his sovereignty over the world is his gift to the world, unifying its scattered events. The coming of God also means that God has the power over the future of those who are under his rule. Thus the circle is closed. Jesus' message of the Kingdom of God implies that the unity of the world is to be expected from its future. Therefore the unity of all things should not be understood in terms of an eternal cosmos but as something to be achieved by a process of reconciling previous schisms and contradictions. Reconciliation is a constitutive aspect of creation.[108]

Two corollary notions immediately surface. First, there is the observed interrelation between the contingency of events and the characterizing of the power which brings them forth as *personal*. Pannenberg has struggled throughout his theology to hold on to the personal character of God, affirming indeed that only if the power of the future over the present can be understood in some way as "personal" can it be designated divine.[109] Initially this concern took the form of a denial that we are persons directly and God is a person derivatively. Pannenberg was determined to counter Fichte's essential linking of personhood with finitude from the beginning of his theological activity, eventually concluding that a person is the very opposite of that which exists presently (*vorhanden*) and thus finitely.[110] What he finally has come to insist upon is that precisely "the contingency of events is a crucial presupposition for understanding the future as personal."[111] But there is more. It is necessary also to be able to conclude that contingent events are more than an erratic multiplicity of happenings. Once again, it is understood to be the pairing of contingency and ultimate unity as dependent upon one and the same power which justifies calling the power of the future personal, hence, God--but precisely only where that meaningful connection is not perceived in dependence upon "deterministic models of reality"[112] but arises out of the free decision of a transcendent being.[113]

God's essential personhood is actually established and defended by Pannenberg on several interrelated levels, which at least merit acknowledgment here even though the latter two will be dealt with at greater length later on. (1) There is, as I have just presented, the emphasis on the personal power of the future to bring forth both contingency and the ultimate unifying of the contingent into a meaningful whole. (2) There is the further observation of the linking of this unifying power with the notion of freedom:

> Man is free only because he has a future, because he can go beyond what is presently extant. And so freedom is in general the power that transforms the present. This means, however, that futurity as a condition of freedom constitutes the very core of the personal . . . . Therefore the power of the

future is personal in contrast to the mere depth of being because it touches every present concretely as its future in the possibilities of its transformation.[114]

This interconnectedness of futurity, power, and freedom will occupy our attention further in section E. (3) Finally, there are more recent developments that have emerged as Pannenberg pursues a doctrine of God as trinitarian, a subject addressed specifically in section F.

The second corollary notion is Pannenberg's affirmation of the "eschatological reversal of the idea of creation,"[115] the vision of creation and eschatology as "partners in the formation of reality,"[116] a point of view which he hailed in Bloch's philosophy but contends to be an independent development in his own unfolding thought. The initial emergence of the idea is triggered by reflection on the futurity of what history and historical events ultimately will be discovered to mean: since "the essence of all things will finally be decided simultaneously with the final end," therefore "creation is still underway to its proper reality," and can be said accordingly to take place "from the side of the end" (*vom Ende her*).[117] But that does not exhaust Pannenberg's meaning of creation *"am Ende,"* and in point of fact his subsequent broadening of the notion *does* follow his contact with Bloch's work. For he comes also to maintain that the power of the future over the present, and over every past present, *to bring it forth into being* entails the realization that it is from the future that all creativity takes place altogether.[118] That is to say, not just *essence* but existence, *appearance*, comes to be understood as created by the eschatological future that is God. It is for Pannenberg, however, the emphasis in Jesus' message on the future of God's lordship as "alone powerful over the present world and decisive for its meaning, its essence,"[119] to which he attributes the originating of this theological insight.

Tied in with the foregoing is the further reflection on Pannenberg's part that, concerning the tradition of the *Deus absconditus*, the "hidden God" whose ways are obscure within the world of human experience, "the absence of God is the negative side of his futurity. In Jesus' message it is only *as future that God is present.* "[120]

The impact of these correlative considerations of the disclosure of God as powerful future can be seen precisely on the categories of theological reflection pursued in the early portion of this exploration. Before summing up the implications that have now emerged, an explanatory comment is first of all in order.

One may well question whether Pannenberg's conclusions follow from his arguments concerning what *must* be the case if a valid doctrine of God is to be conceptualized (end of history, ultimate unity of truth, infinite counterpart to the human experience of world-openness) or whether indeed, as he claims, they derive from the revealing of God in Jesus of Nazareth. There is, obviously, a striking degree of correspondence between what is "needed" and what is perceived to be forthcoming as "revealed." So which is really primary? Is Pannenberg's true starting point the disclosures of revelation or the *religionsgeschichtlich* situation? In a word, *both* function in that manner, interrelatedly. To claim that Pannenberg argues from the need for history's ultimate universality to the eventuality of a God who guarantees it, or from the human questioning to divine answer, widely misses the mark, as I have previously noted. What is important for Pannenberg is precisely the degree of harmony between history as question and God as revealed answer. To be fair to his own understanding, then, one can only conclude that determining what functions as primary consideration in his theology is not unlike analyzing the truth of water in terms of the primacy of one or the other of its components. Does one begin with hydrogen and add oxygen? Only if *both* are present in combination does water appear. So also for Pannenberg, it would seem: God's truth is present for and to us only through the compresence of question and answer.

With that clarification, let us complete this sequence of theses with a backward glance at three of the future-directed questions explored in this study.

1) God and History: Resolving the Quest for Meaning. We were led to discern in chapter three that if history is to have any comprehensible meaning at all, that can only comes about through the arrival of a final future which unifies the multiplicity of events and provisional meaning into an overarching context of universal interrelatedness and discloses from out of that future the true essence of all that has become.[121] So long as that is only a *prerequisite* for the possibility of meaning, ultimate nihilism is a real alternative. Indeed, within history, the transcending of nihilism is characterizable essentially as an act of hope. However, our first summary thesis of Pannenberg's interpretation of the meaning of Jesus' resurrection[122] identified the correlating disclosure that in Jesus' fate the end of history has happened in advance, so that the overturning of the threat of nihilism is now more oriented to an act of *trust* in the faithfulness of the God who raised Jesus from the dead. The further conclusion that we are now led to draw from Pannenberg's insights into God as the power of the future is that it is precisely the ultimate futurity of God, who in the coming of God's Reign determines the true essence of all that has occurred in history, that assures a unity of meaning *flowing forth from out of that very future.*[123]

2) God and Knowledge: Grounding the Possibility of Truth.

Similarly, as illuminated in chapter two, the eventual achievement of unity is as necessary for epistemology as for ontology. The pursuit of knowledge strains after the assurance of the coherent oneness of truth entire, and since truth is understood by Pannenberg to be historical, the possibility of reason's success depends on the ultimate cessation of process in an unsurpassable attainment of the unity of all that has become, whereupon the multiplicity of ideas arising in relation to the process encounters an all-decisive standard of judgment.[124] Once again, we have seen in the fourth summary thesis on the meaning of the resurrection[125] that in Jesus the unifying end is understood to have proleptically broken through into history, assuring thereby the ultimate legitimacy of the quest for truth. Recognizing now that unity and power belong inescapably together, Pannenberg is in a position to conclude that only a vision of the essential futurity of the God who promises that anticipated unity of knowing and known adequately embraces the whole of the process, from in front of it.[126]

The very notion of the verifiability of God's reality is involved here as well.[127] In that God is conceivable as God only as One who succeeds as unifying unity of all that is, including what has not yet become but one day will, it is out of the power of the future that a provisional assessment of the truth of that power is derived. It is certainly the case that "only in the future of his Kingdom will the statement 'God exists' prove to be definitely true. But then it will be clear that the statement was always true."[128] Even so:

> There is no doubt that every answer to this question will remain a matter of dispute so long as human history has not reached that consummation which the biblical hope calls the kingdom of God. Until then there can be no final and indisputable answer to the question about the reality of God.[129]

3) God and Subjectivity: Answering the Question of Humanness.

Finally, the discussion in chapter four concerning human world-openness beyond everything extant in the world, and the possibility of a reality objectively grounding the question character of human subjectivity, reaches its culmination here, in the disclosure of God's essential futurity.[130] It is not merely the case that Jesus' resurrection confirms the hope of human destiny beyond death, as identified in the fifth thesis on resurrection.[131] Beyond that, God as the power of the future legitimates the concept of personhood as applicable to God and *thereby*, derivatively, as ultimately applicable to human beings.[132] It is as the power of the future that God is conceivable as a *personal* reality beyond all human questioning--as real but non-extant, as bearer and bestower of freedom, as *unverfügbar*--and as ground of the futural destiny of human personhood.[133]

By the same token, the subjectivity inherent in the whole history of religious reflection worldwide is understood to receive its center of focus from the unifying event of Jesus as prolepsis.

As the power of the future, the God of the coming reign of God proclaimed by Jesus already anticipates all later epochs of the history of the church and of the non-Christian religions. From this standpoint, the history of religions even beyond the time of the public ministry of Jesus presents itself as a history of the appearance of the God who revealed himself through Jesus.

But even looking back at it from the standpoint of Jesus, the history of religions permits of being understood as the appearance of the God revealed by him. The alien religions cannot be adequately interpreted as mere fabrications of man's strivings after the true God. Ultimately, they have to do with the same divine reality as the message of Jesus.[134]

In other words, the God disclosed by Christianity's Jesus is conceived by Pannenberg to be equally the power of Buddhism's future, of Islam's future, and so on. And the insights into true being that come to expression there, as manifestations of human world-openness, are perceived to be pieces of the eventual whole of truth, not antithetical to it.

D. God, Time, and Eternity

Before concluding the overview of Pannenberg's conceptualizing of God by bringing into view the most recent developments in his theology, namely, his intriguing insights into a reformulation of the doctrine of the Trinity, it is necessary to give careful and extended attention to the notion of God as the power of the future in yet one further and very vital way. I have, up to this point, tended to take the proposal somewhat at face value, spelling out its essential ramifications and correlative implications. But a key task remains. Truly to understand where Pannenberg's theology is going with this provocative shift of focus on the being of God requires a precise analysis of the terms of the defining concept. What does *power* actually mean here? What does *future* mean, in relation to the underlying perspective on eternity and time? This section and the one that follows attempt to dissect those issues, beginning with the latter, as a means of gaining access to the core structure of Pannenberg's post-theistic vision.

To understand adequately how Pannenberg's convictions about eternity and temporality underlie and inform his concept of God's futurity, it is again necessary to distinguish earlier developments in his thought from the perspective that emerges from "The God of Hope" onward. For even as his emphasis on the futural character of God's reality has gone beyond his earlier formulations of God's nature, so has his interpretation of the nature of God's eternity undergone subtle but important shifts in the process. As we sort through these, we need to be alert to the answers Pannenberg gives to several fundamental questions: Is time real for God, and if so, how? How is the notion of eternity to be understood? What is the relation of eternity to time? If truth is historical, what implications does that contain for change and development within God?

Pannenberg began with somewhat inherited notions of time and eternity that he rather quickly discarded. In *What Is Man?*, he referred to God's "eternal present" as involving a single simultaneous sequence of events, experienced from a standpoint outside of and not subject to the flow of time.[135] This mode of conceptualization was subsequently surrendered and the notion of God's eternity as "timelessness" came to be eliminated,[136] even though it must also be acknowledged that from a very early period (1959) Pannenberg was already calling for the reinterpretation of God's timelessness in the direction of God's "lordship over time" and "almighty simultaneity to every time."[137] This emphasis on God's *"Gleichzeitigkeit"* (simultaneity, "compresence") is one that reappears continually in Pannenberg's work, as we shall see shortly. However, an accompanying suggestion in his early period that one derive from the theory of relativity an insight into the "spacial rendering of time," thinking thereby "of the course of the world as a constant present,"[138] was still being put forward a decade later in the guise of a contortion or "deformation of the ordinary form of temporal sequence comparable to the contortion of space according to the theory of relativity."[139] This was strongly repudiated by the scientist-theologian Ian Barbour at that time as an illegitimate appropriation of relativity physics,[140] and Pannenberg's latest investigation into temporality[141] makes no effort to refloat that trial balloon.

Pannenberg moved in "The God of Hope" to a specific correlating of the eternity and essential futurity of God: eternity is not timelessness, or "the endless endurance of something that existed since the beginning of time" but rather should be recognized as "the power of the future over every present."[142] He has since sustained that suggestion, only embryonic there, with the development of the thesis that "the *eschaton* is eternity in the fullest sense," insofar as that "is the mode of God's being in the coming of his Kingdom."[143] This notion, then, of God's eternity as a "final future" which comes to be comprehended as "the totally comprehensive present" opens the way to overcoming "the differences of past, present, and [historical] future" precisely *in the eschaton.*[144] From that vantage point, it becomes possible to discern that it is *as the powerful future* that God is understandable as "contemporaneous [*gleichzeitig*] to every time."[145] And this represents a terminological-conceptual shift of crucial importance, from the

Gleichzeitigkeit of eternity to all historical time to the *Gleichzeitigkeit* of *God's future as mode of the eternal* to all time.

This provides the basic breakthrough for encompassing the insights, emerging earlier in the Christology, into Jesus' new understanding of time as characterized by the power of the future (Reign) in the present. Jesus' message is understood to reflect a sense "that future and present are inextricably interwoven,"[146] a perspective that is already seen to be found in the apocalyptic interweaving of historical future and hidden presence of God's eternity in time,[147] and which leads Pannenberg to the general conclusion that one is justified in speaking of a "remarkable entwining" or "interweaving" (*Verschränkung*) precisely of *eternity* and time.[148]

This key notion of *Verschränkung* is developed in an essay on "Time and Eternity in the Religious Experience of Israel and of Christianity," prepared in 1975 but only published five years later (1980). There Pannenberg champions once again the apocalyptic world view in its presupposition that what is hidden on earth is already disclosable in advance to the apocalyptic seer, which points up the interpenetration of eternity into time and calls even for the conclusion that therein eternity and time may be seen to "coincide" (*koinzidieren*).[149] This is presented by Pannenberg as analogous on the one hand to the seer's breaking through the spatial differentiation between heaven and earth,[150] and on the other hand to the mythic coincidence of *Urzeit* and present which Israel and then especially early Christianity took over and transformed into a coincidence of *Endzeit* and present:[151]

> ...the Christian faith lived out of the hope of the saving future in distinction to the present. Analogously to mythic consciousness, however, even for the eschatological consciousness of faith the separation of the times is not absolute. Just as the foundational *Urzeit* of the myth can be made present in the cult, so does the eschatological saving future become already through the Spirit a presently determinative power in the believer. On what does such a present that overlaps the difference of the times depend? In the interweaving of the times is announced the presence of eternity in time.[152]

The conclusion which Pannenberg then reaches is that the future of God, as "the parousia of God's eternity, already forms the depth dimension of the present time" and precisely "in its time-overlapping [*zeitübergriefend*] presence" is conceivable as God's eternity.[153]

Let us lay this out in a provisional summary. The key terms that interpret the relation of time and eternity, and therefore of historical present and ultimate future, are *Gleichzeitigkeit* and *Verschränkung*: contemporaneity or compresence, and entwining or interweaving. Working from an essential identity between the concepts of eternity and ultimate futurity--or, more precisely, looking to the notion of God's eschatological future as a basis for redefining how eternity is to be conceived--Pannenberg interprets the penetration of the power of the future into the present as an interweaving of eternity itself into time, and therefore can speak of a coinciding of the two. The answer to Pannenberg's question of "how the temporal difference between divine reality and the present is related to the difference between the divine as the 'Eternal One' and all time whatsoever"[154] is found in the overcoming of both indications of any dualistic differentness by the entwining compresence of the future of all into the temporal becoming of all.

But what, exactly, does that mean? More to the point, perhaps, what are the implications that derive from this proposal? Let us investigate the latter question as a way of penetrating the former one. To do that, we need to move backward again, into Pannenberg's earlier wrestling with a related theme that eventually finds definition from just these deliberations--namely, the issue of whether the temporality of truth entails the attributing of change to God.

From the outset of Pannenberg's assessment that history itself is the locus of God's self-disclosure, he has attempted to come to terms with the question of how that history genuinely contributes to the being of the God revealed therein. Under his second thesis on revelation, as happening ultimately at the end of history, Pannenberg observed that history itself does not merely contribute to the disclosure of God extrinsically but belongs to the very essence of God, "which has a history in time."[155] Temporal history is affirmed as "of decisive importance for God himself," and "the eternity of God is itself still *dependent on* the future of the world."[156] But is that not a denial of God's essential immutability? Pannenberg has never been open to that possible consequence. The concept of immutability, he pointed out, needs to be redefined, not simply as enduring sameness but as a corollary of God's self-determined constancy, God's freely enacted faithfulness.[157] In the freedom of God's contingent acting that discloses God as "wholly other," "God assumes properties into his eternal essence through such deeds in that he chooses these and no other events as the form of his contingent operation."[158] Therefore, "the particular, the unique, and the accidental are included in God's eternity,"[159] inasmuch as true being, the truth of God, essentially incorporates into itself the historical.[160] In summary thus far:

> While the god of Greek thought is one with the foundation of the cosmos in such a way that he belongs to the cosmos as its ground, the biblical God is distinct from his creation as one who acts freely and contingently, since he ever again distinguishes himself from it in history. Thus, the Greek truth is superseded in principle by the biblical truth insofar as the latter includes those

features of reality which the Greek idea of truth excluded, though without any less decisive interest in holding fast to the permanent and enduring.[161]

But to this point, the issue has only been joined, not resolved. The question presses itself forward: *How* does this incorporation of historical/temporal truth into the essential/eternal truth of God not *require* divine becoming, change, process? Pannenberg's answer is already forthcoming, however briefly, in his Christology, where, in the context of a discussion of the implications of the incarnation for understanding God's eternality, he states:

> . . . that an element of God's becoming and being in the other, in the reality differentiated from himself, is one with his eternity requires that what newly flashes into view from time to time in the divine life can be understood at the same time *as having always been true in God's eternity.*[162]

That is drawn out in further detail in *Theology and the Kingdom of God*, in the context of a brief critical engagement with the process philosophy of A. N. Whitehead. Pannenberg wants to affirm the process contribution of "incorporating time into the idea of God,"[163] but precisely without allowing for the seemingly incumbent consequence of acknowledging development within God. He avoids that by recapitulating and extending the notion of *retroactive permanence* set forth in the Christology:

> The very essence of God implies time. Only in the future of his Kingdom come will the statement "God exists" prove to be definitely true. But then it will be clear that the statement was always true. . . . It is true that, from the viewpoint of our finite present, the future is not yet decided. Therefore, the movement of time contributes to deciding what the definite truth is going to be, also with regard to the essence of God. But--and here is the difference from Whitehead--what turns out to be true in the future will then be evident as having been true all along. This applies to God as well as to every finite reality. God was present in every past moment as the one who he is in his futurity. He was in the past the same one whom he will manifest himself to be in the future.[164]

Therefore eternity is not the antithesis of change but takes up into itself change--unchangingly![165] The reality of God, as the ultimate future of the becoming of history, "is still in process *for every finite point of view*. But this does not mean that it is in the same way a process on its own terms."[166]

Therefore, it would appear, the implications of the interpenetrating presence of the future into every present come more visibly into the light: Pannenberg is concerned to defend the incorporation of historical truth into God precisely by insisting upon the essential completeness of the future of God *which brings historical truth into being*, as the power of the future over every present. Thus the basis for this remarkable combination of concepts, which affirms both the contribution of history to the eternal truth of God and the absence of genuine development within God, is to be sought, finally, outside the discussion of the significance of time and eternity for the notion of God's futurity. It is to the other term in the fundamental definition that we must look for further clarification if this juxtaposition of ideas is ultimately to hold together. In the understanding of the way in which God is to be comprehended as the *power* of the future are the disturbing antinomies to be probed. To this we now turn.

E. God, Power, and Freedom

Very early in his theological investigations, Pannenberg was concerned to obviate the threat of divine determinism as a significant obstacle to responsible religious faith. In a 1957 essay on "The Influence of the Experience of Temptation upon Luther's Doctrine of Predestination," he endeavored to defend Luther's position against the charge of freedom-denying predeterminism by championing immutability as "the fidelity of God to God's promises" over against a Greek-derived notion of a metaphysical incapacity for change, the "unchangeableness of a hidden first cause."[167] Recognizing, as we have seen, that any legitimate concept of God must be able to knock the props out from under an atheism of human freedom, Pannenberg has continued to be keenly exercised over the necessity of circumventing the pitfalls of a deterministic notion of deity. The very attractiveness of the possibility of God's essential futurity is discernible in the prospects it holds out for grounding human freedom. The traditional conceptualization of divine omnipotence must somehow be transcended:

> If the eternity of God is thought of as the unlimited continuance of a being which has existed from the first, then the omnipotence and omniscient providence of this God must have established the course of everything that takes place in the universe in all its details from the very first. In this case there is no room for genuine freedom on the part of any creature.[168]

Pannenberg is deeply motivated, therefore, to rethink the way in which God is powerful, challenging the supposition that there is here "an insoluble difficulty involved in every idea of God"[169] and seeking to fathom a deeper insight into the power of God to establish, not subvert, creaturely freedom.[170]

Accordingly, the question which focuses my examination of Pannenberg's concept of God's future as *powerful* is precisely the one he has himself set out from: How is power to be understood here, such that the freedom of the other is genuinely authenticated and not made to

270

vanish into the ether of divine determinism? It is perhaps not an exaggerated claim to propose that the whole of Pannenberg's rather brilliant theological enterprise stands or falls on the adequacy and conceptual consistency of the answer he works out to this pivotal issue-- for he himself suggests no less.[171]

Pannenberg worked for a time with designations of God as "all-embracing power" (*die alles umgreifende Macht*)[172] and the "power over everything,"[173] the latter being conjoined explictly with the issue of human freedom:

> Only the ground of all reality, or, better, the power over all reality, is able to guarantee a security that cannot be destroyed by any other power. Therefore, man inquires after a ground which can support himself and all reality, which as the power over all reality is also able to carry him beyond the limits of his own present existence, and which therefore supports him precisely in the openness of his freedom.[174]

Pannenberg was still utilizing that phrase extensively in the year following his penetration into the *essential* futurity of God's power in "The God of Hope."[175] Already in the immediately preceding essay on "The Question of God," however, there is brief reference to God as *"alles bestimmende Wirklichkeit,"* the all-*determining* reality.[176] And it is this theme which soon comes to predominate Pannenberg's interpretation of the nature of the power of the future: God can be meaningfully conceived as God only as *die alles-bestimmende Macht*--the all-determining power of the whole of reality.[177] It is the meaning Pannenberg intends this phrase to convey which holds the key to unraveling the mystery of divine power conjoined with human freedom.

The phrase is not easily clarified. As with the duality of meanings inherent in the corollary noun *Bestimmung* ("destiny" and "determination"), so here also, with *"bestimmend,"* we face a pair of possible interpretations--though this time both are incorporated in the single English equivalent, "determining." On the one hand, Pannenberg may intend to assert only that, since it is the ultimate future which finally decides the essence of what becoming occurrences in history actually *mean,* therefore the future possesses the power of *ascertainment* of the true character of all reality.[178] Not existence per se but the *essence* of what comes to exist is fully a consequence of God's all-determining power, under this perspective. A number of times the phrase is employed without any clear indication of specific intent,[179] but admitting certainly of an interpretation that would see no further meaning in the phrase than this. For the sake of convenience, I shall designate this way of understanding Pannenberg's notion of all-determining power as "soft determinism."

271

On the other hand, there is the possibility that what Pannenberg really has in mind is nothing less than a kind of "hard determinism," that is, the understanding *that the power of the future is a genuine force of creativity out of which history is fully and concretely constituted.* Indeed, the passages that tilt in this direction are truly numerous. Though it may seem slightly repetitive, thorough attention to the various indications of this intention in Pannenberg is warranted here for the sake of an adequate assessment of his post-theistic vision.

Pannenberg can typically allude to the power of God as that which "dominates all" and is "master over all,"[180] and can ascribe to God "constitutive" (*konstituierend*) significance over all of history.[181] The impression one receives is that such a deity is solely accountable for what emerges into being in every historical present. The point of view is strongly subscribed to in *Theology and the Kingdom of God* :

> In every event the infinite future separates itself from the finite events which until then had been hidden in this future but are now released into existence. The future lets go of itself to bring into being our present. And every new present is again confronted by a dark and mysterious future out of which certain relevant events will be released. Thus does the future determine the present.[182]

In regard, then, to these present events which "spring from that future,"[183] one possible qualification might be entertained. Perhaps only the *that* of an event is released into existence, with some degree of self-determination also at hand in regard to its particular contours. Such a suggestion is made by the process theologian Lewis Ford in dialogue with Pannenberg:

> God is the ultimate power of the future, rescuing the world from degeneration into chaos by the relentless provision of ever-new creative possibilities for the world to actualize. . . . Since these possibilities may become distorted in transmission, God is not the *sole* power of the future, although he is the ultimate power. The perversion of the divine is the demonic. Both exercise their power upon us by the lure of the future.[184]

Not so, Pannenberg insists. It is essential for him that "the power of the future should not only create possibilities, but actualities as well," establishing "the *complete dependence* of everything real upon God."[185]

This is singularly consistent with two corollary themes concerning the absolute freedom of God and the doctrine of *creatio ex nihilo.* In regard to the first of these, Pannenberg has championed what he calls "the freedom of God's active omnipotence"[186] from early on, accenting God's transcendence over finite reality in terms of "a living, ever new carrying out of his freedom."[187] Precisely as final future, God is

272

to be thought of as "pure freedom,"[188] as "freedom itself."[189] Indeed, viewed in this light, much of the discussion about the contingency and novelty of events in history seems oriented toward establishing the freedom of the God active therein to bring forth the new rather than be circumscribed by the givenness of what already is. It is "the otherness of the freedom of God precisely in his acts"[190] which establishes the contingent character of God's activity and therefore the contingency of the events themselves. What is at stake is not the genuineness of contingent novelty but the theological affirmation that the freedom of God is in no way held in check by realities external to God's own being. To maintain that some cause other than God's future is also involved in the becoming of the present would be to entail accordingly that the ultimate truth of God incorporates that which is attributable to factors not exclusively derivative from God, which would therefore infringe upon the absolute freedom of God not to be in any way determined by anything other than Godself. It is, indeed, no other than this consideration, of the absolute freedom of God's contingent acting, that ultimately underlies the contention that God is both the essential truth of history's becoming and yet not subject to change and development.

The second corollary is already implied in these reflections. The doctrine of "creation out of nothing" is for Pannenberg not a quasi-scientific thesis about primal origination but a defense of the all-encompassing power of the Creator God.[191] Everything that is must always have derived from God's future. Indeed, though Pannenberg usually defends the doctrine only by referring to its absence in process theology as a basis for rejecting that perspective,[192] the implication one receives is that the idea of creatio ex nihilo is equally relevant in terms of how one understands every moment in the history of ongoing creation.

Thus can Pannenberg declare, as persuasive testimony that defends my imputation of "hard" determinism to his position, that "human history in the midst of its perversions continues to be the creation of the God whose kingdom is coming"[193] and who is even now "already ruling the world from the hiddenness of heaven."[194] Similarly the future of humankind, even to the determination of whether we will blow ourselves off the face of the earth in a nuclear holocaust or achieve global peace, "remains the prerogative of God"![195]

All of this is summed up in a key passage in Theology and the Philosophy of Science which, at the very same time, contains the germ of an idea that may possibly open the way to a genuine alternative so far unpursued. There, Pannenberg observes that the definition of God as all-determining power, nominally "pre-given,"[196] remains incomplete by itself, requiring a more substantive content:

273

The definition presupposes a formal conception of the divine reality as "power," without specifying what particular sort of power, whether of storms, death, law or love. The definition expands this conception by adding the proviso that the power is the power behind "everything." Implicit in this claim is the idea that this all-determining power is itself determined only by itself and not subject to determination by anything else, unless it determines that it should be determined by something else.[197]

Unless it determines that it should be determined by something else: no more crucial qualification has appeared in Pannenberg's explorations into the power of God than this. Although there is no evidence yet of his having extended his reflections about divine and non-divine causation along those lines, we need to keep this possible direction in mind as we turn our attention explicitly to Pannenberg's endeavors to embrace in a significant way a measure of human responsibility positively to live out of God's oncoming future. This builds on a previous discussion in chapter four on the relationship between freedom and the future,[198] but also goes beyond that in seeking now to relate that theme squarely to Pannenberg's concept of futural causality which we are in the process of illuminating here.

We begin by observing a curious tendency on Pannenberg's part to indulge in a subtle but important shift between "being" and "having," between *being* the future and *having* a future, as these relate to the issue of freedom. On the one hand, *God's* being itself *is* "the absolute future of freedom": "absolute future belongs to the essence of freedom, because absolute freedom cannot have any future outside itself and is therefore its own future."[199] Therefore, strictly speaking, "it is only possible to think of freedom as the absolute future of freedom."[200] Freedom is nothing else than "to have future *in* oneself and *out of* oneself."[201] Freedom and future go together as having power over what is extant.[202] But on the other hand, a human being *"is* free only because he *has* a future"; freedom is also to be discerned in our "openness *to* the future."[203] Understandably, this is not original but derivative freedom: we have to be "set free," freed from succumbing to the lure of the transitory, freed for one's true destiny with God.[204]

Working then from this angle of vision, Pannenberg can conclude that "the creature-event has freedom in relation to the power of the creative love that does not let it go."[205] It is sustained in its freedom to transcend the world at hand by the power that originated it and binds it fast to itself. This is in contrast to a merely formal--and insipid and trivial--freedom of choosing "this way or that" about one's transitory mode of existing.[206] Freedom is therefore *substantively* real only when it acknowledges and floats with the currents that flow into the present from out of God's creative future:

274

In relation to the God of the power of the future, man is free: free for a truly personal life, free to accept the provisionality of everything, free with regard to nature and society, free for that creative love that changes the world without destroying it. This creative love proceeds from freedom and is directed toward affirming and creating freedom in the world.[207]

The image that Pannenberg has in mind here would seem to be that we are "free" to fiddle with the dial on the radio but the divine music of our destiny is coming to us only on a certain (divinely determined) wave length and our responsibility is to let ourselves get tuned in. Not to do so, to pick up only cosmic static, is not to be *free* at all, that is, free to hear the music.

It is understood by Pannenberg that when freedom is experienced by humanity in that manner, apparently, then it is that God *effectively* is working *through* God's creatures to achieve the aims of God which are at the same time the highest aims of the created realm.

Divine and human acting do not stand opposed to one another on the same level. Only a base God-concept leads to consequences which would deprive human activity of its own propriety, and subjugate it to compulsion. The activity of God's creatures does not stand over against the working of the Creator. God acts through them, serves them freely, however much God's acting at the same time exceeds the purposes of the creatures.[208]

Viewed thusly, the actual goal of God's lordship in and over history is "the abolition of the antithesis between ruler and ruled."[209]

Thus does God's action in history have to the highest degree the form of the inspiration of human behavior through the vision of human destiny and through the spirit of love, which lets the good fortune of consummation break in already in the present.[210]

This notion of "creative work" that is "inspired by the creative power of God's future"[211]--etymologically, to be "in-Spirit-ed"--is extended by the observation that "man participates in God. . . by active transformation of the world" precisely to the extent that "the power of the future, the coming reign of God, has become influential in the present and has gripped man."[212] Human striving for the good "corresponds with God's intention for the transformation of the world through his rule."[213]

Such terminology as "influence" and "inspiration" and "transformation"--as opposed to the *formation* of the world by the creative power of the future--certainly weighs heavily against a judgment of hard determinism being applied to Pannenberg's position. The direction in which these statements move is toward an affirmation of the Reign of God as an ellipse with two foci: on the one hand, the primacy of *grace*, of the bestowal of God's reign of love upon God's creation; on the other hand, the necessity of *response*, of acting in such a way as genuinely to *receive* the gracious offer. Pannenberg can therefore speak of the human actualization of peace, justice, and love not as human enactments of God's Reign but as particular actions which express the spirit of that Reign[214] and as that *through which* the activity of God actualizes itself-- wherefore "human self-actualization and God's self-actualization are therefore identical; they fulfill themselves in one and the same process."[215] In an early sermon (1962) that drew on the metaphor in Isaiah 40, Pannenberg suggested that, rather than thinking of ourselves as the builders of God's Reign,

> we should build the highway on which the majesty of God will travel forth in triumph. So we are God's road crew. . . . So history becomes the highway on which God's majesty travels forth, always and again running otherwise than we road builders of God suppose; but without our building, it does not come to pass.[216]

We cannot permit ourselves an overreaction to this last clause; sermons are not intended necessarily to possess the same logical rigor and consistency as a theological treatise. But it serves to point up sharply the deep-seated conviction on Pannenberg's part that, *in some way*, room must be made for the issue of a human response to the powerful gift of God's future. Somehow, the difference from the human side between being open toward the future of one's destiny and being alienated from it must be preserved if any real sense is to be made at all of the folly of human behavior. And this Pannenberg strives to do, in defining *sin* specifically in terms of a human self-assertiveness that closes us off from our intended future[217] and causes us to miss our true destiny,[218] resulting in our being shattered on the power that would free us.[219] On the basis of this possibility of failing to accept what God's future holds out to us, one can therefore also speak of God's Reign in terms of judgment as well as fulfillment.[220]

So what remains in a positive sense, as to what is possible for the person open to God's future to accomplish? Pannenberg's response here is both consistent, and illuminating. We are to "prepare this present for the future"[221] and "open up the future to [our] fellow men and women,"[222] not by trying to change the world directly but *by proclaiming to the world what God is doing and intending to do toward the ultimate fulfillment of the world in God's Reign.*[223] Specifically, this leads Pannenberg to great concern for overcoming the divided character of the existing church, since its fragmentation denies its message of *unity* as the goal of the power of the future, the realm of perfect community.[224] It leads him to write eloquently of the need for the church to "seek to make the power of the love that establishes justice effective in the formation of every human society,"[225] and for the use of "the creative freedom of the

276

imagination" through which "love discovers possibilities for promoting understanding, for the life together of those who are apparently hopelessly estranged, and possibilities for reintegrating even lawbreakers into society."[226] But this ever remains oriented in the final analysis toward the work of the church in converting the world to the hope of its fulfillment ultimately in and by God, not toward the direct achievement of peace with justice in the world per se. The call to repentance leads to no new order of the world; it is aimed at individuals, seeking to change the hearts of women and men.[227]

Yet the nagging question remains: Is there really room in Pannenberg's doctrine of God's creative efficacy even for no more than this? That can be so, only if in some way there is genuine space for effective resistance to the power of the future. And *that* can be so, in turn, only if it is somehow possible to acknowledge *the reality of power within that upon which the power of the future is ever at work.* Can this be allowed?

Again, there are passages in Pannenberg's writings which tend to imply such a perception. They take the form of distinguishing between the ultimate sovereignty of God *in* the future and the limitations on that power *of* the future *in the present.* It is, for example, *because* God's rule is "still future" that the true good "is not conclusively possessed but always the object of our striving."[228] Acknowledging that "in some sense atheism has a point in arguing that the world ought to be different if there were a God who cares for man and even for every individual," Pannenberg agrees that the question of "whether the power of God is manifesting itself is not to be evaded. The Christian answer to this can be that the kingdom of God has not yet been established. It is still a matter of the future."[229] What Pannenberg then goes on to refer to specifically as "the absence of God and of his power" leads to the necessity of the "anticipation of a future manifestation of what is so conspicuously absent at present."[230]

But I submit that this is only an apparent way out of the impasse, and the references indicated here do not reflect Pannenberg at his sharpest or most consistent. These observations seem to turn on a carelessness with which the word "future" is employed, in respect to a failure to distinguish clearly between the historical future, which ontologically is no different from any emergent present which at one time was not yet, and the ultimate future, which is ontologically the ground also of that historical future. It is not helpful to suggest that God's power is presently absent because it is "still future" as if that implied that it simply has not arrived yet, when what Pannenberg really intends to maintain is that God's power is *always* present to us precisely *as* future. Indeed, Pannenberg himself can also counteract this misimpression by referring to God's *"apparent* impotence" in the world presently at hand,[231] the impression being that this is not a *real* impotence at all.

In point of fact, the way in which Pannenberg has articulated his response to the theodicy question does not tend to build on such considerations as these at all. If Pannenberg wanted to accent the futurity of God's power in terms of a present degree of absence of that power, the theodicy issue is readily resolvable by identifying the existence of evil in the world as an indication of the resistance of creation to the power of the future that is acting upon it and drawing it toward its true order. But this is not a direction that Pannenberg is willing to take. There are, instead, essentially two components in Pannenberg's answer to the problem of the enduring reality of evil: the notion of eschatological reconciliation, and a suggestion of the participation of God *as Trinity* in the evil and suffering of the world. This latter element will be examined separately, within the context of the subsequent discussion on Pannenberg's doctrine of the Trinity.[232] It is the first which will briefly occupy the focus of our attention here.

What Pannenberg has primarily been inclined to maintain is that "there can be only one valid answer to the reality of evil: the eschatological reconciliation of God with his world by that glorification of his suffering creatures which alone will finally prove his true divinity."[233] It is only in the definitive coming of the eschaton that the counter-current (*"Gegeninstanz"*) of evil will fully be conquered and countermanded (*"aufgehoben"*),[234] wherein at the same time God's divinity will be decisively confirmed.

So we are finally left with no real entry at all into the possible *power* of evil to resist the ultimate power of God's Reign, whose coming is assured (by the resurrection of Jesus) and which even now is understood to be creatively, if hiddenly, at work. Nowhere does Pannenberg provide any ontological basis for establishing the independent capacity of creatures, human or otherwise, effectively to thwart the power of the future.

There seem indeed to be two countervailing tendencies equally at work in Pannenberg's thought, and the one or the other of these comes to expression at various places in his theology depending on where his focus lies at that moment. When the basic concern is to defend the infinite, unrestricted, absolute character of the divine, then the creative all-determining power of the future over the present is asserted comprehensively. But when the concern shifts to didactic expressions of human responsibility for being genuinely open to one's destiny, allowances for the actuality of human sinfulness are made without actually grounding those expressions of sin in any explanation that accounts for their causal origination. Cutting through all the agile mental gymnastics, *no other power than God's* is ever explicitly acknowledged by Pannenberg, even though his own intentionality seems to demand it.

God's "all-determining power is itself determined only by itself and not subject to determination by anything else, unless it determines that it should be determined by something else."[235] We return again to this remarkably pregnant and promising sentence. Does Pannenberg's reflection here set the direction for a way out of the impasse concerning God's power and the lack of its sufficient manifestation within history? Though he has not pursued that possibility, the way seems to be open to do so--and precisely in respect to the realization that the character of the power of the future is ultimately one of love.

Pannenberg has never been reluctant to acknowledge explicitly the power of God as disclosed in the life and message of Jesus to be essentially characterizable as love.

> However, if this love were powerless, then it would not be God; and if it were only one power among others, then it would not be the one God from whom and to whom are all things and who alone can in all seriousness be called God.[236]

Rather, God's power is understood to manifest itself as love in "the present announcement of the imminent Kingdom of God [which] offers man a chance to participate in God's future rather than being overwhelmed by its sudden arrival and being conquered as an adversary of that future,"[237] and also in the unconditional forgiveness of sins. Indeed the lordship of the coming Reign "consists not in domination and might but in the power of forgiving love."[238]

This incipient juxtaposition of power as might and the power of love has been expanded significantly in Pannenberg's 1975 essay on "Christology and Theology," in a passage that bears translating at length. Recognizing that "God does not insert himself into his creation with force [*Gewalt*] in order to be acknowledged as its Lord,"[239] he writes:

> The Jewish idea of God's omnipotence is to be concretized, however, in that the power of the God of Jesus is presently effective precisely in the form of God's apparent impotence. God's futural lordship determines the present world in those places, where one hungers and thirsts for righteousness; where meekness, peaceableness, and warmheartedness reign; where the needy and those who mourn, the suffering and the persecuted, find their consolation in the future of God. Just that is revealed even in the cross of Jesus. . . . Therefore [because God is in league with the weak of the world] the community of God with such human weakness is not to be understood as renunciation, as a setting aside of power and might which God should actually already possess in himself. . . . A Christian understanding of God. . .must think God's divinity from out of God's conduct disclosed in the message and history of Jesus of Nazareth. The

self-binding of God with that which in this world is weak, and fails. . . . cannot be understood as a kind of temporary renunciation by God of God's true nature, not as self-alienation, but rather precisely as God's self-actualization in the exercise of God's lordship over his creation. How else than in such a gentle and silent form should the seizure of power by divine love be accomplished in the present world? That the divine love, in spite of its conspicuous weakness and impotence, nevertheless truly rules this world, is manifested in the fact that all the powers and forces seemingly having mastery over the course of things finally come to nothing. . . .

The omnipotence of the Christian God does not stand in opposition to God's powerless [gewaltlos] love, but shows itself precisely in the power of the seemingly (that is, in the eyes of the one isolated from God) impotent cause of justice, peace and love among people. God's bond with those who, for the sake of justice, peace, and love, are powerless, suffer and fail, is not an expression of a renunciation of God's divinity, but characterizes the way in which the divinity of the God of life, essentially futural for the creation, is already presently powerful, the way, therefore, in which the God of Jesus exercises God's creative power over the life of God's creatures.[240]

Is it not thoroughly appropriate to suggest that when these reflections are set beside the qualifying observation from *Theology and the Philosophy of Science,* a significant breakthrough presents itself for consideration: that just possibly, in Jesus, the God who is all-determining power has disclosed godself, precisely *as love,* to *will* the contribution of others to the process of God's ultimate self-determination? We have only to require that this insight be extended by the recognition that so to understand the character of God's power not as might but as an expression of self-imparting divine love, power as the *empowerment* of the beloved, calls for one further step: the acknowledgment that power as love is a meaningful notion only where there are other centers of power in relation to which that power is lovingly exercised. That direction is mentioned here as one possibility for bringing together motifs in Pannenberg's understanding of God, power, and freedom which we have seen to stand in unresolved tension. A fulller elaboration of this possibility will be set forth in the critical section below, after attention is directed toward the remaining key component of Pannenberg's theology of the science of God.

F. The Trinity

The concern to clarify and defend the Christian doctrine of God as a Trinity has occupied Pannenberg's attention from the outset. Indeed, his insistence on proceeding "from below" christologically was directed precisely at the possibility of arriving at Jesus' divinity as a conclusion instead of taking it for granted as a starting point. This Pannenberg believed he had accomplished, discerning in Jesus' life and especially in his resurrection a disclosure of the truth of God which could be understood as God's own self-communication.[241] Thus could Pannenberg speak of a "revelational unity" of Jesus with God, which comprises the identifying statement of the fourth chapter of his Christology, "Jesus' Divinity in Relation to the Father's Divinity":

> In his revelational unity with God, which constitutes Jesus' own divinity, Jesus at the same time still remains distinct from God as his Father. The beginning of the doctrine of the Trinity lies in this.[242]

It is now readily possible for us to perceive why, for Pannenberg, Jesus' resurrection could have retroactive significance for confirming his *eternal* Sonship to the Father even though this was only *established* at Easter.

> The idea that Jesus' exaltation to participation in the divinity of God was accomplished only through the resurrection is not appropriate because of the confirmatory character that belongs to the Easter event and through which it points back to the pre-Easter life of Jesus. Rather, from the perspective of his resurrection, Jesus is recognized as the one who he was previously. He was not only unrecognizable before Easter, but he would not have been who he was without the Easter event.
> The Easter event points back to the pre-Easter Jesus insofar as it has confirmed his pre-Easter claim to authority. Jesus' unity with God, established in the Easter event, does not begin only with this event--it comes into force retroactively from the perspective of this event for the claim to authority in the activity of the earthly Jesus. Conversely, the pre-Easter Jesus' claim to authority is to be understood as an anticipation of his unity with God that was shown by the Easter event.[243]

Adoptionism is circumvented by the Pannenbergian perspective that retroactivity of meaning is not a special case with this one event but characterizes all of reality, as we have seen: "what turns out to be true in the future will then be evident as having been true all along."[244] Therefore, "if God has revealed himself in Jesus then Jesus' community with God, his Sonship, belongs to eternity."[245]

It is tempting to leap to the conclusion that Pannenberg's relocation of God's essence into the final future opens the way to redefining God as Trinity along temporal lines, and indeed he offers some degree of support for this. The Holy Spirit is occasionally identified as "the present reality of God," "the mode of presence of the coming God."[246] The Spirit is "the reality of the Reign of God in the world and thus the reality, the presence, of God himself."[247] By comparison, the Son may be characterized as having to do with the past, in the history of the person Jesus, and the Father/Creator is now identified with the ultimate future. However, though there are intriguing openings in this direction, that is not the primary approach which Pannenberg takes, particularly in light of his concept of the interpenetration of God's eternity into *all* times, past, present, and future. Rather, as I shall unfold shortly, God as Father, Son, and Spirit is equally relevant to every moment in time but in different ways.

Pannenberg's doctrine of the Trinity has been in many respects the more recent of his theological insights to reach provisional completion, and it is a subject on which he is currently preparing a work of major substance. The outlines of his emerging position are to be found primarily in four essays of relatively recent vintage,[248] centering particularly on the possibility of a post-Fichtean, post-Hegelian, doctrine of divine personhood and subjectivity.

Pannenberg works forward from the wrong turn taken in the classical formulation of the Trinity as one *ousia in three hypostases* in relation to the interpretation of hypostasis as *"individua substantia."*[249] He considers it erroneous to have bound individuality and substance together in such a way as to have clouded the distinction between *person* and substance, and thereby also between person and *subject.*. The core of Pannenberg's trinitarianism lies, indeed, in his insistence on distinguishing between the singular subjectivity of God and the threefold personhood of the Trinity, for the coupling of person and subject leads, in his understanding, toward a position of tri-theism.[250]

> Person, in the sense of the doctrine of the Trinity, and subject, in the sense of the development which leads from the concept of hypostasis to the subjectivity of transcendental philosophy, are not the same. But the working out of their difference is a task of theology yet unaccomplished, a task which at the same time is of considerable anthropological significance.[251]

An opening in the right direction is found by Pannenberg in Hegel's philosophy of the subject, but it is one that does not go far enough. Hegel was finally thwarted by the aporia that the self-generating subject, which comes to itself over against an other posited by it, cannot fully account for its own complete self-identity:

> For either the other, in its origination, is independent of the subject. Then the question arises as to how the subject can be in such an other with *itself*: the subject, as that which it is in the other, will therefore have to be different from the I that it is over against the other. Or on the other hand, the other is generated by the subject, and then Fichte's aporia arises: the generating subject remains an other over against that which it generates. But then the subject with its other is not in the strict sense with itself, that is, not in the sense of a strict identity. The Hegelian formula, that the subject is in the other with itself, does not lose all meaning thereby. It truly describes a phenomenon, and therein its peculiar fascination is grounded. But in the light of Fichte's aporia of the self-generation of the subject, Hegel's formula turns out to be ambiguous: if it is not in the sense of strict identity that the subject can be

282

with itself in the other posited by it, then either it remains with itself in its relation to the other without being able to become identical with it. That is the barrenness of romantic subjectivity, which only circles around itself in every content with which the romantic I occupies itself. Or on the other hand, the subject takes the content seriously, really gives itself up to the other. Then it, itself, becomes thereby an other, and the subject is no longer absolute. The positing of the other is then no longer only a development of what the subject already was beforehand. If the subject becomes an *other* through the other, in that it finds itself in its other, then the subject is no longer the all-encompassing but is the process of the history of its transformation, through which it imparts itself to itself.

It is no accident that the Hegelian formula of the subject, which is with itself in the other, disintegrates upon analysis into the empty self-circling romantic subject on the one side, and into a "subject" which is no longer absolute but is a function of a history which overcomes its subjectivity on the other side.[252]

It is crucial for Pannenberg to be able to transcend this--to be able to hold on to the sense of the subject as coming to itself in the history of a relationship with that which is *other* to it, in which it finds itself, but is at the same time encompassed within its own being all along. And this Pannenberg comes to do, in his conceptualizing of God's innertrinitarian character as that of the one subject, God, having reality precisely in the process of the interrelatedness of the three persons.

According to Pannenberg's understanding, the persons of the Trinity do not partake of the essence of divinity directly, unmediatedly, but only through each other: "the self-distinction from God is constitutive for the trinitarian persons and for their own divinity."[253] In the inner development of the relationship of the persons of the Trinity one to another, the subject "God" is self-constituted and the identity of the three as co-divine is confirmed.

As we find our relation to our human destiny, our human nature and selfhood, only through our relation to other human beings, so also does the Son find his relation to the divine nature--has his divinity--only by reference to the Father, and vice versa. Father and Son are God not for themselves but only through the communion of the Spirit who unites them. The unity of the divine nature does not dissolve into personal relations, to be sure, but is mediated for each of the persons through their relations with the other persons. For each of the persons, the other two persons are the form in which the divine nature appears. For the Son, divinity appears in the form of the Father, and he knows himself to share therein through the Spirit. For the Father, the Son is the actualization of his divinity, his reign and his love, and in the Spirit he has his bond with the Son as well as the certainty of his own divinity. The Spirit, lastly, has its own divinity in the communion of the Father and the Son.[254]

Thereby, God, in the unity of God's being, is not to be conceived as personal per se. Rather, "the 'face" of the one God is threefold, and, to be sure, not only for us but even for the trinitarian persons themselves in their relation to the divine essence."[255] Thus the identity of God can only truly be comprehended in terms of God's threefold personhood.

History becomes then the "space" that the trinitarian God provides for the created order to live in covenantal partnership with its Creator/Reconciler/Redeemer. The created order shares with the trinitarian persons the same intentionality of developing community with God through self-distinction from God. But in Jesus' taking onto himself the sin of the world in his death on the cross, God's own participation in the depth of the suffering of the creation is embraced thereby, wherefore the way is opened for trinitarian theology to resolve finally the theodicy question by virtue of God's uniting godself with the pain and conflict God's Reign will one day overcome.[256] In summary:

> In God's history with the world, mediated fully trinitarianly, God's divinity remains at issue until it is confirmed with the consummation of the Reign of God. For without the coming of God's Reign, God would not be. Therefore the future of God's Reign is the locus of God's reality as well as the truth of history as a history of God's acting. But the futural realm can only be the Reign of God in such a way that its future now already determines the present and in the same way has already determined the present of all that is past. That God's deity is yet at stake within history, and that God's futural reality nevertheless is already at work in the process of history--both are enabled by the doctrine of the Trinity that is expressed through the tension between the creative acting of the Father and his relatedness to the working of the Son and the Spirit toward the realization of the Reign of God as his presence in creation, and creation in him, without dissolving their distinctiveness. The mutuality [*Ineinander*] of unity and distinctiveness in the innertrinitarian relations of the divine persons, as this is revealed in the history of Jesus Christ, embraces the mutuality of the absence and presence of God, the future and present of God's Reign in creation. Thereby the existence as well as the history of the created order, as a way to its full community with God, is first made possible. But in the mutuality of God's presence and absence in the world is grounded even the suffering of God's creatures along the way of their history. . . . In the tension between the power and the impotence of the Creator, in the death of God's Son and with the glorification of both through the Spirit, the trinitarian God takes upon himself the suffering of God's creation. So is God the God of history, and its truth.[257]

G. Unfinished Roadwork on the Way to God

To embark immediately upon a final critical engagement of yet outstanding problems in Pannenberg's post-theistic explorations at this point without first expressing deep appreciation for a remarkable and penetrating reconception of the Christian understanding of God would be something of an insensitive travesty. The very extent of intellectual energy devoted to this study betokens a considerable degree of enduring gratitude for promising vistas opened up by Pannenberg's bold and trailblazing efforts in theological comprehension. The assessment of unresolved aporias in the doctrine of God set forth here is couched within a context of extensive affirmation of the intentionality operative in Pannenberg's approach (to be biblically responsible and conceptually rigorous) and the fundamental direction of his theological reconstruction. This observation is made here as, in part, a reminder that the intent and guiding focus of this venture in critical dialogue is to engage in a basically *internal* critique that seeks to expose the degree of conceptual consistency with which Pannenberg remains true to his own fundamental principles of theological understanding. Let us, therefore, review briefly what I have perceived to be fundamentally operative in Pannenberg's orientation, and identify the significant theological insights uncovered here which evoke a response of keen admiration and considerable thankfulness, before proceeding to the concluding integrative critique.

The basic flow of Pannenberg's eschatologically centered theology seeks the truth about God--if God is to be conceived at all--as answer to the question of truth's unity, as history's guarantor of meaningfulness, as ground of human openness and freedom beyond everything extant in the world. The biblical record is strikingly consistent with those concerns in that it embodies a growing tradition of understanding that God has been and continues to be revealed indirectly in all of history as the faithful One who assures history of its ultimate destiny in the consummating onset of God's Reign. This disclosure is especially and unsurpassably to be detected in the resurrection of Jesus which proleptically actualizes history's and humanity's goal while history remains underway. The fundamental convictions with which Pannenberg works in developing this overall theological vision particularly include the following: (1) that truth must be susceptible of ultimate unification; (2) that theology ought employ no borrowed philosophical constructs without their being transformed by encounter with the disclosure of the divine in history; (3) that the Hebraic notion of truth as happening is correct; (4) that meaning is not something external to an event but is encompassed within it, wherefore (5) history is essentially *Überlieferungsgeschichte,* the history of the transmission of traditions; (6) that the hermeneutical task takes place within the horizon of history in its totality; and (7) that God-talk is not univocal but doxological.

Out of this basic approach to theological understanding have come insights which I find to be significantly persuasive:
    (1) The insistence that theology, as a participant in the quest for truth's overarching unity, must be rationally defensible.
    (2) The insistence that truth is historical, and therefore inclusive of change and contingent novelty rather than oriented toward

unchanging being.

(3) The concomitant emphasis on history as locus of divine revelation--not history sans word but history understood precisely as including word.

(4) The insistence on the necessity of rational historical inquiry into all purported events and experiences in which believing/trusting faith is grounded.

(5) An acceptance, accordingly, of the provisionality of every theological affirmation.

(6) The perception of human existence as unfinished, as on its way toward its essence--as aimed at its destiny to actualize the *imago Dei* fully and unendingly.

(7) The rediscovery of the central theological importance of eschatology as rooted in Jesus' proclamation of the Reign of God.

(8) The recognition that Jesus' message of the coming Reign of God embraces both its futurity and its interpenetration into the present, so that neither future nor present is to be swallowed up in or subsumed by the other.

(9) The focus on the centrality of the Easter event for Christian faith and understanding, and the refusal to relegate it to a realm of transhistorical reality inaccessible to critical inquiry.

(10) The acknowledgment that knowledge of God is genuinely and significantly shaped by the way God is communicated in the message and activity and destiny of Jesus of Nazareth.

With this positive conceptual panorama in mind, let us proceed to an analysis of critical complications that prevent a complete endorsement of the eschatological doctrine of God to which these insights have led Pannenberg, and suggest, in the process, ways in which the key conceptual roadblocks may begin to be surmounted.

APORIA #1: Fundamental tensions in the doctrine of divine casuality. Pannenberg is not representing a resurgence of the role of teleological causation in his understanding of the power of the future to bring about the present. All his comments about God's acting in history from the standpoint of the eschatological future reflect essentially a continuity with notions of efficient causation, though now viewed somewhat in reverse. In this respect, David McKenzie is well wide of the mark when he contends "that Pannenberg has conflated the idea of the future with the future itself, [explaining] only how one aspect of the present, namely, one's idea of the future, is determinative for the present."[258] To the contrary, Langdon Gilkey is very much on target with his telling observation that Pannenberg has retheologized Bloch by "transforming ideals as final causes into a divine reality as an agent or efficient cause."[259] My question has been, and continues to be, whether what comes into momentary existence in history's myriad becoming is

286

also traceable to any additional agents or efficient causes. I have lifted up the element of ambiguity present in Pannenberg's doctrine of God as the all-determining power of the future, recognizing the possibility of "hard" and "soft" determinism therein. In the one case, God is interpreted as fully constituting what emerges in history; in the other, God finally decides what those emergent realities ultimately mean, what their essence is. Let us probe this pair of alternatives, drawing out the implications of Pannenberg's provocative but undeveloped concession in *Theology and the Philosophy of Science*,[260] to see where the two options take us concerning an understanding of divine power and its consequences.

On the other hand, if that concession is not made--if, in other words, one has no reason to conclude that the all-determining power resolves to be determined in part by anything other than itself--the consequences seem absolutely unavoidable that Pannenberg finally is unable to circumvent the verdict of many of his critics that the "openness" of the future is, as in the perception of Gilkey, merely epistemological and not ontological, that is, decided out of God's time-intersecting eternity but not yet known by us.[261] If the concession is not a real one, then the meaning of the contingent novelty of events has reference only to *God's* freedom of non-necessity--a sort of eschatologically recentered Nominalism--and not at all to the conventional understanding of the non-necessity of the events themselves. In this mode of interpretation of Pannenberg's intent the conclusion seems inescapable that human openness *to* the future is nothing more than a process of discovery of what will come to be but is actually already decided (in God's future), in which case the much-heralded concern to develop a doctrine of God that overcomes the atheism of human freedom is vitiated.[262] The final outcome of this line of thought is that Pannenberg has merely substituted for the unpalatable tradition of divine pre-determinism an equally odious divine *post-determinism*[263] which amounts to the same thing--what Gilkey aptly tags "a kind of Calvinism set into temporal reverse gear."[264]

But perhaps Pannenberg *has* opened a door to a quite different set of possibilities. What if, on the other hand, one were to develop the implications allowed for by the consideration that the all-determining power may *will* to give over to the creaturely realm a share in deciding the shape of what comes into being? Immediately a radically different set of factors comes into play. The whole notion of an appeal to persons to be open to the offer of the Reign of God in our lives takes on genuine meaning: the possibility of not doing so is really there. In this perspective, sense can be made of the idea that present (or rather, immediately past) reality acts as a drag on our response to the power of the future to free us from imprisonment in the already-at-hand. Though the effort by Lewis Ford to draw out Pannenberg's reflections in this direction was explicitly rejected by Pannenberg,[265] the option nevertheless seems a real one: God as all-determining power need not *fully* constitute the actuality of what becomes in history *if it is God's absolutely free determination not to do so.*

The significance of this direction of thought is enhanced when one considers the matter from the standpoint of Jesus' message of God and God's Reign. If it is appropriate to maintain that it is *as love* that God is powerful, then that perception is utterly consistent with Pannenberg's unexplored proviso. For to will others to participate in the deciding of their own becoming is precisely to indulge in the *risk* of love. The offer may very well be abused. But the meaning of existence itself is infinitely intensified thereby: what would otherwise be a drama written by a single Author and played out on a cosmic stage now becomes a true adventure into creative novelty, and the participants speak lines of at least partly their own devising. Thereby, the coming of the Reign as *judgment* makes genuine sense, for there are decisions other than God's whose adequacy is to be continually evaluted. And equally the coming of the Reign as *grace* is genuinely affirmed--for the context of possibility of deciding *for* God's oncoming, in-breaking love is ever that sustaining and *empowering* love of God itself (I John 4:19).

Within this orientation, Pannenberg's particular exploration into the true nature of human freedom as a matter of being freed by the power of the future to actualize one's proper destiny is not necessarily repudiated but even underscored: our resistance to the power of the future may be not so much an expression of our willful and free self-determination but a consequence of our unfree entrapment by the seductiveness of our past and present environment or our bondage to the safely familiar.

To say that the aporia of divine causality is readily solved in this way, by seizing upon God's willingness to share decisions of causal efficacy with other centers of power *that God godself creates*, thereby reflecting a position of soft determinism, is hardly so simple however--because *other* implications also flow out from each of these alternative perspectives on Pannenberg's meaning. Does this latter interpretation require the surrendering of other features less readily relinquished than the notion of strict determinism? Indeed it does, as we now move to consider.

APORIA #2: Related tensions in the interpretation of divine eternality and temporality. Pannenberg has linked his interpretation of the essential futurity of God with an understanding of the interpenetration (*Verschränkung*) of the eternity of God's future into every historical present, a perspective on the interlacing of the times of which he particularly finds evidences in the tradition of apocalyptic. There the ultimate future of the Reign of God is perceived to be hidden to earth but already a reality in the eternity of God and therefore disclosable to the apocalyptic seer who is transported into the heavenly realm. Pannenberg champions this perspective on eternity and temporality as but one more facet of apocalyptic which has been authenticated by the message and fate of Jesus. Out of this notion of eternity as God's powerful presence to every time is conveyed the thesis of a divine omnitemporality which can maintain God's transcending of real change and development: what arises as contingent novelty in *our* midst is that to which God as eternal is related, and therefore only from our temporally finite point of view does it *appear* that God changes as God encompasses change.

Now we see why the aporia of divine determinism cannot be so quickly resolved in the direction I have indicated: *Pannenberg's doctrine of God's changeless eternal co-presence to every moment depends utterly on the hard meaning of God's all-determining power.* It is only because God, in God's eternity, *totally* determines all that emerges as historical truth--truth incorporated into its ultimate consummation--that the novelties of history make no contribution of their own to God's fullness of being. Process and change come to be incorporated as constitutive for ultimate truth only because it is ultimately God who is fully constitutive of process and change.[266]

On the other hand, acknowledgment that God wills to allow other instances of causal agency than God's own to contribute to the becoming of history leads inexorably to the realization that history is also the *divine* adventure, full of novelty and uncontrolled twists and turns even for God. Such a perspective explicitly overturns the distinction between merely (mis-)perceived and truly real development in God, and calls for the irresistible conclusion that time, precisely in its temporal distinctions of already and not yet, affects God also. For if what God "releases" into existence from out of God's powerful future includes the provision for a degree of self-determination in the shape of what comes into being at that moment, then God is increased by the knowledge of the decision now made which God wills not to control. God is therefore affected by what is brought forth "from time to time" within the temporal process.

The notion that the historical is the real, which began to focus Pannenberg's energies over a quarter of a century ago, is decidedly enhanced in this interpretation. But that gain is in direct tension with a thesis Pannenberg holds onto with great tenacity: the lack of real development within the deity. We cannot avoid the conclusion, however, that Pannenberg can retain this facet of his doctrine of God only by denying not only the alternative possibility of soft determinism in the becoming of events in history but also the truly genuine reality of temporal process itself.[267]

APORIA #3: The ontologically unsustained thesis of the eschatological futurity of God's essential being. There is simply no gainsaying the fact that, more than two decades after he began to raise the fascinating prospect of a theology oriented toward the ontological primacy of the future and the future as God's mode of being, Pannenberg still has not carried through with the requisite development of a full-fledged "eschatological ontology." Even Pannenberg's friendliest critics have been calling now for some time for a thoroughly worked-out demonstration of the philosophical theses that would render Pannenberg's futural vision coherent, consistent, and cogent.[268] Beyond exploratory essays such as "Zeit und Ewigkeit . ." that only begin to probe the critical issues in a merely germinal way, this he has not really embarked upon at all. The forcefulness and persuasiveness of Pannenberg's vision is diminished by the lack of sufficient philosophical precision being directed toward the possibility of conceptualizing the future (*as genuine future* and not just as codeword for eternity) as having its own present ontological status. Bloch's endeavors in that direction do not function at all for Pannenberg as a contribution to that possibility, as we have seen. What remains is the suspicion that an ontology of the future may not really be conceptualizable at all.

This lack renders problematic such expressions as God's reality as "absolute future"[269] and God being "future" not merely in relation to us but "in himself."[270] Ford pursues this lead in the direction of a conceptualizing of God as "forever future,"[271] bringing to bear upon the temporal process "the power of an absolute, inexhaustible future."[272] Of course, Pannenberg's coupling of God's futurity "in himself" with an emphasis on the eventuality of history's terminating consummation (see the fourth aporia) is overtly opposed to that notion. But Ford's suggestion lifts up the ambiguity in Pannenberg's underdeveloped thesis of the futurity of God--even at the same time that it extends the credibility of Pannenberg's insights.

For Ford tellingly adds another component to the arguments of Pannenberg against the notion of a presently extant deity: Einstein's theory of special relativity discloses that there is no single absolute present in the universe, but rather "a vast number of cosmic present moments for each event in Einsteinian space-time."[273] Ford believes accordingly that "the situation now with regard to time is quite analogous to the Copernican revolution with regard to space."[274] What this points to is that the attempt to relocate God's subjectivity into the future is not necessarily so alien to common sense after all, inasmuch as the cosmic presentness of God from moment to moment has unresolved problems of its own. But Pannenberg's lack of sufficient conceptual clarity thus far in providing the ontological underpinnings of his alternative vision leaves the outlines of his eschatological theology at a far more provisional stage than one would ordinarily wish for from theological scholarship.

APORIA #4: The inadequate conceptualizing of a final telos of becoming and meaning. The declaration of the ultimate consummation of history as a necessary condition for truth and meaning suffers in part, once again, from the inadequately developed conceptual imaging of the ontological primacy of the future. Pannenberg's protestations that theology has no obligation to give explicit content to the notion of the End of things[275] is difficult to endorse, for too much weight is imposed on the viability of the concept to treat it so cavalierly. Some imaging must be put forward.

There is a strong temptation to accuse Pannenberg of ultimately selling out the Hebraic conceptuality of truth as dynamic happening, in the direction of a Greek orientation toward truth as permanent and unchanging being, the difference arising only in the sense that now the one eventually follows upon and replaces the other. To this tendency one would have to observe that the Greeks were misled by their erroneous perception that *rest* is a natural condition of matter and *motion* is to be explained. To the contrary, nothing is completely at rest anywhere in the universe--except, just possibly at the center of black holes, and that hardly represents much enhancement of value. It would seem that the notion of an *unmoved* mover is a rather deficient conceptualization. To image the consummation of the Reign of God in terms that eliminate all dynamic continuation whatsoever would seem to be the very antithesis of creation's ultimate perfection.

But to be fair to Pannenberg, he has endeavored to distance himself from implications of the notion of an ultimate End of history which would require the absolute cessation of all dynamic process.[276] The problem remains precisely in the lack of conceptual clarification in speaking both of an end of history and an ongoing though somehow transformed process of eternal life rather than static lifelessness. The supposition seems to be that temporal successiveness is only an accident of process, not an essential characteristic thereof. But the conceptual apparatus to support this is nowhere presented, other than in the discredited notion of a "contortion of time."

It is just possible that the anticipation of an eschatological termination of history, discerned in apocalyptic and ostensibly confirmed in the Easter event, is not only conceptually vapid but also both unnecessary and ungrounded. Certainly its tenability is diminished by the unresolved aporias attendant to it: the absence of a cognitively meaningful model; the unexplored clash of concepts between a God who *must* be non-extant vis-a-vis human openness and a God who comes to be extant precisely in the consummation of God's Reign; the lack of clarity on how God can be both absolute future in godself and the determinate coming of the Reign in a future present. All of these militate against the persuasiveness of the idea.

But why is it, after all, so essential? What is it that requires the positing of an ultimate consummation of history, human and cosmic? Beyond what appears to Pannenberg to be the self-evident character of the definition of God as *all*-determining power--which, of course, requires a final perspective from which that hypothesis can be definitively confirmed or denied--there is the crucial discernment that Jesus' fate validates the truth of the notion in representing the proleptic dawning of the ultimate *telos* already within history. The background for this mode of intepretation is the perception of a fundamental continuity between Jesus and the tradition of apocalyptic that renders valid the conviction that his resurrection presages an end of history and the arrival of the eschaton. But I have had occasion to take issue with this entire mode of appropriation of the meaning of the Easter event, concluding that, contrary to Pannenberg's argumentation, there is in Jesus' disclosure of God and God's Reign no championing of essential apocalyptic features and equally in his fate no confirmation of its verity. What we are therefore left with, accordingly, is the suggestion that if God is in fact not revealed in Jesus as guarantor of an ultimate unambiguous display of all-encompassing power, then perhaps it is incumbent to suspend the doctrine of a necessary end to historical process and develop the dynamic of unity and meaning and power in some other way than through dependence on Hegelian and post-Hegelian categories of thought. Such an alternative might be explored in seeing God's unifying of the many as a dynamic consummation, forever being superseded by God's new act of unification; in recognizing that new expressions of meaning regarding past events are themselves not extensions of events as open-ended but *new events*, so that happenings do not require a final "closure" to be meaning-full; and in grasping God's power in history as that which is never totally thwarted by adversity but ever remains capable of injecting new possibilities of empowering love into the ongoing historical process.[277]

APORIA #5: The insufficiency of a theodicy of eschatological reconciliation. The shifting of the locus of God's fullness of being and power into the future appeared at first glance to provide a striking resolution of the theodicy issue: evil reigns in the world now because God's power, God's Reign, is still in the future. Certainly the experiential evidence that all is not presently for the best in a best of all possible worlds serves as considerable justification for referring to the Reign of God as something not presently and fully actual, as something yet to come. But we have seen how this turns out not to be what Pannenberg really has in mind when he speaks of the futurity of God, in spite of whatever impulses may have initially triggered that reflection. God is understood by Pannenberg to be even now already determining the course of events, from out of God's powerful future. Thus the theodicy issue re-emerges with renewed fury: if God is already at work in a world of suffering and injustice and evil, what does that say about God's goodness and righteousness, or God's power?

The question is one to which Pannenberg is necessarily sensitive, for the criticism of his theology frequently focus on this particular issue.[278] It is striking that one very significant option has not been explored by him, concerning the recognition that God may will to share the process of the determination of what becomes. If that is indeed so, the theodicy problem is overcome in the recognition of the risk necessarily entailed in offering to creation itself the possibility of co-creatorhood. What goes wrong in the historical process is to be explained not in terms of divine indifference or impotence or moral neutrality but in respect to the very real openness of possibility that ensues, for good *or* for evil, when God wills not to control the process.

But the route that Pannenberg has taken is quite a different one, and one which I find extremely unsatisfactory. Pannenberg lifts up the element of divine trinitarian participation in the pain of history, particularly through the suffering of the Son, and completes that with the observation that all unjust suffering will, in the full coming of the Reign of God unambiguously, be taken up into the glorification of God's creation and thereby somehow nullified, cancelled out, *aufgehoben*. Thus theodicy is especially tied up with the previously discussed aporia of an ultimate end, and Daniel D. Williams' observation is very much to the point in noting that life's seriousness is somewhat blunted if there awaits the oncoming of one final "absolute good" embracing "the essence of every event, no matter what relation to good and evil it may sustain."[279] There is, Williams reflects, no real risk of lostness of being; the essence of events which were monstrously evil and destructive is equally taken up into the *telos*. I share this sense of alienation from Pannenberg's view. It is somehow not enough to project a theology of God that embraces the horror of the Holocaust with a vision of ultimate eschatological transformation and consummation which suggests somehow that the End justifies the meantime.[280]

Behind the Aporias. One final note is appropriate. The unresolved aporias which have been identified here in regard to Pannenberg's doctrine of God as the all-determining power of the future seem to be fundamentally traceable to an overlapping quartet of considerations, varyingly touched on already within the discussion but briefly summarized here in conclusion. (1) There remains a drastically underdeveloped ontology of the future which is strongly called for by a conceptual scheme that leaves too much unexplored and unclarified. (2) There remains in Pannenberg's approach to the understanding of God's self-disclosure in history a residue of insufficiently reconstructed philosophical concepts, particularly concerning the nature of power and the changelessness of the Absolute, but also including the Hegelian insistence on an ultimate resolution of historical ambiguity, which have not been thoroughly penetrated by the revelatory data at hand. (3) The fateful championing of perceived features in the apocalyptic tradition, regarded as essentially substantiated in Jesus' message and resurrection, opens the door for Pannenberg to an uncritical appropriation of apocalyptic's failure of nerve concerning the uncertainty of the future, namely, in endorsing the presupposition there that history's ultimate future is actually already fully decided but merely hidden from present view, and that history will necessarily come to a final eschatological end. (4) The thesis that the truth of God is especially discernible in the way God is disclosed by Jesus of Nazareth has not been substantively developed in the direction of allowing *all* one's notions of deity to be critically revised by their exposure to that illuminating and transforming mediator of radically good news.

NOTES

[1] Pannenberg, *Theology and the Philosophy of Science*, p. 297.

[2] *Ibid.*, p. 299.

[3] *Ibid.*, pp. 300f. Moltmann had earlier observed that Pannenberg's argument that the unity of reality requires for its ultimate completion the existence of God reopens the issue of the validity of the *cosmological* argument (*Theology of Hope*, pp. 77f.), but that verdict rested on a fundamental misperception: Pannenberg never maintained that such a unity was *necessarily* forthcoming. Ultimate cosmic nihilism is a legitimate possibility, while history runs its course. Here Pannenberg is suggesting rather than any substantiation of the God hypothesis, depending on nothing external to the very *idea* of God (as "all-determining reality": see section E of this chapter), would in effect amount to an *ontological* "self-proof" of God's being. (*TPS*, p. 300.)

[4]There is also a fourth--or rather, the first of four: the "atheism of mechanistic physics" originating with Laplace's development of a mechanistic system of finite causation as self-sufficient in causal explanation. But for Pannenberg this emergence of "a new theistic metaphysics as a substructure for its self-enclosed picture of the world as an infinity of finite things and processes" was in fact no more than the presuppositional world-view which lies behind the distinctive developments of modern atheisms per se--which have taken the necessary second step of explaining away the religious ideas of God themselves. See "Types of Atheism and Their Theological Significance," *BQT* II, pp. 184-86 (p. 185 for the passage quoted here).

[5]"Types of Atheism," *BQT* II, pp. 196f.

[6]For the flow of the argument, see *supra*, pp. 4-5.

[7]"Types of Atheism," *BQT* II, p. 199.

[8]*Ibid.*, pp. 186f.

[9]*Ibid.*, pp. 189f.

[10]"Anthropology and the Question of God," *IGHF*, p. 87. See also "Speaking about God in the face of Atheist Criticism," *IGHF*, p. 106, and *AC*, pp. 24f.

[11]"Types of Atheism," *BQT* II, pp. 192f.

[12]*Ibid.*, p. 193.

[13]*Supra*, pp. 100-02.

[14]"Types of Atheism," *BQT* II, pp. 195f.

[15]*Ibid.*, p. 200.

[16]"The God of Hope," *BQT* II, p. 235. These phrases are in question form in the text, but the indicative is overtly implied.

[17]"The Appropriation of the Philosophical Concept of God as a Dogmatic Problem of Early Christian Theology," *BQT* II, pp. 119-83. Originally published in 1959.

[18]*Ibid.*, p. 134.

[19] *Ibid.*, p. 136.

[20] *Ibid.*, p. 139.

[21] *Ibid.*, pp. 139f. See also *AC*, p. 34.

[22] The notion first appears in 1961, in "What is a Dogmatic Statement?," *BQT* I, pp. 202ff.

[23] See Edmund Schlink, *The Coming Christ and the Coming Church*, trans. I. H. Nielson (Philadelphia: Fortress Press, 1968), pp. 16-84, especially pp. 19-34, 41f., and 77f. Original German publication: 1961. Pannenberg's fullest elaboration of his use of the idea appeared in his contribution to the Schlink Festschrift, "Analogie und Doxologie," *Dogma und Denkstrukturen*, ed. W. Joest and W. Pannenberg (Göttingen: Vandenhoeck & Ruprecht, 1963), pp. 96-115, subsequently appearing in *BQT* I, pp. 211-38.

[24] Schlink, *op. cit.*, p. 22.

[25] "Analogy and Doxology," *BQT* I, pp. 216f. The door which Pannenberg opens here is one through which we surely will want to pass as we probe the meaning of God's *power*.

[26] "What is a Dogmatic Statement?," *BQT* I, pp. 203f.; *JGM*, pp. 184.

[27] "Analogy and Doxlogy," *BQT* I, pp. 228-30.

[28] "What is a Dogmatic Statement?," *BQT* I, p. 205.

[29] "Analogy and Doxology," *BQT* I, pp. 237f. See *supra*, p. 37.

[30] So Pannenberg himself observed, in "God's Presence in History," *Theologians in Transition*, ed. James M. Wall (New York: The Crossroad Publishing Company, 1981), p. 93. (Pannenberg's contribution to the "How My Mind Has Changed" series in *The Christian Century*, March 11, 1981.)

[31] Albert Camus, *The Stranger*, trans. Stuart Gilbert (New York: Alfred A. Knopf, 1946), p. 152.

[32] "The God of Hope," *BQT* II, pp. 240, 242.

[33] *TKG*, p. 56, my italics.

[34] Karl Barth, *Church Dogmatics* II:1: *The Doctrine of God*, trans. T. H. L. Parker, W. B. Johnston, H. Knight, and J. L. M. Haire (Edinburgh: T. & T. Clark, 1957), pp. 619, and ff. Pannenberg wishes, essentially, to make this aspect primary and to include the other two within it: for example, to propose that God is pre-temporal *qua* the future of even the earliest moment of time.

[35] *Ibid.*, p. 629.

[36] *Ibid.*, pp. 608, 612.

[37] *Ibid.*, p. 629.

[38] *Ibid.*, p. 630, my italics.

[39] *Ibid.*, p. 631 ("the God of all hope" my italics). Thus Barth also anticipates Pannenberg's concentration on futural revelation: The "vindication" of God's truth "will be the revelation of the kingdom of God. For the kingdom of God consists in the fact that in some sense He is all in all. It is only in its revelation that the kingdom of God is post-temporal and therefore lies in the future. Already pre-temporally God was, and supra-temporally He is, all in all without reservation or reduction. But if we believe this and recognise it in faith, we believe in its future revelation. God's revelation stands before us as the goal and end of time. We wait for it even as we look back on its occurrence in the middle of time and grasp it as the kingdom of God that has drawn near" (630).

[40] Robert W. Jenson, "The Futurist Option in Speaking of God," *Lutheran Quarterly* 21, 1969, pp. 209f.

[41] Barth, *Church Dogmatics* II:1, p. 635.

[42] The third edition of Fredrich Gogarten, *Der Mensch zwischen Gott und Welt* (Stuttgart: Friedrich Vorwerk Verlag, 1956) is quoted from herein.

[43] *Ibid.*, p. 389.

[44] *Ibid.*, pp. 395-99.

[45] *Ibid.*, pp. 369f. So does Gogarten also interpret Exodus 3:14 as "I am who I will be" (395).

[46] *Ibid.*, p. 406.

[47] Heinrich Ott, *Eschatologie* (Zollikon: Evangelischer Verlag A. G., 1958), p. 9.

[48] *Ibid.*, p. 11, italics his. Ott also anticipates here Pannenberg's thesis that it is the future in its eschatological sense which discloses the meaning of the present (13) and that Jesus' resurrection is the inbreaking of the eschaton wherein the revelation of the *endzeitlich* lordship of God is gained (15).

[49] "Heilsgeschehen und Geschichte," *GsT* I, p. 41, from a portion of the essay that was irresponsibly omitted in the English translation. Ulrich Hedinger correctly points out the distinction between Pannenberg's concept of God as *Zukunft* and Gogarten's concept of the *Zukünftigkeit* of God (*Hoffnung zwischen Kreuz und Reich* [Zurich: EVZ-Verlag, 1968], pp. 318f., note 9), although Pannenberg retains the utilization of both terms. But the point of interest here is the acknowledgment of a conceptual climate in the context of which Pannenberg's doctrine of God was maturing.

[50] "Heilsgeschehen und Geschichte," *GsT* I, p. 74, ft. 68. (Cf. the less than informative translation in *BQT* I, p. 74, ft. 144.)

[51] "Dogmatische Thesen," *OaG*, p. 97.

[52] "On the Theology of Law," *Ethics*, trans. Keith Crim (Philadelphia: The Westminster Press, 1981), p. 52. (On the publishing and editing history of the essay, see *ibid.*, p. 199, note 1.)

[53] *Ibid.*, p. 54. See also p. 56: "What confronts mankind in the world is to be surpassed day by day in the direction of that future of God which has not yet appeared."

[54] "The Revelation of God in Jesus of Nazareth," *TaH*, p. 113. Cf. also, from the same year, the "Nachwort" to the second edition of *OaG*, p. 147: "The conclusive unmasking of that which happened in Jesus Christ will first bring the future of God."

[55] *JGM*, p. 366.

[56] "The Question of God," *BQT* II, p. 233. The essay was originally a lecture delivered in the summer of 1964, being published the following year. Three years later, in private conversation, Pannenberg summarized his reasoning on God's being as "non-extant" (*nicht vorhanden*) thusly: (1) God would be *a* being alongside others; (2) phenomenologically, God has no spatiality; (3) God could only exist presently as *finite*, not infinite, being. Subsequently (in "Can Christianity Do without an Eschatology?," *The Christian Hope*, p. 32, and also "Speaking about God in the Face of Atheist Criticism," *IGHF*, p. 109), Pannenberg added the qualification that an extant God would

298

conflict with the reality of human freedom, a consideration that will occupy our attention in the context of section E below.

[57]"Der Gott der Hoffnung," in *Ernst Bloch zu ehren,* ed. Siegfried Unseld (Frankfurt am Main: Suhrkamp Verlag, 1965), pp. 209-25, subsequently appearing in *BQT* II, pp. 234-49.

[58]Such did prove to be the case with Moltmann, another contributor to that volume, who had (according to Hans Walter Wolff) introduced Pannenberg to Bloch's championing of eschatological thinking while the two men were colleagues at Wuppertal. But Pannenberg later recollected, in private conversation (10-21-82), that "I agreed to write for the Bloch Festschrift because I thought he had rendered theology a service. That was not intended to mean he had rendered that service to my own personal development." See *infra*, pp. 255, for my summary conclusions on the validity of this judgment.

[59]Key writings thereto are *Das Prinzip Hoffnung* (Frankfurt am Main: Suhrkamp Verlag, 1959) and *Philosophische Grundfragen I: Zur Ontologie des Noch-Nicht-Seins* (Frankfurt am Main: Suhrkamp Verlag, 1961). Of the considerable secondary literature that burst upon the scene in the late sixties and early seventies, the best basic introduction still remains Wolf-Dieter Marsch's *Hoffen worauf? Auseinandersetzung mit Ernst Bloch* (Hamburg: Furche-Verlag, 1963). For access to Bloch in English, see particularly *Man on His Own* (New York: Herder and Herder, 1970), a translation (by E. B. Ashton) of a volume of selected writings which includes key passages from *Das Prinzip Hoffnung;* and *Atheism in Christianity: The Religion of the Exodus and the Kingdom,* trans. J. T. Swann (New York: Herder and Herder, 1972).

[60]Bloch, *Philosophische Grundfragen I*, pp. 18f.

[61]Bloch, *Das Prinzip Hoffnung*, p. 1412; similarly, pp. 1457f.: Yahweh had come to be perceived as "a God of the end of days, with *futurum* as mode of being."

[62]*Ibid.*, p. 1408, translated in *Man on His Own*, p. 156. See also *Das Prinzip Hoffnung*, pp. 1411-13, 1523-28.

[63]*Ibid.*, pp. 1529-33.

[64]This summarization is basically dependent upon *Philosophische Grundfragen I*, pp. 7-9, 16-18, 21-24.

[65]Bloch, *Das Prinzip Hoffnung*, p. 1628.

[66]*Ibid.*, p. 1625, and "Kann Hoffnung enttäuscht werden?," in Bloch, *Auswahl*

aus seinen Schriften, ed. Hans Heinz Holz (Frankfurt am Main: Fischer Bücherei, 1967), p. 181.

[67] Bloch, *Das Prinzip Hoffnung,* pp. 357f., and *Philosophische Grundfragen I,* pp. 25-31.

[68] Bloch, *Das Prinzip Hoffnung,* pp. 363f., 1531-33, 1548-50, 1624.

[69] Bloch, "Kann Hoffnung enttäuscht werden?," *Auswahl aus seinen Schriften,* p. 181.

[70] "The God of Hope," *BQT* II, p. 237f.

[71] *Ibid.,* pp. 238, 241.

[72] *Ibid.,* p. 243.

[73] *Ibid.,* pp. 241f.

[74] *Ibid.,* pp. 239f.

[75] *Ibid.,* p. 242.

[76] All but three of his citations of Bloch in the article relate to but two short sections of *Das Prinzip Hoffnung* (pp. 1405-17 and 1524-34).

[77] There is some unresolved confusion as to just how early Pannenberg was encountering Bloch's thought. Although there are references in Pannenberg's writings to some of Bloch's work from as early as 1962 ("On the Theology of Law," originally a lecture in June of that year), Olive reports that Pannenberg began to "read Bloch seriously" only in 1963 (Don Olive, *Wolfhart Pannenberg* [Waco, Texas: Word Books, 1973], p. 30, and note 34, p. 110), and Tupper states that Pannenberg read *Das Prinzip Hoffnung* only after finishing the initial draft of his Christology (*The Theology of Wolfhart Pannenberg,* p. 26). In private conversation in 1971, Pannenberg recalled the date of significant contact as even later (1965!), but that may have been due to his concern to assure his basic independence from germinal Blochian influence--for Pannenberg did point out at that time that his insight into creation as eschatological, "*am Ende,*" preceded his contact with Bloch's similar idea. That notion first puts in an appearance in Pannenberg in 1963, in "Analogy and Doxology," *BQT* I, p. 237. (See also the earlier discussion of this issue *supra,* Ch. 4, note 46.)

[78] See *supra,* especially pp. 190-92.

[79]"Can Christianity Do without an Eschatology?," *The Christian Hope*, p. 31.

[80]See *supra,* especially p. 192.

[81]*TKG*, p. 55.

[82]*E.g.,:* "Toward a Theology of the History of Religions," *BQT* II, p. 104; "Speaking about God in the face of Atheist Criticism," *IGHF*, pp. 111, 115; *Thesen zur Theologie der Kirche* (München: Claudius Verlag, 1970), p. 11; "Future and Unity," *HGM*, p. 65; *AC*, p. 25; "Dogmatische Erwägungen zue Auferstehung Jesu," *GsT* II, p. 170.

[83]"The God of Hope," *BQT* II, p. 240. The concluding phrase is a quote from Bloch, *Das Prinzip Hoffnung,* p. 1458: *"futurum also Seinsbeschaffenheit. ."*

[84]We have encountered already the tendency on Pannenberg's part to want to have it both ways: God is *already* revealed in Jesus /God *will be* revealed *am Ende*. The issue parallels the matter of God's futural Reign being proleptically present in Jesus: just so is God's ultimate self-disclosure proleptically on view in Jesus' resurrection. See the discussion *supra,* pp. 200f.

[85]"The God of Hope," *BQT* II, p. 242.

[86]The summary is derived from *TKG*, p. 60, and "Christian Theology and Philosophical Criticism," *IGHF*, p. 131. The quoted phrase is my translation from the original of the latter, *GmF*, p. 64.

[87]"Future and Unity," *HFM*, pp. 61f. "Futurology" and "eschatology" are therefore decisively at odds.

[88]It is in this sense that Pannenberg is writing when he observes that "if the future of all creatures is a universal one, that is, if each instance of reality has the same future, then the future to which I look forward today is the same future that confronted every earlier present. My future now was also Julius Caesar's future, the future of the prehistoric saurians and the future of the first physical processes approximately ten billion years ago. Thus I come to view past events as having eventuated from the same future to which I look forward. And, of course, those past event were the *finite* future of yet earlier events." (*TKG*, p. 61, my italics--for pointing up the distinction between universal/ultimate and historical/finite future.)

[89]In English, one can readily identify this distinction by using upper and lower case, "Future" and "future." Though Pannenberg has acknowledged to me that he has no objection to this procedure, he himself has not chosen to do so in his own English-

language essays and addresses, so I will resist doing so here--even though much confusion might possibly be avoided by employing that convention.

[90]The term is problematic only if one misses the fact that this post-historical future is decisively immediate to every moment *within* history, as pointed out in the next paragraph.

[91]"On Historical and Theological Hermeneutic," *BQT* I, p. 178, including ft. 43.

[92]*TKG*, p. 54. The presentness of the future as reflected in Jesus' message is also reflected in a lengthy passage from "Appearance as the Arrival of the Future," *TKG*, p. 133, already quoted *supra*, pp. 32f.

[93]"The God of Hope," *BQT* II, pp. 240, 241.

[94]"Speaking about God in the face of Atheist Criticism," *IGHF*, p. 110. (See *GmF*, pp. 41f.) It is instructive to interrelate this notion with the orientation of process thought. There, precisely the *opposite* is maintained: Only that which has reality can be regarded as an adequate source of accounting for what becomes. See Alfred North Whitehead, *Process and Reality*, corrected edition edited by David R. Griffin and Donald W. Sherburne (New York: The Free Press, 1978), pp. 18f.

[95]*TKG*, p. 63. Section D of this chapter endeavors to unpack the implications contained here (as elsewhere) concerning God and temporality.

[96]All quotes in this paragraph are from "The God of Hope," *BQT* II, p. 242. Cf. also "Dogmatische Erwägungen zur Auferstehung Jesu," *GsT* II, p. 171.

[97]*TKG*, p. 59.

[98]*TKG*, p. 54 (both quotes).

[99]*Ibid.*, p. 70.

[100]"A Liberal Logos Christology: The Christology of John Cobb," *John Cobb's Theology in Process*, p. 138, and p. 148, note 13. See also "The Doctrine of Creation and Modern Science," *Zygon* 23, 1988, pp. 12-14. The earlier discussion of energy fields in "The Doctrine of the Spirit and the Task of a Theology of Nature" (*Theology* 75, 1972, p. 15--reprinted in *Faith and Reality* under the title, "The Spirit of Life") did not relate to the issue of *divine* energy.

[101]*TKG*, p. 70. Several motifs in this summary go beyond the preceding

discussion and will yet receive individual attention in the present chapter--specifically, the eschatological doctrine of creation, the references to freedom (God's and ours), and God's power as characterized by love.

[102]It is, of course, more properly the case that the resurrection of Jesus provides the solution to those hypothesized explorations, as was demonstrated in chapter seven. But the specific shape of the doctrine of God that emerges thereby offers a crucial perspective on those themes precisely when it is as the power of the future that this revealed God is understood. That is what this section will subsequently lift up.

[103]See *supra*, pp. 75f.

[104]"Christian Theology and Philosophical Criticism," *IGHF*, p. 131.

[105]*TKG*, p. 57.

[106]*Ibid.*, p. 58.

[107]*Ibid.*, p. 59.

[108]*Ibid.*, pp. 59f.

[109]"The God of Hope," *BQT* II, pp. 244-46; "On Historical and Theological Hermeneutic," *BQT* I, p. 157; "Speaking about God in the Face of Atheist Criticism," *IGHF*, pp. 111f.

[110]See the discussion *supra*, pp. 97-99, especially pp. 98f.

[111]*TKG*, p. 57. See also "Analogy and Doxology," *BQT* I, pp. 232f.

[112]*TKG*, p. 57.

[113]See "The God of Hope," *BQT* II, pp. 245f.

[114]*Ibid.* See also "Anthropology and the Question of God," *IGHF*, p. 96.

[115]"The God of Hope," *BQT* II, p. 243.

[116]*TKG*, p. 60.

[117] "Analogy and Doxology," *BQT* I, p. 237. Cf. *AC,* p. 39: "God creates the world in the light of its latter end, because it is only the end which decides the meaning of the things and beings with which we have to do in the present."

[118] "The God of Hope," *BQT* II, p. 243.

[119] *Ibid.*

[120] *TKG,* p. 68 (italics his). See also "The God of hope," *BQT* II, p. 241.

[121] See *supra,* especially pp. 67f., 76-78.

[122] *Supra,* pp. 198f.

[123] *TKG,* p. 60.

[124] See *supra,* especially pp.28f., 34-37, 45-47.

[125] *Supra,* pp. 202f.

[126] See, again, *TKG,* p. 60, middle paragraph.

[127] See *supra,* pp. 43-45.

[128] *TKG,* p. 62.

[129] *AC,* p. 36.

[130] See *supra,* especially pp. 93-97, 106-12.

[131] *Supra,* pp. 203-05.

[132] *Supra,* pp. 97-99.

[133] See "Person und Subjekt," *GsT* II, pp. 91f.

[134] "Toward a Theology of the HIstory of Religions," *BQT* II, p. 115.

[135] *WIM,* pp. 70f. Allan Galloway (*Wolfhart Pannenberg* [London: George Allen & Unwin Ltd., 1973] p. 95) discerns a fundamental continuity here with the classical

theism of Thomas Aquinas, though he acknowledges that Pannenberg has struggled to move beyond that.

[136] "The Hope of God," *BQT* II, p. 244. Cf. also Tupper's quote of a personal communication from Pannenberg in 1971: "I would not speak today as I did then of a standpoint outside the flow of time but rather of the absolute future of God." (Tupper, *The Theology of Wolfhart Pannenberg*, p. 289.)

[137] "The Appropriation of the Philosophical Concept of God as a Dogmatic Problem of Early Christian Theology," *BQT* II, p. 180. (See also pp. 173f.) Pannenberg would seem to regard God's ubiquity in a similar way, as God's powerful lordship over every space. (Cf. *e.g., WIM*, p. 76, and "Zeit und Ewigkeit in der religiösen Erfahrung Israels und des Christentums," *GsT* II, p. 200.)

[138] *WIM*, p. 73.

[139] "Future and Unity," *HFM*, p. 71.

[140] Unpublished response of Barbour to Pannenberg at the conference on "Hope and the Future of Man." See also the discussion *supra*, pp. 68f.

[141] "Zeit und Ewigkeit in der religiösen Erfahrung Israels und des Christentums," *GsT* II, pp. 188-206. This section focuses careful attention on that essay.

[142] "The God of Hope," *BQT* II, p. 244. See also *TKG*, p. 62: "The God of the coming Kingdom must be called eternal because he is not only the future of our present but has been also the future of every past age."

[143] *TKG*, p. 64. Cf. also "Future and Unity," *HFM*, p. 72, where eschatological future and "eternal essence" are affirmed as coincident.

[144] *TKG*, pp. 63f.

[145] "Dogmatische Erwägungen zur Auferstehung Jesu," *GsT* II, p. 171.

[146] *TKG*, p. 53.

[147] *AC*, p. 173; "Zeit und Ewigkeit," *GsT* II, p. 199. The novelty in Jesus is identified in the recognition that the essential future comes to be acknowledged as interwovenly present not only in God but for us as well. ("Zeit und Ewigkeit," *GsT* II, p. 202.)

[148] "Zeit und Ewigkeit," *GsT* II, p. 201.

[149] *Ibid.*, pp. 199f., the latter notion repeated on p. 202.

[150] *Ibid.*, p. 200.

[151] *Ibid.*, pp. 190f., 195-99.

[152] *Ibid.*, p. 199. This perspective enables Pannenberg to understand the Johannine approach to eschatological data as already real in the present: see pp. 200f.

[153] *Ibid.*, p. 202. (The last clause appears in question form in the text, but the indicative is implicitly legitimated by the context.) See also "Constructive and Critical Functions of Christian Eschatology," *Harvard Theological Review* 77, 1984, p. 136, where eternity is characterized as "a simultaneous presence of what is separated in the sequence of time."

[154] *Ibid.*, p. 190.

[155] "Dogmatische Thesen," *OaG*, p. 97 (cf. *RaH*, pp. 133f.).

[156] *AC*, p. 174, my italics (from a somewhat later date than *OaG* but essentially repeating its thesis). See also the recent "Problems of a Trinitarian Doctrine of God," *Dialog* 26, 1987, p. 255, where he remarks that "God, through the creation of the world, made himself radically dependent on this creation and on its history." (Original is in italics.)

[157] "The Appropriation of the Philosophical Concept of God," *BQT* II, pp. 161f.

[158] *Ibid.*, p. 181.

[159] *WIM*, p. 76.

[160] "What is Truth?" *BQT* II, p. 9.

[161] *Ibid.*, p. 10.

[162] *JGM*, p. 32, my italics.

[163] *TKG*, p. 62.

[164] *Ibid.,* pp. 62f.

[165] *Ibid.,* p. 63.

[166] "A Theological Conversation with Wolfhart Pannenberg," *Dialog* 11, 1972, p. 294, my italics. See also "Der Gott der Geschichte," *GsT* II, pp. 118f.

[167] "Der Einfluss der Anfechtungserfahrung auf den Prädestinationsbegriff Luthers," *KuD* 3, 1957, pp. 136f.

[168] "Speaking about God in the Face of Atheist Criticism," *IGHF,* p. 108.

[169] *Ibid.,* p. 93.

[170] See already the earlier exploration into this theme in regard to Pannenberg's theological anthropology, *supra,* pp. 99-102.

[171] See "Speaking about God," *IGHF,* p. 106--the sentence quoted *supra,* p. 101.

[172] *GC,* p. 43, in a sentence unaccountably omitted from *JGM:* "Gott *heisst* ja die alles umgreifende Macht." (My italics.) The phrase also appears in the *earlier* version of "The Crisis of the Scripture Principle" as translated in *Dialog* 2, 1963, p. 308. The later version in *BQT* I reflects Pannenberg's shift to the terminology of "all-determining" power identified below. (See the publishing history of the essay, *BQT* I, p. 1.)

[173] "*Die Macht über alles Wirkliche,*" in *GsT* I, p. 378 ("The Question of God," *BQT* II, p. 223). See also "Toward a Theology of the History of Religions," *BQT* II, pp. 104f.

[174] "The Question of God," *BQT* II, p. 223.

[175] This is the phrase that appears throughout Pannenberg's "Response to the Discussion" (*TaH*) from 1965-66. (See the references already identified, *supra,* Ch. 5, note 55.

[176] "The Question of God," *BQT* II, p. 201 (*GsT* I, p. 361): "Anyone who tries to speak of God today can no longer count on being immediately understood--at least, not if he has in mind the living God of the Bible *as the reality which determines everything,* as the creator of the world." (My italics.)

[177] The key phrase puts in an appearance in "On Historical and Theological

307

Hermeneutic" (*BQT* I, pp. 156-58, 178), an essay hailing from 1964 but extensively revised for publication in *BQT*. It is also anticipated in a footnote in "Response to the Discussion" where Pannenberg speaks of the future as "the power determining the present" (*TaH*, p. 267, ft. 77). It becomes especially prominent in *TKG*, the content there dating from 1966, and its use is widespread in Pannenberg thereafter. The point of these references is to clarify that the definition of God as all-determining power, though anticipated earlier, comes to decisive expression only subsequent to the penetration into God as *die Macht der Zukunft*. *I.e.*, it is explicitly as the power of the future that God can be comprehended as the all-determining power of the whole of reality. (In conversation, 10-21-82, Pannenberg observed that he regards the understanding of God as "all-determining power" to embody "a *minimal* description of what the concept of God logically must contain, while *die Macht der Zukunft* is meant to comprise, though not to spell out in detail, a distinctively *Christian* understanding of God.")

[178]See, *e.g., TKG* , p. 60; *AC*, p. 38. David McKenzie finally comes to just this conclusion in the article derived from his dissertation on Pannenberg, contending that "the bulk of Pannenberg's work" points to the understanding that "the future determines the present . . . only in that it shows the essence of the present," not in the mode of an agent exercising influence over the course of events. ("Pannenberg on God and Freedom," *JR* 60, 1980, p. 322.) The ensuing paragraphs in the text here tend utterly to dispel that curious illusion. Indeed, McKenzie's own considerable confusion over Pannenberg's "fundamentally unclarified" (323) concept of the power of the future is reflected in his equal acknowledgment of the lack of space for human "free will as contracausal freedom" in Pannenberg's understanding of God (308) and his quoting of a Pannenbergian passage that explicitly sets forth God's creating not only possibilities but actualities as well (328; see *infra*, p. 272). (Pannenberg has, in fact, explicitly rejected this interpretation, emphasizing in conversation with me, 10-21-82, that "I want, of course, to say more than" this--namely, that God only "determines the *essence*, the ultimate *meaning*, of historical occurrences. God is *creator*," and all that concretely comes to be is "comprehended by the action of God."

[179]*E.g.*, "Speaking about God in the Face of Atheist Criticism," *IGHF*, p. 107; "The Nature of a Theological Statement," *Zygon* 7, 1972, pp. 12, 16; *TPS*, p. 300; "Christologie und Theologie," *GsT* II, p. 137.

[180]*TKG*, p. 55.

[181]"On Historical and Theological Hermeneutic," *BQT* I, pp. 157, 158; "A Liberal Logos Christology," *John Cobb's Theology in Process*, p. 136.

[182]*TKG*, p. 59.

[183]*Ibid.*

[184] Lewis Ford, "A Whiteheadian Basis for Pannenberg's Theology," *Encounter* 38, 1977, p. 314. The latter sentences are a footnote to the first one quoted.

[185] Pannenberg and Lewis Ford, "A Dialog about Process Philosophy," *Encounter* 38, 1977, p. 319, 320 (my italics). See also "The Significance of the Categories 'Part' and 'Whole' for the Epistemology of Theology," *JR* 66, 1986, p. 379: God as unifying unity of the whole is "not only the source of the unity of the parts but also source of the parts themselves. Only in this manner would God be conceived as the *creative* source of the world."

[186] "The Appropriation of the Philosophical Concept of God," *BQT* II, p. 175.

[187] "Response to the Discussion," *TaH*, p. 250.

[188] *TKG*, p. 63. He continues there: "For what is freedom but to have future in oneself and out of oneself?"

[189] *TPS*, p. 309, ft. 615. See also "The Significance of Christianity in the Philosophy of Hegel," *IGHF*, p. 174.

[190] "The Appropriation of the Philosophical Concept of God," *BQT* II, p. 181. See also therein pp. 138, 162, 169, 171, 179; and "What is Truth?," *BQT* II, p. 10.

[191] "The Appropriation of the Philosophical Concept of God," *BQT* II, pp. 142-47, especially pp. 145f.

[192] "Future and Unity," *HFM*, p. 64; "Der Gott der Geschichte," *GsT* II, p. 119.

[193] "Future and Unity," *HFM*, pp. 65f. (my italics).

[194] *Ibid.*, p. 72. Cf. *AC*, p. 174, where a similar point about the "material identity" between the still hidden future life and the life of the present is made.

[195] "Die Auferstehung Jesu und die Zukunft des Menschen," *GsT* II, pp. 174f.

[196] *TPS*, p. 303. (See also *supra*, Ch. 8, note 177.)

[197] *TPS*, p. 302.

[198] See *supra*, p. 100.

[199]"The Significance of Christianity in the Philosophy of Hegel," *IGHF*, p. 174 (the latter clause is a footnote to the phrase before the colon).

[200]*Ibid.*

[201]*TKG*, p. 63.

[202]"Speaking about God in the face of Atheist Criticism," *IGHF*, p. 111.

[203]"The God of Hope," *BQT* II, p. 245 (my italics). In a similar vein, Pannenberg can slip into suggesting that "only he who *has* a future is in possession of power" (*TKG*, p. 60, my italics), although, according to his reversal of ontological priorities, one ought more properly to say that the future "has" *us*.

[204]"Man--the Image of God?," *Faith and Reality*, p. 47.

[205]*TKG*, p. 66.

[206]"Man--the Image of God?," *FR*, p. 47.

[207]*TKG*, p. 69.

[208]"Der Gott der Geschichte," *GsT* II, p. 116.

[209]*AC*, p. 125.

[210]"Weltgeschichte und Heilsgeschichte," *Probleme biblischer Theologie*, pp. 365f.

[211]*TKG*, p. 117.

[212]"The God of Hope," *BQT* II, p. 248. Cf. also "Der Sozialismus--Das wahre Gottesreich?," *Müssen Christen Sozialisten sein?*, ed. Wolfgang Teichert (Hamburg: Lutherisches Verlagshaus, 1976), p. 63: "First when people no longer exercise lordship over each other but God himself reigns among us directly will peace and justice finally lodge with us." The Christian awaits the actualizing of a just society "from God alone. . . . the *'Jenseits'* is now already the power for the *'Diesseits'*. . . .Only to the extent that God comes to dominion in human hearts are peace and justice in their full human sense now already possible."

[213]*TKG*, p. 111.

214 *Ibid.*, p. 118.

215 "Christologie und Theologie,"*GsT* II, p. 144.

216 Pannenberg, *Gegenwart Gottes: Predigten* (München: Claudius Verlag, 1973), pp. 67f. (Hereafter: *GG:P.*) Similarly, from a decade later: "The reign of peace will not be created by us. It is there where God comes to us. It needs only to be received: That, and that alone, can transform the spirit of the world" (192).

217 *TKG*, p. 69.

218 *GG:P*, p. 135.

219 "Facts of History and Christian Ethics," *Dialog* 8, 1969, p. 294.

220 Pannenberg, *Human Nature, Election, and History* (Philadelphia: The Westminster Press, 1977), pp. 93f.

221 *TKG*, p. 126.

222 "On the Theology of Law," *Ethics*, p. 52.

223 See, *e.g., TKG*, p. 85; "On the Theology of Law," *Ethics*, pp. 52-56; *GG:P*, p. 120.

224 See, *e.g.,* Pannenberg, "The Working of the Spirit in the Creation and in the People of God," in *Spirit, Faith, and Church*, by W. Pannenberg, Avery Dulles, S. J., and Carl E. Braaten (Philadelphia: The Westminster Press, 1970), p. 30; *GG:P*, p. 192.

225 "On the Theology of Law," *Ethics*, p. 53.

226 *Ibid.*, p. 54.

227 *GG:P*, p. 192.

228 *TKG*, p.111.

229 "Can Christianity Do without an Eschatology?" *The Christian Hope*, p. 31.

230 *Ibid.*, p. 32.

[231] "Christologie und Theologie," *GsT* II, p. 140 (my italics). The context of this expression will be set forth shortly, in discussing the characterizing of God's power as love.

[232] See "Der Gott der Geschichte," *GsT* II, p. 127, in particular, for an expression of this notion.

[233] Pannenberg, "Postscript," in E. Frank Tupper, *The Theology of Wolfhart Pannenberg*, p. 304. See also "Future and Unity," *HFM*, pp. 63f.

[234] Pannenberg, "Vom Nutzen der Eschatologie für die christliche Theologie (Eine Antwort)," *KuD* 25, 1979, pp. 93f.

[235] *TPS*, p. 302.

[236] "Response to the Discussion," *TaH*, p. 232, ft. 10.

[237] *TKG*, pp. 64f.

[238] Gottebenbildlichkeit und Bildung des Menschen," *GsT* II, p. 225.

[239] "Christologie und Theologie," *GsT* II, p. 144.

[240] *Ibid.*, pp. 140f.

[241] See *supra*, summary thesis number three on the meaning of the resurrection, pp. 200-02.

[242] *JGM*, p. 115.

[243] *Ibid.*, p. 137 (see also p. 135).

[244] *TKG*, p. 63. See *supra*, p. 269, for the more extended quote of his passage and the discussion of its implications.

[245] *JGM*, p. 154.

[246] *AC*, pp. 140, 141.

[247] "Der Gott der Geschichte," *GsT* II, p. 124.

[248] "Person und Subjekt" (1976), "Der Gott der Geschichte" (1977), and "Die Subjektivität Gottes und die Trinitätslehre: Ein Beitrag zur Beziehung zwischen Karl Barth und der Philosophie Hegels" (1977), all appearing in the volume of collected writings, *GsT* II; and "Problems of a Trinitarian Doctrine of God," *Dialog* 26, 1987, pp. 250-57.

[249] "Person and Subjekt," *GsT* II, pp. 82f.

[250] *Ibid.*, pp. 82f., 85f.

[251] *Ibid.*, p. 85.

[252] *Ibid.*, p. 87.

[253] "Der Gott der Geschichte," *GsT* II, p. 124.

[254] "Person and Subjekt," *GsT* II, pp. 92f. See also "Der Gott der Geschichte," *GsT* II, p. 124.

[255] "Person und Subjekt," *GsT* II, p. 95.

[256] "Der Gott der Geschichte," *GsT* II, pp. 125-27.

[257] *Ibid.*, pp. 127f.

[258] David McKenzie, "Pannenberg on God and Freedom," *JR* 60, 1980, p. 321.

[259] Langdon Gilkey, "Pannenberg's *Basic Questions in Theology*: a Review Article," *Perspective* 14, 1973, p. 51.

[260] *TPS*, p. 302. See *supra*, pp. 274ff., 279f.

[261] Gilkey, *op. cit.*, pp. 46, 53.

[262] Pannenberg's tape-recorded comments (10-21-82) repudiating an opening toward a degree of human self-determination only reinforce this conclusion. Polk: "Is there any degree of self-expression that is not determined by God?" Pannenberg: "No, I don't think so. . . . Even everything we do in shaping our lives is an effect of God's creative action. They don't work on the same level, and therefore they can't possibly be in competition. If the human person is a *creature* of God, so everything that belongs to that creature, including its self-creative, self-determining potential, is already an effect of the work of the Creator."

[263]Pannenberg objects strongly to this interpretation of his position, insisting that the temporal shift is vitally important in the overcoming of deterministic thinking. In conversation with me (10-21-82), he called the attribution of "post-determinism" an illusory notion; "to change the temporal mode has consequences concerning the nature of causality," in that the cause now no longer is understood to come before its effect. But how this by itself denies what "post-determinism" expresses remains a mystery to me.

[264]Gilkey, *op. cit.*, p. 53. "Only an ontological and so theologically conceptual limitation on the divine sovereignty--whether from eternity, from the present *or* from the future--can guarantee the openness of history, not a mere change in the temporal locus of God's being and work" (54). Gilkey's 1973 review-article on *BQT* I and II is still the most perceptive critique of the problems of Pannenberg's doctrine of the futurity of God to have appeared in print, in English or German. Its penetrating analysis is rendered all the more convincing by the fact that Pannenberg has never (in published form) addressed himself to Gilkey's arguments in the decade and a half since.

[265]See *supra*, p. 272.

[266]See the preliminary raising of this issue, *supra*, pp. 33f., and critical question #4, p. 48.

[267]Johannes Metz expressed just this latter concern in the discussion of Pannenberg's theses at the 1971 hope conference, insisting that where there is no "real time" as a qualification of the being of God, then what finally emerges is a kind of non-temporal identity of creation and consummation which cancels both. Metz accused Pannenberg's understanding of being essentially continuous not with Hebraic thought but with the Greek concept of reality as unchanging. (From a taped record of the proceedings.) So also, Peter Eicher, in his review of the critical discussion of Pannenberg's theology through 1972, calls "the question of the *understanding of time* which is at the root of this theology of history" the "underlying systematic problem" yet unresolved." (Eicher, "Geschichte und Wort Gottes: Ein Protokoll der Pannenbergdiskussion von 1961-1972," *Catholica* 32, 1978, p. 353.) I submit that it still is--or rather, that it is one of them.

[268]*Inter alia*, see Philip Hefner, "Questions for Moltmann and Pannenberg," *Una Sancta* 25, 1968, pp. 44 and ff.; Frank Tupper, *op. cit.*, p. 299; Allan Galloway, *op. cit.*, pp. 71, 83f., 97, 131, 136f. See also Gilkey, *op. cit.*, pp. 46, 54: "his eschatological theology remains at several crucial points unintelligible and inconsistent without the ontological understanding which likewise he both presupposes and vigorously adjures" (54).

[269]"The Significance of Christianity in the Philosophy of Hegel," *IGHF*, p. 174.

[270] *TKG*, p. 63. See the discussion *supra*, pp. 257ff., especially p. 258.

[271] Lewis S. Ford, "God as the Subjectivity of the Future," *Encounter* 41, 1980, p. 292.

[272] Ford, "A Whiteheadian Basis for Pannenberg's Theology," *Encounter* 38, 1977, p. 315.

[273] Ford, "God as the Subjectivity of the Future," *Encounter* 41, 1980, p. 288. See also John Macquarrie, *Christian Hope* (New York: The Seabury Press, 1978), p. 126.

[274] Ford, "God as the Subjectivity of the Future," *Encounter* 41, 1980, p. 288.

[275] See the discussion *supra*, pp. 68f.

[276] See particularly, "A Theological Conversation with Wolfhart Pannenberg," *Dialog* 11, 1972, p. 288, as quoted *supra* , p. 69.

[277] See the preliminary suggestion of this alternative, *supra*, pp. 142f.

[278] See, *e.g.*, Felix Flückiger, *Theologie der Geschichte: Die biblische Rede von Gott und die neuere Geschichtstheologie* (Wuppertal: Theologischer Verlag Rolf Brockhaus, 1970), p. 97; Traugott Koch, "Das Böse als theologisches Problem,"*KuD* 24, 1978, pp. 290-92; Tupper, *op. cit.,* pp. 300-02.

[279] Daniel Day Williams, "Response to Wolfhart Pannenberg," *HFM*, p. 87.

[280] Pannenberg's remark, in personal correspondence (letter of 1-11-83), that he felt so misunderstood by Williams' comment that he did not consider it merited a response--because of his view of the role of *judgment* in the eschatological Reign, separating good from evil--is certainly cogent. But one cannot evade the nagging concern that the place of judgment has not been sufficiently probed in a theological perspective that embraces the *whole* of what becomes in history, the evil as well as the good, within the exclusive causality of *God* as all-determining power.

BIBLIOGRAPHY

I. WORKS BY PANNENBERG

A. *Books*

Anthropology in Theological Perspective. Tr. by Matthew J. O'Connell. Philadelphia: The Westminster Press, 1985. (*Anthropologie in theologischer Perspektive.* Göttingen: Vandenhoeck & Ruprecht, 1983.)

The Apostles' Creed: In the Light of Today's Questions. Tr. by Margaret Kohl. Philadelphia: The Westminster Press, 1972. (*Das Glaubensbekenntnis.* Hamburg: Siebenstern Taschenbuch Verlag, 1972.)

Basic Questions in Theology, Volumes I and II. Tr. by George H. Kehm. Philadelphia: Fortress Press, 1970 (I), 1971 (II). (*Grundfragen systematischer Theologie,* Band I. Göttingen: Vandenhoeck & Ruprecht, 1967.)

Christian Spirituality. Philadelphia: The Westminster Press, 1983.

The Church. Tr. by Keith Crim. Philadelphia: The Westminster Press, 1983. (*Ethik und Ekklesiologie,* Part II. Göttingen: Vandenhoeck & Ruprecht, 1977.)

Ethics. Tr. by Keith Crim. Philadelphia: The Westminster Press, 1981. (*Ethik und Ekklesiologie,* Part I. Göttingen: Vandenhoeck & Ruprecht, 1977.)

Faith and Reality. Tr. by John Maxwell. Philadelphia: The Westminster Press, 1977. (*Glaube und Wirklichkeit.* München: Chr. Kaiser Verlag, 1975.)

Gegenwart Gottes: Predigten. München: Claudius Verlag, 1973.

Grundfragen systematischer Theologie, Band II. Göttingen: Vandenhoeck & Ruprecht, 1980.

Human Nature, Election, and History. Philadelphia: The Westminster Press, 1977.

317

The Idea of God and Human Freedom. Tr. by R. A. Wilson. Philadelphia: The Westminster Press, 1973. (*Gottesgedanke und menschlihe Freiheit.* Göttingen: Vandenhoeck & Ruprecht, 1972. Also: *Christentum und Mythos.* Gütersloh: Gütersloher Verlagshaus Gerd Mohn, 1972. Also: "Eschatologie und Sinnerfahrung," *Toekomst van de Religie: Religie van de Toekomst?* Uitgeverij Emmaus [N. V. Desclee de Brouwer], 1972, pp. 134-148.) (Published in Great Britain as *Basic Questions in Theology,* Volume III.)

Jesus--God and Man. Tr. by Lewis L. Wilkins and Duane A. Priebe. Philadelphia: The Westminster Press, 1968. 2nd ed.: 1977. (*Grundzüge der Christologie.* Gütersloh: Gütersloher Verlagshaus Gerd Mohn, 1964. 5th ed.: 1975.)

Die Prädestinationslehre des Duns Skotus. Göttingen: Vandenhoeck & Ruprecht, 1954.

Reformation zwischen gestern und morgen. Gütersloh: Gütersloher Verlagshaus Gerd Mohn, 1969.

Theology and the Kingdom of God. Philadelphia: The Westminster Press, 1969.

Theology and the Philosophy of Science. Tr. by Francis McDonagh. Philadelphia: The Westminster Press, 1976. (*Wissenschaftstheorie und Theologie.* Frankfurt am Main: Suhrkamp Verlag, 1973.)

Thesen zur Theologie der Kirche. München: Claudius Verlag, 1970.

What Is Man? Tr. by Duane A. Priebe. Philadelphia: Fortress Press, 1970. (*Was ist der Mensch?* Göttingen: Vandenhoeck & Ruprecht, 1962.)

Pannenberg, Wolfhart, Avery Dulles, and Carl Braaten, *Spirit, Faith, and Church.* Philadelphia: The Westminster Press, 1970.

_____ and Pinchas Lapide, *Judentum und Christentum: Einheit und Unterschied.* München: Kaiser Verlag, 1981.

_____, ed., *Die Erfahrung der Abwesenheit Gottes in der modernen Kultur.* Göttingen: Vandenhoeck & Ruprecht, 1984.

_____, ed., *Revelation as History.* Tr. by David Granskou. New York: The Macmillan Company, 1968. (*Offenbarung als Geschichte.* Göttingen: Vandenhoeck & Ruprecht, 1961.)

_____ and Wilfried Joest, eds., *Dogma und Denkstrukturen: Festschrift für Edmund Schlink.* Göttingen: Vandenhoeck & Ruprecht, 1963.

B. Articles and Essays

"Aggression und die theologische Lehre von der Sünde," *Zeitschrift für Evangelische Ethik,* 21 (1977), 161-173.

"Antwort auf G. Sauters Uberlegungen," *Evangelische Theologie*, 40 (1980), 168-181.

"Atom, Duration, Form: Difficulties with Process Philosophy," *Process Studies*, 14 (1984), 21-30.

"Bewusstsein und Geist," *Zeitschrift für Theologie und Kirche*, 80 (1983), 332-51.

"Can Christianity Do without an Eschatology?" in G. B. Caird et al, *The Christian Hope*. London: Society for Promoting Christian Knowledge, 1970.

"Christentum und Platonismus: Die kritische Platonrezeption Augustins in ihrer Bedeutung für das gegenwärtige christliche Denken," *Zeitschrift für Kirchengeschichte*, 96 (1985), 147-61.

"Das christliche Gottesverständnis im Spannungsfeld seiner jüdischen und griechischen Wurzeln," in *EKD Texts 15: Der christliche Glaube und seine jüdisch-griechische Herkunft.* Hannover: Kirchenamt der EKD, 1986.

"Christliche Rechtsbegründung," in *Handbuch der christlichen Ethik*, Band 2. Ed. by Anselm Hertz (et al). Gütersloh: Gütersloher Verlagshaus Gerd Mohn, 1978.

"Christlicher Glaube und menschliche Freiheit," *Kerygma und Dogma*, 4 (1958), 251-280.

"The Christological Foundation of Christian Anthropology," in *Humanism and Christianity* (*Concilium*, Vol. 86). Ed. by Claude Geffre. New York: Herder and Herder, 1973.

"Civil Religion? Religionsfreiheit und pluralistischer Staat: Das theologische Fundament der Gesellschaft," in *Die religiöse Dimension der Gesellschaft*. Ed. by Peter Koslowski. Tübingen: J. C. B. Mohr (Paul Siebeck), 1985.

"Constructive and Critical Functions of Christian Eschatology," *Harvard Theological Review*, 77 (1984), 119-39.

"The Crisis of the Scripture-Principle in Protestant Theology," *Dialog*, 2 (1963), 307-313.

"Did Jesus Really Rise from the Dead?" *Dialog*, 4 (1965), 128-135.

"The Doctrine of Creation and Modern Science," *Zygon*, 23 (1988), 3-21.

"Der Einfluss der Anfechtungserfahrung auf den Prädestinationsbegriff Luthers," *Kerygma und Dogma*, 3 (1957), 109-139.

"Facts of History and Christian Ethics," *Dialog*, 8 (1969), 287-296.

"Foundation Documents of the Faith: XI. The Place of Creeds in Christianity Today," *Expository Times*, 91 (1980), 328-32.

"Freedom and the Lutheran Reformation," *Theology Today*, 38 (1981), 287-297.

"Future and Unity," in *Hope and the Future of Man*. Ed. by Ewert H. Cousins. Philadelphia: Fortress Press, 1972. (Also appearing as chapter 9 in *Ethics*.)

"Geist und Energie," *Acta Teilhardiana*, 8 (1971), 5-12.

"Glaube und Wirklichkeit im Denken Gerhard von Rads," in *Gerhard von Rad: Seine Bedeutung für die Theologie*. Ed. by Hans Walter Wolff. München: Chr. Kaiser Verlag, 1973.

"God's Presence in History," in *Theologians in Transition*. Ed. by James M. Wall. New York: The Crossroad Publishing Co., 1981.

"Gott V: Theologiegeschichtlich," *Die Religion in Geschichte und Gegenwart*, II, 1717-1732. Dritte Auflage. Ed. by Kurl Galling et al. Tübingen: J. C. B. Mohr (Paul Siebeck), 1958.

"I Believe in God the Father Almighty. . ," in *A New Look at the Apostles' Creed*. Ed. by Gerhard Rein. Tr. by David LeFort. Minneapolis: Augsburg Publishing House, 1969.

"Kontingenz und Naturgesetz," in *Erwägungen zu einer Theologie der Natur*, by A. M. Klaus Müller and W. Pannenberg. Gütersloh: Gütersloher Verlagshaus Gerd Mohn, 1970.

"Die Krise des Ethischen und die Theologie," *Theologische Literaturzeitung*, 87 (1962), 7-16.

"A Liberal Logos Christology: The Christology of John Cobb," tr. by David P. Polk, in *John Cobb's Theology in Process*. Ed. by David R. Griffin and Thomas J. J. Altizer. Philadelphia: The Westminster Press, 1977.

"Lima: pro und contra," *Kerygma und Dogma*, 32 (1986), 35-51.

"Mythus und Wort. Theologische Überlegungen zu Karl Jaspers' Mythusbegriff," *Zeitschrift für Theologie und Kirche*, 51 (1954), 167-185.

"Nachwort," in *Geschichte, Offenbarung, Glaube*, by Ignace Berten. München: Claudius Verlag, 1970.

"Nachwort zur zweiten Auflage," in *Offenbarung als Geschichte*, 3rd ed. (1965). Ed. by W. Pannenberg. Göttingen: Vandenhoeck & Ruprecht, 1961.

"The Nature of a Theological Statement," *Zygon*, 7 (1972), 6-19.

"Person," *Die Religion in Geschichte und Gegenwart*, V, 230-235. Dritte Auflage. Ed. by Kurl Galling et al. Tübingen: J. C. B. Mohr (Paul Siebeck), 1961.

"Die politische Dimension des Evangeliums," in *Die Politik und das Heil*. Ed. by R. Hörl. Mainz: Matthias-Grünewald-Verlag, 1968.

"Postscript," in *The Theology of Wolfhart Pannenberg,* E. Frank Tupper. Philadelphia: The Westminster Press, 1972.

"Problems of a Trinitarian Doctrine of God," *Dialog,* 26 (1987), 250-57.

"Report from Bangalore," *Mid-Stream,* 18 (1979), 52-62.

"Response to Dr. J. N. D. Anderson," *Christianity Today,* 12 (1968), 681-683.

"Response to the Discussion," and: "The Revelation of God in Jesus of Nazareth," in *Theology as History.* Ed. by James M. Robinson and John B. Cobb. New York: Harper & Row, 1967.

"Der Schlussbericht der anglikanisch-römisch-katholischen Internationalen Kommission und seine Beurteilung durch die römische Glaubenskongregation," *Kerygma und Dogma,* 29 (1983), 166-73.

"The Significance of Eschatology for the Understanding of the Apostolicity and Catholicity of the Church," *One in Christ,* 6 (1970), 410-429.

"The Significance of the Categories 'Part' and 'Whole' for the Epistemology of Theology," *The Journal of Religion,* 66 (1986), 369-85.

"Der Sozialismus--Das wahre Gottesreich?" in *Müssen Christen Sozialisten sein?* Ed. by Wolfgang Teichert. Hamburg: Lutherisches Verlagshaus, 1976.

"A Theological Conversation with Wolfhart Pannenberg," *Dialog,* 11 (1972), 286-295.

"Theological Questions to Scientists," *Zygon,* 16 (1981), 65-77.

"Die Theologie und die neuen Fragen nach Intersubjektivität, Gesellschaft und religiöser Gemeinschaft," *Archivio di Filosofia,* 54 (1986), 411-25.

"Unity of the Church--Unity of Humankind: A Critical Appraisal of a Shift in Ecumenical Direction," *Mid-Stream,* 21 (1982), 285-90.

"Vom Nutzen der Eschatologie für die christliche Theologie (Eine Antwort)," *Kerygma und Dogma,* 25 (1979), 88-105.

"Weltgeschichte und Heilsgeschichte," in *Probleme biblischer Theologie: Festschrift für Gerhard von Rad.* Ed. by Hans Walter Wolff. München: Chr. Kaiser Verlag, 1971.

"Wirkungen biblischer Gotteserkenntnis auf das abendländische Menschenbild," *Studium Generale,* 15 (1962), 586-593.

Pannenberg, Wolfhart, and Lewis Ford, "A Dialogue about Process Philosophy," *Encounter,* 38 (1977), 318-324.

_____ and Gerhard Sauter, "Im Fegefeuer der Methode: Wolfhart Pannenberg und Gerhard Sauter im Gespräch über Theologie als Wissenschaft," *Evangelische Kommentare*, 6 (1973), 4-10.

II. WORKS CONCERNING PANNENBERG

Althaus, Paul, "Offenbarung als Geschichte und Glaube. Bemerkungen zu W. Pannenbergs Begriff der Offenbarung," *Theologische Literaturzeitung*, 87 (1962), 321-330.

Apczynski, John. "Truth in Religion: A Polanyian Appraisal of Wolfhart Pannenberg's Theological Program," *Zygon*, 17 (1982), 49-73.

Berten, Ignace, *Geschichte, Offenbarung, Glaube: Eine Einführung in die Theologie Wolfhart Pannenbergs*. Tr. from French by Sigrid Martin. München: Claudius Verlag, 1970.

Betz, Hans Dieter, "The Concept of Apocalyptic in the Theology of the Pannenberg Group," *Journal for Theology and the Church 6: Apocalypticism*. Ed. by Robert W. Funk. New York: Herder and Herder, 1969.

Bollinger, Gary, "Pannenberg's Theology of the Religions and the Claim to Christian Superiority," *Encounter*, 43 (1982), 273-85.

Braaten, Carl E. "The Current Controversy on Revelation: Pannenberg and his Critics," *The Journal of Religion*, 45 (1965), 225-237.

_____, "Toward a Theology of Hope," *Theology Today*, 24 (1967), 208-226.

_____, "Wolfhart Pannenberg," in *A Handbook of Christian Theologians*, Enlarged Edition. Ed. by Martin E. Marty and Dean G. Peerman. Nashville: Abingdon Press, 1988.

_____ and Philip Clayton, eds., *The Theology of Wolfhart Pannenberg*. Minneapolis: Augsburg Press, 1988.

Burhenn, Herbert, "Pannenberg's Argument for the Historicity of the Resurrection," *Journal of the American Academy of Religion*, 40 (1972), 368-379.

_____, "Pannenberg's Doctrine of God," *Scottish Journal of Theology*, 28 (1975), 535-549.

Clayton, Philip, "The God of History and the Presence of the Future," *The Journal of Religion*, 65 (1985), 98-108.

Cobb, John B., Jr., "A New Trio Arises in Europe," in *New Theology No. 2.* Ed. by Martin Marty and Dean Peerman. New York: The Macmillan Company, 1965.

_____, "Responses to Critics," in *John Cobb's Theology in Process.* Ed. by David R. Griffin and Thomas J. J. Altizer. Philadelphia: The Westminster Press, 1977.

_____, "Wolfhart Pannenberg's 'Jesus: God and Man'," *The Journal of Religion,* 49 (1969), 192-201.

_____, review of *Theology and the Philosophy of Science, Religious Studies Review,* 3 (1977), 213-215.

Craig, William Lane, "Pannenbergs Beweis für die Auferstehung Jesu," *Kerygma und Dogma,* 34 (1988), pp. 78-104.

Eicher, Peter, "Geschichte und Wort Gottes: Ein Protokoll der Pannenbergdiskussion von 1961-1972," *Catholica,* 32 (1978), 321-354.

Enquist, Roy J., "Utopia and the Search for a Godly Future," *Dialog,* 19 (1980), 131-140.

Escribano-Alberca, Ignacio, *Das vorläufige Heil: Zum christlichen Zeitbegriff.* Düsseldorf: Patmos-Verlag, 1970.

Fischer, Hermann, "Fundamentaltheologische Prolegomena zur theologischen Anthropologie: Anfragen an W. Pannenbergs Anthropologie," *Theologische Rundschau,* 50 (1985), 41-61.

Flückiger, Felix, *Theologie der Geschichte: Die biblische Rede von Gott und die neuere Geschichtstheologie.* Wuppertal: Theologischer Verlag Rolf Brockhaus, 1970. (Pp. 93-103.)

Ford, Lewis S., "God as the Subjectivity of the Future," *Encounter,* 41 (1980), 287-292.

_____, "A Whiteheadian Basis for Pannenberg's Theology," *Encounter,* 38 (1977), 307-317.

Foster, Durwood, "Pannenberg's Polanyianism: A Response to John V. Apczynski," *Zygon,* 17 (1982), 75-81.

Fuchs, Ernst, "Theologie oder Ideologie? Bemerkungen zu einem heilsgeschichtlichen Programm," *Theologische Literaturzeitung,* 88 (1963), 257-260.

Fuller, Daniel P., "A New German Theological Movement," *Scottish Journal of Theology,* 19 (1966), 160-175.

Galloway, Allan D., "The New Hegelians," *Religious Studies,* 8 (1972), 367-371.

_____, "Today's Word for Today: II. Wolfhart Pannenberg," *Expository Times,* 92 (19820, 69-73.

_____, *Wolfhart Pannenberg*. London: George Allen & Unwin Ltd., 1973.

Geense, Adriaan, *Auferstehung und Offenbarung*. Göttingen: Vandenhoeck & Ruprecht, 1971.

Geyer, Hans-Georg, "Geschichte als theologische Problem. Bemerkungen zu W. Pannenbergs Geschichtstheologie," *Evangelische Theologie*, 22 (1962), 92-104.

_____, "Gottes Sein als Thema der Theologie," *Verkundigung und Forschung*, 11:2 (1966), 3-37.

Gilkey, Langdon, "Pannenberg's *Basic Questions in Theology:* A Review Article," *Perspective*, 14 (1973), 34-56.

Goebel, Hans Theodor, *Wort Gottes als Auftrag. Zur Theologie von Rudolf Bultmann, Gerhard Ebeling und Wolfhart Pannenberg*. Neukirchen-Vluyn: Neukirchener Verlag, 1972.

Gray, Donald P., "Response to Wolfhart Pannenberg," in *Hope and the Future of Man*. Ed. by Ewert H. Cousins. Philadelphia: Fortress Press, 1972.

Griffiss, James E., review of *Basic Questions in Theology*, Vol. II, *Anglican Theological Review*, 54 (1972), 219-225.

Halsey, Jim S., "History, Language, and Hermeneutic: The Synthesis of Wolfhart Pannenberg," *Westminster Theological Journal,* 41 (1979), 269-290.

Harder, Helmut G., and W. Taylor Stevenson, "The Continuity of History and Faith in the Theology of Wolfhart Pannenberg: Toward an Erotics of History," *The Journal of Religion*, 51 (1971), 34-56.

Hefner, Philip, "The Concreteness of God's Kingdom: A Problem for the Christian Life," *The Journal of Religion*, 51 (1971), 188-205.

_____, "Questions for Moltmann and Pannenberg," *Una Sancta,* 25 (1968), 32-51.

Henke, Peter, *Gewissheit vor dem Nichts: Eine Antithese zu den theologischen Entwürfen Wolfhart Pannenbergs und Jürgen Moltmanns*. Berlin, New York: Walter de Gruyter, 1978.

Hesse, Franz, "Wolfhart Pannenberg und das Alte Testament," *Neue Zeitschrift für systematische Theologie und Religionsphilosophie*, 7 (1965), 174-199.

Hick, John, "A Note on Pannenberg's Eschatology," *Harvard Theological Review*, 77 (1984), 421-23.

Hill, William J., "The Historicity of God," *Theological Studies*, 45 (1984), 320-33.

Hodgson, Peter C., "Pannenberg on Jesus: a Review Article," *Journal of the American Academy of Religion,* 36 (1968), 373-384.

_____, review of *Theology and the Philosophy of Science, Religious Studies Review,* 3 (1977), 215-218.

Jellouschek, H., "Zum Verhältnis von Wissen und Glauben," *Zeitschrift für Katholische Theologie,* 93 (1971), 309-327.

Jenson, Robert W., "The Futurist Option in Speaking of God," *Lutheran Quarterly,* 21 (1969), 17-25.

_____, "'Gott' als Antwort," *Evangelische Theologie,* 26 (1966), 368-378.

Jentz, Arthur H., Jr., "Personal Freedom and the Futurity of God: Some Reflections on Pannenberg's 'God of Hope'," *Reformed Review,* 31 (1978), 148-154.

Johnson, Elizabeth A., "The Ongoing Christology of Wolfhart Pannenberg," *Horizons,* 9 (1982), 237-50.

_____, "The Right Way to Speak about God? Pannenberg on Analogy," *Theological Studies,* 43 (1982), 673-92.

Kienzler, Klaus, *Logik der Auferstehung: Eine Untersuchung zu R. Bultmann, G. Ebeling und W. Pannenberg.* Freiburg: Verlag Herder, 1976.

Klappert, Bertold, *Die Auferweckung des Gekreuzigten.* Neukirchen-Vluyn: Neukirchener Verlag, 1971.

_____, "Tendenzen der Gotteslehre in der Gegenwart," *Evangelische Theologie,* 35 (1975), 189-208.

Klein, Günter, "Offenbarung als Geschichte?" *Monatschrift für Pastoraltheologie,* 51 (1962), 65-88.

_____, *Theologie des Wortes Gottes und die Hypothese der Universalgeschichte.* München: Chr. Kaiser Verlag, 1964.

Koch, Kurt, "Gottes Handeln in der Geschichte und die Bestimmung des Menschen: Zur geschichtstheologischen Neuinterpretation des christlichen Erwählungsglaubens bei Wolfhart Pannenberg," *Catholica,* 33 (1979), 220-239.

Koch, Traugott, "Das Böse als theologisches Problem," *Kerygma und Dogma,* 24 (1978), 285-320.

Konrad, Franz, *Das Offenbarungsverständnis in der evangelischen Theologie.* München: Max Hueber Verlag, 1971.

Leuze, Reinhard. "Möglichkeiten und Grenzen einer Theologie der Religionsgeschichte," *Kerygma und Dogma,* 24 (1978), 230-243.

Lonning, Per, "Zur Denkbarkeit Gottes: in Gespräch mit Wolfhart Pannenberg und Eberhard Jüngel," *Studia Theologica,* 34 (1980), 39-71.

McCullagh, C. B., "The Possibility of an Historical Basis for Christian Theology," *Theology,* 74 (1971), 513-522.

McDermott, Brian O., "Pannenberg's Resurrection Christology: a Critique," *Theological Studies,* 35 (1974), 711-721.

McGrath, Alister, "Christology and Soteriology: A Response to Wolfhart Pannenberg's Critique of the Soteriological Approach to Christology," *Theologische Zeitschrift,* 42 (1986), 222-36.

McKenzie, David, "Pannenberg on Faith and Reason," *Dialog,* 18 (1979), 222-24.

_____, "Pannenberg on God and Freedom" *The Journal of Religion,* 60 (1980), 307-329.

_____, *Wolfhart Pannenberg and Religious Philosophy.* Washington, DC: University Press of America, 1980.

Macquarrie, John, "Theologies of Hope: A Critical Examination," *The Expository Times,* 82 (1971), 100-105.

Michaelson, Gordon E., "Pannenberg on the Resurrection and Historical Method," *Scottish Journal of Theology,* 33 (1980), 345-59.

Mühlenberg, Ekkehard, "Gott in der Geschichte: Erwägung zur Geschichtstheologie von W. Pannenberg," *Kerygma und Dogma,* 24 (1978), 244-261.

Muschalek, George, S. J., and Arnold Gamper, S. J., "Offenbarung in Geschichte," *Zeitschrift für Katholische Theologie,* 86 (1964) 180-196.

Neie, Herbert, *The Doctrine of the Atonement in the Theology of Wolfhart Pannenberg.* Berlin, New York: Walter de Gryter, 1979.

Neuhaus, Richard John, "History as Sacred Drama," *Worldview,* 22 (1979), 23-26.

_____, "Pannenberg Jousts with the World Council of Churches," *The Christian Century,* 99 (1982), 74-76.

_____, "Wolfhart Pannenberg: Profile of a Theologian," in *Theology and the Kingdom of God.* Philadelphia: The Westminster Press, 1969.

Nicol, Iain G., "Facts and Meanings: Wolfhart Pannenberg's Theology as History and the Role of the Historical-Critical Method," *Religious Studies,* 12 (1971), 129-139.

North, Robert, "Pannenberg's Historicizing Exegesis," *The Heythrop Journal,* 12 (1971), 377-400.

Obayashi, Hiroshi, "Future and Responsibility: A Critique of Pannenberg's Eschatology," *Studies in Religion*, 1 (1971), 191-203.

_____, "Pannenberg and Troeltsch: History and Religion," *Journal of the American Academy of Religion*, 38 (1970), 401-419.

O'Collins, Gerald G., S. J., "Christology from Below," *Interpretation*, 23 (1969), 228-232.

_____, "The Christology of Wolfhart Pannenberg," *Religious Studies*, 3 (1967-8), 369-376.

_____, *Foundations of Theology*. Chicago: Loyola University Press, 1971. (Pp. 115-131.)

_____, "Revelation as History," *The Heythrop Journal*, 7 (1966), 394-406.

Oden, Thomas C., "The Human Potential and Evangelical Hope," *Dialog*, 13 (1974), 121-128.

Olive, Don H., *Wolfhart Pannenberg*. Waco, Texas: Word Books, 1973.

Olson, Robert E., "The Human Self-Realization of God: Hegelian Elements in Pannenberg's Christology," *Perspectives in Religious Studies*, 13 (1986), 207-23.

_____, "Pannenberg's Theological Anthropology," *Perspectives in Religious Studies*, 13 (1986), 161-69.

_____, "Trinity and Eschatology: The Historical Being of God in Jürgen Moltman and Wolfhart Pannenberg," *Scottish Journal of Theology*, 36 (1983), 213-27.

Osborn, Robert T., "Pannenberg's Programme," *Canadian Journal of Theology*, 13 (1967), 109-122.

Owens, J. M., "Christology and History," *The Reformed Theological Review*, 26 (1967), 54-64.

_____, "A First Look at Pannenberg's Christology," *The Reformed Theological Review*, 25 (1966), 52-64.

Parker, Thomas D., "Faith and History: a Review of Wolfhart Pannenberg's *Jesus--God and Man*," *McCormick Quarterly*, 22 (1968-9), 43-82.

Pasquariello, Ronald D., "Pannenberg's Philosophical Foundations," *The Journal of Religion*, 56 (1976), 338-347.

Peters, Ted, "Truth in History: Gadamer's Hermeneutics and Pannenberg's Apologetic Method," *The Journal of Religion*, 55 (1975), 36-56.

327

_____, "The Whirlwind as Yet Unnamed," *Journal of the American Academiy of Religion*, 42 (1974) 699-709.

Petri, Heinrich, "Die Entdeckung der Fundamentaltheologie in der evangelischen Theologie," *Catholica*, 33 (1979), 241-61.

Placher, William C., "Pannenberg on History and Revelation," *Reformed Review*, 30 (1976), 39-47.

_____, "The Present Absence of Christ: Some Thoughts on Pannenberg and Moltmann," *Encounter*, 40 (1979), 169-179.

Rendtorff, Trutz, "Überlieferungsgeschichte als Problem der systematischen Theologie," *Theologische Literaturzeitung*, 90 (1965), 81-98.

Rhem, Richard A., "A Theological Conception of Reality as History--Some Aspects of the Thinking of Wolfhart Pannenberg," *Reformed Review*, 26 (1972), 178-188, 212-223.

Robinson, James M., "The Historicality of Biblical Language," in *The Old Testament and Christian Faith*. Ed. by Bernhard W. Anderson. New York: Herder and Herder, 1969.

_____ and John B. Cobb, Jr., eds., *Theology as History (New Frontiers in Theology, Vol. 3)*. New York: Harper & Row, 1967.

Ross, J. Robert, "Historical Knowledge as Basis for Faith," *Zygon*, 13 (1978), 209-224.

Russell, Robert John, "Contingency in Physics and Cosmology: A Critique of the Theology of Wolfhart Pannenberg," *Zygon*, 23 (1988), 23-43.

Santmire, H. Paul, review of *Revelation as History* and *Theology as History*, *Dialog*, 9 (1970), 142-145.

Sauter, Gerhard, "Fragestellungen der Christologie," *Verkundigung und Forschung*, 11:2 (1966), 37-68 (56-61).

_____, "Überlegungen zu einem weiteren Gesprächsgang über 'Theologie und Wissenschaftstheorie'," *Evangelische Theologie*, 40 (1980), 161-168.

Scharlemann, Robert P., review of *Jesus--God and Man*, *Dialog*, 8 (1969), 74-77.

Schmid, George, "Erkennen und Erwägen," *Zeitschrift für Religions- und Geistesgeschichte*, 30 (1978), 289-305.

Schwarzwäller, Klaus, *Theologie oder Phänomenologie*. München: Chr. Kaiser Verlag, 1966. (Pp. 90-118.)

Simpson, Gary M., "Whither Wolfhart Pannenberg? Reciprocity and Political Theology," *The Journal of Religion*, 67 (1987), 33-49.

Stead, Christopher, "Die Aufnahme des philosophischen Gottesbegriffes in der früchristlichen Theologie: W. Pannenbergs These neu bedacht," *Theologische Rundschau*, 51 (1986), 349-71.

Steiger, Lothar, "Revelation-History and Theological Reason: A Critique of the Theology of Wolfhart Pannenberg," in *History and Hermeneutic (Journal for Theology and the Church*, Vol. 4). Ed. by Robert W. Funk. New York: Harper & Row, 1967.

Stock, Konrad, "Ist die Bestimmung der Person noch offen?," *Evangelische Theologie*, 45 (1985), 290-97.

Suhl, Alfred, "Zur Beurteilung der Überlieferung von der Auferstehung Jesu in Wolfhart Pannenbergs 'Grundzüge der Christologie'," *Neue Zeitschrift für systematische Theologie*, 12 (1970), 294-308.

Tracy, David, review of *Jesus--God and Man* and *Revelation as History, The Catholic Biblical Quarterly*, 31 (1969), 285-288.

_____, review of *What Is Man? Basic Questions in Theology*, Vol. I, & *Spirit, Faith, and Church, Journal of the American Academy of Religion*, 39 (1971), 543-548.

Tupper, E. Frank, *The Theology of Wolfhart Pannenberg*. Philadelphia: The Westminster Press, 1972.

Van Huyssteen, J. W. V., "Systematic Theology and the Philosophy of Science: The Need for Methodological and Theoretical Clarity in Theology," *Journal of Theology for Southern Africa*, 34 (1981), 3-16.

Venema, Cornelis P., "History, Human Freedom and the Idea of God in the Theology of Wolfhart Pannenberg," *Calvin Theological Journal*, 17 (1982), 53-77.

Wagner, Falk, "Vernünftige Theologie und Theologie der Vernunft," *Kerygma und Dogma*, 24 (1978), 262-284.

Walsh, Brian J., "A Critical Review of Pannenberg's *Anthropology in Theological Perspective*," *Christian Scholar's Review*, 15 (1986), 247-59.

_____, "Pannenberg's Eschatological Ontology," *Christian Scholar's Review*, 11 (1982), 229-49.

Weischedel, Wilhelm, "Von der Fragwürdigkeit einer philosophischen Theologie," *Evangelische Theologie*, 27 (1967), 113-138.

White, Harvey W., "A Critique of Pannenberg's *Theology and the Philosophy of Science*," *Studies in Religion*, 11 (1982), 419-36.

Wicken, Jeffrey S., "Theology and Science in the Evolving Cosmos: A Need for Dialogue," *Zygon*, 23 (1988), 45-55.

Wilken, Robert L., "Who Is Wolfhart Pannenberg?" *Dialog*, 4 (1965), 140-142.

Williams, Daniel Day, "Response to Wolfhart Pannenberg," in *Hope and the Future of Man*. Ed. by Ewert H. Cousins. Philadelphia: Fortress Press, 1972.

_____, review of *What Is Man?*, *Theology Today*, 28 (1971), 107-109.

Wood, Laurence, "History and Hermeneutics: a Pannenbergian Perspective," *Wesleyan Theological Journal*, 16 (1981), 7-22.

330

INDEX

331

Hegel, G. W. F., 11f., 14, 25, 34f., 41, 48, 53f., 55, 65, 69, 72, 78, 99, 133, 202f., 282f., 293, 309f., 314
Heidegger, Martin, 23, 65, 85, 186
Herrmann, Wilhelm, 23, 185, 225
Hesse, Franz, 136, 141, 147, 149
Hick, John, 45
Hodgson, Peter, 228

Jaspers, Karl, 8, 16
Jenson, Robert, 16, 251, 297
Johnson, Elizabeth A., 17

Kähler, Martin, 59, 183, 185, 225, 247
Käsemann, Ernst, 2, 12, 16, 187, 226, 231
Kant, Immanuel, 23, 30, 41, 66, 106
Kierkegaard, Soren, 3, 33, 109
Klein, Günter, 201, 236, 244
Knierim, Rolf, 141, 144f., 149
Koch, Klaus, 10, 144, 159f., 162, 178-80
Koch, Traugott, 315
Künneth, Walter, 207f., 240

Landmann, Michael, 116
Laplace, Pierre Simon de, 295
Löwith, Karl, 8f., 16, 62-65, 78, 84
Luther, Martin, 9, 17, 270, 307

McKenzie, David, 286, 308, 313
Macquarrie, John, 315
Marsch, Wolf-Dieter, 299
Martin, H. V., 230
Marxsen, Willi, 212, 214, 221, 242-44
Melanchthon, Philipp, 23
Metz, Johannes, 314
Moltmann, Jürgen, 10, 15, 18, 62, 82f., 121, 223, 243f., 251, 257, 294, 299, 314
Murdock, William, 156, 158, 161, 176f., 179

Neuhaus, Richard, 3, 13, 15, 17, 19
Nickelsberg, George W. E., 178, 180f.
Nicholas of Cusa, 30, 40

Nicol, Iain, 244
Niebuhr, Richard R., 196, 233
Nietzsche, Friedrich, 247
Nissen, Andreas, 156-58, 161f., 176
North, Robert, 17

Ockham, William of, 106
O'Collins, Gerald, 91, 212, 242, 244
Olive, Don, 300
Ott, Heinrich, 251, 298
Otto, Rudolf, 230

Parmenides, 32f.
Pascal, Blaise, 94
Perrin, Norman, 186, 194, 226-28, 232
Plato, 27, 32f., 40, 106
Plessner, Helmuth, 116, 122
Portmann, Adolf, 116
Preuss, H. D., 173
Priebe, Duane, 116, 119

Rad, Gerhard von, 8f., 16f., 18, 62, 82, 159-61, 177-79
Rendtorff, Rolf, 10, 17, 61, 128-32, 134f., 144f.
Rendtorff, Trutz, 10, 17, 82f.
Rhem, Richard, 89f., 149
Rist, Martin, 169f., 182
Ritschl, Albrecht, 23
Robinson, James M., 3, 13, 15f., 18f., 61, 70, 81f., 88f., 131, 144, 214f., 225, 243
Rössler, Dietrich, 10, 17, 151, 154-60, 174f., 178
Russell, D. S., 160, 169, 178, 181

Santmire, Paul, 16
Sauter, Gerhard, 55, 83, 122, 174, 231
Scheler, Max, 116
Schelling, F. W. J., 25
Schleiermacher, Friedrich, 116f.
Schlink, Edmund, 8f., 248, 296
Schmitals, Walter, 160f., 179
Schweitzer, Albert, 2, 12, 185, 189, 254
Seils, Martin, 159, 177
Soden, Hans von, 28, 53f.

David P. Polk is the H. G. Brown Associate Professor of Pastoral Ministry at Brite Divinity School, Texas Christian University. Active in several areas of theological scholarship, he holds a Ph.D. in systematic theology from the Claremont Graduate School. He previously taught at Drury, Coe, and Mt. Mercy colleges, as well as Lexington Theological Seminary. He currently serves as president of the Association of Practical Theology and works with the Process and Faith program of the Center for Process Studies.